W9-DHY-093

The Universal Guide to DB2 for Windows NT®

ISBN 0-13-099723-4

90000

9 780130 997234

IBM DB2 Certification Guide Series

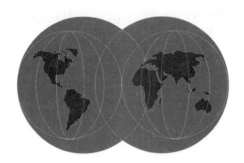

DB2 Universal Database Certification Guide, Second Edition
  edited by Janacek and Snow

DB2 Cluster Certification Guide
  by Cook, Janacek, and Snow

DB2 Universal DRDA Certification Guide
  by Brandl, Bullock, Cook, Harbus, Janacek, and Le

DB2 Universal Replication Certification Guide
  by Cook and Harbus

DB2 Universal Database and SAP R/3, Version 4
  by Bullock, Cook, Deedes-Vincke, Harbus, Nardone, and Neuhaus

Universal Guide to DB2 for Windows NT
  by Cook, Harbus, and Snow

The Universal Guide to DB2 for Windows NT®

JONATHAN COOK ■ ROBERT HARBUS ■ DWAINE SNOW

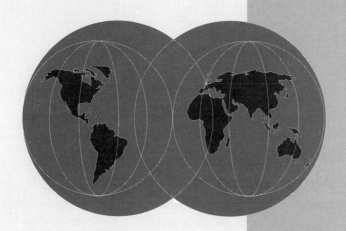

International Technical Support Organization
Austin, Texas 78758

ISBN 0-13-099723-4

90000

9 780130 997234

PRENTICE HALL PTR, UPPER SADDLE RIVER, NEW JERSEY 07458

Editorial/production supervision: *Maria Molinari*
Cover design director: *Jayne Conte*
Cover designer: *Bruce Kenselaar*
Manufacturing manager: *Pat Brown*
Marketing manager: *Kaylie Smith*
Acquisitions editor: *Mike Meehan*
Editorial assistant: *Bart Blanken*

Published by Prentice Hall PTR
Prentice-Hall, Inc.
A Simon & Schuster Company
Upper Saddle River, NJ 07458

Prentice Hall books are widely used by corporations and government agencies for training, marketing, and resale.
The publisher offers discounts on this book when ordered in bulk quantities.
For more information, contact Corporate Sales Dept.; Phone 800-382-3419; FAX: 201-236-7141
E-mail (Internet): corpsales@prenhall.com
Or write: Prentice Hall PTR, Corp. Sales Department, One Lake Street,Upper Saddle River, NJ 07458
The following terms are trademarks or registered trademarks of the IBM Corporation in the United States and/or other countries: ADSTAR, Distributed Database Connection Services, DRDA, DATABASE 2, DB2, Distributed Relational Database Architecture, AIX, AS/400, OS/400, VSE/ESA, OS/2, SQL/DS, MVS/ESA, IBM, VM/ESA.

The following terms are trademarks of other companies as follows: HP-UX, Hewlett-Packard Company; Lotus, 1-2-3, Lotus Development Corporation; Microsoft, Windows, Windows 95, Windows NT, OpenDatabase, Connectivity, Microsoft Corporation; PostScript, Adobe Systems, Incorporated; IPX/SPX, NetWare, Novell, Novell, Inc.; Solaris, SUN Microsystems, Inc.; UNIX, X/Open, X/Open Company Limited.

UNIX is a registered trademark in the U.S. and other countries licensed exclusively through X/Open Company Limited.
DB2 information on the Internet-http://www.software.ibm.com/data/db2
DB2 certification information on the Internet http://www.ibm.com/certify

All other products or servies mentioned in this book are the trademarks or service marks of their respective companies or organizations.

Printed in the United States of America

10 9 8 7 6 5 4 3 2 1

ISBN 0-13-099723-4

Prentice-Hall International (UK) Limited, *London*
Prentice-Hall of Australia Pty. Limited, *Sydney*
Prentice-Hall Canada Inc., *Toronto*
Prentice-Hall Hispanoamericana, S.A., *Mexico*
Prentice-Hall of India Private Limited, *New Delhi*
Prentice-Hall of Japan, Inc., *Tokyo*
Simon & Schuster Asia Pte. Ltd., *Singapore*
Editora Prentice-Hall do Brasil, Ltda., *Rio de Janeiro*

Contents

Figures. xi

Tables. xix

Preface. xxi
How This Book is Organized xxi
The Team That Wrote This Book xxii

Chapter 1. Overview. 1
1.1 DB2 Family of Products 1
1.2 DB2 UDB Family of Products 3
   1.2.1 DB2 UDB Personal Edition 5
   1.2.2 DB2 Workgroup Edition 6
   1.2.3 DB2 Enterprise Edition 8
   1.2.4 DB2 Universal Database Enterprise-Extended Edition 9
   1.2.5 DB2 Connect 10
   1.2.6 DB2 Developer's Edition. 13
1.3 DB2 UDB in the Windows NT Environment. 16
   1.3.1 Introduction of Windows NT 16
1.4 DB2 UDB for Windows NT Scenarios 17
   1.4.1 Small Workgroup Example 17
   1.4.2 Trusted Domain Example 18
   1.4.3 Enterprise Example 20
1.5 Summary 22

Chapter 2. DB2 UDB and Windows NT Security 23
2.1 Windows NT Security Concepts 25
   2.1.1 Workgroups in Windows NT 25
   2.1.2 Domains in Windows NT. 29
2.2 Groups and User Authentication. 33
   2.2.1 User Accounts 34
   2.2.2 Global Groups 35
   2.2.3 Local Groups 37
   2.2.4 Domain Scenario 39
   2.2.5 Windows NT Authentication 40
2.3 Trust Relationships Between Domains 42
   2.3.1 Trusted Domains 42
   2.3.2 Creating a Trust Relationship 44
   2.3.3 Models of Domain Trust 46
2.4 DB2 UDB for Windows NT Authentication and Security 53
   2.4.1 DB2 UDB for Windows NT Group Resolution 53

2.4.2 Forcing Local Authentication. 55
2.4.3 Authority Levels 56
2.4.4 Controlling Client Access to DB2 Databases. 61
2.4.5 DB2 Authentication Methods. 61
2.4.6 Example Scenarios. 63
2.5 The DB2 for Windows NT Environment 66
2.5.1 User ID and Group ID Limitations 67
2.5.2 DB2 for Windows NT Security Server Service. 69
2.5.3 DB2 Instances and Windows NT Services 70
2.5.4 Planning for DB2 UDB in a Windows NT Environment 71
2.5.5 Example Scenarios. 73
2.5.6 Frequently Asked Questions. 79

Chapter 3. DB2 UDB Installation 83
3.1 Installing DB2 UDB Servers 83
3.1.1 Pre-Installation 83
3.1.2 Running the Installation Program 85
3.1.3 Post-Installation 102
3.1.4 Summary of the Installation 104
3.2 Uninstalling DB2 UDB 106
3.2.1 Stop All DB2 Applications and Processes. 107
3.2.2 Execute the DB2 UDB Uninstall Program 109
3.2.3 Summary of the Uninstall Process 109
3.3 Installing DB2 UDB Clients. 110
3.3.1 Pre-Installation 110
3.3.2 Installing the DB2 Client Application Enabler 112
3.3.3 Installing the DB2 Software Developer's Kit 117
3.4 Applying a DB2 UDB Fixpack 118

Chapter 4. DB2 UDB Client/Server Communications 123
4.1 DB2 UDB Client/Server Overview. 123
4.2 Discovery 125
4.2.1 Search Discovery 126
4.2.2 Known Discovery 128
4.2.3 Configuring Discovery. 130
4.2.4 Restricting Discovery 132
4.3 DB2 Administration Server (DAS) Instance. 133
4.3.1 Creation of a DAS instance. 136
4.3.2 DAS Instance Owner 139
4.3.3 Managing a DAS Instance 140
4.3.4 Configuring DAS Instance Communications After Installation . . .143
4.4 Client Configuration Assistant. 148
4.4.1 Search Discovery Using the CCA 150

    4.4.2 Known Discovery Using the CCA 156
4.5 Access Profiles. 165
    4.5.1 Server Access Profiles 165
    4.5.2 Client Access Profiles. 170
4.6 Manual Configuration Using the CCA 175
    4.6.1 Using TCP/IP 175
    4.6.2 Using NetBIOS 179
    4.6.3 Named Pipes 180
    4.6.4 Using IPX/SPX 182
    4.6.5 Using APPC 184
4.7 Configuration Using the Control Center 186
    4.7.1 Adding Databases to the Control Center. 186
    4.7.2 Changing the Communications Settings for an Instance 189
4.8 Summary 190

Chapter 5. DB2 UDB Graphical Tools 191
5.1 Overview of the Graphical Tools. 191
    5.1.1 Enabling Remote Administration. 195
    5.1.2 Control Center 196
    5.1.3 Command Center 206
    5.1.4 Script Center 209
    5.1.5 Journal. 213
    5.1.6 DB2 UDB SmartGuides 217

Chapter 6. Backup and Recovery 223
6.1 Overview of Database Recovery 223
    6.1.1 Crash Recovery 223
    6.1.2 Restore Recovery. 225
    6.1.3 Roll-forward Recovery 226
6.2 Recovery Concepts and Issues 227
    6.2.1 Unit of Work or Transaction 227
    6.2.2 Point of Recovery. 228
    6.2.3 Database Logs 228
    6.2.4 Database Configuration Parameters. 230
    6.2.5 Database and Table Space Backup 233
    6.2.6 Using the Control Center Backup Database Notebook 234
    6.2.7 Backup File Format 237
    6.2.8 Database and Table Space Restore 239
    6.2.9 Redefining Table Space Containers During Restore. 247
    6.2.10 Recovery History File 248
6.3 Database Backup and Recovery Using the SmartGuides 249
    6.3.1 Backup Database SmartGuide 249
    6.3.2 Restore Database SmartGuide. 252

6.4 DB2 UDB for Windows NT Tape Support 254
   6.4.1 Backing Up To Tape 259
   6.4.2 Restoring From Tape 260
   6.4.3 Disaster Recovery Considerations 262

Chapter 7. DB2 UDB Enterprise-Extended Edition 263
7.1 DB2 UDB EEE Concepts 263
   7.1.1 Database Partition Servers per Machine 264
   7.1.2 Coordinator Node 265
   7.1.3 Nodegroups 265
   7.1.4 The DB2 Node Configuration File 267
   7.1.5 Partitioning 269
7.2 Managing DB2 UDB EEE Instances 271
   7.2.1 Creating a Multipartition Instance 271
   7.2.2 Updating a DB2 instance to a Multipartition System 274
   7.2.3 Listing Instances 275
   7.2.4 Starting a DB2 Instance 275
   7.2.5 Stopping a DB2 Instance 276
   7.2.6 Adding the DB2 Instance to the Control Center 277
   7.2.7 Removing a DB2 Instance 280
7.3 Managing DB2 Database Partitions 281
   7.3.1 Listing Database Partition Servers 281
   7.3.2 Connecting to a Logical Node 281
7.4 Installing DB2 UDB EEE 283
   7.4.1 Installation Pre-Requisites 283
   7.4.2 Pre-Installation Tasks 284
   7.4.3 Run the Installation Program 289

Chapter 8. Failover Support with DB2 UDB EEE 301
8.1 Microsoft Cluster Server 301
   8.1.1 MSCS Concepts 302
   8.1.2 Clusters of Nodes 302
   8.1.3 Resources in MSCS 303
   8.1.4 Virtual Server 307
   8.1.5 Failover 308
   8.1.6 Shared Disk versus Shared Nothing 310
8.2 DB2 UDB EEE Failover Support 311
   8.2.1 DB2 UDB EEE Failover Configurations 311
   8.2.2 Implementing a DB2 UDB EEE Instance with Failover Support . 313
   8.2.3 Using DB2MSCS to Enable MSCS Support 315
   8.2.4 Using the Cluster Administrator to Enable MSCS Support 321
   8.2.5 Registering Database Drive Mappings 333
   8.2.6 Changing DB2 Node Configuration Information 337

8.2.7 Disabling DB2 Resource Failover to the second MSCS node . . 338
8.2.8 Failback Considerations 339
8.2.9 Application Support Considerations 340
8.2.10 Miscellaneous DB2 UDB EEE Concepts 341
8.3 Administering DB2 in an MSCS Environment 342
8.3.1 Starting and Stopping DB2 Resources 343
8.3.2 Running Scripts 343
8.3.3 Database Considerations 348
8.3.4 Windows NT User and Group Support 349
8.3.5 Communications Considerations. 349
8.3.6 System Time Considerations 350
8.3.7 Administration Server and Control Center Considerations 350
8.3.8 Limitations and Restrictions 351
8.4 DB2 UDB EEE Two-Node Mutual Takeover Example 351
8.4.1 Creating the MSCS Cluster. 352
8.4.2 Configuring DB2 UDB EEE and MSCS for Failover Support . . . 364
8.4.3 Registering Database Drive Mappings for DB2 390
8.4.4 Configuring the DB2 Administration Server for MSCS Failover . 391
8.4.5 Additional Configuration to Support FCM communications 393
8.4.6 Verifying Failover and Failback. 397

Chapter 9. Performance Monitoring 401
9.1 Windows NT Performance Monitor 401
9.1.1 Registering DB2 Performance Counters 402
9.1.2 Using the NT Performance Monitor with DB2 403
9.2 DB2 UDB Monitoring 418
9.2.1 Snapshot Monitoring. 419
9.2.2 Event Monitoring. 430

Chapter 10. Problem Determination 441
10.1 Approach to DB2 UDB Problem Determination 441
10.2 Describing the Problem 442
10.2.1 Example Problem Descriptions 443
10.3 Gathering the Appropriate Diagnostic Information 443
10.3.1 Choosing the Correct Diagnostic Level 444
10.3.2 The DB2 Trace Facility 445
10.3.3 CLI/ODBC Traces 451
10.3.4 The Windows NT Event Log 453
10.3.5 Database Analysis and Repair Tool 456
10.4 Examining the Diagnostic Information. 458
10.4.1 DB2DIAG.LOG File Entry Format 458
10.4.2 Dump Files 461
10.4.3 Trap Files 462

10.4.4 Formatting the DB2 Trace. 464
10.4.5 The Format of a Trace Entry. 465
10.4.6 Trace Information That is Not Captured 466
10.4.7 Verifying That the Error Has Been Captured. 467
10.4.8 Examining a CLI/ODBC Trace 467
10.5 Determining the Source of the Problem 474
10.5.1 Online Help. 474
10.5.2 DB2 Technical Library on the Web 478
10.6 Installation Problems 483
10.6.1 Common Installation Errors 484
10.7 Information to Collect for IBM Support 487
10.7.1 What to Collect. 487
10.7.2 History of Reported Problems. 488

Appendix A. Related Publications. 491
A.1 International Technical Support Organization Publications 491
A.2 Other Publications. 491

Index 493

Figures

1. DB2 Universal Database 2
2. Remote Client Accessing DB2 Server Using CAE. 4
3. DB2 UDB Personal Edition 6
4. DB2 Workgroup Edition with Remote Clients 7
5. Accessing Internet Data. 9
6. DRDA Application Flow 11
7. DRDA Flow in DB2 Connect Personal Edition. 12
8. DRDA Flow in DB2 Connect Enterprise Edition. 13
9. DB2 Personal Developer's and Universal Developer's Edition 15
10. Positioning of Windows NT 16
11. Small Workgroup Example 18
12. Trusted Domain Example 19
13. DB2 in an Enterprise Environment. 21
14. Workgroup Security 26
15. Creating a Windows NT Share 27
16. Setting Permissions on a Share. 28
17. Setting File Permissions 29
18. Domain Security. 30
19. Server Manager 32
20. Creating a User Account 35
21. Creating a Global Group 36
22. User Manager Showing Global Groups 37
23. Creating a Local Group 38
24. Local Groups in a Domain 40
25. User Authentication in the Windows NT Environment 41
26. Domain A Trusts Domain B 43
27. Trust Relationships Between Domains A, B, and C. 44
28. Creating a Trust Relationship between Domains. 45
29. The Single Domain Model 46
30. The Master Domain Model. 48
31. The Multiple Master Domain Model 50
32. The Complete Trust Model 52
33. Cross-Domain Authentication 54
34. DB2 Access Control Hierarchy 56
35. Database Authorities 60
36. Authentication on Windows 95/98 and Windows NT 64
37. Setting DB2 Security Service to Start Automatically 70
38. DB2 Instances as Windows NT Services. 71
39. Security in a Workgroup. 75
40. Security in a Single Domain. 77

41. Client Authentication in a Master Account Domain 79
42. Welcome Panel 86
43. Select DB2 Products 87
44. Select Installation Type 88
45. Select DB2 Components 89
46. Graphical Tools Subcomponents 90
47. Online Books 91
48. Select Start Options 92
49. Customize Communication Protocols 93
50. Customize DB2 Instance 94
51. NetBIOS Settings for the DB2 Instance 94
52. TCP/IP Settings for the DB2 Instance 95
53. TCP/IP Settings for the DAS Instance 96
54. Username and Password for the DAS Instance 96
55. Setup Cannot Verify db2admin's Password 97
56. Summary of Components 98
57. Copying Files During Installation 100
58. Complete Setup 101
59. DB2 UDB First Steps 102
60. License Use Runtime 103
61. Nodelock Administration Tool 104
62. Windows NT Registry Editor 105
63. Search the DB2 Online Books 106
64. Check DB2 Processes from Task Manager 108
65. Confirm DB2 Deletion 109
66. Uninstall Completed 109
67. Enable Remote Administration Option 113
68. Select DB2 Components 114
69. Customize NetBIOS 115
70. Summary of Installation 115
71. Complete Setup 116
72. Select Components for DB2 SDK 118
73. Space Required for DB2 Fixpack 119
74. Windows NT Registry Entries for DB2 UDB 120
75. DB2 Client/Server 124
76. Search Discovery 126
77. Limitation of Search Discovery with Router/Bridge 127
78. Known Discovery 129
79. Discovery Hierachy 133
80. DB2 Server Instances and DAS Instance 134
81. Sample DAS Instance Configuration 135
82. Customize Communications Protocols 137
83. Customizing the Administration Server 138

84. DAS Username and Password Panel 139
85. Control Center - Add DAS Instance 144
86. Setup Communications 145
87. Comparison of Communications Settings for the DAS Instance 148
88. Client Configuration Assistant, Main Panel 149
89. Add Database Smartguide 151
90. Add Database Using Search Discovery 152
91. Add Database Search Results 153
92. Add Database Search Results Expanded 153
93. Add Database, Alias Page 154
94. Add Database, ODBC Page 155
95. Database Connection Test 155
96. Test Connection 156
97. Successful Connection 156
98. Add Database Smartguide 157
99. Add Database Using Known Discovery 158
100. Add System for the Different Protocols 159
101. Add Database, Target Database Page 161
102. Add Database, Alias Page 162
103. Add Database, ODBC Page 163
104. Database Connection Test 163
105. Test Connection 164
106. Successful Connection 164
107. Generate Server Access Profile 166
108. Sample Extract from a Server Access Profile 167
109. Importing a Server Access Profile 169
110. Server Access Profile, Three Tiers 169
111. Client Configuration Assistant, Export Client Access Profile 171
112. Databases to Export 171
113. Sample Extract from a Client Access Profile 173
114. Import Client Access Profile 174
115. Add Database - Protocol 176
116. Add Database - TCP/IP 177
117. Add Database - Target Database 177
118. Add Database - Alias 178
119. Add Database - ODBC 178
120. Add Database - Protocol 179
121. Add Database - NetBIOS 180
122. Add Database - Protocol 181
123. Add Database - Named Pipe 182
124. Add Database - Protocol 183
125. Add Database - IPX/SPX 184
126. Add Database - Protocol 185

127. Add Database - APPC. 185
128. Control Center - Systems Menu 187
129. Control Center - Add system. 188
130. Add Instance 188
131. Control Center - Add database 189
132. Choosing a Configuration Method. 190
133. Windows NT Desktop Showing Contents of DB2 Folders. 192
134. Roadmap to the GUI Tools in DB2 UDB V5 193
135. Main Components of the Control Center. 196
136. The Database Manager Configuration Notebook 198
137. Get Database Manager Configuration Command Output 199
138. List and Force Application Options 200
139. Database Administrative Tasks, Roll-Forward Recovery 201
140. Syntax of the Rollforward Command. 202
141. Loading a Table Using the Control Center 203
142. Column Panel for Loading. 204
143. Count Panel, Load Modes and Count Options 205
144. Syntax of the Load Command. 206
145. Command Center 207
146. Command Center Showing Results on Scrollable Window. 208
147. Saving a Command Script 209
148. Script Center 210
149. Script Center Options 211
150. Creating an Example Script in the Script Center. 212
151. Scheduling the Example Script in the Script Center 213
152. Journal Tool Showing the Pending Job. 215
153. Journal Tool Showing Job History. 216
154. Job Results in Journal 217
155. Client Configuration Assistant, Add Database SmartGuide 218
156. Performance Configuration SmartGuide 219
157. Database Status from the Control Center 224
158. Crash Recovery. 225
159. Restore Recovery 226
160. Roll-Forward Recovery 227
161. Circular Logging 229
162. Archival Logging 229
163. Database Configuration Parameters Related to Database Logging 231
164. Backup Database Options in the Control Center 234
165. Backup Page in Backup Database Notebook 235
166. Options Page in the Backup Database Notebook. 236
167. Script Center Showing the Backup Database and Table Space Scripts . 237
168. Backup File Format Example 238
169. Restore to New Database 239

170.The Restore Database Notebook 240
171.Table Spaces Page on the Restore Database Notebook 241
172.Roll-Forward Page on the Restore Database Notebook 242
173.Options Page in Recover Database Notebook 243
174.Restore Table Space Using the Control Center 244
175.Restore Table Space Notebook, Backup Image 245
176.Restore Table Space Notebook, Roll-Forward Page 246
177.Restore Table Space Using the Redirect Option 247
178.Backup Database SmartGuide, Availability Panel. 250
179.Backup Database SmartGuide, Rate of Change Panel 251
180.Backup Database SmartGuide, Recommendations Panel 252
181.Restore Database SmartGuide, Restore Status Panel 253
182.Restore Database SmartGuide, Roll Forward Panel. 254
183.SCSI Adapter Tape Devices 255
184.Tape Device Properties. 256
185.Windows NT Backup Tool 257
186.Initialize Tape Command. 258
187.Script Used to Backup Databases to Tape 259
188.Script Used to Restore Databases from Tape. 261
189.DB2 UDB EEE Concepts 264
190.Default Nodegroups 267
191.Data Placement in DB2 UDB EEE 270
192.Syntax of the db2icrt Command 272
193.Syntax of the db2iupdt Command 274
194.Starting a Database Instance from the DB2 UDB Control Center 276
195.Adding an Instance to the Control Center List. 278
196.Choosing an Instance to be Added. 279
197.New List of Instances 279
198.Syntax of the db2nlist command 281
199.Installation Choices for DB2 UDB EEE 287
200.DB2 Select Products Window 290
201.Select an Installation Option 290
202.Configure the Instance Owning Database Partition Server. 291
203.Enter a TCP/IP Port Number for the DB2 Performance Monitor 292
204.Customize Communications Protocols 292
205.Enter Username and Password for the Administration Server 293
206.Completion of the DB2 Installation Procedure 294
207.Select Products Window 295
208.Select an Installation Option 295
209.Select the Instance Owning Machine 296
210.Configure the New Node. 297
211.DB2 First Steps 298
212.Basic Configuration of an MSCS Cluster 303

213.Hot-Standby Failover Configuration 312
214.Mutual Takeover Failover Configuration 313
215.Syntax of the DB2MSCS utility 321
216.Verifying Installation of DB2 Resource Type...................... 322
217.Syntax of the db2icrt Command 329
218.Syntax of the db2iclus migrate Command......................... 330
219.Syntax of the db2iclus add Command............................ 331
220.Syntax of the db2ncrt Command................................. 332
221.Syntax of the db2ncrt Command................................. 334
222.Syntax of the db2drvmp reconcile Command 336
223.Syntax of the db2nchg Command................................ 337
224.Syntax of the db2iclus drop Command 338
225.Initial Server Configuration 353
226.Forming a New MSCS Cluster 354
227.Naming the New MSCS Cluster 354
228.User Account Information for DB2LAB7 355
229.Shared Drive for the DB2CLUS MSCS Cluster Quorum Files 356
230.Network Information for Network Adapter IBMFE1 on DB2LAB7 357
231.Network Information for Network Adapter AMDPCN2 on DB2LAB7.... 357
232.Prioritizing Internal Network Communications on DB2LAB7.......... 358
233.Defining the IP Address for the DB2CLUS cluster 359
234.Verifying Cluster Server is Started 359
235.Joining an Existing MSCS Cluster............................... 360
236.Name of the Cluster to Join.................................... 361
237.User Account Information for DB2LAB5 362
238.Network Information for Network Adapter AMDPCN2 on DB2LAB5.... 363
239.Cluster Administrator Tool on DB2LAB7.......................... 364
240.The DB2MSCS Input File, cluster.cfg 367
241.Verifying the Installation of the DB2 Resource Type................ 369
242.Creating a New MSCS Group 370
243.Creating the DB2 Node 0 Cluster Group......................... 371
244.Nominating Preferred Owners.................................. 371
245.Successful Creation of the Cluster Group........................ 372
246.Changing the Group for a Disk Resource 372
247.Confirming Resource Group Changes 373
248.Moving Disk Resources....................................... 373
249.Creating a New Disk Resource 374
250.Assigning a Disk to a Disk Resource 375
251.Creating a File Share for the Instance Directory 376
252.Assigning a Drive Dependency for the Instance Directory 377
253.File Share Parameters for the Instance Directory.................. 378
254.Creating the IP Address Resource for DB2........................ 379
255.Parameters for the IP Address Resource for DB2 380

256.Creating a New Network Name for DB2 381
257.Dependencies for the Network Name for DB2 382
258.Network Name DB2WOLF0 for the DB2 Instance 382
259.Creating the DB2MPP-0 DB2 Resource 383
260.Dependencies for the DB2MPP-0 DB2 Resource. 384
261.Configuration of DB2 Node 0 Group in the Cluster Administrator Tool . . 385
262.Nominating Preferred Owners for the Second MSCS Group 386
263.Changing Ownership of Disk Group 3 387
264.Change of Ownership of Disk Group 3 387
265.Configuration of the DB2 Node 1 Group 388
266.Creating the DB2DAS00 DB2 Resource. 392
267.Selecting the DB2DAS00 Service 393
268.Changing the Startup Type for the DB2DAS00 Service 393
269.Adding the FCM IP Address as a Dependency to DB2MPP-0 395
270.Adding the FCM IP Address as a Dependency to DB2MPP-1 396
271.Failback Properties for DB2 Node 0 397
272.NT Performance Monitor. 404
273.Add to Chart 405
274.NT Performance Monitor - Local Database Connections 406
275.Chart Options 407
276.Chart - Histogram Option 407
277.Windows NT Performance Monitor - Alert. 408
278.Add to Alert 409
279.Alert Added 410
280.Alert Options 410
281.NT Performance Monitor - Log 411
282.Add to Log. 412
283.Log Options - Start Logging 412
284.Log Options - Stop Logging. 413
285.NT Performance Monitor - Report. 414
286.Add to Report 415
287.Sample Report 415
288.Timeframe of Logged Data 416
289.Selecting a Remote NT Machine to Monitor 417
290.DB2 Control Center - Configure Instance 420
291.Configure Instance - Monitor Tab 421
292.Performance Monitor Profile 424
293.Table Monitoring Enabled 425
294.Performance Monitor Details. 426
295.Performance Graph. 427
296.Alert Center 427
297.Creating an Event Monitor. 432
298.Create Event Monitors - Options 433

299. Stop Event Monitoring 435
300. Event Analyzer 436
301. Monitored Periods View 437
302. SQL Statements View 438
303. SQL Statement Details 439
304. DB2 Trace Facility 450
305. Trace Formatting Options 451
306. Configuring for a CLI/ODBC Trace 453
307. Viewing Windows NT Application Event Log 455
308. Web Page of DB2 Technical Library 479
309. DB2 Library Search Facility 480
310. Example of a Technical Note Related to a Problem 483

Tables

1. List of Definitions 23
2. Sizing the SAM Database 31
3. Related DB2 Processes. 108
4. Parameters that Affect Discovery 130
5. List of SmartGuides 221
6. USEREXIT and LOGRETAIN Parameters. 232
7. Monitor Switches 419
8. Event Monitor Records 434
9. Messages Available from the Command Line Processor 476
10. DB2 for Windows NT Common Installation Errors. 484

Preface

DB2 Universal Database is an award-winning database management system available on a wide range of platforms. This means you have more choice and flexibility than ever before in deciding where to store your valuable data, and which platforms your users and decision makers can use to access this data. DB2 Universal Database (or UDB) allows you to build robust, industrial-strength database applications to address all of your business requirements, no matter how complex.

Written by DB2 experts from around the globe, this book is unique in its coverage of DB2 Universal Database on the Windows NT platform. Everything from configuring client/server communications to exploiting the security features in Windows NT is covered in a step-by-step, easy to follow manner.

If you are a database administrator, system administrator or programmer and you need to implement and maintain a database system which will be accessed by local or remote clients, or if you need to understand and use DB2 Universal Database on the Windows NT platform, this book is a must!

How This Book is Organized

- "Overview" on page 1

  This provides an overview of the DB2 products, in particular DB2 for Windows NT.

- "DB2 UDB and Windows NT Security" on page 23

  This provides an overall view of security within Windows NT. Also discussed is how security for the DB2 products work in a Windows NT environment.

- "DB2 UDB Installation" on page 83

  The installation of a range of DB2 UDB products is covered in this chapter.

- "DB2 UDB Client/Server Communications" on page 123

  Everything about using the Discovery function to configure clients to connect to a DB2 UDB database server is covered in this chapter. Also presented is connectivity to a DRDA host database.

- "DB2 UDB Graphical Tools" on page 191

This provides an overview of the functions of the graphical tools included in DB2 Universal Database, including the Control Center, the Command Center, Journal and Script Center.

- "Backup and Recovery" on page 223

This provides an overview of how to backup and restore databases and table spaces using DB2 UDB.

- "DB2 UDB Enterprise-Extended Edition" on page 263

This section covers the version of DB2 UDB which runs on a cluster of Windows NT machines. A step-by-step example of installing DB2 UDB Enterprise-Extended Edition (EEE) is given.

- "Failover Support with DB2 UDB EEE" on page 301

Using Microsoft's MSCS support, two Windows NT machines can be setup to provide failover support for each other. This chapter shows how to use DB2 UDB in this environment.

- "Performance Monitoring" on page 401

This chapter looks at the performance tools available within Windows NT that you can use to monitor and tune your DB2 UDB for Windows NT environment. Also discussed are some of the facilities within DB2 for performance monitoring.

- "Problem Determination" on page 441

This provides helpful tips and techniques in diagnosing problems that you may encounter in a DB2 UDB for Windows NT environment.

The Team That Wrote This Book

This book was produced by a team of specialists from around the world working at the International Technical Support Organization in Austin, Texas.

Jonathan Cook is the DB2 Project Leader at the International Technical Support Organization (ITSO), Austin Center. He has ten years of experience as a database specialist working in the areas of application development and database administration. He has been with IBM since 1992, working in both the United Kingdom and France before joining the Austin ITSO. He writes extensively and teaches IBM classes worldwide on DB2 for the UNIX and Intel platforms.

Robert Harbus is the DB2 Universal Database Certification and Education coordinator at the IBM Toronto Lab. A member of the DB2 UDB team since its inception in 1991, Robert provided Technical Marketing and Electronic customer support and direct customer support most recently as a member of the DB2 Universal Database Enterprise - Extended Edition (EEE) support team. Robert is currently responsible for the DB2 UDB certification program and testing, and works with the ITSO and Education & Training to ensure that DB2 UDB education courses, training and material are available to meet the needs of DB2 UDB users. Robert teaches DB2 internals and certification courses worldwide and is involved in producing certification guides and redbooks.

Dwaine Snow has worked with DB2 Universal Database and its predecessors for the past 8 years. During this time, he has written and designed applications using DB2. He has also worked in the DB2 UDB Customer Service Team. Dwaine has written a number of DB2-related articles and has contributed to a number of DB2 redbooks. He has presented at DB2 conferences and has taught DB2 UDB courses worldwide.

Anthony Cunningham has been working with DB2 since joining IBM in 1994. Initially he was involved with internal DB2/390 systems, covering a multitude of services ranging from installation through to disaster recovery. Later he became interested in DB2 Common Server and moving onto DB2 UDB, gaining an interest in connectivity and cross platform support. Today Anthony works for the UK Software Business providing technical pre-sales support.

Rubina Goolamhussen is a Data Management Products support specialist in IBM Portugal. She supports DB2 on Intel and UNIX platforms. She has been working with related DB2 products for over three years.

Cheng Gu has been an IBM technical specialist since 1996, providing technical support on IBM Data Management products and solutions, working with DB2, Visual Warehouse and DB2 OLAP Server. Cheng also provides technical support on major Enterprise Resource Planning solutions with DB2, such as SAP and Baan. He has certified in the areas of DB2 Database Administration and SAP R/3 on DB2 Installation.

Nancy Miller is a part of IBM's Personal Solutions System Center, which performs services and support for DB2 and many other products on the Intel platform. She has been working with and supporting DB2 since 1992.

Yu-Phing Ong has worked in the IBM Support Centre of Australia, for the last 4 years. He is the country specialist in Australia, for DB2 on the PC and Unix platforms, and is a member, and the team leader, of the ISC group which supports the Asia Pacific (South) region in the suite of Information/Knowledge management products from IBM.

A special thanks to Dale Hagen of the IBM Toronto Lab for providing assistance and scenarios in the area of DB2 and Windows NT security. His assistance was invaluable.

Thanks also to the following people for their significant contributions to this project:

Peter Pau
IBM Toronto Lab

Lan Pham
IBM Toronto Lab

Juliana Hsu
IBM Toronto Lab

Calene Janacek
IBM Austin

The following people were invaluable for their expertise and moral support:

Elizabeth Barnes
IBM ITSO Austin

Catherine Cook
IBM France

Chapter 1. Overview

This chapter gives you an overview of the DB2 family of products, in
particular DB2 Universal Database (UDB) on the Windows NT platform. The
chapter is organized as follows:

- Introduction to the DB2 family of database servers
- Introduction to DB2 Universal Database components and products
- Overall information about Windows NT, including sample configurations
- How DB2 is integrated with Windows NT

Throughout this chapter, we illustrate some of the features that are found in
DB2 UDB for Windows NT. Although the versions of DB2 on the different
supported platforms are very similar, the implementation of DB2 on Windows
NT may be slightly different due to particular functions of the operating
system.

1.1 DB2 Family of Products

The term *universal* in DB2 Universal Database means the ability to store all
kinds of electronic information. This includes traditional relational data as well
as structured and unstructured binary information, documents and text in
many languages, graphics, images, multimedia (audio and video), maps,
insurance claims forms or any other type of electronic information.

The DB2 database products are collectively known as the *DB2 Family.* The
DB2 family is divided into two main groups:

- DB2 for midrange and large systems. Supported platforms are OS/400,
  VSE/VM and OS/390.

- DB2 UDB for Intel and UNIX environments. Supported platforms include
  OS/2, Windows NT, Windows 95/98, AIX, HP-UX, and Sun Solaris.

The features and implementations of the midrange and large system
members of the DB2 Family are very similar to DB2 UDB. When there are
differences, they are very often due to the differing features of the operating
systems.

DB2 UDB provides seamless database connectivity using the most popular
network communications protocols, including NetBIOS, TCP/IP, IPX/SPX,
Named Pipes, and APPC. The infrastructure (but not the protocol) that DB2
database clients use to communicate with DB2 database servers is provided
by DB2.

In Figure 1, some of the DB2 Universal Database products are shown. DB2 UDB is supported on hardware platforms ranging from laptops to massively parallel systems with hundreds of nodes. This provides extensive and granular growth.

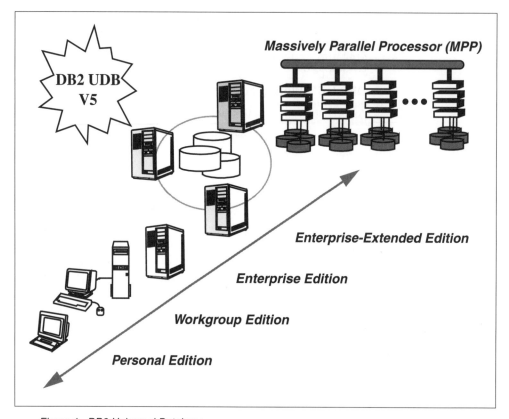

Figure 1. DB2 Universal Database

1.2 DB2 UDB Family of Products

There are three main DB2 UDB products, namely:

1. **DB2 Universal Database**. There are four versions (known as editions) of the DB2 Universal Database product, as shown in Figure 1:

   - **DB2 UDB Personal Edition**

     An RDBMS engine that **will not** support remote clients. This is available on the Intel platform only.

   - **DB2 UDB Workgroup Edition**

     An RDBMS engine that **will** support remote clients. This is available on the Intel uniprocessor machines only.

   - **DB2 UDB Enterprise Edition**

     Similar to the Workgroup Edition, but is also available for SMP machines. In addition, this product allows remote client applications to access data on a host database using the Distributed Relational Database Architecture (DRDA).

   - **DB2 UDB Enterprise-Extended Edition**

     Similar to the Enterprise Edition, with additional support for clusters of database servers in a partitioned database environment.

2. **DB2 Connect.** This product provides the ability to access a host database using DRDA. There are two versions of this product: DB2 Connect Personal Edition and DB2 Connect Enterprise Edition.

3. **DB2 Developer's Edition**. This product provides the ability to develop and test a database application for one user. There are two versions of this product: DB2 Personal Developer's Edition (PDE) and DB2 Universal Developer's Edition (UDE).

All DB2 products have a common component called the DB2 Client Application Enabler (CAE). Once a DB2 application has been developed, the DB2 Client Application Enabler component must be installed on each workstation where the application is executed. Figure 2 shows the relationship between the application, CAE and the DB2 Database Server. If the application and database are installed on the same workstation, the application is known as a *local client*. If the application is installed on a workstation other than the DB2 server, the application is known as a *remote client*.

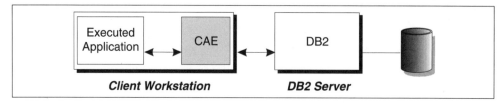

Figure 2. Remote Client Accessing DB2 Server Using CAE

The Client Application Enabler provides functions other than the ability to communicate with a DB2 UDB server or DB2 Connect gateway. Using the CAE, you can do any of the following:

- Issue an interactive SQL statement on a remote client which accesses data on a remote UDB server.
- Graphically administer and monitor a UDB database server.
- Run applications that were developed to comply with the Open Database Connectivity (ODBC) standard or Java Database Connectivity (JDBC).

There are no licensing requirements to install the Client Application Enabler component. Licensing is controlled at the DB2 UDB server.

The version of the CAE that you need to install depends on the operating system on the client machine. For example, if you have a database application developed for AIX, you need to install the Client Application Enabler for AIX.

There is a different CAE for each supported DB2 client operating system. The supported platforms include OS/2, Windows NT, Windows 95/98, Windows 3.x, AIX, HP-UX, MacIntosh, DOS, Sun Solaris, SCO Unixware and Silicon Graphics IRIX. The CAE component should be installed on all end-user workstations

A complete set of CAEs is provided with Workgroup Edition, Enterprise Edition, Enterprise-Extended Edition, and with the DB2 Connect Enterprise Edition products. This set of CAEs is provided on a CD-ROM, and is referred to as the *DB2 CAE Client Pack*.

Let's take a look in more detail at the DB2 UDB products.

1.2.1 DB2 UDB Personal Edition

DB2 UDB Personal Edition provides the same engine functions found in Workgroup, Enterprise and Enterprise-Extended Editions. However, DB2 Personal Edition cannot accept requests from a remote client.

As the product name suggests, DB2 Personal Edition is licensed for one user to create databases on the workstation in which it was installed. DB2 Personal Edition can be used as a remote client to a DB2 UDB server where either Workgroup, Enterprise or Enterprise-Extended is installed, since it contains the Client Application Enabler component. Therefore, once the DB2 Personal Edition product has been installed, you can use this workstation as a remote client connecting to a DB2 Server, as well as a DB2 Server managing local databases.

The DB2 Personal Edition product may be appropriate for the following users:

- DB2 mobile users who use a local database and can take advantage of the replication feature in UDB to copy local changes to a remote server.
- DB2 end-users requiring access to local and remote databases.

Figure 3 shows an example of a DB2 Personal Edition installation. In this example, the user can access a local database on their mobile workstation (laptop) and access remote databases found on the database server. From the laptop, the user can make changes to the database throughout the day and replicate those changes as a remote client to a UDB remote server.

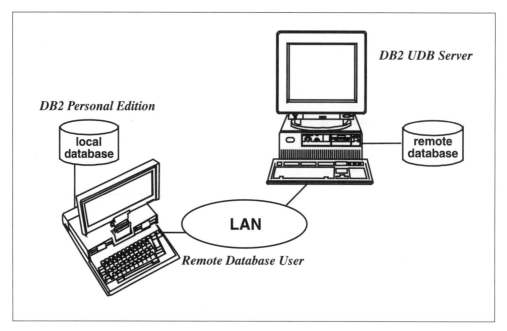

DB2 Personal Edition

DB2 UDB Server

local
database

remote
database

LAN

Remote Database User

Figure 3. DB2 UDB Personal Edition

DB2 Personal Edition includes graphical tools that enable you to administer, tune for performance, access remote DB2 servers, process SQL queries, and manage other servers from a single workstation.

In addition to Windows NT, this product is available for the OS/2, and Windows 95/98 operating systems. DB2 Personal Edition is licensed for a single user.

1.2.2 DB2 Workgroup Edition

DB2 Workgroup Edition contains all DB2 Personal Edition product functions with the added ability to accept requests from remote clients. Like DB2 Personal Edition, DB2 Workgroup Edition is for the Intel platform only. In Figure 4 on page 7, a mobile user who occasionally connects to a LAN is using DB2 Personal Edition. This mobile user can access any of the databases on the workstation where DB2 Workgroup Edition is installed.

DB2 Workgroup Edition is designed for use in a LAN environment. It provides support for both remote and local clients. A workstation with DB2 Workgroup Edition installed can be connected to a network and participate in a client/server environment as shown in Figure 4:

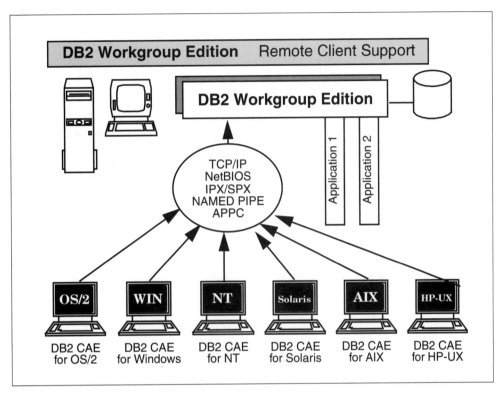

Figure 4. DB2 Workgroup Edition with Remote Clients

In Figure 4, *application 1* and *application 2* are local database applications. Remote clients can also potentially execute *application 1* and *application 2*, if the proper client/server setup has been performed. A DB2 application does not contain any specific information regarding the physical location of the database. DB2 client applications communicate with DB2 Workgroup Edition using a supported protocol and the DB2 CAE. Depending on the client and server operating system involved, DB2 Workgroup Edition supports the following protocols: TCP/IP, NetBIOS, IPX/SPX, Named Pipes and APPC.

DB2 Workgroup Edition includes Net.Data for Internet support and the graphical management tools that are also found in DB2 Personal Edition. In addition, the DB2 Client Pack is shipped with DB2 Workgroup Edition. The DB2 Client Pack contains all of the current DB2 Client Application Enablers

DB2 Workgroup Edition is licensed on a per-user basis. The base license is for one concurrent or registered DB2 user. It is available for OS/2 and SCO UnixWare as well as Windows NT. Additional entitlements (user licenses) are available in multiples of 1, 5, 10 or 50. DB2 Workgroup Edition is licensed for a machine with one to four processors only. Entitlements are required for additional users.

1.2.3 DB2 Enterprise Edition

DB2 UDB Enterprise Edition includes all of the function provided in the Workgroup Edition, plus support for host database connectivity. It allows access to DB2 databases residing on host systems such as DB2 for OS/390 Version 5.1, DB2 for OS/400, and DB2 Server for VSE/VM Version 5.1. The licensing for DB2 Enterprise Edition is based on the number of users, number of machines installed and processor type. The base license is for one concurrent or registered DB2 user.   Additional entitlements are available for 1, 5, 10 or 50 users. The base installation of DB2 Enterprise is on a uni-processor. Tier upgrades are available if the machine has more than one processor.   With the first tier upgrade, you receive the rights to a free entitlement for 50 users.

In addition to Windows NT, DB2 Enterprise Edition is available on OS/2 and the following UNIX platforms: AIX, HP-UX, Sun Solaris and SCO UnixWare.

1.2.3.1 Sample Scenario Using DB2 Enterprise Edition

The popularity of the Internet and the World Wide Web has created a demand for web access to enterprise data. The DB2 UDB server product includes the Net.Data product, which plays an important role in the configuration shown in Figure 5:

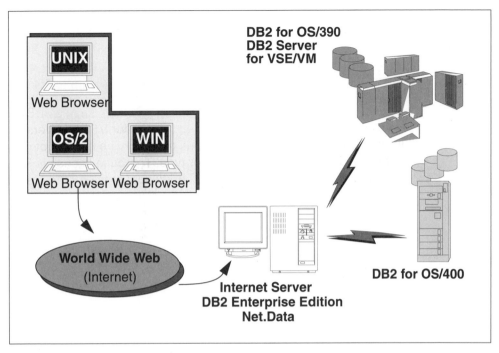

Figure 5. Accessing Internet Data

Applications that are built with Net.Data may be stored on a web server and can be viewed from any web browser. From the web browser interface, users can either select automated queries or define new ones that retrieve specified information directly from a DB2 UDB database. Figure 5 illustrates how DB2 Enterprise Edition acts as the database server and the gateway to access data stored in DB2 for OS/400, DB2 for OS/390 and DB2 Server for VSE/VM. The ability to connect to a host database (DB2 Connect) is packaged with DB2 Enterprise Edition.

1.2.4 DB2 Universal Database Enterprise-Extended Edition

This product contains all the features and functions of DB2 Enterprise Edition. It also provides the ability for a database to be partitioned within/across multiple independent computers of the same platform. To the end-user or application developer, the database appears to be on a single computer. While DB2 Workgroup and DB2 Enterprise Edition can handle large databases, Enterprise-Extended Edition is designed for applications where the database is simply too large for a single computer to handle efficiently. SQL operations can operate in parallel on the individual database partitions, thus increasing the execution of a single query.

DB2 Enterprise-Extended Edition licensing is similar to that of DB2 Enterprise Edition. However, the licensing is based on the number of registered or concurrent users, the type of processor and the number of database partitions. You must have a license for each database partition (node) in your configuration. The base license for DB2 Enterprise-Extended Edition is for machines ranging from a uni-processor up to a 4-way SMP. The base number of users is different in Enterprise-Extended Edition than in Enterprise Edition. The base user license is for one user with an additional 50 users, equaling 51 users for that database partition. Tier upgrades also are available. The first tier upgrade for a database partition provides the rights to a 50 user entitlement pack for that database partition or node. Additional user entitlements are available for 1, 5, 10 or 50 users.

In addition to Windows NT, DB2 Enterprise-Extended Edition (EEE) is available on the AIX and Sun Solaris platforms.

1.2.5 DB2 Connect

The DB2 Connect product allows clients to access data stored on database servers that implement the Distributed Relational Database Architecture. The target database server for a DB2 Connect installation is known as a *DRDA Application Server*. Figure 6 on page 11 shows the flow of database requests through DB2 Connect.

DB2 Connect supports the APPC and TCP/IP communication protocols to provide communications support between DRDA Application Servers and DRDA Application Requesters. Any of the supported network protocols can be used for the DB2 client (CAE) to establish a connection to the DB2 Connect gateway.

The database application must request the data from a DRDA Application Server through a DRDA Application Requester. The DB2 CAE component is not a DRDA Application Requester.

The DB2 Connect product provides *DRDA Application Requester* functionality.

The DRDA Application Server accessed using DB2 Connect could be any of the following DB2 Servers:

- DB2 for OS/390. Only Version 5.1 or higher supports TCP/IP in a DRDA environment.
- DB2 for OS/400. Only Version 4.2 or higher supports TCP/IP in a DRDA environment.
- DB2 Server for VSE/VM.

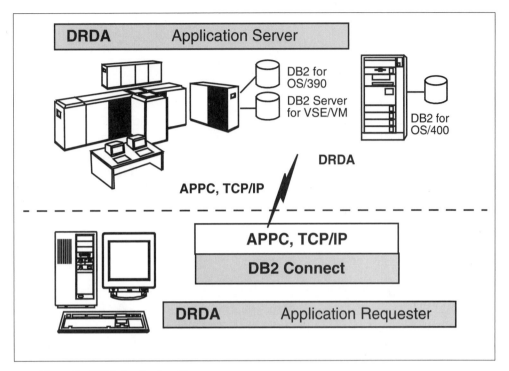

Figure 6. DRDA Application Flow

1.2.5.1 DB2 Connect Personal Edition

DB2 Connect Personal Edition is available only on the Intel platform: OS/2, Windows NT, Windows 95/98 and Windows 3.x. It provides access to host databases from the workstation where it is installed. Figure 7 on page 12 shows the DRDA flow between the Application Requester and the Application Server using the DB2 Connect Personal Edition product.

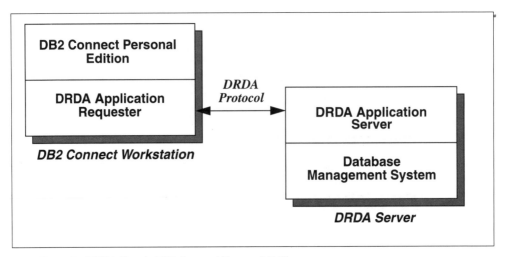

Figure 7. DRDA Flow in DB2 Connect Personal Edition

1.2.5.2 DB2 Connect Enterprise Edition

The DB2 Connect Enterprise Edition product provides the ability for multiple clients to access host data. A DB2 Connect gateway routes each database request from the DB2 clients to the appropriate DRDA Application Server database. Figure 8 on page 13 shows the addition of a remote client. The remote client communicates with the DB2 Connect workstation using any of the supported communication protocols supported by the DB2 Connect gateway platform.

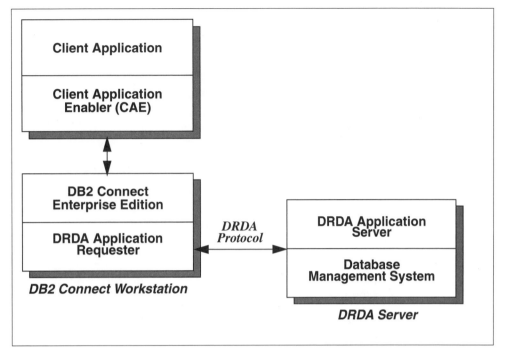

Figure 8. DRDA Flow in DB2 Connect Enterprise Edition

The licensing for DB2 Connect Enterprise is user-based. That is, it is licensed on the number of concurrent or registered users. The base license is for one user with additional entitlements of 1, 5, 10 or 50 users. DB2 Connect Enterprise Edition is supported on OS/2, Windows NT, AIX, HP-UX and Sun Solaris.

1.2.6 DB2 Developer's Edition

The DB2 Developer's Edition is a separate product that can be installed on either the DB2 server or on a DB2 client. It provides all of the necessary data access tools for developing SQL applications. It is available in DB2 Personal Developer's (PDE) Edition and DB2 Universal Developer's Edition (UDE). DB2 Personal Developer's Edition is available only for the Intel platforms. DB2 Universal Developer's Edition is available for all server platforms except Enterprise-Extended Edition.

The application development environment provided with both versions of the Developer's Edition allows application developers to write programs using the following methods:

• Embedded SQL

- Call Level Interface or CLI (compatible with the Microsoft ODBC standard)
- DB2 Application Programming Interfaces (APIs)
- DB2 data access through the World Wide Web
- Java with embedded SQL (SQLJ)

The programming environment also includes the necessary programming libraries, header files, code samples and pre-compilers for the supported programming languages. Several programming languages, including COBOL, FORTRAN, REXX, C, C++ and Java are supported by DB2 (depending on the operating system platform)

Figure 9 on page 15 shows the contents of both the DB2 Universal Developer's Edition and the DB2 Personal Developer's Edition. Both products contain the following

- Software Developer's Kit (SDK) - Provides the environment and tools you need to develop applications that access DB2 databases using embedded SQL or DB2 Call Level Interface (CLI). This is found in both PDE and UDE. The SDK in the PDE is for OS/2, Windows 16-bit and 32-bit 3.x, Windows 95/98 and Windows NT. The SDK in the UDE is for all DB2 platforms.

- Extender Support - Provides the ability to define large object data types, and includes related functions that allow your applications to access and retrieve documents, photographs, music, movie clips or fingerprints.

- Visual Age for Java - A suite of application development tools for building Java-compatible applications, applets, and JavaBean components that run on any Java Development Kit (JDK) enabled browser. It contains Enterprise Access Builder for building JDBC interfaces to data managed by DB2. It can also be used to create DB2 stored procedures and DB2 user-defined functions.

- Net.Data - A comprehensive World Wide Web (WWW) development environment to create dynamic web pages or complex web-based applications that can access DB2 databases.

- Lotus Approach - Provides a graphical interface to perform queries, develop reports and analyze data. You can also develop applications using LotusScript, a full-featured, object-oriented programming language. This is found in both the PDE and the UDE products.

- Domino Go WebServer - A scalable, high-performance web server that runs on a broad range of platforms. It offers the latest in web security and supports key internet standards. This is found only in the UDE product.

- ODBC and JDBC are supported in PDE and UDE. versions of the Developer's Edition.

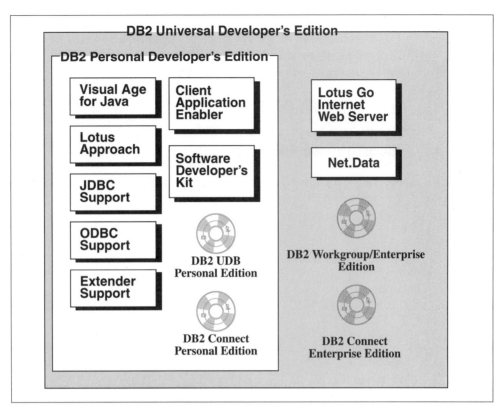

Figure 9. DB2 Personal Developer's and Universal Developer's Edition

Figure 9 shows that the DB2 UDB Server and Connect products are part of the Developer's Edition. The DB2 Personal Developer's Edition contains DB2 UDB Personal Edition and DB2 Connect Personal Edition. This allows a single application developer to develop and test a database application. DB2 Personal Developer's Edition is a single-user product available for OS/2, Windows 3.1, and Windows 95/98 as well as Windows NT.

DB2 Universal Developer's Edition is available on all platforms that support the DB2 Universal Database server product, except for the Enterprise-Extended Edition product (partitioned database environment). DB2 Universal Developer's Edition is intended for application development and testing only. The database server can be on a platform that is different from the platform on which the application is developed. It contains the DB2 UDB Personal Edition, Workgroup and Enterprise Editions of the database server product. Also, DB2 Connect Personal and Enterprise Edition are found in the UDE product. The UDE is licensed for one user. Additional entitlements are available for 1,5 or 10 concurrent or registered DB2 users.

1.3 DB2 UDB in the Windows NT Environment

This section looks at the Windows NT operating system, its interaction with DB2 UDB and supported clients that you may find in a DB2 Universal Database for Windows NT environment.

1.3.1 Introduction of Windows NT

Microsoft's different operating systems target different customer needs. Windows NT is positioned in the enterprise area as a system that fits your needs from a small department server to a centralized enterprise system.

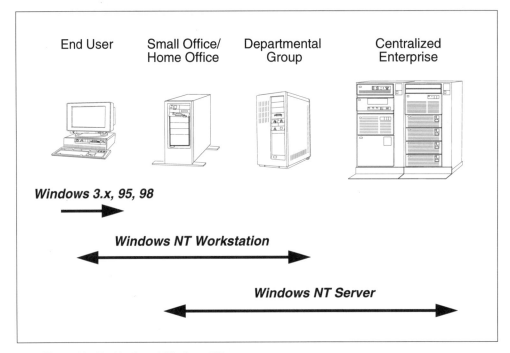

Figure 10. Positioning of Windows NT

Windows NT has two different strategic implementations which are designed for different requirements:

- Windows NT Workstation

    This version is designed as an interactive desktop operating system. It is focused on interaction with local users sharing their resources such as the CD-drive, disk and software in a small workgroup. Priority for system resources is first given to the local user, and then remote clients. Each workstation has its own user administration.

- Windows NT Server

  This version is a superset of Windows NT workstation with several enhancements such as domain-based naming and logon support. These enhancements make it more suitable for sharing resources in an environment with a large number of client machines. The primary focus of a Windows NT Server is to serve remote clients as a high performance system. There are three different roles of a Windows NT Server:

  - Member Server. This system serves applications and resources to users in a network.
  - Primary Domain Controller (PDC). This system provides user administration and authorization checking for a domain.
  - Backup Domain Controller (BDC). This system functions as a backup for the PDC.

  For more detail on definitions and functions of the different server versions, please see "DB2 UDB and Windows NT Security" on page 23.

1.4 DB2 UDB for Windows NT Scenarios

This section gives a few sample scenarios using various DB2 UDB for Windows NT products. Also, some of the terminology specific to the Windows NT environment will be introduced.

1.4.1 Small Workgroup Example

A small number of programmers are developing applications to access data from a DB2 database server. They are using Windows NT workstations running an application development tool and they want to write database applications. All developers will access the same database server.

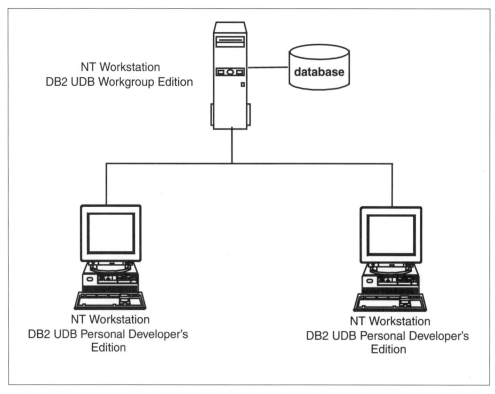

NT Workstation
DB2 UDB Workgroup Edition

database

NT Workstation
DB2 UDB Personal Developer's
Edition

NT Workstation
DB2 UDB Personal Developer's
Edition

Figure 11. Small Workgroup Example

One possible configuration is shown in Figure 11. Each application developer
has DB2 UDB Personal Developer's Edition for NT installed on their Windows
NT workstation. There is one DB2 for Windows NT database server on a
central Windows NT workstation. In addition, each developer could create
their own test database. With a larger number of users, Windows NT Server
could be installed on the DB2 database server machine instead of the
Windows NT Workstation.

1.4.2 Trusted Domain Example

This scenario involves a small to medium enterprise with a larger number of
end users. There is a DB2 UDB for Windows NT database server. This group
uses a trusted and a trusting domain. There are users in the domain of the
database server, but most of them are located in one domain, the trusted
domain. This reduces the amount of user administration, since a database
installed on Windows NT cannot span two domains. The concept of a trusted
domain and a trusting domain are explained in "DB2 UDB and Windows NT
Security" on page 23.

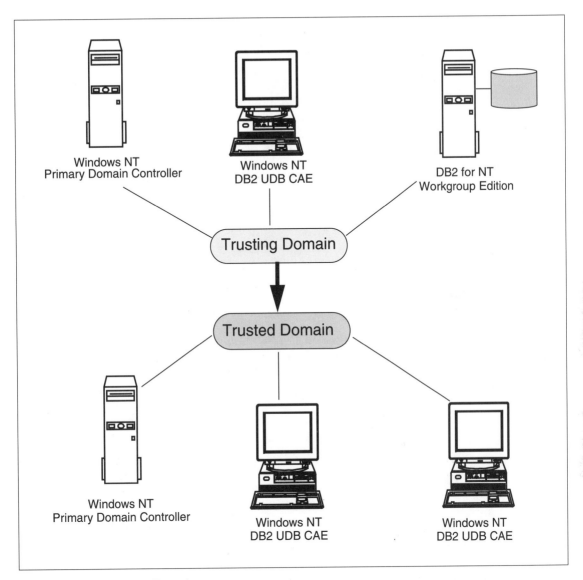

Figure 12. Trusted Domain Example

The characteristics of the scenario in Figure 12 are:

- There is only one database server, which is shared in the environment.
- User administration is reduced to a minimum.
- Different departments also need resources that will not be shared with other users.

- Users execute applications, either ODBC-enabled or otherwise, which access the databases on the database server.

End users executing ODBC applications need only the DB2 CAE installed on their Windows NT Workstation machines.

DB2 UDB for Windows NT can either be installed on Windows NT Workstation or Windows NT Server. The installation of a Primary Domain Controller (PDC) or Backup Domain Controller (BDC) on the same machine is not recommended, in order to avoid resource conflicts.

Figure 12 shows this scenario based on the domain concept of Windows NT. The main user administration will be done in the trusted domain. The arrow in the figure indicates the direction of the trust. If a user logs on in a trusting domain and is not in the local security database, the primary domain controller of the trusting domain will ask the primary domain controller of the trusted domain to authenticate the user. DB2 will also involve the primary domain controller of the trusted domain for group enumeration.

1.4.3 Enterprise Example

In this scenario, Windows NT Workstation will be used on end users and development workstations. There will also be a need to access data from a host database. Some of the data used by the host applications is distributed over the LAN to be used on DB2 for Windows NT database servers.

The end users execute ODBC-enabled applications such as Lotus Approach to access data from remote DB2 for MVS and DB2 for Windows NT databases. Application developers need to be able to write and test database access modules for the LAN and host database systems. One of the immediate goals is to start developing these host and LAN database applications with a minimum number of workstations. Another additional requirement is that host applications may need to access data from a DB2 for Windows NT database server.

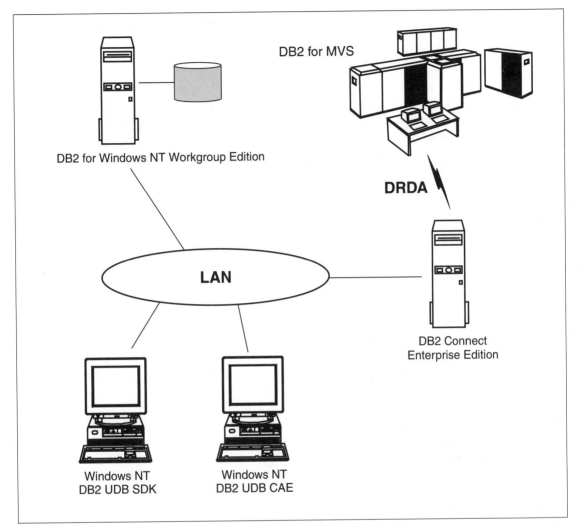

Figure 13. DB2 in an Enterprise Environment

Figure 13 shows a possible configuration. Here, we have chosen to place the DB2 Connect Enterprise Edition product on one Windows NT workstation, while the DB2 UDB for Windows NT Workgroup Edition product is on another Windows NT workstation. Depending on the system resources, namely memory, disk and CPU on the database server, and the number of clients accessing either the gateway or the database server, this functionality could be achieved by installing DB2 UDB Enterprise Edition on a single workstation.

There are two possible kinds of clients in this enterprise:

- An end user using an ODBC-enabled application, such as Lotus Approach, needs the DB2 CAE and required communication protocol.
- An application developer needs the DB2 SDK and communication protocol for the operating system platform.

Notice that both types of remote clients need only the LAN communication protocol on their workstation. The DB2 Connect Enterprise Edition gateway will have both the LAN communication protocol and an APPC or TCP/IP product installed (depending on which protocol is used for the DRDA connection). The LAN protocol can be either TCP/IP, NetBIOS, IPX/SPX or APPC or Named Pipes.

1.5 Summary

This chapter has provided an introduction to the DB2 Universal Database products, as well as an high level overview of Windows NT. There are many features of Windows NT that make it a desirable platform on which to run DB2 UDB. For example:

- DB2 UDB can take advantage of the multi threading processor in Windows NT to allow the execution of multiple jobs in parallel.

- DB2 UDB supports two methods of storage for database objects, the native NT file system and raw devices.

- DB2 UDB instances and other processes are implemented as Windows NT Services and can be started automatically when the system is started.

- You have the choice of either using the Windows NT Performance Monitor or the DB2 Performance Monitor.

- Entries for DB2 UDB are automatically added in the Windows NT Registry.

- You are able to install DB2 UDB on different workstations without an additional local CD-ROM drive, from a code server running a script file.

- DB2 uses Windows NT for authorization and group resolution. This allows you to have a central administration control point in Windows NT.

- All system messages generated by DB2 will be logged in the Windows NT Event Viewer. This assists you in analyzing problems by isolating the source.

Chapter 2. DB2 UDB and Windows NT Security

Security is one of the most important features of any database management system. It is key to keeping data safe and limiting data access to those with a need to know. DB2 UDB has many security features of its own, but on Windows NT it also relies on the security features of the Windows NT operating system itself. The Windows NT operating system was designed with integrated security, and security controls almost all system objects. To understand security for DB2 UDB on Windows NT, we must understand not only the many security features of DB2 UDB but also the Windows NT security model and how it's used by DB2 UDB.

Let's take a moment to look first at the security issues that must be resolved. What exactly are the problems we're solving by implementing security features?

First, providing security for a database management system means providing a means of authentication. Authentication means "are you who you say you are?". This must be answered before you have any access at all to the database management system. The Windows NT security system may be involved in providing this authentication. Authentication can take place at any one of a number of levels: locally at the client, at the DB2 server, at the domain level, or through a trusted domain. We'll look at these scenarios as we discuss the Windows NT security model.

Second, once you have been authenticated and DB2 UDB knows who you are, what can you do? You may need to protect data from some users but not others. You may need to give some users the ability to perform administrative functions on the database system but not see the data. Control over what any individual user can do is maintained through privileges. We'll discuss these in depth as we discuss DB2 UDB's security features.

Before we proceed, a few definitions, listed below in Table 1, will help to clarify some of the terms we use throughout the book, especially in this chapter.

Table 1. List of Definitions

Terms	Definition (for this book)
Windows NT	Either Windows NT Workstation or Windows NT Server. Reference will be made to the common Windows NT features of the two products.

Terms	Definition (for this book)
Windows NT Workstation	The Windows NT Workstation product. Cannot be a domain controller.
Windows NT Server	The Windows NT Server product. It is a superset of the NT Workstation product. A machine running Windows NT Server may be a Windows NT Workstation or a domain controller.
Domain	A domain is an arrangement of client and server computers referenced by a specific (unique) name that share a single security permissions (domain) database.
Domain Controller	Refers to the computer running Windows NT Server that manages all aspects of user-domain interactions and uses the information in the directory (domain) database to authenticate users logging onto domain accounts.
Primary Domain Controller	In a Windows NT domain, the computer running the Windows NT Server that authenticates domain logons and maintains the directory database for the domain. There can be only one per domain. It can also be referred to as the PDC.
Backup Domain Controller	These are servers that contain up-to-date and accurate copies of the security and user databases. These servers can also authenticate workstations in the absence of a primary domain controller (PDC). They can also be referred to as BDCs.
Server	This is a Windows NT Server that is part of a domain as a file or print server, but is not a domain controller.
Workstation	A machine running Windows NT Workstation or Windows NT Server in a domain that is not a domain controller or a file / print server.
Right	The ability of a user or group of users to perform a Windows NT operation. Examples of rights are logging on to a server and performing backups. Rights apply to the system (computer or domain) as a whole, as opposed to permissions, which apply to specific objects. These can also be termed *user rights*.
Permission	Authority in Windows NT granted to a user or group of users to perform operations on specific objects, such as files, directories, printers, and other resources. Examples of permissions are read, change, full control and no access. Permissions are applied on a user-by-user or group-by-group basis.

Terms	Definition (for this book)
Privilege	Within DB2 UDB, the right of a particular user or group of users to create, access or modify an object.

2.1 Windows NT Security Concepts

In this section we'll look at some of the Windows NT concepts that are key to understanding how DB2 UDB utilizes the Windows NT security model. In Chapter 1, the section entitled "Windows NT" introduced some of these concepts. Now we'll look at them in more detail.

Windows NT has three models for creating a logical organization of computers: the workgroup, the client-server and the domain model. For our purposes we will discuss only the workgroup and the domain models.

Both workgroups and domains provide ways to share resources such as file and printing services. They do have some significant differences however, the primary one being security.

2.1.1 Workgroups in Windows NT

A *workgroup* is most simply described as a collection of Windows workstations. It can contain computers running any number of operating systems, including DOS, Windows 3.x, Windows for Workgroups, Windows 95/98, Windows NT Workstation and Windows NT Server, and is identified by a unique name.

Windows NT Server (installed as a stand-alone/member server) or Windows NT Workstation installations in the workgroup can share their objects with other members (clients) of the workgroup. These shared resources, or *shares*, might include directories or printers. A share will have a share name associated with it. Figure 14 on page 26 shows items that might be shared in a workgroup.

Although these resources are shared, user logons are specific to each computer in the workgroup. Therefore, if a user requires access to all file servers in a workgroup, an account must be created for that user on each machine.

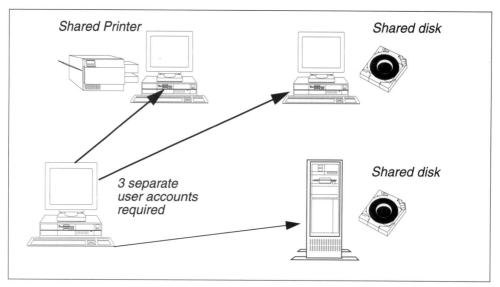

Figure 14. Workgroup Security

Although the workgroup model can work well in a small organization where centralized security is not required, security can be a concern in this environment. Shared objects on a network can be made more secure by either hiding the share or by putting a password on them. Hiding a share means that it will not appear on browse lists on other machines in the workgroup and has to be known by anyone who wants to use it.

Figure 15 on page 27 shows the creation of a share under Windows NT. To obtain the screen shown in Figure 15, right-click the mouse on the object (the DB2LOG directory in this example) that you want to share in Windows NT Explorer. Select the **Sharing** option, choose the **Sharing** tab and then click on **Shared As**. Either replace the share name with one you want and/or add a dollar sign ($) to make it hidden. You can also set the number of users who can concurrently connect to this share. (The setting up of a share can also be done through My Computer.)

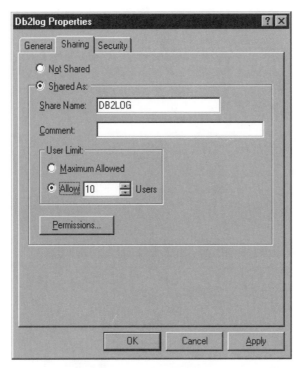

Figure 15. Creating a Windows NT Share

Having a password on a shared object is a way to control security. However, a share can only have one password for the entire network.

Windows NT machines can also enhance workgroup security at the user level. A particular user can be granted one of the following permissions to a share:

- No access
- Read
- Change
- Full Control

Figure 16 on page 28 is an example of applying permissions on a share. The default when a share is created is to grant Everyone (a Windows NT pre-defined group that includes all users who can access the computer) full control. To apply restrictions, remove this group from the permissions list and add users or groups with the desired type of access.

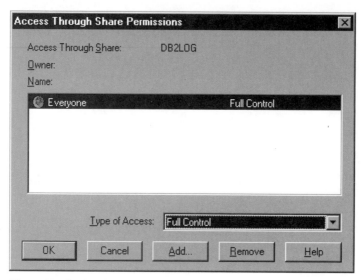

Figure 16. Setting Permissions on a Share

Windows NT comes with a number of default shares, namely:

- Each hard disk partition and CD-ROM drive have a share at their root directory. Those shares are C$, D$, E$ and so on.

- The directory that contains the Windows NT programs (\Winnt). That share is ADMIN$.

- In the case of domain controllers, the directory that contains the logon scripts (\Winnt\System32\Repl\Import\Scripts) is a default share. This share is NETLOGON.

All but the NETLOGON share are hidden shares. Another term for all of these shares is administrative shares, because only administrators can access them. They are automatically created when Windows NT is booted. However, in Windows NT 4.0, these default shares can be unshared. To do this, select the directory with the right mouse button, choose **Sharing...** , and click on **Not Shared**.

If Windows NT is formatted with an NTFS volume, then permissions on this NTFS volume can also be set on files and directories. An example of this is shown in Figure 17, where administrators are updated to have full control on files and directories.

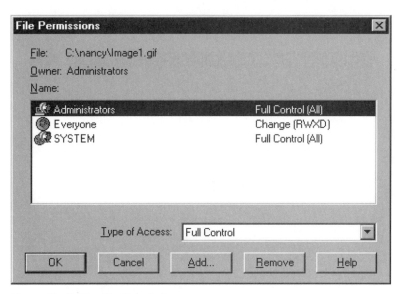

Figure 17. Setting File Permissions

2.1.2 Domains in Windows NT

A Windows NT *domain* (hereafter referred to as a domain) is an arrangement of client and server computers referenced by a specific (unique) name that share a single security permissions (domain) database. The key difference between a Windows NT workgroup and a Windows NT domain is that the computers that make up the domain share a centralized user logon database. This is an important concept which differentiates the implementation of DB2 UDB on Windows NT from its implementation on all other platforms.

A domain can contain Windows NT Servers and LAN Manager 2.x Servers. However, a LAN Manager Server cannot authenticate a Windows NT client. (Authentication will be covered in detail in "Windows NT Authentication" on page 40.) Therefore if LAN Manager Servers are going to be part of a domain, there should be at least two Windows NT Servers in case one fails. Furthermore, a LAN Manager server cannot be a Primary Domain Controller.

Figure 18 on page 30 illustrates the Windows NT model for domain security. Unlike the model for workgroup security shown in Figure 1 on page 8, the userid and password only need to be defined at the Primary Domain Controller to be able to access network resources. In contrast, the Windows NT workgroup environment would require the userid and password to be defined on each machine the user wanted to access.

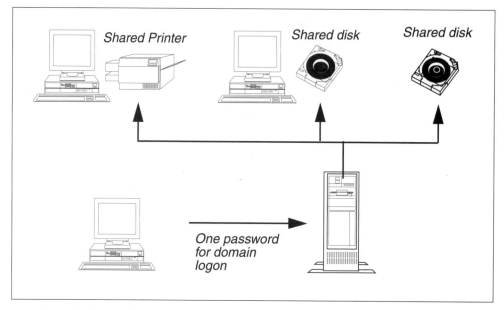

Figure 18. Domain Security

2.1.2.1 Primary Domain Controllers

A domain is established when a Windows NT Server is created as a domain controller in a new domain. This can be done when a Windows NT Server is installed. During the setup procedure you may select to either create a primary domain controller in a new domain, a backup domain controller in a known domain, or a stand-alone server in a known domain. Selecting controller in a new domain will make that server the *Primary Domain Controller (PDC)*. A domain name must be supplied. The domain name must not be the same as any other domain on your network or any machine name within another domain. Each domain contains only one PDC.

As the PDC, a Windows NT Server will have the master copy of the *Security Access Manager (SAM)* database. The SAM database contains information about which users can log onto the domain, their passwords and which groups they belong to. It also records which machine names are members of the domain and which other domains this domain knows about and trusts. It is encrypted and resides in the following file:

`\WINNT\SYSTEM32\CONFIG\SAM`

All other servers added to the domain as Backup Domain Controllers (BDC) will hold a copy of the SAM database which is regularly synchronized against the master copy on the PDC. When Windows NT machines are booted, a copy of the SAM database is copied into memory.

To assist in the exercise of planning domain requirements, the size of a given SAM database file can be estimated fairly accurately. Table 2 summarizes the figures.

Table 2. Sizing the SAM Database

SAM Component	Size SAM increases by
User account	1024 bytes (1K)
Computer or machine account	512 bytes (0.5K)
Global group	12 bytes/user + 512 bytes
Local group	36 bytes/user + 512 bytes

There are a few considerations that may help you in planning for the SAM database:

- The SAM database gets read into memory on each PDC and BDC. This is a fixed RAM cost on every domain controller. This overhead is something to be aware of if you are planning to have your database server be a domain controller, as this is memory that will not be available for database buffers.

- The larger the SAM database, the longer a domain controller server will take to boot.

2.1.2.2 Backup Domain Controller

Once a domain has been established (a Primary Domain Controller was created), other Windows NT Servers can be added to the domain as either normal servers or as domain controllers. If added as another domain controller, a Windows NT Server is called a Backup Domain Controller.

The major difference between a PDC and a BDC is the implementation of the SAM database. A BDC holds a copy of the SAM database from the PDC. The BDC can authenticate users to the domain on behalf of the PDC. Any updates made to the SAM at the BDC are actually made at the PDC transparently to the administrator.

The PDC broadcasts changes made to the SAM database at a configurable time interval following a series of predefined steps.

The amount of data to be sent to a particular BDC is determined by how out of synchronization the SAM at the BDC is with the SAM at the PDC. The PDC can determine to send only a set of changes, or it can determine to send the entire SAM database to the particular BDC.

The BDCs can also be manually synchronized with the PDC through the Synchronize Entire Domain option on Server Manager (see Figure 19).

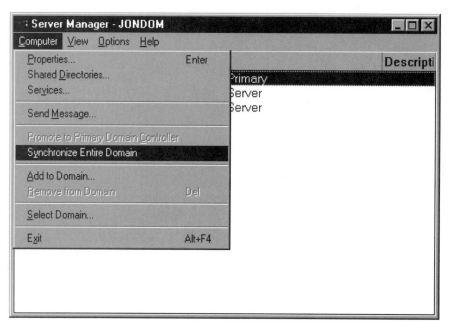

Figure 19. Server Manager

Deciding how many BDCs to have in a domain can provide some challenges. The physical distribution of the network and enterprise architecture are the main considerations in determining how many BDCs to have in a domain. BDCs can offer faster logon times for users, as well as redundancy for the system, should the PDC fail. However, backup domain controllers generate network traffic, and this could cause network slowdown during synchronization. You must also consider the cost of multiple BDC servers.

Depending on the size of a domain, it is often desirable to keep the PDC as a dedicated server if the resources are available. "DB2 UDB for Windows NT in a Domain" on page 72 discusses the placement of DB2 on PDCs and BDCs.

The main purpose of a BDC is to provide redundancy in the domain should the PDC fail. If the PDC fails, a BDC can be promoted to PDC through the Server Manager. If the PDC is active when a BDC is promoted, then the PDC is automatically and dynamically demoted to BDC.

If a PDC fails and a BDC is promoted to assume the PDC duties, then when the original PDC is started again, Server Manager will show there are two PDCs in the domain. One of them must be demoted to a BDC. This is done through the Demote to Backup Domain Controller option on Server Manager. This only displays when two PDCs exist.

2.1.2.3 Windows NT Server and Windows NT Workstation

When Windows NT Server is installed on a domain as a stand-alone server (not a domain controller), it can operate as a file, print or applications server. A workstation with Windows NT Server installed behaves much like a system with Windows NT Workstation installed.

A computer running Windows NT Workstation or Windows NT Server can belong to either a workgroup, a domain or neither (stand-alone), but cannot belong to both a workgroup and a domain. A Windows NT Server that is not a domain controller has its own local SAM database.

A Windows NT Workstation machine will have a local SAM database as well. It can authenticate users logging in locally and decide what rights users have when logging on from that machine. This Windows NT machine is not capable of becoming a Backup or Primary Domain Controller. To become a domain controller, Windows NT Server must be installed.

2.2 Groups and User Authentication

Users are defined on Windows NT by creating user accounts within the Windows NT administrative tool called the User Manager. An account which contains other accounts, called members, is a *group*. Groups give Windows NT administrators the ability to grant rights and permissions to a number of users at once, without having to maintain each user individually. Groups are also used to grant DB2 privileges and authorities. Groups, like user accounts, are defined and maintained in the SAM database of Windows NT machines.

There are two types of groups in the Windows NT architecture:

- Local groups
- Global groups

A *local group* can include user accounts that have been created in the local accounts database. If the machine is part of a domain, it can also contain global accounts and global groups from the Windows NT domain. On a Windows NT Workstation, a local group can be granted permissions and rights only for its own workstation. On Windows NT Server, a local group can be granted permissions and rights only for the servers of its own domain.

A *global group* exists only on a domain controller and contains user accounts from the domain's SAM. A global group can be used in servers and workstations of its own domain, and in trusting domains. It can become a member of local groups on those machines.

The Primary Domain Controller holds the SAM for the domain. This SAM is replicated to any BDCs in the domain. Domain controllers do not have a *local* SAM database. They hold user and group data for the domain. In this sense, any groups created on the PDC, local or global, are domain groups.

Windows NT machines that are not domain controllers (NT Workstations and some NT Servers) will each have their own SAM databases. User accounts and groups created on those machines are local to that machine. There is no Create Global Group option on machines that are not domain controllers.

Let's look at user accounts and groups in more detail.

2.2.1 User Accounts

Each user in a Windows NT environment will have a user account. This is essentially a record of a user ID, password and the groups which the user is a member, along with a few other details, such as logon restrictions, logon scripts to be executed, the user's home directory, mandatory profile, and account expiration. Figure 20 on page 35 shows the screen in User Manager used to create a new user account. Once a user account has been created, it can be made a member of a group.

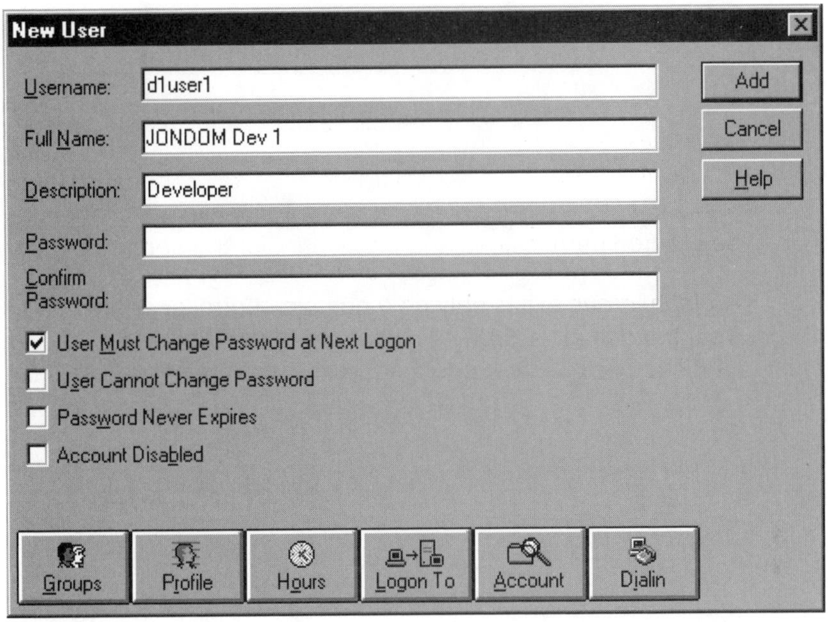

Figure 20. Creating a User Account

2.2.2 Global Groups

Global groups are domain objects. They can only be created on a PDC. Figure 21 on page 36 shows the User Manager screen used to create a global group. They are called global groups because they can be accessed by any machine in a domain and can be seen across domains.

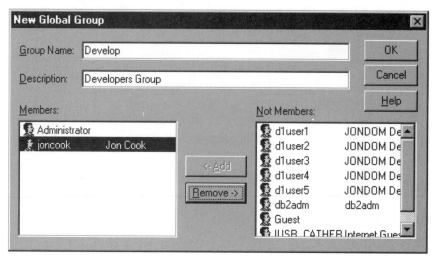

Figure 21. Creating a Global Group

A global group can only contain user accounts from the domain on which it is created. It cannot contain any other groups as members. However, once created, global groups can be seen and used by any machine in the domain or by other machines in trusting domains. (See "Trusted Domains" on page 42).

Windows NT Server comes with a number of default global groups. Those groups are:

- Domain Users
- Domain Admins
- Domain Guests

The Domain Users group contains all user accounts created on the domain.

The Domain Admins group contains designated administrator accounts. By default, Domain Admins contains only the Windows NT default administrator account called Administrator.

The Domain Guests group contains all guest accounts for the domain. By default, Domain Guests contains only the default guest user account called Guest.

Within User Manager, global groups are identified by a picture of a globe being included in the icon, as opposed to a computer for a local group icon. This is shown in Figure 22 on page 37, where the three last groups are global groups.

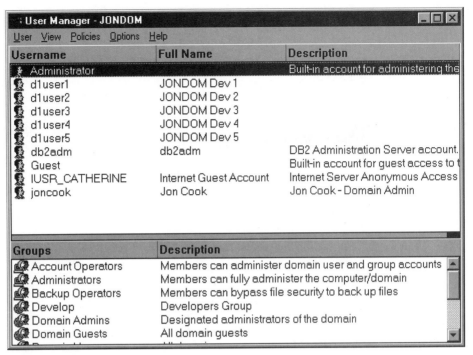

Figure 22. User Manager Showing Global Groups

2.2.3 Local Groups

Local groups are local to the Windows NT machine on which they are created. Remember that group information is stored in a machine's SAM database. A local group created on a workstation is specific to that workstation. A local group created on a domain controller, however, applies to all domain controllers in that domain because the SAM is propagated to all domain controllers on a regular basis.

Local groups can contain individual user accounts which are defined in the local SAM database, any users from within the domain or users from trusted domains. In addition a local group can contain as a member a global group from the domain or a trusted domain. (Trusted domains are explained in detail in "Trusted Domains" on page 42).

Global groups from trusted domains can be seen in the New Local Group window of User Manager, under the List Names From drop-down window (see Figure 23).

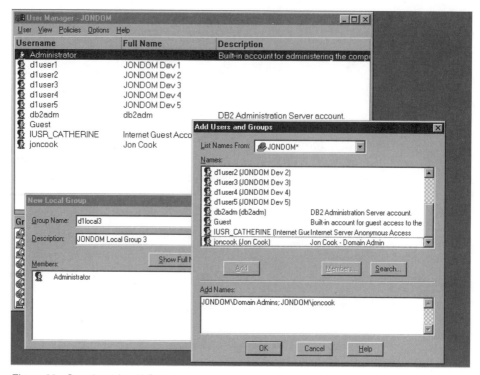

Figure 23. Creating a Local Group

A local group cannot contain other local groups.

Windows NT has a number of default local groups established at installation. The default local groups are:

- Account Operators (Windows NT Server only)
- Administrators
- Backup Operators
- Guests
- Power Users (Windows NT Workstation only)
- Print Operators (Windows NT Server only)
- Replicator
- Server Operators (Windows NT Server only)
- Users

There is one additional group called Everyone. This group does not appear on the list of groups in User Manager. However, it can be assigned rights and permissions. Anyone who has a user account in the domain, including all local and remote users, is a part of the Everyone local group. The Everyone group also contains all global groups of any trusted domains.

The Administrators group is the most powerful group. By default, it contains only the default administrator account called Administrator. The Administrators local group on the Primary Domain Controller is the Administrators group for all domain controllers of that domain.

When a Windows NT Workstation or Windows NT Server joins a domain (but not as a domain controller, in the case of Windows NT Server), the Domain Admins global group is added to the Administrators local group on the machine. This gives any member of the Domain Admins group administrative privileges on that machine.

Members of the Users group have minimal rights on machines running Windows NT Server, but they do have rights on Windows NT Workstations. They have the right to manage and create local groups. When a Windows NT machine joins a domain (not as a domain controller, in the case of Windows NT Server), the Domain Users global group is added to the Users local group on the machine. This allows all domain users to log on to the domain from that machine.

Note

A user ID must be known to at least one local group on a Windows NT machine before that user is allowed to log on at that machine.

2.2.4 Domain Scenario

To help illustrate the concept of groups, let's examine a domain scenario. Figure 24 on page 40 is a representation of a domain. This domain has the following:

- a PDC (machine A)
- Two BDCs (machines B and C)
- Another Windows NT Server (machine D)
- Two Windows NT Workstations (machines E and F)

A global group was created on machine A, the PDC, and will therefore also exist on machines B and C, the BDCs. This group will be global to the entire domain. This implies that it can be made a part of any local group in this domain (on A, D, E or F) or a local group in a trusting domain. Such a global group could only contain user accounts defined on the domain MYDOMAIN.

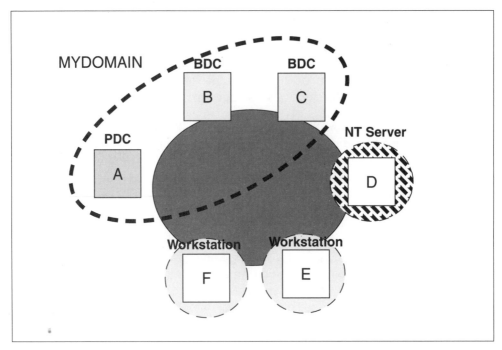

Figure 24. Local Groups in a Domain

A local group created on machine A is local only on the domain controllers. That is, if a user account was created and made only a member of a local group on machine A, that user could only log on to machines A, B or C. A local group on machine A could contain individual user accounts or global groups defined either on MYDOMAIN or from a trusted domain.

Machines B and C, the Backup Domain Controllers, cannot and do not have their own local groups. This is because their SAM is a copy from the PDC.

A local group defined on D, E or F will be local to that machine. Such a local group can contain user accounts that are locally defined or are domain accounts on MYDOMAIN. It could also contain global groups from MYDOMAIN or from a trusted domain.

2.2.5 Windows NT Authentication

We have discussed the concepts of Windows NT user accounts, local and global groups and domains. The next logical topic is authentication. The actual process of user authentication is relatively simple. Authentication is verifying that a user is who they say they are.

Recall that user IDs and passwords are stored in the SAM database on Windows NT machines, but a user's user ID and password does not necessarily have to reside on the machine from which they log on. When Windows NT authenticates a user, it follows a simple hierarchy to look for a user ID and password. This hierarchy of authentication is summarized in Figure 25.

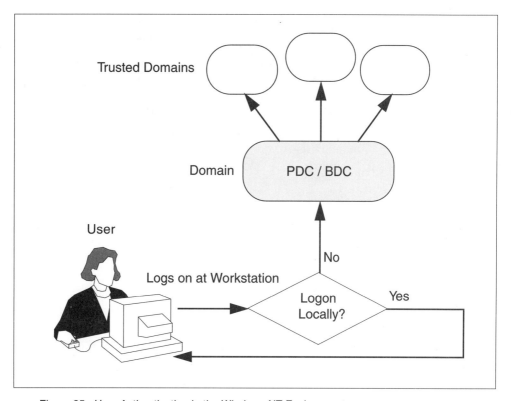

Trusted Domains

Domain   PDC / BDC

User

Logs on at Workstation

No

Logon Locally?   Yes

Figure 25. User Authentication in the Windows NT Environment

If you choose a workstation or local logon, Windows NT will only look at the local SAM. If the user is not in the local SAM, authentication will fail.

If you choose domain authentication the domain controller that does the authentication can be either the PDC or a BDC. BDCs have a copy of the PDC's SAM database. To determine which domain controller will perform the authentication, a broadcast message is sent out from the user's machine, and the first domain controller to respond to the message will perform the authentication.

If the user is not known to the domain, (that is, the user ID is not in the SAM database of the PDC), then domain controllers of any trusted domains are queried. The concept of trusted domains is discussed in "Trusted Domains" on page 42. Either the PDC or a BDC can respond to an authentication request from a trusting domain.

Once the userid has been found and the password authenticated, any account or policy restrictions are determined, as well as a list of groups of which the user is a member.

2.3 Trust Relationships Between Domains

We have discussed the concept of a single domain; however, an enterprise may wish to establish more than one domain. These domains do not have to exist independently, nor do separate user accounts have to exist for each domain a given user wishes to log into. Interdependent multiple domains can be achieved through relationships between domains called trusts.

2.3.1 Trusted Domains

Trust relationships between domains are established so that users from one domain can access resources in another domain without being re-authenticated.

There are two characteristics of a trust relationship:

1. One domain trusts another to authenticate users on its behalf and therefore grants access to resources in its domain without re-authenticating users.

2. An administrator from one domain trusts an administrator from another domain to administer resources in that domain.

The two domains in a trust relationship are called the *trusting* and the *trusted* domain. A scenario representing this relationship is shown in Figure 26 on page 43. A trust relationship lets an administrator of one domain (the trusting domain) grant rights and permissions to global groups and users of another domain (the trusted domain). The administrator of the trusted domain must be, in turn, trusted since this administrator can control which users are members of global groups.

Trust is uni-directional. Figure 26 represents a trust relationship created between two domains, A and B.

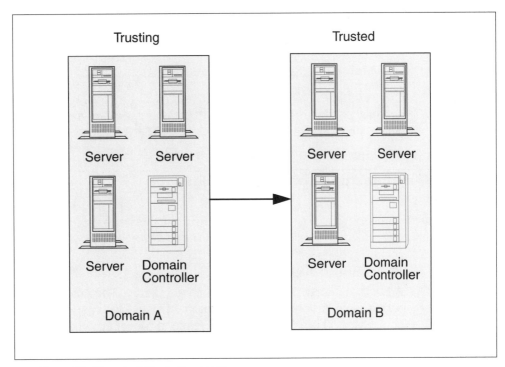

Figure 26. Domain A Trusts Domain B

In Figure 26, Domain A trusts Domain B to authenticate users on its behalf and therefore will grant resource access to users from domain B. In this example, B is the trusted domain and A is the trusting domain. In practice, users logging onto Domain B would see both domains in the domain drop-down menu on the Windows NT log on box, while users in Domain A would see only Domain A.

Note

Trust relationships are not transitive. This means that explicit trust relationships need to be established in each direction between domains. There is no concept of an implicit or piggybacked trust relationship.

Figure 27 on page 44 represents three domains where Domain A trusts Domain B and Domain B, in turn, trusts Domain C. With just these two relationships, Domain C cannot authenticate users on behalf of Domain A. Domain A does not trust Domain C.

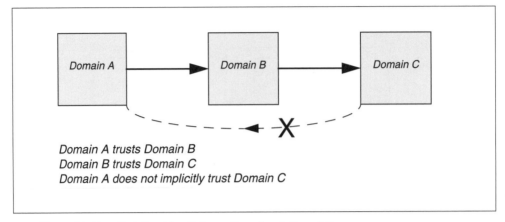

Domain A trusts Domain B
Domain B trusts Domain C
Domain A does not implicitly trust Domain C

Figure 27. Trust Relationships Between Domains A, B, and C

2.3.2 Creating a Trust Relationship

A trust relationship is relatively simple to setup. The configuration of a trust relationship is done by administrators in User Manager on both domain controllers. The relationship first needs to be set up on a domain controller in what is to be the trusted domain, then completed on the trusting domain.The following steps must be completed.

First, on the PDC of the *trusted* domain:

1. In User Manager for Domains, select **Policies | Trust Relationships**.

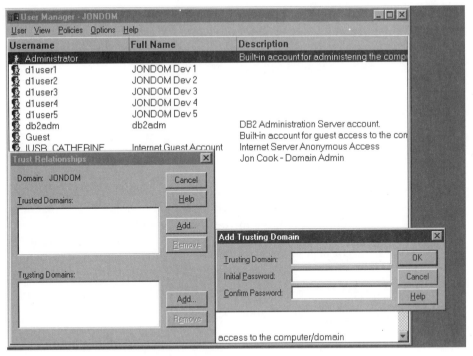

Figure 28. Creating a Trust Relationship between Domains

2. In the *Trust Relationships* dialog box, click on the **Add...** button next to Trusting Domains.

3. In the *Add Trusting Domain* dialog box, enter the name of the domain that will be the trusting domain.

4. Enter and confirm a password that the administrator of the trusting domain will use to complete the relationship (See Figure 28).

Second, on the PDC of the *trusting* domain:

1. In User Manager for Domains, select **Policies | Trust Relationships**.

2. In the *Trust Relationships* dialog box, click on the **Add...** button next to Trusted Domains and enter the name of the trusted domain and the password selected to be the administrator of the trusted domain. The trust relationship is now complete.

If the relationship needs to be broken, then it must be removed from both domains. This is performed in the same way as adding a trust relationship except select **Remove**.

2.3.3 Models of Domain Trust

Choosing the right domain trust architecture for an enterprise can be an involved and complex task, with a number of considerations to be taken into account. To assist in this process, let's look at four common models of domain organization. They are:

1. The Single Domain Model

2. The Master Domain Model

3. The Multiple Master Domain Model

4. The Complete Trust Model

These should be treated as models. Organizations should configure their domain(s) to best suit their individual needs. We will examine each of these models briefly and consider how the model might be used with DB2. Other important factors will influence the model an organization chooses. Consult a Windows NT planning reference for more information.

2.3.3.1 The Single Domain Model
Figure 29 represents the single domain model.

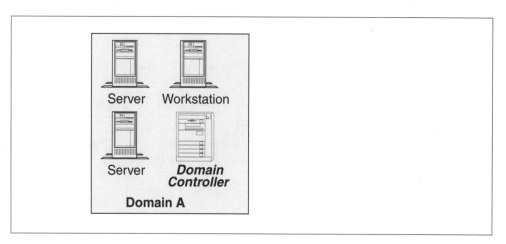

Figure 29. The Single Domain Model

All servers and workstations belong to one domain. There are no trust relationships to any other domain.

Advantages of this model include:

- It's easy to implement.
- It's a suitable design for a small to medium sized network.

- There are no trust relationships to establish or maintain.
- You have one set of administrators.

Disadvantages of this model include:

- The list of users and machines can grow to an undesirable size.
- Network and server performance problems may arise.

An example of a single domain model might be a small network with an independent domain. This could be a production environment, where it is desirable to keep the production data separate from the development environment. You might also have a number of small domains for an organization where the sharing or dividing of resources such as databases is not required. The ability to administer each domain separately also is not an issue.

The most compelling reason not to implement this model, especially in a production environment, is generally the size of the domain, specifically the number of users and machines. These factors affect the size of the SAM database on the domain controllers.

2.3.3.2 The Master Domain Model

Figure 30 illustrates the master domain model:

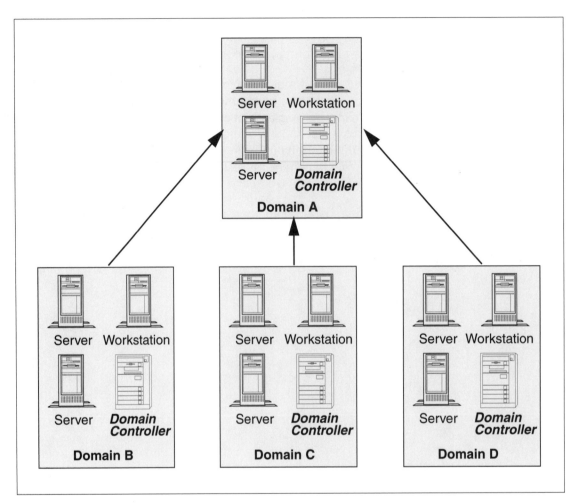

Figure 30. The Master Domain Model

The master domain, Domain A in the illustration, is the domain where all users are defined. All other domains trust the master domain. Domains other than the master domain have no users defined. The other domains are called *resource* or *slave domains*.

Advantages of this model include:

• Administration for the enterprise is centralized.

- It supports logical grouping of resources (such as divisions or departments).
- It supports geographical division of an enterprise.
- Global groups are defined only once.

Disadvantages of this model include:

- Performance may degrade on a WAN or with a large number of users.
- Local groups must be defined on each domain.
- Global administration can be cumbersome to establish.
- Master domain can be a single point of failure.

You might find the master domain model implemented where each department in an organization is on its own domain. However, all administration and authentication occurs in the master domain. The enterprise is split geographically and resources are grouped accordingly. However, users are all defined and administered centrally. This model easily supports movement of personnel across domains.

2.3.3.3 The Multiple Master Domain Model

Figure 31 shows the multiple master domain model.

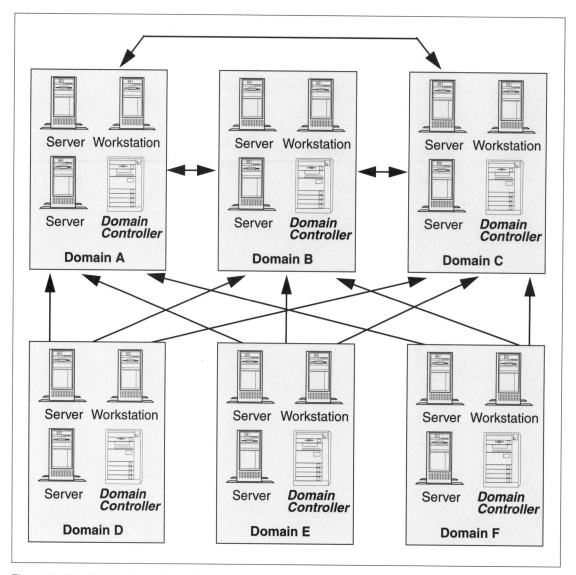

Figure 31. The Multiple Master Domain Model

In this example, Domains A, B, and C are master domains where the user accounts are held. Domains D, E, and F are resource domains. The master domains have trust relationships between one other and can each authenticate for the resource domains.

Advantages of this model include:

- It supports a large number of users with acceptable performance.
- Resources are grouped logically.
- Resource domains can be managed independently for security.

Disadvantages of this model include:

- Groups may need to be defined more than once for different domains.
- There are many trust relationships to manage.
- Maintenance of user accounts is more difficult because they are in multiple domains.

A multiple master domain may be established for the same reasons as a master domain. You may choose the multiple master model if you have too many users for one domain to handle all the authentication requests. To ease network traffic and speed user authentication requests, multiple master domains are created to service the resource domains.

2.3.3.4 The Complete Trust Model

Figure 32 shows the complete trust model.

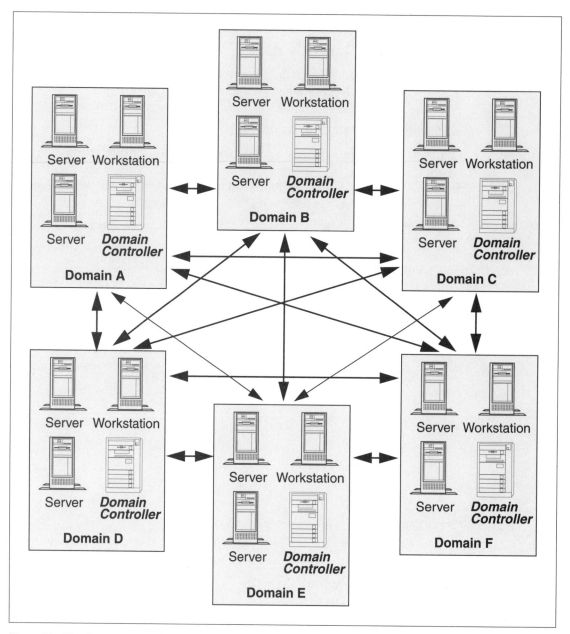

Figure 32. The Complete Trust Model

In a complete trust model, domains exist with trust relationships to and from all other domains on the network.

Advantages of this model include:

- It supports a large number of users.
- It does not require central administration.
- Resources and users are grouped logically into domains (from a browser perspective).
- Resources are managed independently for each domain.

Disadvantages of this model include:

- Lack of central administration can cause potentially severe network problems.
- There are a large number of trust relationships to manage.

An example of a suitable environment where the complete trust model might be implemented is a development environment.

2.4 DB2 UDB for Windows NT Authentication and Security

We have looked at Windows NT security and authentication. Now let's examine those concepts from a DB2 UDB for Windows NT perspective. DB2 UDB supports the use of groups in the granting of privileges and in the determination of authority levels. DB2 will use the groups you define to Windows NT, assuming they conform to the naming rules for DB2 UDB user names.

DB2 allows you to specify either a local group or a global group when granting privileges or defining authority levels. A user is determined to be a member of a group if the user's account is defined explicitly in the local or global group or implicitly by being a member of a global group defined to be a member of a local group.

2.4.1 DB2 UDB for Windows NT Group Resolution

For DB2 UDB for Windows NT to be able to authenticate and grant privileges to a user, that user can be one of the following:

- a locally defined user
- a user defined on the domain
- a member of a local group
- a member of a global group
- a member of a global group that is in turn a member of a local group.

Not only can the user be found on either a local or global group, but with DB2 UDB the user ID and group can actually be in trusted domains and DB2 will resolve ownership. In other words, the ID and the group can be in different SAM databases if an appropriate trust relationship exists.

To put it another way, DB2 UDB will determine whether a user account is defined in the local machine's SAM, the SAM of the domain controller or the SAM of a domain controller in a domain trusted by the domain containing the DB2 UDB server. By default, DB2 will then go to the machine where that account is defined to enumerate groups (including the definition of an administrator). If that account is a domain account then the machine is a domain controller for that domain. This means that the Domain Administrator is responsible for defining groups that are to be used by DB2 Administrators.

Figure 33 on page 54 illustrates how DB2 can handle privileges for users and groups in a trusted Master Domain (Master Account Domain) configuration.

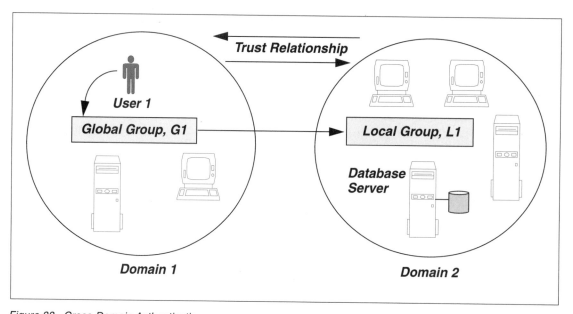

Figure 33. Cross-Domain Authentication

In this example, the user account for USER1 is held in Domain 1. USER1 is included in global group G1 on Domain 1.

A local group L1 is defined on Domain 2, which is trusted by Domain 1. The global group G1 is a member of the local group L1.

Assuming that all default privileges were revoked, any one of the following SQL statements will now allow USER1 access to a database on the DB2 UDB database server if it is part of Domain 2:

```
GRANT CONNECT ON DATABASE TO USER1
GRANT CONNECT ON DATABASE TO L1
GRANT CONNECT ON DATABASE TO G1
```

2.4.2 Forcing Local Authentication

DB2 uses a Windows NT API call to find the SAM database where the user is defined. The search order used by this API call is:

1. Local machine SAM

2. Domain controller

3. Trusted Domain controllers

DB2 will be told where the user account was validated, and by default DB2 will use that location to enumerate groups.

DB2 UDB can be directed to enumerate groups on the local machine rather than on the Domain controller. This creates an extra level of administration overhead, but allows the DB2 Administrator (assuming he/she is also a local Administrator) to control the groups that DB2 UDB sees (you may not want to have a general Windows NT Administrator to have this power).

To force DB2 to enumerate groups on the local machine, you must set the DB2 registry variable DB2_GRP_LOOKUP on the DB2 server machine as follows.

To set it globally (for all instances on the DB2 Server):

```
db2set -g db2_grp_lookup=local
```

To set it for the current instance on a DB2 server:

```
db2set -i instancename db2_grp_lookup=local
```

After issuing this command, you must stop and start the DB2 instance(s) for the change to take effect.

If all user accounts are specified locally on the DB2 machine, then there is no need to use this registry variable. However if the user accounts are domain accounts, then you may wish to consider its use.

If DB2_GRP_LOOKUP is set to local, this will indicate to DB2 to not go to the domain controller for group enumeration, but rather to enumerate locally. If you do this, then you would have to also do one of the following:

1. Create a local group that has the userid defined in it, in the form domainname\userid

2. Create a local group which has a global group defined in it and have the userid defined in that global group on the domain.

2.4.3 Authority Levels

An *authority level* is a set of rights to create or access database manager resources. These authorities are assigned to a group of users. Figure 34 on page 56 illustrates the hierarchy of authority levels.

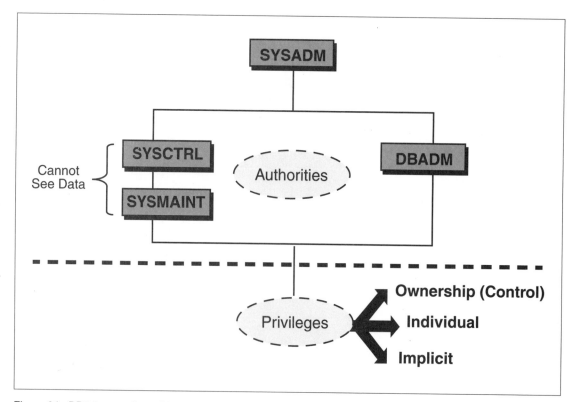

Figure 34. DB2 Access Control Hierarchy

At the top of this hierarchy is the DB2 System Administrator or **SYSADM**. Any member of the SYSADM user group is able to perform any of the DB2 administration operations as well as access all database objects. SYSADM members are the only users allowed to configure the DB2 instance.

System administration authority for a particular instance is given to any user belonging to the group specified by the SYSADM_GROUP parameter in the DB2 database manager configuration file. When the instance is created, that parameter is set to null. Until the SYSADM_GROUP parameter is given a value, user names that are members of the Administrators group are considered to have system administrator (SYSADM) privileges. By default, it is the Administrators group on the machine where the account is defined. If it is a Domain account, then it must be a Domain Administrator.

Generally you will not want all Windows NT Administrators to have SYSADM authority over your database instances, nor will you necessarily want your database administrators to be Windows NT administrators. Thus you will need to update the SYSADM_GROUP parameter promptly after installing DB2 UDB or after creating an instance. But before you do, ensure that:

1. The group exists. Use the Windows NT User Manager administrative tool to create groups.

2. Users that you wish to have SYSADM authority for the instance are members of that group.

To specify group names, update the database manager configuration file using one of the following methods:

- The Command Line Processor (or the Command Center), documented in the *DB2 UDB Command Reference.* For example:

```
db2 update dbm cfg using sysadm_group dbadmin
```

- The Control Center. Right click on the instance name, select **Configure...**, and select the **Administration** tab. Then enter the appropriate local group name for *System administration authority group*.

- The configuration API, if you are developing your own application.

A user with SYSADM authority can perform both database manager and maintenance operations, as well as database operations. DB2 UDB provides two additional levels of system control authority, *SYSCTRL* and *SYSMAINT.* Like SYSADM, users receive these authority levels through membership in groups.

These group names must be entered in the database manager configuration file as values for the SYSCTRL_GROUP and SYSMAINT_GROUP parameters. Initially these parameters are set to null, meaning that no user has these authority levels.

SYSCTRL provides the ability to perform most administration commands. A member of the SYSCTRL user group does not have authority to access database objects nor modify the instance configuration file (DBM configuration). SYSCTRL offers almost complete control of database objects defined in a DB2 instance, but cannot access user data directly, unless explicitly granted the privilege to do so. A user with this authority, or higher, can perform the following functions:

- Update the database, node and DCS directory entries
- Update database configuration parameters
- Create or drop a database
- Force applications
- Start/Stop the DB2 instance
    - Note that starting and stopping a DB2 instance on Windows NT implies starting and stopping the service that represents the instance. As such, the user must also have the authority to start and stop a service on Windows NT.
- Quiesce a database
- Execute the RESTORE/BACKUP/ROLLFORWARD commands
- Create or drop a table space

SYSMAINT authority allows the execution of maintenance activities but not access to user data. Only users with this level of authority (or higher) can do the following tasks:

- Update database configuration files
- Backup databases and table spaces
- Restore an existing database
- Restore table spaces
- Start and stop the DB2 instance
    - Note that starting and stopping a DB2 instance on Windows NT implies starting and stopping the service that represents the instance. As such, the user must also have the authority to start and stop a service on Windows NT.
- Run the Database Monitor

The authority levels of SYSCTRL and SYSMAINT provide access to instance-level commands and a limited number of database-level commands for the purpose of system maintenance. No direct access to data within the database is permitted for users that have only these authorities.

At the database administration level, there is the *DBADM* authority. The creator of a database will automatically have DBADM authority for the new database. Other users can be granted DBADM authority using the SQL GRANT statement. It is possible to hold DBADM authority for multiple databases. DBADM provides authority to perform some common administration tasks, such as loading data, creating database objects and monitoring database activity. A user with DBADM authority does have access to data in that database as well.

A *privilege* is the right of a particular user or group to create or access a database resource. There are three types of privileges: Ownership, Individual, and Implicit.

1. **Ownership or control privileges**. For most objects, the user or group who creates the object has full access to that object. Control privilege is automatically granted to the creator of an object. There are some database objects, such as views, that are exceptions to this rule. Having control privilege is like having ownership of the object. You have the right to access the object and grant access to others. Privileges are controlled by users with ownership or administrative privileges. They provide other users with access using the SQL GRANT statement.

2. **Individual privileges**. These are privileges that allow you to perform a specific action. These privileges include select, delete and insert, and are granted by a user with ownership or control privileges.

3. **Implicit privileges**. An implicit privilege is one that is granted to a user automatically when that user is explicitly granted certain higher level privileges. These privileges are not revoked when the higher level privileges are explicitly revoked.

We have talked about the possible classes of users and their related authority levels. Note that the first three (SYSADM, SYSCTRL, and SYSMAINT) are controlled outside of DB2 and recorded in the database manager configuration file, while DBADM is controlled within DB2 through the SQL GRANT statement and the SQL REVOKE statement.

Table 35 shows the valid authorities for the various DB2 levels.

Figure 35. Database Authorities

Function	SYSADM	SYSCTRL	SYSMAIN	DBADM
CATALOG/UNCATALOG DATABASE	YES			
CATALOG/UNCATALOG NODE	YES			
CATALOG/UNCATALOG DCS	YES			
UPDATE DATABASE MANAGER CONFIGURATION FILE	YES			
GRANT/REVOKE DBADM	YES			
ESTABLISH/CHANGE SYSCTRL	YES			
ESTABLISH/CHANGE SYSMAINT	YES			
FORCE USERS	YES	YES		
CREATE/DROP DATABASE	YES	YES		
QUIESCE DATABASE	YES	YES		
CREATE/DROP/ALTER TABLESPACE	YES	YES		
RESTORE TO NEW DATABASE	YES	YES		
UPDATE DATABASE CONFIGURATION FILE	YES	YES	YES	
BACK UP DATABASE/TABLESPACE	YES	YES	YES	
RESTORE TO EXISTING DATABASE	YES	YES	YES	
PERFORM ROLL FORWARD RECOVERY	YES	YES	YES	
START/STOP INSTANCE	YES	YES	YES	
RESTORE TABLESPACE	YES	YES	YES	
RUN TRACE	YES	YES	YES	
OBTAIN MONITOR SNAPSHOTS	YES	YES	YES	
QUERY TABLESPACE STATE	YES	YES	YES	YES
UPDATE LOG HISTORY FILES	YES	YES	YES	YES
QUIESCE TABLESPACE	YES	YES	YES	YES
LOAD TABLES	YES			YES

Function	SYSADM	SYSCTRL	SYSMAIN	DBADM
SET/UNSET CHECK PENDING STATUS	YES	YES		YES
READ LOG FILES	YES	YES		YES
CREATE/ACTIVATE/DROP EVENT MONITORS	YES	YES		YES
USE IMPORT/EXPORT UTILITY	YES			YES

Assigning Authorities

SYSADM, SYSCTRL, SYSMAINT and DBADM should be restricted to avoid the risk of compromising system and data integrity. These authority levels are not required for general use. For a more detailed discussion of privileges and authorizations, see the *DB2 UDB Administration Guide.* For a complete list of the minimum authority level needed to execute DB2 commands and SQL statements, see the *DB2 UDB Command Reference* or the *DB2 UDB SQL Reference.*

2.4.4 Controlling Client Access to DB2 Databases

Controlling database access involves the control of access both to DB2 resources and to your data. A plan for controlling database access should be developed by defining your objectives for a database access control scheme, and specifying who shall have access to what resources and under what circumstances. This plan should also describe how to meet these objectives by using database functions, functions of other programs, and administrative procedures.

This section describes how to control access to the database manager and how the database manager controls access within itself. It also describes how you can customize access to the databases in your instance.

2.4.5 DB2 Authentication Methods

We've looked at how authentication occurs within Windows NT. DB2 UDB gives you some additional options as to where a user will be authenticated. You may wish user verification to occur at the client, at the server, or at a host. These options are provided through *authentication types*.

The authentication type is stored in the database manager configuration file at the database server. It is initially set when the instance is created and all databases will have the same authentication type as the instance in which the database was created.

DB2 UDB provides the following authentication types:

- **SERVER.** Specifies that authentication occurs on the DB2 server. The user name and password must be specified during the connection or attachment attempt and are validated at the server to determine if the user is permitted to access the instance. This is the default.

- **CLIENT.** This authentication type provides *Single Signon*. Once a user signs on to the desktop, no further authentication is required. A userid and password are not required on a connection or attachment request. If a userid and password are provided, it is by default verified on the client machine.

  Since an explicit logon to the server is not required, this authentication type is secure in a Windows NT domain where all machines are running Windows NT and all users log on to Domain accounts only. If all clients are *not* Windows NT clients, you should consider using Server authentication or limiting Client authentication to *trusted* clients. Trusted clients are defined to be clients that have a native security system. Specifically, all UNIX, OS/2, Windows NT, OS/400, OS/390, and VM clients have security systems and are regarded as *trusted*, whereas Macintosh, Windows 3.1, and Windows 95/98 clients are not. Because of this distinction in client security systems, DB2 UDB has two database manager configuration parameters to help you deal with untrusted clients. These parameters are active ONLY when authentication for the remote instance is set to CLIENT.

  1. *TRUST_ALLCLNTS*

     This parameter may be set to YES or NO. When set to YES, all clients are treated as trusted clients. A userid/password combination is not required on connection or attachment requests to the DB2 server. This is the default setting.

     If set to NO, untrusted clients must provide a userid and password when connecting to the server. Trusted clients will not have to provide a userid and password.

> **Untrusted Clients**
>
> If you are using Authentication CLIENT, DB2 UDB will not validate untrusted clients when *TRUST_ALLCLNTS* is set to YES. If you have untrusted clients in your environment connecting to your DB2 server, be sure to set *TRUST_ALLCLNTS* to NO.

2. *TRUST_CLNTAUTH*

> This parameter may be set to CLIENT or SERVER, and defaults to CLIENT. It determines where authentication will take place if a trusted client provides a userid and password on a connection or attachment request.
>
> If set to CLIENT, the userid and password are validated on the client machine. If set to SERVER, the userid and password are validated at the server.
>
> Note that this parameter is invoked only if a userid and password are provided. If the client is trusted, and no userid or password are provided, authentication is assumed to have taken place at the client.

It is recommended that in a Domain environment if you decide on Client authentication, that you set TRUST_ALLCLNTS to NO and set TRUST_CLNTAUTH to SERVER. However, if you have a mix of Windows NT and Windows 95/98 clients, there are ways to set up the Windows 95/98 machines to force a Domain logon. In this case, it should be safe to specify TRUST_ALLCLNTS to YES.

A major advantage of using TRUST_CLNTAUTH = SERVER in a domain is the reduction in RPC connections to the domain controller if the client machines are connecting and providing a userid and password combination for authentication. The DB2 UDB server machine will maintain one persistent connection to the Domain controller.

- **DCS.** Specifies that authentication occurs at the DRDA Application Server (AS). If the DB2 Connect product is not being used to access a DRDA AS, DCS is the same as SERVER and verification is at the DB2 UDB database server.

- **DCE.** Specifies that the user is authenticated using DCE Security Services.

2.4.6 Example Scenarios

As we have seen, several elements contribute to DB2 UDB's authentication scheme in the Windows NT environment: the security system of Windows NT itself, the security system (or lack of security system) of clients, domain authentication, trusted domains, and the ability to specify authentication type. To help clarify how these elements work together, let's look at some example scenarios.

The configuration is as follows:

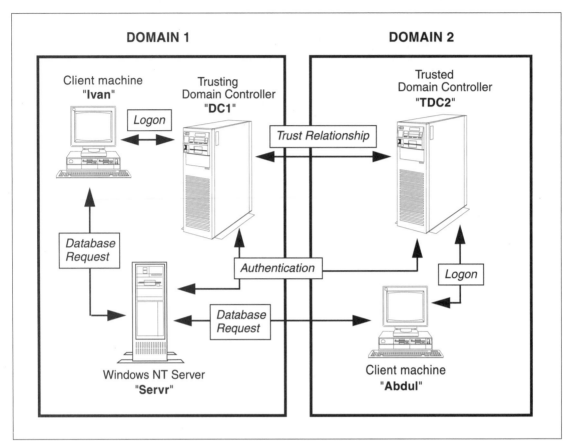

DOMAIN 1 — DOMAIN 2

Client machine "Ivan" — Trusting Domain Controller "DC1"

Trusted Domain Controller "TDC2"

Logon

Trust Relationship

Database Request

Authentication

Logon

Database Request

Windows NT Server "Servr"

Client machine "Abdul"

Figure 36. Authentication on Windows 95/98 and Windows NT

Each machine has a security database, Security Access Management (SAM), unless one or both of the client machines are running Windows 95/98. Windows 95/98 machines do not have a SAM database. DC1 is the domain controller, in which the client machine, Ivan, and the DB2 for Windows NT server, Servr, are enrolled. TDC2 is a trusted domain for DC1 and the client machine, Abdul, is a member of TDC2's domain. The *TRUST_ALLCLNTS* parameter is set at the default. Let's look at three possible scenarios for this example configuration.

2.4.6.1 Server Authentication

In this example:

1. Abdul logs on to the TDC2 domain (that is, he is known in the TDC2 SAM database).

2. Abdul then connects to a DB2 database that physically resides on Servr:

```
db2 connect to remotedb user abdul using abdulpw
```

3. Abdul has logged into the TDC2 domain. As a result of the trust relationship between TDC2 and DC1, Abdul has access to the DC1 domain as well. The search for the user Abdul will first be done at the local machine, then the domain controller DC1 and then any trusted domains. In this case, the user name Abdul is found on TDC2.

4. The DB2 machine called Servr then does the following:

   a. Validates the user name and password with TDC2.

   b. Finds out whether Abdul is an administrator by asking TDC2.

   c. Enumerates all Abdul's groups by asking TDC2.

2.4.6.2 Client Authentication and Windows NT Client Machines
In this example:

1. The administrator logs on to Servr and changes the authentication for the database instance to *Client*:

```
net stop myinst
db2 update dbm cfg using authentication client
net start myinst
```

2. Ivan, at a Windows NT client machine, logs on to the DC1 domain (that is, he is known in the DC1 SAM database).

3. Ivan then connects to a DB2 database that is cataloged to reside on Servr:

```
db2 connect to remotedb user ivan using ivanpw
```

4. The search for the user name will be done first at the local machine, then at the domain controller DC1 before trying any trusted domains. In this case, user Ivan is found on DC1.

5. Ivan's machine then validates the user name and password with DC1.

6. The DB2 database server, Servr then:

   a. Determines where Ivan is known.

   b. Finds out whether Ivan is an administrator by asking DC1.

c. Enumerates all Ivan's groups by asking DC1.

2.4.6.3 Client Authentication and Windows 95/98 Clients
In this example:

1. The administrator logs on to Servr and changes the authentication for the database instance to Client:

```
net stop myinst
db2 update dbm cfg using authentication client
net start myinst
```

2. Ivan, at a Windows 95/98 client machine, logs on to the DC1 domain (that is, he is known in the DC1 SAM database).

3. Ivan then connects to a DB2 database that is cataloged to reside on Servr:

```
db2 connect to remotedb user ivan using ivanpw
```

4. Ivan's Windows 95/98 machine cannot validate the user name and password. The user name and password are therefore assumed to be valid.

5. Servr then:

   a. Determines where Ivan is known.

   b. Finds out whether Ivan is an administrator by asking DC1.

   c. Enumerates all Ivan's groups by asking DC1.

Because a Windows 95/98 client cannot validate a given user name and password, client authentication under Windows 95/98 is not secure. If the Windows 95/98 machine has access to a Windows NT security provider, however, some measure of security can be imposed by configuring the Windows 95/98 system for validated pass-through logon. For details on how to configure your Windows 95/98 system in this way, refer to the Microsoft documentation for Windows 95/98.

2.5 The DB2 for Windows NT Environment

This section discusses some of the considerations that you need for logging into a DB2 for Windows NT environment, especially the first time the database manager is started. You'll need to understand the restrictions that

DB2 imposes on user and group IDs and passwords. Then, you'll need to understand the default Windows NT environment and what to change before logging into DB2.

2.5.1 User ID and Group ID Limitations

Once a user is authenticated, the user is identified within DB2 using an SQL authorization name known as an *authid*. The authid is used to track authorities and privileges and as the default high-level qualifier. On the Windows NT platform, DB2 UDB uses the Windows NT userid as the DB2 authid. Therefore, userids that will be used to connect to DB2 databases must follow certain DB2 naming conventions.

User IDs, group ids and passwords are limited to a maximum of eight characters. There are other restrictions as well:

- Cannot start with a digit (0 to 9) or end with a dollar sign ($).
- Can be one to eight characters long and may contain the following characters:
  - Upper or lower case characters A to Z.
  - Special characters #, @ or $.
  - Digits 0 to 9.
- Cannot be PUBLIC, USERS, ADMINS, LOCAL or GUESTS, or any SQL reserved word, or a name that starts with IBM, SYS or SQL.

Note

Passwords in Windows NT are case-sensitive, although user IDs are not. This can be a common cause for logon failure.

2.5.1.1 Authority to Install DB2 UDB for Windows NT

This section covers some important details for starting the database manager for the first time in a Windows NT environment.

To install DB2 UDB or start it the first time, you need to log on to Windows NT with an administrator user ID. The Windows NT default administrator (Administrator), although longer than eight characters, is now supported for installation. You can create another account that conforms to the DB2 user and group ID limitations, and is a member of the administrator group on the machine in which DB2 for Windows NT will be installed.

The db2admin ID

If you attempt to install DB2 UDB for NT while logged on with the default Administrator ID or other non-qualifying ID, DB2 UDB now continues with the installation process and creates a valid userid for its use during the installation process. This userid is deleted after the install is complete unless it is the same userid used for the DB2 Administration Server instance.

Being an administrator means you are part of the group in Windows NT User Manager called Administrators. All members of the Windows NT Administrators group receive SYSADM privileges, by default, until such time as a group is defined in the database manager configuration file for SYSADM_GROUP.

2.5.1.2 Authority to Start DB2 UDB for Windows NT

The DB2START command launches DB2 as a Windows NT Service. It also is run as a service when started from the Windows NT Control Panel / Services dialog box or with the NET START command.

Because DB2START launches a Windows NT service, a user attempting to start DB2 must meet Windows NT's requirements for starting a service. Specifically, the user account must satisfy *either* of the following criteria:

- The user must be a Windows NT Administrator.

- The user must be part of either the SYSADM_GROUP, SYSCTRL_GROUP or SYSMAINT_GROUP as defined in the database manager configuration file *and* also have the right to start a Windows NT Service (by being a member of the Administrators, Server Operators or Power Users group on Windows NT).

The DB2 service will run under the default SYSTEM account. The SYSTEM account cannot access LAN resources. A common source of failure is to place User Defined Functions or Stored Procedures (both are DLLs) on a LAN drive and attempt to access them from the DB2 service (or a process spawned by the DB2 process). The solution to this problem is to run the DB2 Service under a user account that has Administrator authority. Changing the account from the SYSTEM account to a user account/password can be accomplished through the Services Dialog box in the Windows NT Control Panel. You need to highlight the DB2 Service you want to change, and press the **Startup** button. Then change the *Log On As* option to specify a user account and password.

In addition to the above, the account must have the following Advanced rights (assignable through the Windows NT User Manager Policies/User Rights dialog):

- Act as Part of the Operating System
- Create a Token Object
- Log on as a service
- Replace a process level token

2.5.2 DB2 for Windows NT Security Server Service

The DB2 for Windows NT Security Service is installed as a part of the Client Application Enabler for Windows NT. The previous versions of DB2 on Windows NT required that the DB2 for Windows NT Security Service be started on the database server to authenticate users. However in DB2 UDB the authentication of user names and passwords has been integrated into the DB2 System Controller, and the DB2 Security Service is not used on database server machines. The DB2 Security Service is now required only on Windows NT client machines when connecting those clients to a DB2 server that is configured for authentication CLIENT and TRUST_CLNTAUTH is set to CLIENT and you specify a userid/password on the connect

This service is normally configured to autostart.

The service can be manually started (and stopped) in two ways.

1. The first is to enter the following command from a command window:

```
NET START DB2NTSECSERVER
```

2. Open **Services** within the Control Panel. Select **DB2 Security Server** by clicking on it and then select the **Start (Stop)** button.

To have the service start automatically with Windows NT, open **Services** within the Control Panel. Select **DB2 Security Server** and then select **Startup**. A Service window will appear. Click on the **Automatic** radio button under Startup type and click on **OK**. Note that you have to be logged onto the machine with an account that is a member of the Administrators group to change the Services configuration.

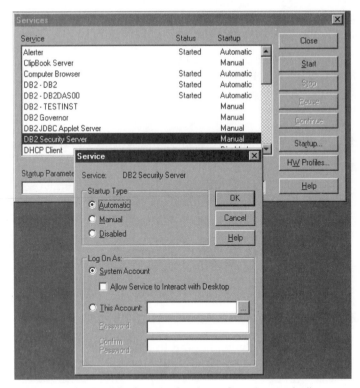

Figure 37. Setting DB2 Security Service to Start Automatically

Notice that in Figure 37 on page 70 there is an option to Log On As. The default is to log on as System Account. This should not be changed because the security server requires system privileges.

2.5.3 DB2 Instances and Windows NT Services

DB2 instances generally should be configured to start automatically as Windows NT Services. There will be a service for each DB2 instance in the Control Panel / Services dialog box. For example, in Figure 38, there are two regular DB2 instances: DB2 (the default instance) and TESTINST.

The DB2START and DB2STOP commands will also start and stop the instance as a service unless you use the /D switch, which will start it as a process. Be aware that if you start DB2 as a process, it will be stopped if you log off of Windows NT. In general you should always run your DB2 instances as services.

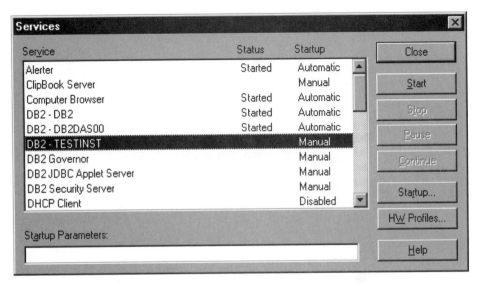

Figure 38. DB2 Instances as Windows NT Services

2.5.4 Planning for DB2 UDB in a Windows NT Environment

This section looks at where you might install DB2 UDB Server in a Windows NT environment and looks in detail at what is required if it is installed on a Backup Domain Controller.

An important point when considering where to install DB2 is the type of authentication that will occur between clients and server. This will partly be driven by the types of clients on the network (see "DB2 Authentication Methods" on page 61 for notes on trusted clients). Also consider the types of clients in any trusted domains.

2.5.4.1 DB2 UDB for Windows NT in a Workgroup

If you are considering installing DB2 for Windows NT in a workgroup, first consider if a workgroup is suitable for your needs. DB2's notion of Client level security provides Single Signon, but since in a Workgroup there are many SAM databases, there is no guarantee that when you grant a privilege to user JON that a JON account will not exist on more that one client machine. Despite this exposure, Client level security is very convenient (Single Signon is provided and if you choose not to use groups you could eliminate the need for duplicate account maintenance) for many small offices where access to data is either not restricted or can be controlled by the types of programs that the users can access. If you need tighter security, then the only option is to set the DB2 instance to Server level authentication. This then requires that the user provide a userid and password during a connect or attachment and also requires that you maintain duplicate accounts at each DB2 server. In either case, groups are enumerated on the DB2 Server machine.

2.5.4.2 DB2 UDB for Windows NT in a Domain

There are two basic options for installing DB2 UDB for Windows NT in a domain.

1. On a workstation. This could be a Windows NT Server that is not a domain controller or a Windows NT Workstation where Peer-to-Peer services are enabled.

2. On a Domain Controller. In a Windows NT LAN environment, a user can be authenticated at either a Primary or Backup Domain Controller. This ability to authenticate on multiple machines is very important in large distributed LANs with one central PDC and one or more BDCs at each site.

DB2 UDB for Windows NT on a Non-Domain Controller

This option could be used with either DB2 authentication client or server. This implementation of DB2 is actually the one used in the examples given for how DB2 authentication occurs in "Example Scenarios" on page 63.

One of the big advantages of putting DB2 UDB for Windows NT on a dedicated server is that it can be tuned and secured specifically for that task. Also the DB2 application would not have to compete for server resources were it performing as a domain controller.

On the negative side, regardless of which type of authentication DB2 is configured for, Windows NT authentication may have to occur on another server in its own or another domain.

DB2 UDB for Windows NT on a Primary Domain Controller

DB2 could be installed on a Primary Domain Controller. The biggest advantage of installing DB2 UDB for Windows NT on a PDC is that authentication can occur on the same machine. Also, there is less chance of encountering difficulties with the resolution of group membership for user accounts.

Implementing DB2 on a PDC also avoids some of the extra configuration that is discussed in the next section, "DB2 UDB for Windows NT on a Backup Domain Controller" on page 73. However, it is recommended, especially in larger networks, that the Primary Domain Controller be maintained as a dedicated server.

Once installed and configured, DB2 administrators and Windows NT administrators can and should be kept separate. In a larger enterprise or network, it would not be desirable, from a domain administration point of view, to have DB2 administrators logging on and performing DB2 maintenance on the PDC. The opposite is also true from a DB2 viewpoint. You would not want PDC administrators logging into a DB2 instance as SYSADM.

DB2 UDB for Windows NT on a Backup Domain Controller

Installing DB2 for Windows NT on a Backup Domain Controller offers all of the same advantages as those for a Primary Domain Controller. Users can be authenticated on the BDC at their site (and, in fact, on the same machine) in a distributed environment instead of requiring a call to the PDC for authentication. However, in order to enable DB2 to use the security database on the BDC, you must set a DB2 registry variable called DB2DMNBCKCTLR.

If the DB2DMNBCKCTLR registry variable is not set or is set to blank, DB2 UDB for Windows NT performs authentication at the PDC.

To set this registry variable to the name of the domain that the BDC is a member of, use the `db2set` command. For example:

```
DB2SET DB2DMNBCKCTLR=db2ntdmn
```

If the DB2DMNBCKCTLR registry variable is set to a question mark (that is, DB2DMNBCKCTLR=?), then DB2 UDB for Windows NT will attempt to determine the domain that this machine is a BDC for. If you know the domain, we recommend that you set the registry variable as above.

2.5.5 Example Scenarios

It is important to see how the above information about security can be related to some concrete examples. In this section we provide you with some scenarios of DB2 UDB in several different Windows NT environments.

In the following examples, these abbreviations are used:

- WGCN - Workgroup NT Client Machine
- WGCW - Workgroup Windows 95/98 client machine
- WGDB - Workgroup DB2 Server Machine
- PDC - Primary Domain Controller
- BDC - Backup Domain Controller
- TPDC - Trusted Domain Controller
- DMDB - Domain DB2 Server Machine
- DMCN - Domain NT Client Machines

We also assume that the CONNECT privilege has been granted to PUBLIC (this is the default when the database is created).

2.5.5.1 Client Authentication in a Workgroup

When user Dale on WGCN connects to WGDB and does not provide a userid/password DB2 extracts the userid from the operating system and sends it to the server (see Figure 39 on page 75). WGDB searches the local SAM to determine if Dale is known. If the account is *not* found then groups are *not* enumerated and Dale has access to all data granted to PUBLIC or to DALE explicitly.

When user Dale on WGCN connects to WGDB as user FRED with FREDPW, DB2 will attempt to validate the password on the client machine. The DB2 Security Service will be contacted to do the validation. A common error in this scenario happens when the DB2 Security Service is not running. The application receives:

```
SQL1402 Unable to authenticate user due to unexpected system
error.
```

If the account is found and the password is valid, the userid FRED is sent to WGDB and processing continues as above.

When user Dale on WGCW connects to WGDB as user FRED with FREDPW, DB2 cannot validate the password since Windows 95/98 does not have a native security system. DB2 trusts that the password provided is valid and passes the userid FRED to WGDB and processing continues as above.

In the scenarios above, if you want to use local groups then you *must* create duplicate user accounts on WGDB. If you want to prevent the user on WGCW from accessing WGDB without authentication, set TRUST_ALLCNTS to NO. If you don't want to run the DB2 Security Service on the client machine and want the userid/password validated at the server, set TRUST_CLNTAUTH to SERVER.

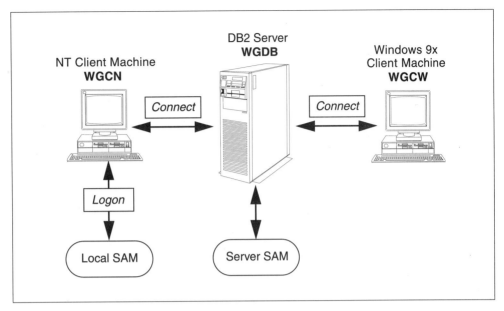

Figure 39. Security in a Workgroup

2.5.5.2 Server Authentication in a Workgroup

When user Dale on WGCN connects to WGDB and does not provide a userid/password, DB2 extracts the userid from the operating system and sends it to the server (see Figure 39). WGDB determines that the DB2 instance has server authentication and rejects the request.

Note

If the application were running on the WGDB machine a userid/password would *not* be required even though the authentication type is SERVER.

When user Dale on WGCN (or on WGCW) connects to WGDB as user FRED with FREDPW, DB2 will validate the password on the server machine. The account *must* exist on WGDB or the connection request will fail. Once the account is validated, groups and authorities will be enumerated by using the Security Database on WGDB.

2.5.5.3 Client Authentication in a Single Domain

When domain account Dale on DMCN connects to DMDB without providing a userid/password, the account name is passed to DMDB (see Figure 40 on page 77). DB2 will search the local SAM and if the account is not found it will search the Domain Controller. When the account is known to be a domain account, DB2 will communicate with the PDC machine to enumerate groups. The group enumeration search order described earlier is another common source of error. DB2 does not flow domainname\userid to the server, only the userid is sent. If the userid exists in both the local SAM and in the domain SAM, DB2 will find the local userid first and enumerate groups on the local machine.

> **Note**
>
> You should ensure that there are no accounts on the local server that have the same name as accounts in the domain.

When domain account Dale on DMCN connects to DMDB as FRED using FREDPW the account name and password is verified on the client machine by communicating with the DB2 Security Service. The DB2 Security Service will search the local SAM and if the account is not found it will search the Domain Controller. When the account is known to be a domain account, DB2 will communicate with the PDC machine to validate the password. If the password is valid, DB2 will pass the account FRED to the server machine and processing will continue as described above. If TRUST_CLNTAUTH was set to SERVER then the userid/password would be validated at the DB2 server machine. This is the desired behavior since it would dramatically reduce the number of RPC connections required to the PDC machine.

If the DBA of the DMDB machine wishes to control the definition of groups and potentially eliminate load on the PDC, he could create local groups on the DMDB machine and include NTDOMAIN\Dale and NTDOMAIN\Fred and set DB2_GRP_LOOKUP to local. Many installations choose this option since it allows the separation of DB2 groups from system groups defined by the Domain Administrator and does not preclude the inclusion of domain global groups in the local groups on DMDB.

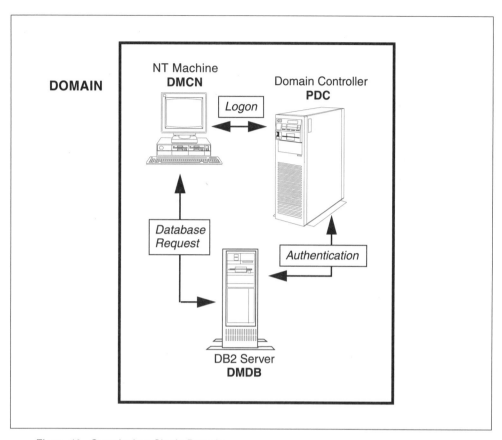

Figure 40. Security in a Single Domain

2.5.5.4 Server Authentication in a Single Domain

When domain account Dale on DMCN connects to DMDB without providing a userid/password, the account name is passed to DMDB (see Figure 40). DMDB determines that the DB2 instance has server authentication and rejects the request.

Note

If the application were running on the DMDB machine a userid/password would not be required even though the authentication type is SERVER.

When domain account Dale on DMCN connects to DMDB as Dale using DALEPW the account name (user id) and password is verified on DMDB. DB2 will search the local SAM and if the account is not found it will search the

Domain Controller. When the account is known to be a domain account, DB2 will communicate with the PDC machine to validate the password. If the password is valid, DB2 will continue to enumerate groups on the Domain Controller.

As discussed with Client Authentication, the DB2 administrator can change where groups are enumerated by setting DB2_GRP_LOOKUP to local.

2.5.5.5 Client Authentication in a Master Account Domain

The examples discussed under the Single Account Domain Environment apply to the Master Account Domain (Master Domain) environment, except that DB2 will enumerate groups across the trust relationship. As an illustration, we discuss the default Client security scheme as it applies to a Master Domain.

User Dale logs on to a domain account in the Master Account Domain (see Figure 41 on page 79). The machine DMCN is in this domain and the domain controller for this domain is TPDC. The DB2 server DMDB is in the resource domain whose domain controller is PDC. A trust relationship exists between TPDC and PDC. When Dale connects to a database on DMDB, the userid is sent to the DB2 server.

DB2 searches the local SAM, then the SAM of the PDC in the resource domain and finally the SAM in the Master Account Domain. The account is found and the machine TPDC is used to enumerate groups. Again a common problem in this environment is having duplicate accounts in either the local SAM or in the Resource Domain SAM. For this to work properly, ensure a single name space.

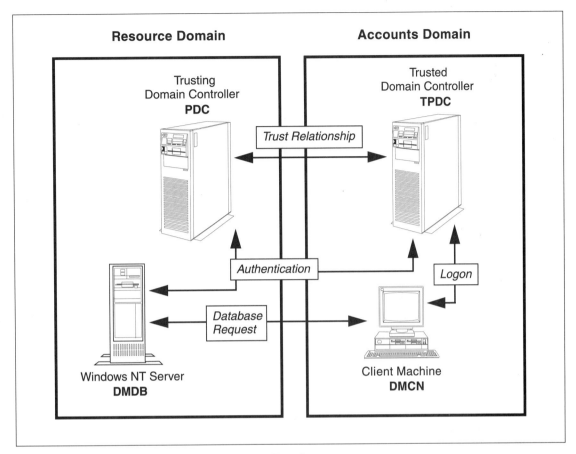

Resource Domain
Accounts Domain

Trusting
Domain Controller
PDC

Trusted
Domain Controller
TPDC

Trust Relationship

Authentication

Logon

Database
Request

Windows NT Server
DMDB

Client Machine
DMCN

Figure 41. Client Authentication in a Master Account Domain

As described previously, the DBA on DMDB can decide to control group
membership (and reduce connection overhead) by setting
DB2_GRP_LOOKUP to local.

2.5.6 Frequently Asked Questions

We conclude this chapter by presenting a number of frequently asked
questions related to DB2 UDB for Windows NT and security:

1. **Q**. All my accounts are domain accounts. I do not want the Windows NT
   Domain Administrator controlling the definition and membership of groups
   that by DB2 DBA will use in the granting of DB2 privileges.What can I do?

   A. In this case, you should create local groups on the DB2 UDB server and
   in these local groups explicitly specify the domain accounts that you want

to include (that is domainname\userid). You can include global groups if you choose, but then you are affected by any changes made to those global groups by the Windows NT Domain Administrator.

Once you create your local groups, you should set the DB2 registry variable DB2_GRP_LOOKUP=local and restart your DB2 instance. All group enumeration will now be performed on the local machine (this includes the definition of DB2 authority levels).

2. **Q**. How do I get someone other than a local administrator or a domain administrator to be an administrator or DB2?

   A. In this situation you should create another group, for example ADMDB2, and include in it the user accounts you want to have administer DB2 UDB. You should then update the DB2 database manager configuration file to set the SYSADM_GROUP parameter to ADMDB2.

3. **Q**. I log onto a domain account, but DB2 UDB cannot find the groups I am a member of. What is the problem?

   A. You must remember that DB2 does not qualify the name of a user with the domain name! When the account is presented to the DB2 server, DB2 first searches the local SAM, then the domain SAM and finally the SAM of any trusted domains. Once the user account is found, the groups are enumerated at that machine. A common problem is to have a local account the same as a domain account. DB2 finds the account on the local machine first and searches the local SAM for the groups that the user belongs to. In this case, delete the local account.

4. **Q**. My domain account is a member of the local Administrator's group. I cannot administer DB2 however. Why?

   A. There are two possibilities here. The most likely is that since DB2 has found your account on the domain controller, it is going to the domain controller to determine if you are an Administrator. Since you are not a domain Administrator, you are not (by default) a DB2 administrator. To get around this situation, you can tell DB2 to look on the local machine for its group definitions (use DB2_GRP_LOOKUP=local). You could also define an alternate group to be used as the SYSADM_GROUP and update the DB2 database manager configuration file parameter appropriately.

   The second possibility is that you are not a member of the group defined in the DB2 database manager configuration file SYSADM_GROUP field. This field will override the use of the Windows NT Administrator's group.

5. **Q**. I define all my domain accounts in local groups, but DB2 does not seem to recognize them. What should I do?

A. You should set DB2_GRP_LOOKUP=local to have DB2 UDB look on the local machine for group definitions. By default, DB2 looks on the machine where it finds the definition of the account (userid), in this case, the domain controller.

Chapter 3. DB2 UDB Installation

In Chapter 1, we described the different versions (or editions) of the DB2 Universal Database product and the functions available in each version. In this chapter, we go through the process of installing some of these product versions.

This chapter covers installing DB2 Universal Database for:

- DB2 UDB Servers - Workgroup/Enterprise Edition
- DB2 UDB Clients - Client Application Enabler/Software Developer's Kit

The installation of DB2 UDB Enterprise-Extended Edition is covered in "DB2 UDB Enterprise-Extended Edition" on page 263.

We also look at applying a fixpack to an existing DB2 UDB system.

3.1 Installing DB2 UDB Servers

This section covers the installation of the Workgroup and Enterprise Editions of DB2 UDB.

3.1.1 Pre-Installation

There are things to check and tasks to perform before installation begins:

1. What other software products need to be installed first?

   DB2 UDB Workgroup or Enterprise Editions can be installed on a Windows NT system at Version 3.51 or Version 4.0 or higher. If you need to connect to use APPC communications, you will need an SNA product installed on your system, such as:

   - IBM Communications Server for NT Version 5.0 or
   - Microsoft SNA Server Version 2.11 or later

   The Windows NT base operating system provides NetBIOS, IPX/SPX, Named Pipes, and TCP/IP protocol stacks.

2. How much memory and disk are required?

   The amount of memory you require depends on the number of concurrent users you will have and also the complexity of the applications you will run. For a simple static SQL application, you will need at least 32 MB of memory to accommodate 5 concurrent clients. For 25 concurrent clients, 48 MB of memory is required, and for 50 concurrent clients, you will need 64 MB of memory. Bear in mind that these are minimum requirements, and that installing more memory than these recommendations will certainly improve the performance of your DB2 UDB server.

The disk space required by DB2 UDB server products depends on the options you choose during the installation. The maximum total size of all the files included in Enterprise Edition at Version 5.2 is about 130 MB, of which around 40 MB is the online documentation. For Workgroup Edition, the maximum size is a few MB less. The maximum total size of all the graphical tools files is around 40 MB. The amount of disk actually allocated to the DB2 UDB files depends on the type of file system (FAT or NTFS) you use. As the online documentation consists of a large number of small files, using a FAT partition with a large (16/32 KB) cluster size is not recommended.

3. What configuration tasks need to be done first?

   • The Installation User:

   To perform the installation, you can be logged in as Administrator, or a member of the Administrator Group, or create a new user which is a member of the Administrator Group. If you create a new user, you will need to close all programs and then logon as this user before running the DB2 UDB installation program.

   Note that the user performing the installation does not have to comply with DB2's naming rules, so you can use the default Windows NT user Administrator. If the username does not comply with DB2's naming rules, but has the "Act as part of the operating system" advanced user right, the setup program will create the username db2admin to perform the installation. This username will be removed from the system when the installation is complete (as long as it is not being used as the DAS instance owner).

   • The User Account for DAS Instance Owner:

   By default, setup will suggest db2admin as the DAS instance owner, with the password db2admin. For minimal security, you should at least change the password during the installation process (see Figure 54 on page 96). If you need better security, then you should add a new user, following the required rules. These rules are given in "DB2 UDB Client/Server Communications" on page 123. You can do this before the installation, or let the installation program create this new user for you.

   • Check the existing PATH environment variable:

The setup program does not support PATH environment variables with a value exceeding 512 bytes. A typical installation will add these directories to PATH:

```
C:\IMNNQ_NT;C:\ifor\WIN\BIN;C:\ifor\WIN\BIN\EN_US;C:\SQLLIB\BIN;
C:\SQLLIB\FUNCTION;C:\SQLLIB\SAMPLES\REPL;C:\SQLLIB\HELP
```

Check the current setting for PATH to determine whether the total length might exceed 512 bytes after installation.

- Check for previous versions of DB2:

  To check if DB2 UDB (or DB2 Common Server V2) is installed on your system, run the Windows NT Registry Editor (c:\winnt\regedit.exe), and look for the following registry key:

  ```
  HKEY_LOCAL_MACHINE\SOFTWARE\IBM\DB2
  ```

  The existence of this key means that you have a version of DB2 already installed on your system.

  If DB2 UDB is already installed and you want to re-install DB2 UDB, you should first follow the uninstall process as detailed in "Uninstalling DB2 UDB" on page 106.

  If you have DB2 Common Server installed, and you need to migrate you current environment to DB2 Universal Database, refer to the DB2 UDB V5 Quick Beginnings for Windows NT in the "Migrating from Previous Versions" chapter. Alternately, you can choose to completely uninstall DB2 Common Server.

Note

To delete a version of DB2 from your system, you should always use the Uninstall utility provided with DB2. You should not uninstall from the Windows NT Add/Remove Programs, or by trying to delete files manually.

3.1.2 Running the Installation Program

If your Windows NT CD-ROM has been configured with autorun, when you insert the DB2 UDB product CD, the DB2 UDB installation program is launched automatically.

> **Note**
>
> Throughout this chapter, X: is used to refer to the CD-ROM drive into which the DB2 products CD is placed, C:\SQLLIB is where the DB2 products are installed, C:\ is the Windows NT boot disk, and C:\WINNT is the Windows NT system directory. The screen captures are from a DB2 UDB Version 5.0 installation.

If not, then you should execute X:\setup.exe. The *Welcome Panel* is displayed (Figure 42):

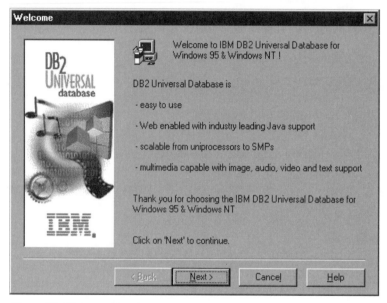

Figure 42. Welcome Panel

The installation program (we will refer to it as *setup*) checks whether the current user has sufficient authority to install DB2 UDB and if there are any DB2 UDB products already installed. Click **Next** to display the *Select Products* screen (Figure 43).

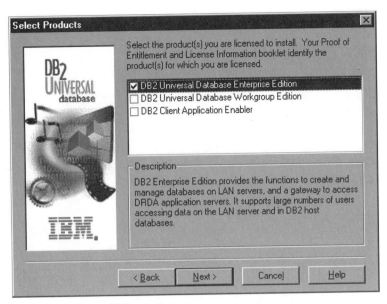

Figure 43. Select DB2 Products

From this screen, you can choose to install DB2 UDB Enterprise Edition (EE), DB2 UDB Workgroup Edition (WE), or DB2 Client Application Enabler (CAE).

The main difference between the Enterprise and Workgroup Editions is that Enterprise Edition includes the DB2 Connect component. We will cover the installation of the CAE in "Installing DB2 UDB Clients" on page 110.

In this example, we have chosen to install DB2 UDB Enterprise Edition. Click **Next** to display the *Select Installation Type* screen (Figure 44).

Note

There is context-sensitive on-line help available throughout setup. For instance, if you click on a particular product, and then click **Help**, a description of the product and its components is displayed.

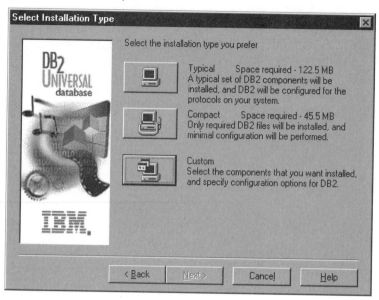

Figure 44. Select Installation Type

There are three types of installation: Typical, Compact and Custom. A Typical install uses the most popular options; a Compact install installs the minimum options possible; and a Custom install allows you to choose the options.

If you select Custom Install, Figure 45 shows the components you can select or deselect.

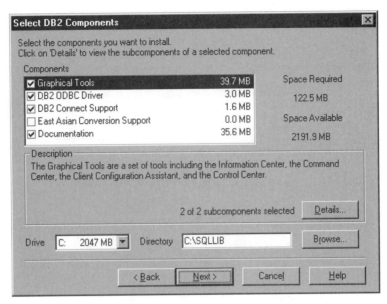

Figure 45. Select DB2 Components

This screen also shows how much space is available on each disk, how much disk space each component will use, and the total space required. You can choose the disk and directory where DB2 UDB will be installed.

You can display more details about a component by clicking on **Details**. For instance, the Graphical Tools component includes the subcomponents, Control Center and Client Configuration Assistant. A description is provided for the highlighted subcomponent (Figure 46).

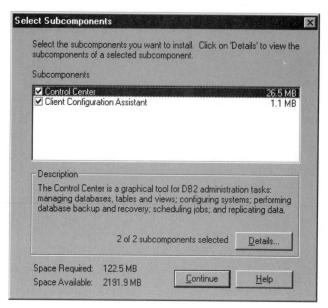

Figure 46. Graphical Tools Subcomponents

If you click on **Details** for the Documentation subcomponent, you can see all the online books (in HTML format) available for installation (Figure 47). As the total size of all these files is around 30-40 MB (depending on the version of DB2 UDB), you may choose to install the books on one server in your network, and access the HTML files from your other machines via a browser.

Figure 47. Online Books

After you have selected the components you want install on your system, you can choose whether the DB2 instance and Control Center should be automatically started when your system boots (Figure 48). Note that the DAS Instance will automatically start at boot time in any case.

Both the DB2 and the DAS instance are implemented as Windows NT Services, so you can change their startup behavior after installation from the Services settings in the Windows NT Control Panel. If you choose to automatically start the Control Center at boot time, then an entry is made in the Windows NT system Startup folder.

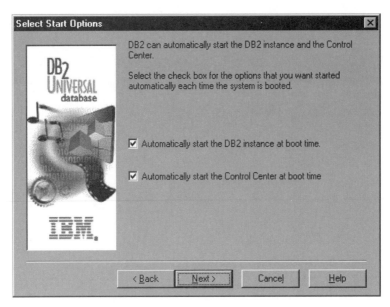

Figure 48. Select Start Options

Setup creates a default DB2 instance called DB2, and an Administration
Server (DAS) instance DB2DAS00. It also detects the networking protocols
which are installed and configured, and sets various DB2 UDB configuration
parameters and registry variables based on the settings for these protocols.
This process happens for both the DB2 and the DAS instance. The NetBIOS,
TCP/IP, IPX/SPX, Named Pipes, and APPC protocols are supported by DB2
UDB and these can all be detected during installation. "DB2 UDB
Client/Server Communications" on page 123 gives more details about the
automatic configuration of communications-related parameters.

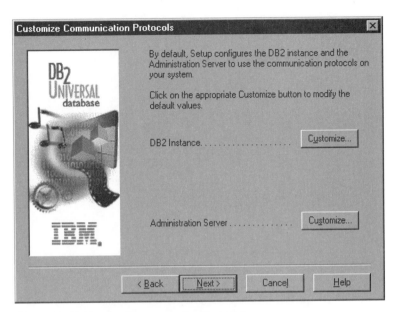

Figure 49. Customize Communication Protocols

You can examine (and change) the communications settings that setup generates by clicking on **Customize** against one of the two instances (Figure 49).

The settings for the protocols which are marked (detected) may be modified by clicking the **Properties** button (Figure 50). If you need to modify the settings of the other protocols, just click in the check box against the protocol, and then click on **Properties**.

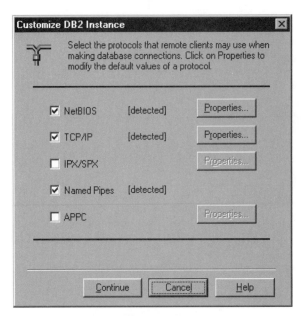

Figure 50. Customize DB2 Instance

Figure 51 shows the settings for the NetBIOS protocol for the DB2 instance. To support NetBIOS, the setup program generates a value for the Workstation name (NNAME) and a value for Adapter number. You can modify these values if required. The NNAME value is stored in the database manager configuration file for the DB2 instance.

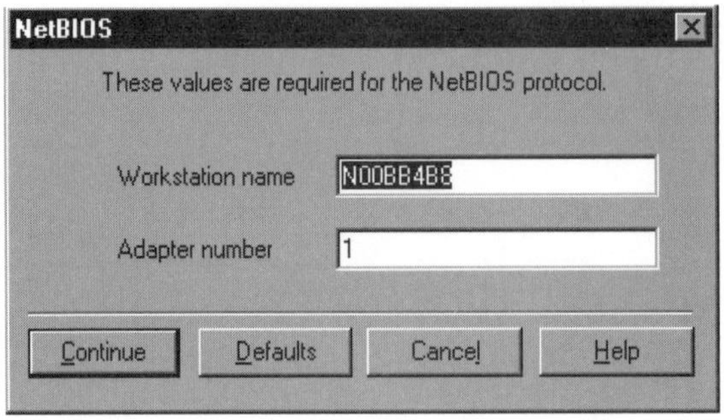

Figure 51. NetBIOS Settings for the DB2 Instance

For the TCP/IP protocol, setup assigns a value (like db2cDB2) to Service Name (SVCENAME in the DBM configuration file) and a value (like 50000) for the Port number (Figure 52).

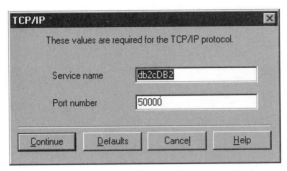

Figure 52. TCP/IP Settings for the DB2 Instance

Setup will also add two ports for the DB2 instance in the Windows NT services file (C:\winnt\system32\drivers\etc\services). The two entries look like this:

```
db2cDB2 50000/tcp    # Connection port for DB2 instance DB2
db2iDB2 50001/tcp    # Interrupt port for DB2 instance DB2
```

The SVCENAME parameter in the database manager configuration file is set to the value for Service name (usually db2cDB2). By default, the Port number for the Connection port is set to 50000 but if this is already used then setup will find the first non-used number over 50000. The second (Interrupt) port, which is used to support DB2 V1 clients, always uses a number one greater than the Connection port. So, for example, if the Port number is 50000, then the Interrupt port will use 50001.

You can also examine and change the settings for the IPX/SPX and APPC protocols for the DB2 instance.

For the TCP/IP settings for the Administration Server (DAS) instance, setup uses 523 as the Port number (Figure 53). This port number is reserved for the DAS instance and should not be changed. No entry is made in the services file as this is a well-known port.

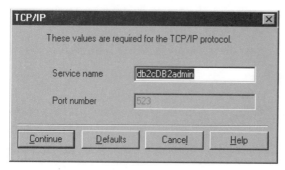

Figure 53. TCP/IP Settings for the DAS Instance

For the IPX/SPX settings for the DAS instance, setup will use the Socket number 87A2.

The DAS instance must be assigned a user that it will use to log on to the system, also known as the DAS instance owner. By default, the username and password are both set to db2admin (Figure 54).

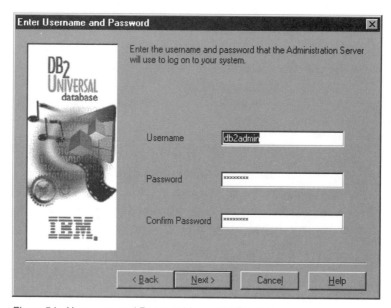

Figure 54. Username and Password for the DAS Instance

For security reasons, it is recommended to change the defaults for the username and password. The setup program will check to see if the username specified for the Administration Server exists. If it does exist, the setup program will verify that the username is a member of the Administrators group. However the setup program will not check the password against the password that is already defined for the user in Windows NT (Figure 55). You should make sure the password you enter is the same as the password already defined in Windows NT for that user. Otherwise, the DAS instance Windows NT Service will fail to start.

Figure 55. Setup Cannot Verify db2admin's Password

If you provide your own username, you must ensure that it is eight characters or less, and complies with DB2's naming rules (see "User ID and Group ID Limitations" on page 67). If you use the default username, db2admin, you should at least change the password to a different value.

If you ever need to change the password for the DAS instance owner after installation, you should:

- Change the password for the DAS instance owner using the User Manager in the Windows NT Administration Tools.

- Change the password for the DB2-DB2DAS00 service on the Services Panel to match the new password that you specified for the DAS instance owner using User Manager.

Figure 56. Summary of Components

As shown in Figure 56, before setup copies the DB2 UDB code to your system, a summary of what you have selected is displayed. You can scroll up and down to see all the settings. If you need to make changes, click **Back** to repeat any of the previous steps.

This summary is saved in a file called C:\DB2LOG\db2.log after installation. Here is an example of this file:

```
Products to Install:
     DB2 Universal Database Enterprise Edition

Setup Type:
     CUSTOM

Components to Install:
     Required DB2 components
     Graphical Tools
          -Client Configuration Assistant
          -Control Center
               -Performance Monitor
               -Visual Explain
     DB2 ODBC Driver
     East Asian Conversion Support
          -Simplified Chinese Conversion Support
     Documentation
          -Administration Guide
          -Administration: Getting Started
          -Command Reference
          -DB2 Universal Database Quick Beginnings
          -Glossary
          -Master Index
```

```
                    -Messages Reference
                    -SQL Getting Started
                    -SQL Reference
                    -System Monitor Guide and Reference
                    -Troubleshooting Guide
                    -DB2 Connectivity Supplement
                    -Replication Guide and Reference
                    -Installing and Configuring DB2 Clients

DB2 System Name:JC6004E

DB2 Instance Configuration:
      NetBIOS
              Workstation Name:N000E04C
              Adapter Number:1
      TCP/IP
              Service Name:db2cDB2
              Port Number:50000
      Named Pipes

Administration Server Configuration:
      Log On Username:db2admin
      NetBIOS
              Workstation Name:N010E04C
              Adapter Number:1
      TCP/IP
              Service Name:db2cDB2admin
              Port Number:523
      Named Pipes

Target Directory:
      C:\SQLLIB

Program Folder:
      DB2 for Windows NT
```

Figure 57. Copying Files During Installation

When you click on **Install**, setup copies the DB2 UDB files to your system
(Figure 57). After this, setup will modify registry variables and configuration
parameters. When this is complete, you will be prompted to restart the
system (Figure 58).

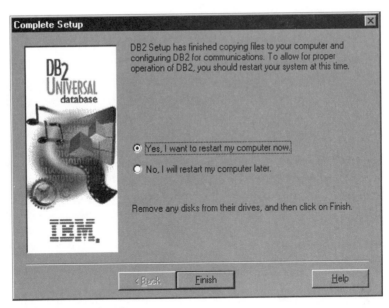

Figure 58. Complete Setup

If you want to know more details about what happened behind the scenes, or check whether the installation was successful or not, check the file db2.log in the directory C:\DB2LOG.

The installation program creates the folder DB2 for Windows NT in the Windows NT Programs folder, and other subfolders and icons within this folder. For example:

```
Program Folders:DB2 for Windows NT
Sub Program Folder: Administration Tools
    Alert Center
    Control Center
    Event Analyzer
    Journal
    Script Center
    Tool Settings
Sub Program Folder: Problem Determination
    Support through Internet
    Trace
Certification
Command Center
Command Line Processor
Command Window
First Steps
Information Center.
Release Notes
Registration
Client Configuration Assistant
Start HTML Search Server
Stop HTML Search Server
Uninstall
```

The Start HTML Search Server and First Steps shortcuts are added to the system StartUp folder. After the first boot, the First Steps icon is deleted.

3.1.3 Post-Installation

The final stage of the DB2 UDB installation process takes place the first time the system is restarted after the DB2 UDB installation program has completed.

3.1.3.1 First Steps

After restarting the system, the First Steps program is run (Figure 59). This allows you to perform some basic tasks in DB2 UDB, such as creating a sample database, using SQL statements, and accessing the online manuals. The First Steps program will only be run automatically at reboot the first time you restart the system after installing DB2 UDB.

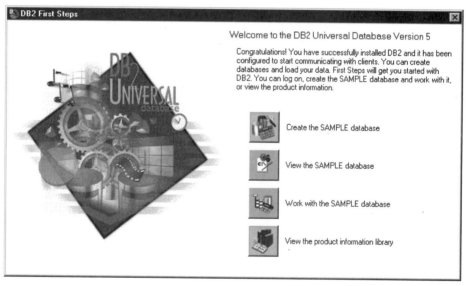

Figure 59. DB2 UDB First Steps

To verify that DB2 UDB was installed successfully, you can click the first button in First Steps to create a sample database.

If you click the second button, marked *View the SAMPLE database*, it will open the Command Center graphical tool and provides a script to connect to and select data from the SAMPLE database.

Clicking the third button will open Control Center, another graphical tool. Using this tool, you can create databases, and other database objects, like tables, table spaces, or indexes. You can also use Control Center to administer your local or remote database system.

By clicking the fourth button, the Information Center graphical tool will be started. This tool is the central point for all the online documentation for DB2 UDB, including the manuals in HTML, sample programs and useful Internet addresses.

3.1.3.2 Nodelock Administration Tools
The license for DB2 UDB is managed by a product called License Use Runtime, which is installed along with DB2 UDB (if not already installed).

As shown in Figure 60, after installation, the *License Use Folder* is displayed.

Figure 60. License Use Runtime

Using the Nodelock Administration Tool (Figure 61), you can view the license key (or *nodelock*) for your copy of DB2 UDB.

Note

The product license key is provided on the product media itself and is added to your system automatically during the installation process.

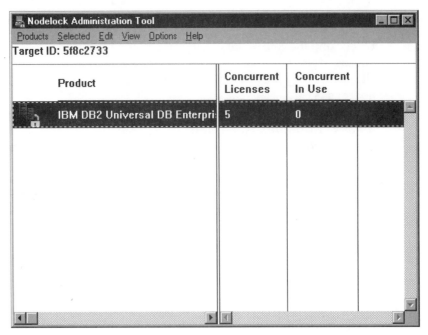

Figure 61. Nodelock Administration Tool

Using the Nodelock Administration Tool, you can monitor the total number of concurrent users who are connecting to DB2.

If you need to add a new License Key, click on **Products** on the Menu Bar of Nodelock Administration Tool, then click on the **New...** item from the dropdown menu. You can then input your License key manually, or import it from a License Key file.

3.1.4 Summary of the Installation

The setup program can potentially change many aspects of your Windows NT configuration. Here is a summary of the changes:

1. Windows NT Registry:

   When you install DB2 UDB on your system, setup creates registry entries for the DB2 instance, the DAS instance and the global profile settings for the DB2 system.

   For example, you can use the Registry Editor (c:\winnt\regedit.exe) to check which directory DB2 UDB has been installed in (Figure 62). Under the registry key:

   HKEY_LOCAL_MACHINE\SOFTWARE\IBM\DB2\GLOBAL_PROFILE

you can see the setting for the Global Profile Registry Variable DB2PATH, among others.

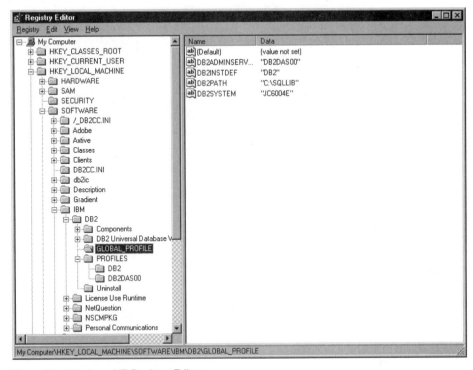

Figure 62. Windows NT Registry Editor

2. Windows NT Services:

   When you install DB2 UDB, some DB2 UDB programs are configured as Windows NT services. For instance:

   - DB2 - DB2: The default DB2 instance.
   - DB2 - DB2DAS00: The Database Administration Server Instance.
   - DB2 Governor: This service can control application behavior by settings limits and defining actions when the limits are exceeded.
   - DB2 Java Applet Server: To support Java Applets.
   - DB2 Security Server: This service lets users get convenient single sign-on, providing transparent access to any authorized enterprise resource.

3. HTML Search Server:

If you choose to install the online books, then the setup program will also install a tool which enables you to search the online books (Figure 63). This tool, known as the HTML Search Server, is in fact the NetQuestion product bundled with Internet Connection Server Lite, an HTTP server. An icon called *Start HTML Search Server* is added to the system Startup folder, so every time the system is booted, the HTML Search Server is started automatically.

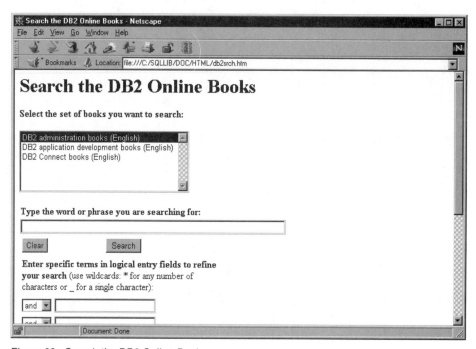

Figure 63. Search the DB2 Online Books

Note

If you do experience any errors or problems during the installation process, refer to "Installation Problems" on page 483.

3.2 Uninstalling DB2 UDB

You may need to uninstall DB2 UDB as the first step in performing a clean installation. For instance, if your Windows NT system lost power during the installation process, or if you had a pre-release version of DB2 UDB installed on your system. To uninstall DB2 UDB, you should always use the uninstall utility provided with the DB2 UDB product. To uninstall DB2 UDB, follow these steps:

3.2.1 Stop All DB2 Applications and Processes

Follow these steps:

1. Check that there are no DB2 applications running, using:

```
C:\>db2 list applications
SQL1611W No data was returned by Database System Monitor.
```

If there are some DB2 applications running, then you should quit these applications, or stop them using:

```
C:\>db2 force application all
DB20000I The FORCE APPLICATION command completed successfully.
DB21024I This command is asynchronous and may not be effective
immediately.
```

2. If you have databases that you wish to keep, you should back them up. If you wish to keep a record of the current configuration, then you should make a copy of your instance and database configuration files. For instance, from a DB2 Command Window:

```
C:\> db2 get dbm cfg > dbmcfg.out
C:\> db2 get db cfg for sample > samplecfg.out
```

3. Stop DB2, using the Windows NT Services panel or a DB2 Command Window. For example:

```
C:\SQLLIB\BIN>db2stop
SQL1064N DB2STOP processing was successful.
```

If DB2 is not running, you may see:

```
SQL1032N No start database manager command was issued.
```

4. Stop the Administration Server using the Windows NT Services panel or a DB2 Command Window. For example:

```
C:\SQLLIB\BIN>db2admin stop
SQL4407W The DB2 Administration Server was stopped successfully.
```

5. If you see any other DB2 UDB Services which are running in the Services Panel, you should stop these also. For example, the DB2 Governor, DB2 Security Server or DB2 Java Applet Server.

6. Stop the HTML Search Server (if it is running), by selecting Stop HTML Search Server in the DB2 Windows NT folder.

7. Check that all DB2 UDB related processes are stopped by running the Windows NT Task Manager.

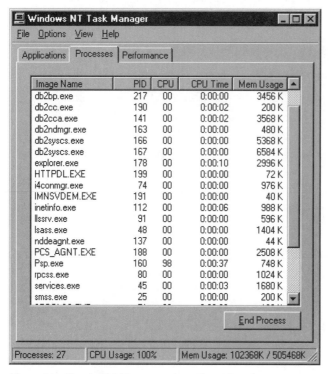

Figure 64. Check DB2 Processes from Task Manager

Figure 64 shows a selection of the possible DB2 UDB processes that may be running on your system. These processes are summarized in Table 3:

Table 3. Related DB2 Processes

Process	Description
db2bp.exe	DB2 CLP or Command Center background process
db2cc.exe	Control Center or other graphic tools
db2govds.exe	DB2 Governor
db2cca.exe	Client Configuration Assistant
db2jds.exe	DB2 JDBC Applet Server
db2licd.exe	License daemon process
db2ndmgr	DAS Node Manager
db2sec.exe	DB2 Security Server
db2syscs.exe	DB2 or DAS instance

Process	Description
HTTPDL.EXE	Lite Web Server
IMNSVDEM.EXE	NetQuestion (HTML Search Server)

You should make sure that none of the processes are running on your system before running the Uninstall program.

3.2.2 Execute the DB2 UDB Uninstall Program

To run the DB2 UDB Uninstall program:

1. Click on the **Uninstall** icon in the DB2 for Windows NT folder.

2. Click **Yes** on the confirmation window (Figure 65).

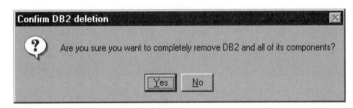

Figure 65. Confirm DB2 Deletion

3. If the uninstall completes successfully, you will see the message "The DB2 Product have been successfully removed" (Figure 66).

Figure 66. Uninstall Completed

3.2.3 Summary of the Uninstall Process

To help you resolve any problems if DB2 UDB does not uninstall successfully, here is a description of the steps that the DB2 UDB uninstall program will attempt:

1. The DB2 UDB files are deleted from C:\SQLLIB. If there are some files in this directory other than the original installed files, these files or directories may not be deleted. You can delete these files or directories manually.

2. The NetQuestion (and Internet Connection Server Lite) files are deleted from C:\IMNNQ_NT.

3. The DB2 entries in the Windows NT Registry are deleted from:

   `HKEY_LOCAL_MACHINE\SOFTWARE\IBM`

4. The Windows NT Services related to DB2 UDB are removed.

5. If your DB2 UDB system was previously configured for TCP/IP, then the following entries (or similar entries) are deleted from the Windows NT TCP/IP Services file in C:\winnt\system32\drivers\etc:

```
db2cDB2        50000/tcp   # Connection port for DB2 instance DB2
db2iDB2        50001/tcp   # Interrupt port for DB2 instance DB2
```

6. The folders related to DB2 UDB are deleted from the Windows NT Desktop.

7. The uninstall process keeps a record of its actions in the log file C:\DB2LOG\db2.log. If you need more details of what happened behind the scenes, you should check the contents of this file.

3.3 Installing DB2 UDB Clients

This section covers the installation of the DB2 UDB Client Application Enabler (CAE) and DB2 UDB Software Developer's Kit (SDK) products.

3.3.1 Pre-Installation

There are things to check and tasks to perform before installation begins:

1. What other software products need to be installed first?

   DB2 UDB CAE or SDK can be installed on a Windows NT system at Version 3.51 or Version 4.0 or higher. If you need to connect to use APPC communications, you will need an SNA product installed on your system, like:

   • IBM Communications Server for NT Version 5.0 or
   • Microsoft SNA Server Version 2.11 or later

   The Windows NT base operating system provides NetBIOS, IPX/SPX, Named Pipes, and TCP/IP protocol stacks.

2. How much memory and disk are required?

The amount of memory you require depends on whether the client needs to run the graphical tools or not. You will need a minimum of 24 MB of memory to run the graphical tools on a client. Otherwise, the amount of memory you need depends on the database applications you want to run. Bear in mind that these are minimum requirements, and that installing more memory than these recommendations will certainly improve the performance of your DB2 UDB client.

The disk space required by DB2 UDB client products depends on the options you choose during the installation. The maximum total size of all the files in the CAE at Version 5.2 is around 90 MB, of which 40 MB is the online documentation. For the SDK, the maximum total size is a few MB more. The maximum total size of all the graphical tools files is around 40 MB. The amount of disk actually allocated to the DB2 UDB files depends on the type of file system (FAT or NTFS) you use. As the online documentation consists of a large number of small files, using a FAT partition with a large (16/32 KB) cluster size is not recommended.

3. What configuration tasks need to be done first?

- The Installation User:

  To perform the installation, you can be logged in as Administrator, or a member of the Administrator Group, or create a new user which is a member of the Administrator Group. If you create a new user, you will need to close all programs and then logon as this user before running the DB2 UDB installation program.

  Note that the user performing the installation does not have to comply with DB2's naming rules so you can use the default Windows NT user Administrator. If the username does not comply with DB2's naming rules, but has the "Act as part of the operating system" advanced user right, the setup program will create the username db2admin to perform the installation. This username will be removed from the system when the installation is complete (as long as it is not being used as the DAS instance owner).

- Check the existing PATH environment variable:

  The setup program does not support PATH environment variables with a value exceeding 512 bytes. A typical installation will add these directories to PATH:

  ```
  C:\IMNNQ_NT;C:\ifor\WIN\BIN;C:\ifor\WIN\BIN\EN_US;C:\SQLLIB\BIN;
  C:\SQLLIB\FUNCTION;C:\SQLLIB\SAMPLES\REPL;C:\SQLLIB\HELP
  ```

  Check the current setting for PATH to determine whether the total length might exceed 512 bytes after installation.

- Check for previous versions of DB2:

  To check if DB2 UDB (or DB2 Common Server V2) is installed on your system, run the Windows NT Registry Editor (c:\winnt\regedit.exe), and look for the following registry key:

  HKEY_LOCAL_MACHINE\SOFTWARE\IBM\DB2

  The existence of this key means that you have a version of DB2 already installed on your system.

  If DB2 UDB is already installed and you want to re-install DB2 UDB, you should first follow the uninstall process as detailed in "Uninstalling DB2 UDB" on page 106.

  If you have DB2 Common Server installed, and you need you migrate your current environment to DB2 Universal Database, refer to the DB2 UDB V5 Quick Beginnings for Windows NT, in the "Migrating from Previous Versions" chapter. Alternately, you can choose to compeletely uninstall DB2 Common Server.

> **Note**
>
> To delete a version of DB2 from your system, you should always use the Uninstall utility provided with DB2. You should not uninstall from the Windows NT Add/Remove Programs, or by trying to delete files manually.

3.3.2 Installing the DB2 Client Application Enabler

You can install DB2 CAE from the DB2 Client Pack CD or from the DB2 Server CD and select the DB2 CAE option. The installation of the CAE is similar to the installation of Enterprise or Workgroup Editions. The setup program gives you the option to install the Graphical Tools, DB2 ODBC driver and Documents.

If your Windows NT CD-ROM has been configured with autorun, when you insert the DB2 UDB product CD, the DB2 UDB installation program is launched automatically. If not, then you should execute X:\setup.exe. The *Welcome Panel* is displayed.

If you are installing from the DB2 UDB Server CD, select the DB2 Client Application Enabler option. The next screen displays an option to *Enable Remote Administration* (Figure 67):

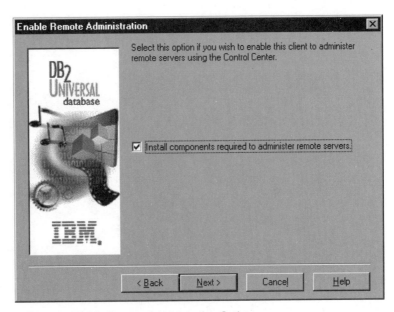

Figure 67. Enable Remote Administration Option

If you want this system to be an administration workstation, then select this option, and you will install the DB2 UDB graphical administration tools (for example, Control Center). If you do not select this option, the only graphical tool you install is the Client Configuration Assistant (assuming a Typical install in both cases).

There are three types of installation, Typical, Compact and Custom. A Typical install uses the most popular options; a Compact install installs the minimum options possible; and a Custom install allows you to choose the options.

For Typical and Compact installs, you only need choose which disk and which directory you want DB2 CAE to be installed in.

If you select Custom Install, Figure 68 shows components you can select or deselect. You also choose the disk and directory for the DB2 CAE files, and whether to automatically start the Control Center (if you have selected it to be installed).

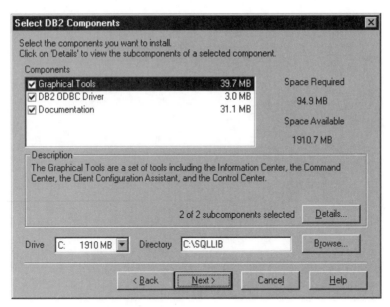

Select DB2 Components

Select the components you want to install.
Click on 'Details' to view the subcomponents of a selected component.

Components

		Space Required
☑ Graphical Tools	39.7 MB	94.9 MB
☑ DB2 ODBC Driver	3.0 MB	
☑ Documentation	31.1 MB	Space Available
		1910.7 MB

Description
The Graphical Tools are a set of tools including the Information Center, the Command
Center, the Client Configuration Assistant, and the Control Center.

2 of 2 subcomponents selected   Details...

Drive C: 1910 MB ▼   Directory C:\SQLLIB   Browse...

< Back   Next >   Cancel   Help

Figure 68. Select DB2 Components

The DB2 CAE needs a Workstation name and Adapter number to support the
NetBIOS protocol. If you have installed and configured the NetBIOS protocol,
the setup program will detect it (Figure 69) and choose some default settings.
You can modify the settings by clicking on **Properties**.

If TCP/IP is installed and configured you can use this protocol on a DB2 client
without specifying any communications settings. This explains why there is
no screen to Customize TCP/IP.

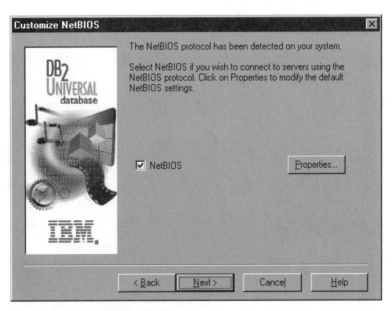

Figure 69. Customize NetBIOS

Before installing the DB2 UDB files to your system, you can verify the installation options you have chosen (Figure 70). If you need to modify any of them, you can click on **Back** and repeat any of the preceding screens.

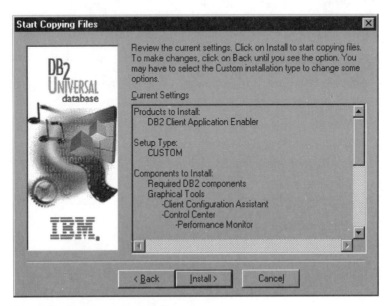

Figure 70. Summary of Installation

When the installation of the DB2 UDB code has finished, the Complete Setup screen is displayed (Figure 71):

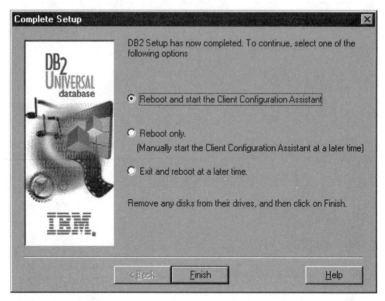

Figure 71. Complete Setup

If you select "Reboot and start the Client Configuration Assistant", then you can setup connections to remote databases using the CCA after rebooting the system. More details about using the CCA are available in "DB2 UDB Client/Server Communications" on page 123.

3.3.2.1 Summary of the Installation

The setup program can potentially change many aspects of your Windows NT configuration. Here is a summary of the changes:

1. Windows NT Registry:

   When you install DB2 UDB CAE on your system, setup creates registry entries for the local DB2 instance, and the global profile settings for the DB2 system in the following Registry key:

   `HKEY_LOCAL_MACHINE\SOFTWARE\IBM\DB2`

2. Windows NT Services:

   When you install DB2 UDB, some DB2 UDB programs are configured as Windows NT services. For instance:

   • DB2 JDBC Applet Server: To support Java Applets.

- DB2 Security Server: This service lets users get convenient single sign-on, providing transparent access to any authorized enterprise resource.

3. HTML Search Server:

   If you choose to install the online books, then the setup program will also install a tool which enables you to search the online books (Figure 63). This tool, known as the HTML Search Server, is in fact the NetQuestion product bundled with Internet Connection Server Lite, an HTTP server. An icon called *Start HTML Search Server* is added to the system Startup folder, so every time the system is booted, the HTML Search Server is started automatically.

4. Log file of DB2 Installation:

   The installation process keeps a record of its actions in the log file C:\DB2LOG\db2.log. If you need more details of what happened behind the scenes, you should check the contents of this file.

3.3.3 Installing the DB2 Software Developer's Kit

The steps to install the DB2 UDB Software Developer's Kit (SDK) are similar to those for installing DB2 CAE. The setup program gives you the same options as the CAE, with the addition of the tools and environment you need to develop applications that access DB2 databases using embedded SQL or the DB2 Call Level Interface.

You install the DB2 SDK by running the file `x:\setup.exe` from the DB2 SDK CD. There is an extra component compared to the DB2 UDB CAE called Sample Applications (Figure 72).

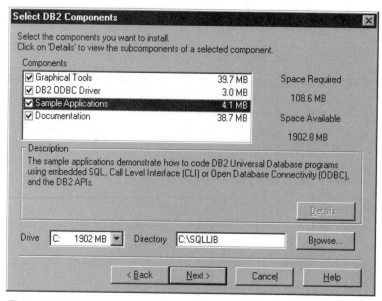

Figure 72. Select Components for DB2 SDK

After installing the DB2 SDK, you can connect to DB2 local and remote databases as with the DB2 CAE. You can also view the header files and libraries for developing DB2 UDB database applications in the C:\sqllib\include directory. This directory should be in the list of directories in the setting of the PATH system environment variable. Sample programs are supplied in the C:\sqllib\samples directory.

3.4 Applying a DB2 UDB Fixpack

A DB2 UDB Fixpack is a version of the DB2 UDB software which is released between major versions to provide improvements and solve known problems.

To apply a DB2 UDB Fixpack, follow these steps:

1. Check the level of DB2 UDB

    To apply a DB2 UDB Fixpack, you must have DB2 UDB already installed on your system. To determine the version and level of DB2 UDB, run the Windows NT Registry Editor (c:\winnt\regedit.exe), and check in the following registry key:

    HKEY_LOCAL_MACHINE\SOFTWARE\IBM\DB2\<product name>\Current Version

    Then examine the values for these keys:

    Version   "0x00000005" (5)

```
Release              "0x00000000" (0)
Modification         "0x00000000" (0)
Service Level        ""
```

In this example, DB2 UDB is installed at 5.0 with no Fixpacks (Service Level) installed. You can get more details about which versions of DB2 UDB are pre-requisites of this Fixpack by reading the readme.txt file in the setup directory on the distribution media.

2. Stop all DB2 Applications, Services and Processes

You should make sure that applications which use DB2 UDB are stopped. Then ensure that all DB2 UDB Services and processes are stopped. See "Stop All DB2 Applications and Processes" on page 107.

3. Space Required

You should allow for enough free disk space for the installation of the DB2 Fixpack. Generally, setup will estimate that it needs approximately X MB of free space, where X is the amount of MB taken by the existing DB2 UDB code. Setup does not take into account that certain files will be replaced during the installation. This means that after the installation completes, a lot of disk space will be freed (Figure 73).

If it appears that there is not enough space to install the chosen product(s), setup will warn you of this fact, but notify you that this does not take into account that existing files will be replaced. If you choose to continue without freeing up space, you must ensure that there is in fact enough space. Once no space is left, you will have to either free up more space to continue, or manually kill the setup process.

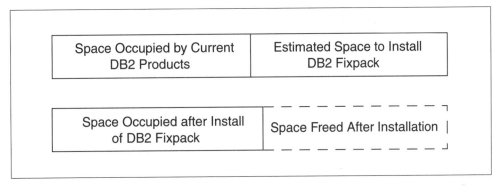

Figure 73. Space Required for DB2 Fixpack

4. Run the Fixpack Installation Program

The steps to install the fixpack are similar to an installation of the DB2 UDB code (see "Installing DB2 UDB Servers" on page 83). The directory where the DB2 fixpack is installed is the same as the existing DB2 code directory and you cannot change the selected components. You can however choose whether the default DB2 Instance and Control Center will be automatically started as system boot. At the end of the installation process, you will be prompted to restart the system.

5. Verify the Fixpack installation

You can verify if the Fixpack installed successfully by checking in the Windows NT Registry.

If you have successfully installed the DB2 Fixpack, you should see there is a value, like "WR09034", in the key "Service Level " under the registry key:

HKEY_LOCAL_MACHINE\SOFTWARE\IBM\DB2\DB2 Universal Database Enterprise Edition\CurrentVersion

As shown in Figure 74, this example is for DB2 UDB Enterprise Edition. You will see similar entries for the other DB2 UDB products.

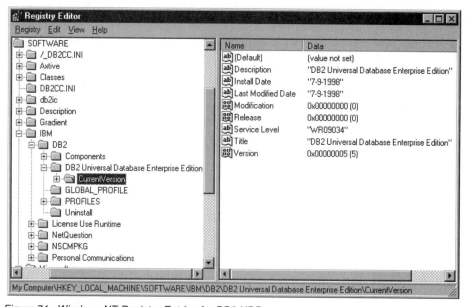

Figure 74. Windows NT Registry Entries for DB2 UDB

6. Post Installation Tasks

After the fixpack installation, you should rebind your applications and DB2 utilities against all your databases using the new bind (.bnd) files shipped with the fixpack. The procedure of rebinding only needs to be performed once per database.

7. The fixpack installation process keeps a record of its actions in the log file C:\DB2LOG\db2.log. If you need more details of what happened behind the scenes, you should check the contents of this file.

Chapter 4. DB2 UDB Client/Server Communications

This chapter covers the features of DB2 UDB on the Windows NT platform that are related to DB2 client/server communications. We will give examples of how to configure DB2 UDB for client/server communications using a selection of different methods.

The following topics are included in this chapter:

- DB2 UDB Client/Server Overview
- DB2 Discovery
- DB2 Administration Server Instance
- The Client Configuration Assistant
- Access Profiles
- Manual Configuration
- The Control Center

4.1 DB2 UDB Client/Server Overview

As in any client/server model, application processing is shared by both the client and server systems. These systems must have the appropriate communications protocols installed and configured to allow the transfer of data between the them. Support for clients in DB2 UDB is provided to users and applications by a common component of the DB2 UDB code, the DB2 Client Application Enabler or CAE. The CAE provides the functions to access DB2 data stored in IBM DB2 relational database servers. If used in conjuction with DB2 Connect, data stored in databases that comply with the Distributed Relational Database Architecture (DRDA) can also be accessed.

DB2 UDB on Windows NT can use any of the following protocols to communicate in a client/server environment:

- NetBIOS
- TCP/IP
- IPX/SPX
- APPC
- Named Pipes

Figure 75 on page 124 illustrates a simple example of a DB2 UDB client/server scenario, showing the flow between the client and the server:

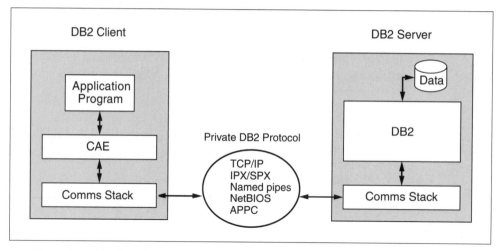

Figure 75. DB2 Client/Server

The protocol used for data transfer in a DB2 client/server environment is a private DB2 database protocol. This private protocol, used to exchange data between the client and the server, uses one of the communications protocols shown in Figure 75 as a transport mechanism to pass data between the client and the server.

When using a DB2 client to request data from a DB2 server, the client needs to know details about how to reach the DB2 server where the data resides. The DB2 client must be provided with the necessary communications information about the DB2 server it wishes to contact. Although both the client and the server need to be configured for communications, only the client needs to know how to contact the DB2 server. The DB2 server does not need to know how to contact all the clients that may access it. There are two methods for configuring a DB2 client:

- **Manual**:

  For manual configuration, you need to know the necessary communications information in order to contact the DB2 server. You can use one of the DB2 GUI tools (DB2 Control Center or DB2 Client Configuration Assistant), or a command prompt (DB2 Command Window or DB2 Command Line Processor) to configure a connection to a DB2 server.

- **Automated:**

For automated configuration, you do not need to provide any detailed communications information to contact the DB2 server. Automated configuration involves one of these methods:

1. Using DB2 Discovery to locate other DB2 UDB servers on your network. Discovery works in one of two ways:

   - Search Discovery - the DB2 client searches for DB2 UDB servers on the network.

   - Known Discovery - one particular server is queried for information about the instances and databases defined there.

2. Using an access profile generated from a server or a client. We cover "Access Profiles" on page 165.

Let's start by taker a closer look at Discovery.

4.2 Discovery

As we have mentioned, DB2 UDB provides a function called *Discovery* which is used to search the network and gather information from DB2 UDB servers located on the network. The information gathered by the Discovery process is then used by the DB2 client to enable it to establish a connection to the DB2 server.

The advantage of using Discovery is that you do not need to know all the details of the communications setup of a DB2 server to establish a connection to it and catalog any remote databases located there. You can use the Client Configuration Assistant (CCA) or the Control Center to automatically locate a DB2 server, update the local communications information and catalog a remote database at your DB2 client. This means that you do not have to manually enter communications protocol information to establish a connection with a remote DB2 server and then manually catalog a database located there. Currently the protocols supported by Discovery are TCP/IP, NetBIOS, IPX/SPX and Named Pipes. However, Search Discovery is only possible using TCP/IP or NetBIOS.

Note

Discovery is only able to locate DB2 UDB V5 (and later) servers.

The Discovery function is provided on DB2 servers by a special instance called the DB2 Administration Server (DAS) instance. The DAS instance listens for discovery requests that are sent from DB2 clients. When the DAS instance receives a request from a remote DB2 client, it replies to the client with configuration information that the DB2 client uses to configure connections. See "DB2 Administration Server (DAS) Instance" on page 133 for more details.

As we have already stated, there are two types of Discovery: Search and Known. Let's take a closer look at each in turn.

4.2.1 Search Discovery

When using Search Discovery, a DB2 client searches for DB2 UDB servers on the network (Figure 76). You are not required to know any communications information about a DB2 server to establish a connection with it, either at instance or database level.

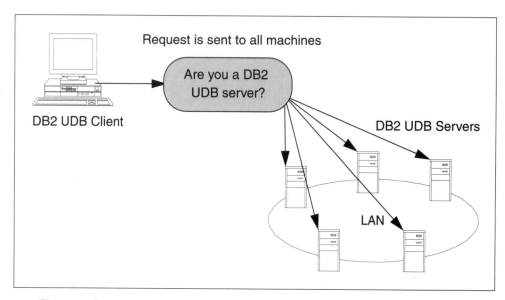

Figure 76. Search Discovery

Although Search Discovery may appear to be a simple way of finding the DB2 servers on your network, it is not guaranteed to find all of them. This is because network routers and bridges in large networks can filter out the messages used to locate other DB2 servers (Figure 77 on page 127). Search Discovery uses broadcast messages to find DB2 servers. These messages can result in a large amount of network traffic being generated. For this reason, most bridges and routers are configured to filter out any broadcast messages so they do not get propagated out to the whole network. This can result in an incomplete list of DB2 servers when you use Search Discovery.

If you need to configure a connection to a DB2 server which is not found by Search Discovery, you can use Known Discovery, where you must specify how the machine is identified on the network.

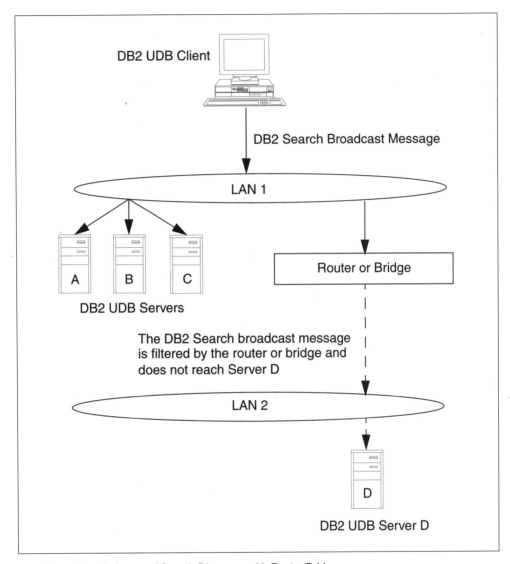

Figure 77. Limitation of Search Discovery with Router/Bridge

The DAS instance on a given DB2 server that is listening for Search Discovery requests will respond to DB2 clients if it detects an incoming request. Incoming requests are listened for using the protocols specified by the value of DISCOVER_COMM parameter in the DAS instance configuration file on the DB2 server. Search Discovery can use two communications protocols:

- TCP/IP
- NetBIOS

To be able to use these communications protocols the appropriate communications stack must be installed and configured on your Windows NT machine. The DAS instance at the DB2 server also needs to be configured for the installed communications protocols. If the communications protocols you wish to use are installed and configured before you install DB2 UDB, then the DAS instance should be automatically configured correctly for Discovery. Details about the various Discovery-related configuration parameters is given in "Configuring Discovery" on page 130.

For an example of using Search Discovery via the CCA, see "Search Discovery Using the CCA" on page 150.

4.2.2 Known Discovery

When using Known Discovery, one particular server is queried for information about its instances and databases (Figure 78). Using this information, a DB2 client can configure connections to those instances and databases. You do need to know minimal communications information about the chosen DB2 server, except in the case that a connection to the DB2 server is already configured at the DB2 client (a known system).

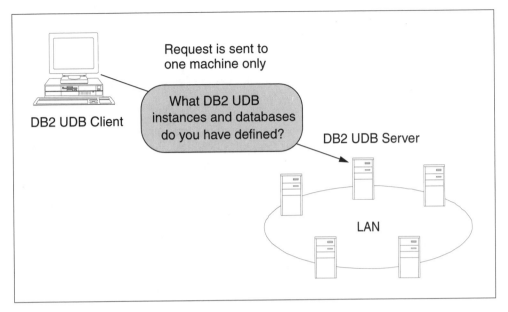

Figure 78. Known Discovery

To use Known Discovery, you will usually need to know the following information about the DB2 server you wish to connect to:

- The communications protocol(s) configured on the remote DB2 server.
- How to identify the DB2 server on the network using a certain protocol.

A good example of when to use Known Discovery instead of Search Discovery is in a large, complex network. As already mentioned, Search Discovery may not work in a large network with bridges and routers. In cases where a DB2 server is not found using Search Discovery, you should try using Known Discovery.

The DAS instance on a given DB2 server that is listening for Known Discovery requests will respond to DB2 clients if it detects an incoming request. Incoming requests are listened for using the protocols specified by the value of DB2COMM in the DAS instance on the DB2 server. Known Discovery is possible using TCP/IP, NetBIOS, IPX/SPX or Named Pipes.

Unlike Search Discovery that broadcasts on the network to find DB2 servers, Known Discovery attempts to establish a direct connection to a particular DB2 server. To establish a connection, Known Discovery can use any of the following communications protocols:

- TCP/IP

- NetBIOS
- IPX/SPX
- Named Pipes

As with Search Discovery, to be able to use these communications protocols, the appropriate communications stack must be installed and configured on your client and server machines.

For an example of using Known Discovery via the CCA, see "Known Discovery Using the CCA" on page 156.

4.2.3 Configuring Discovery

As well as needing to have the communication protocols installed and configured, there are various parameters that need to be configured correctly for Discovery to work. As we mentioned previously, as long as DB2 UDB is installed after the communications protocols have been installed and configured, these Discovery-related parameters should be set automatically. However, if you add a new communications protocol after DB2 UDB is installed, or if Discovery is not working, you may need to check the parameter settings. Table 4 shows the configuration parameters that affect Discovery on both the client and the server:

Table 4. Parameters that Affect Discovery

Client Settings	Server Settings		
DB2 Instance	DAS Instance	DB2 Instance	Database
DISCOVER	DISCOVER	DISCOVER_INST	DISCOVER_DB
DISCOVER_COMM	DISCOVER_COMM	DB2COMM	
	DB2COMM		

We shall now briefly discuss each parameter and its function:

- **DB2 Instance parameters at the Client:**
  - *DISCOVER* - This is a parameter in the database manager configuration file (dbm cfg). The default setting for this parameter is SEARCH. If this parameter is set to SEARCH, then either Search or Known Discovery can be used from the client. If this parameter is set to KNOWN then only Known Discovery can be used. If this parameter is set to DISABLE, then both Known and Search Discovery are disabled.
  - *DISCOVER_COMM* - This is a parameter in the database manager configuration file (dbm cfg). When configured on the client, this

parameter specifies which communications protocol(s) will be used for issuing Search Discovery messages. This parameter can be configured with a single setting or multiple settings separated by commas. When using Search Discovery, it should be set to TCPIP or NETBIOS or both depending on the communications protocol you wish to use. Note that this parameter has no effect on Known Discovery.

- **DAS Instance parameters at the Server:**

  - *DISCOVER* - This is a parameter in the DAS instance configuration file (admin cfg). The default setting for this parameter is SEARCH. If this parameter is set to SEARCH, then the server can respond to either Search or Known Discovery requests. If this parameter is set to KNOWN then only Known Discovery requests can be responded to. If this parameter is set to DISABLE, then both Known and Search Discovery requests are rejected.

  - *DISCOVER_COMM* - This is a parameter in the DAS instance configuration file (admin cfg). It specifies the communication protocols that a DAS instance will listen to for Search Discovery requests. This parameter can be configured with a single setting or multiple settings separated by commas. When using Search Discovery, it should be set to TCPIP or NETBIOS or both depending on the communications protocol you wish to use. Note that this parameter has no effect on Known Discovery.

  - *DB2COMM* - This is a Profile Registry variable for the DAS instance. Setting the DB2COMM variable for the DAS instance informs the DAS instance which communications protocols to listen to for Discovery requests. It is set during installation depending on the communications protocols you have installed and can also be changed manually at any time.

- **DB2 Instance parameters at the Server:**

  - *DISCOVER_INST* - This is a parameter in the database manager configuration file (dbm cfg). This parameter can be set to ENABLE or DISABLE. If set to ENABLE then the DB2 instance can be discovered. If however this parameter is set to DISABLE then the DB2 instance cannot be discovered. This gives you the ability to hide a DB2 instance from discovery. If the discovery of an instance is disabled then all of the databases associated with that instance will be hidden also. The default setting for this parameter is ENABLE. See "Restricting Discovery" on page 132.

  - *DB2COMM* - This is a Profile Registry variable for the DB2 instance. Setting the DB2COMM variable for the DB2 instance makes this DB2 instance accessible to clients. It is set during installation depending on the communications protocols you have installed and can also be changed manually at any time.

- **Database parameters at the Server:**

  - *DISCOVER_DB* - This is a parameter in the database configuration file (db cfg) for a particular database. This parameter acts in a similar fashion to the DISCOVER_INST DB2 instance parameter. The difference is this parameter enables you to hide a list of database from discovery. For each database in a DB2 instance you can set this parameter to either ENABLE or DISABLE. This enables you to control which databases in an instance are shown on a Discovery request. The default setting for this is ENABLE. See "Restricting Discovery" on page 132.

Note

The DISCOVER and DISCOVER_COMM parameters in the database manager configuration file (dbm cfg) on a DB2 server affect Discovery only if a Discovery request is initiated from the DB2 server. In other words, when the DB2 server behaves as a client to another DB2 server.

4.2.4 Restricting Discovery

As well as enabling discovery for either the Search and Known methods, it is also possible to disable discovery so your DB2 server cannot be located on the network. This is achieved by setting the DAS instance parameter DISCOVER to DISABLE. It is also possible to configure Discovery on a DB2 server in a hierachical manner. You can disable or enable at the DB2 server level, instance level and database level. This provides you with the ability to enable discovery of your DB2 server, while hiding certain instances and/or databases (Figure 79 on page 133).

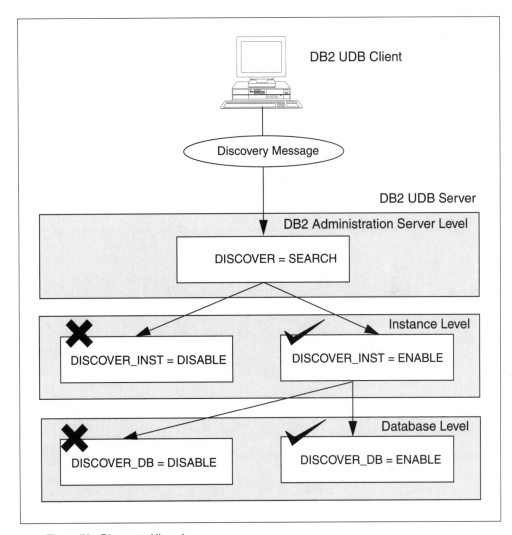

DB2 UDB Client

Discovery Message

DB2 UDB Server

DB2 Administration Server Level

DISCOVER = SEARCH

Instance Level

DISCOVER_INST = DISABLE

DISCOVER_INST = ENABLE

Database Level

DISCOVER_DB = DISABLE

DISCOVER_DB = ENABLE

Figure 79. Discovery Hierachy

4.3 DB2 Administration Server (DAS) Instance

The DB2 Administration Server instance (also known as the DAS instance) is a special type of DB2 instance introduced in DB2 UDB Version 5. The DAS instance is similar to a normal DB2 instance, but it does not contain any databases. The DAS instance has two basic functions:

1. To support the administration of local and remote servers. The DAS instance can:

- Start or stop DB2 instances.
- Attach to an instance to perform administration tasks at the instance or database level.
- Set up the communications for a DB2 server.

2. To enable Discovery.

- The DAS instance at the server collects information which is passed back to the client.

The DAS instance is used by the DB2 administration tools (for instance, the Control Center and the Client Configuration Assistant) to process local or remote requests.

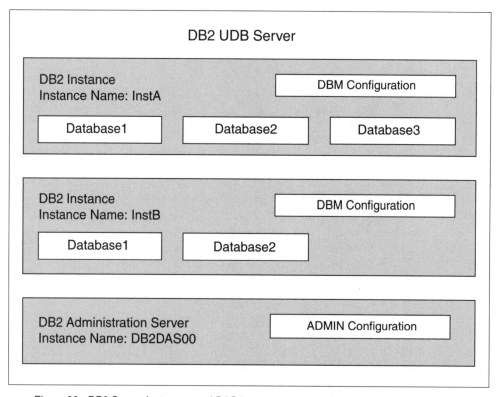

Figure 80. DB2 Server Instances and DAS Instance

Figure 80 shows two DB2 server instances, instA and instB, and the databases created in these two instances. The DAS instance (DB2DAS00) does not contain any databases. Each DB2 server can contain multiple DB2 instances which can co-exist and be active but only one DAS instance can exist on a machine at a time.

Also shown in Figure 80 are the configuration files for the DB2 instances and the DAS instance, which hold each of the instances individual configuration details. The DAS instance configuration file contains parameters which affect the communications configuration, Discovery settings, security settings, and the level of diagnostics. These parameters are described in detail in the DB2 UDB Administration Guide. To display the contents of the DAS instance configuration, you can use the `db2 get admin cfg` command, as shown in Figure 81:

Figure 81. Sample DAS Instance Configuration

The DAS instance enables administration tasks to be performed on a DB2 server from a remote DB2 client. When performing remote administration tasks from a DB2 client the tasks are sent to the DAS instance on the DB2 server and then executed locally on the DB2 server. The results of the task are then returned to the user at the DB2 client. When administering a DB2 server from a remote DB2 client remember that you must use the DAS instance owner user (as defined at the DB2 server).

As mentioned in "Discovery" on page 125, the DAS instance is also to enable the DB2 Discovery methods. If the DAS instance is configured to listen for search requests from DB2 clients, it will respond by sending the DB2 server configuration information back to the DB2 client. The client will then use this information to configure a connection to the DB2 server. See "Client Configuration Assistant" on page 148 for examples of using DB2 Discovery via the Client Configuration Assistant.

4.3.1 Creation of a DAS instance

A DAS instance is created either by the DB2 UDB installation process, or later by using the `db2admin` command. If the DAS instance is created during installation, then the installation program performs the following tasks:

- Detects the communications protocols installed on the machine.
- Obtains protocol information required by DB2, such as workstation name if NetBIOS is detected.
- Sets the properties for each communications protocol with the previously obtained information.
- Allows the user to optionally customize the communications protocols properties (via the Custom install option).
- Sets the communication-related parameters and registry variables for the DAS instance and the DB2 instance using the configuration settings of the installed protocols.
- Creates the DAS instance.

When installing DB2 UDB, if you choose the Custom option (not the Typical or Compact options), you can customize the settings for the communications protocols in both the default DB2 instance and the DAS instance. This is true for any communications protocols that the installation program detects. Customization is usually not necessary though, as the default values will be sufficient in most cases. It is also possible for the user to customize communications that have not been detected (for example, those not yet installed on the system), but the user will have to provide the parameters for these protocols. The DAS instance will not be able to set these parameters because it can not gather information from communications protocols which have not yet been installed. Furthermore, if a communications protocol is not installed, the protocols configuration cannot be updated as required files will be missing from the system. For example, if TCP/IP has not yet been installed, then the DB2 installation program will not be able to add entries into the TCP/IP Services file. The protocols that DB2 supports on Windows NT, are NetBIOS, TCPIP, IPX/SPX, Named Pipes and APPC.

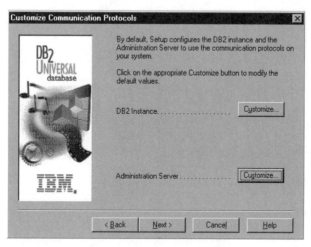

Figure 82. Customize Communications Protocols

Figure 82 shows the installation panel that enables you to customize the DB2 and DAS instance communications protocols. In order to customize the DAS instance communications protocols:

- Click on **Customize** for the Administration Server.

- Click on **Properties** for the communications protocol you wish to configure.

- Enter the values you wish to use or accept the defaults.

- Click on **Continue** to proceed.

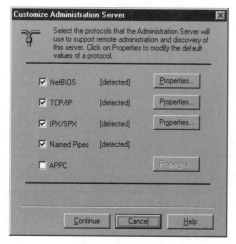

Figure 83. Customizing the Administration Server

Figure 83 shows the panel used for customizing the DAS instance communications protocols. The protocols that are marked (*detected*) have default settings generated for them. By default, any protocols that are detected will automatically be selected for configuration, as shown by a tick in the selection box next to the protocol name.

Note

The detection of APPC communications is supported in DB2 UDB Version 5.2 for Personal Communications (PCOMM) and Communications Server for Windows NT.

If you need to create a DAS instance after installation then you can do so by using the db2admin create command from the command line. Here is the syntax:

```
DB2ADMIN CREATE /USER:<username> /PASSWORD: <password>
```

Where username and password are the username and password of a Windows NT user that will be the DAS instance owner (see "DAS Instance Owner" on page 139). This user must be in the Administrators Group on the Windows NT machine where the DAS instance is created.

This command will create a new DAS instance, if one does not already exist. Remember that only one DAS instance can exist on a DB2 system at one time.

4.3.2 DAS Instance Owner

When a DAS instance is created, it is associated with a Windows NT user account. This user is known as the DAS instance owner and is the administrator of the DAS instance. The DAS instance process is implemented in Windows NT as a service and uses the DAS instance owner as its *Log On As* user account.

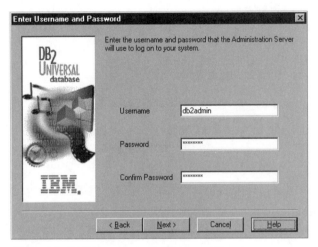

Figure 84. DAS Username and Password Panel

During installation you will be presented with a panel, as shown in Figure 84, in which you are prompted to enter the userid and password you would like the DAS instance to use as its owning user account. The default username that the installation program uses is db2admin. If you wish to use a different username, then it must be 8 characters or less and comply to the following DB2 naming rules:

- Can contain 1 to 8 characters
- Can include letters, numbers, @, # or $
- Cannot begin with IBM, SYS, SQL or a number
- Cannot be a DB2 (USERS, ADMIN, GUESTS, PUBLIC, LOCAL) or an SQL reserved word
- Cannot end with a $
- Cannot include accented characters

The installation program checks for the existence of the user. If the user does not exist then the installation program will create it for you. If it does exist, the installation program will:

- Check that user is a member of the Windows NT Administrators Group.

- Check that the username is not the same as the computer name or the domain name.

Provided that the current logged-in user has the *Act as part of the operating system* advanced user right, the setup program will also assign the following user rights to the DAS instance owner user, so it can be logged on as an Windows NT service:

- Log on as a service
- Act as part of the operating system
- Create a token object
- Increase quotas
- Replace a process level token

Note

The username Administrator should not be used as the DAS instance owner name as it does not comply with the DB2 username rules. Also note that Windows NT passwords are case sensitive (usernames are not).

Here is a summary of the steps the DB2 UDB installation program will perform in relation to the creation and subsequent configuration of a DAS instance:

1. The DAS instance is created as an Windows NT Service.

2. The DAS instance owner user is created and assigned user rights or an existing user is validated for use as the DAS instance owner.

3. These profile registry variables are set:

   - Global Profile: DB2ADMINSERVER = DB2DAS00 (or DB2DAS0n).
   - Global Profile: DB2SYSTEM = Windows NT Computer Name of the machine
   - DAS Instance Profile: DB2COMM = Communications protocols used by the DAS instance

4. The DAS instance and DB2 instance configuration files are updated with communications information gathered during the installation.

4.3.3 Managing a DAS Instance

A DAS instance is similar in some respects to a DB2 instance. One of these similarities is that they both store their individual configurations in a configuration file. The DAS instance stores its configuration in a DAS instance configuration file and the DB2 instance stores its configuration in a Database Manager (DBM) configuration file.

4.3.3.1 Configuring the DAS Instance

The following commands are used to display and alter the current configuration of the DAS instance:

- DB2 GET ADMIN CFG - This command is used to display the current DAS instance configuration. An example of the output from this command can be seen in Figure 81 on page 135.

- DB2 UPDATE ADMIN CFG - This command is used to change the current DAS instance configuration settings. The format for the command is:

```
DB2 UPDATE ADMIN CFG USING <config-keyword> <value>
```

where config-keyword is a reference to a DAS instance configuration keyword (such as DISCOVER_COMM) and value is the value you wish to set it to. For example, to set DISCOVER to KNOWN you would issue the following command:

```
DB2 UPDATE ADMIN CFG USING DISCOVER KNOWN
```

Once the command has been run you need to stop and restart the DAS instance for the changes to take effect. The config-keywords that can be used with the UPDATE ADMIN CFG command are:

- AGENT_STACK_SZ
- AUTHENTICATION
- CATALOG_NOAUTH
- DIAGLEVEL
- DIAGPATH
- DISCOVER
- DISCOVER_COMM
- FILESERVER
- IPX_SOCKET
- NNAME
- OBJECTNAME
- QUERY_HEAP_SZ
- SYSADM_GROUP
- SYSCTRL_GROUP
- SYSMAINT_GROUP
- TPNAME
- TRUST_ALLCLNTS
- TRUST_CLNTAUTH

- DB2 RESET ADMIN CFG - This command is used when you have altered your DAS instance configuration and wish to return to the installation defaults. This command will only become effective once you have stopped and restarted the DAS instance.

4.3.3.2 Using the db2admin Command

There are also other commands used to manage a DAS instance. These commands are used for starting, stopping, deleting, creating and changing the owner of a DAS instance.

- `DB2ADMIN CREATE` - This command is used to create a new DAS instance. It can be used when you do not create a DAS instance during installation or after a DAS instance has been dropped using the `DB2ADMIN DROP` command. It can also be used in the following format to specify an instance owner and password:

  `DB2ADMIN CREATE /USER:<username> /PASSWORD: <password>`

  If you already have a DAS instance on your local machine and try to create a new one using this command you will receive a error message informing you that a DAS instance already exists. Only one DAS instance can exist per DB2 system.

- `DB2ADMIN DROP` - This command is used to remove a DAS instance from your DB2 system. If you remove a DAS instance from your machine you will lose the configuration associated with it. Before you can drop a DAS instance you must use the `DB2ADMIN STOP` command to stop the instance.

- `DB2ADMIN START` - You use this command to manually start a DAS instance. The DAS instance is normally started automatically as an Windows NT service during system boot.

- `DB2ADMIN STOP` - This command is used to stop a DAS instance. This is needed before you drop a DAS instance or if you have altered the configuration and need to stop and restart the DAS instance for the changes to take effect. You can also stop the DAS instance by stopping the Windows NT service called DB2 - DB2DAS00.

- `DB2ADMIN SETID` - This command is used to alter or set the logon account of the DAS instance. This user account is the DAS instance owner. The format for the command is:

  `DB2ADMIN SETID <username> <password>`

- `DB2ADMIN` - Can be used to display the setting of the profile registry variable `DB2ADMINSERVER,` which contains the DAS instance name.

- `DB2ADMIN /h` - This command is used to display the help text for the db2admin commands.

4.3.3.3 Managing the Admin Node Directory

The Admin Node Directory is used to store catalog information about local and remote DAS instances at a client machine.

There are two commands used to manage the Admin Node Directory:

- DB2 CATALOG ADMIN [LOCAL,TCPIP,IPXSPX,NETBIOS,NPIPE] NODE - This command is used to catalog a remote DAS instance. The command is a variation of the DB2 CATALOG NODE command. The full syntax can be found in the *DB2 Command Reference*. Although it is possible to catalog a remote DAS instance, and then to attach to it, this serves no real purpose as the cataloged remote DAS instance is intended to be used by the Client Configuration Assistant (CCA) and the Control Center. Note that you cannot directly issue commands to the remote DAS instance from a command line. You can only configure the remote DAS instance through the Control Center. Once a remote DAS instance has been cataloged, the remote DB2 server will be shown in the Control Center and you can then remotely administer that DB2 server using the Control Center (via the DAS instance on that DB2 server).

- DB2 LIST ADMIN NODE DIRECTORY (SHOW DETAIL) - This command is used to display all the DAS instances that are cataloged on your DB2 system, both local and remote.

4.3.4 Configuring DAS Instance Communications After Installation

In Figure 82 on page 137, we saw that most communications protocols are detected and configured for the DAS instance during the installation process. This section describes how the DAS instance communications settings can be configured after installation.

If you install and configure a new communications protocol after the DAS instance has been created (usually during the DB2 installation), then you should update the DAS instance configuration on your machine. This is the only time you should need to modify these settings. You can use either the Control Center or a Command Window to do this.

4.3.4.1 Updating the DAS Instance Using the Control Center

To use the Control Center to update the DAS instance communications settings, you need to add the DAS instance to the Control Center, using the following steps:

1. Start the Control Center. Select **Start**, then **Programs**, then **DB2 for Windows NT**, then **Administration Tools**, and then **Control Center.**

2. Find the required DB2 system from the list in the display panel.

3. Click on the **[+]** to expand your DB2 system.

4. On the **Instances** folder click the right mouse button and click **Add.**

5. An Add Instance window appears (Figure 85).

6. In the **Remote instance** and **Instance name** fields enter the name of your local DAS instance. Enter a **Comment** if you required.

7. Once you have entered the values click **Apply.**

This will add the DAS instance to your systems instance folder in the Control Center.

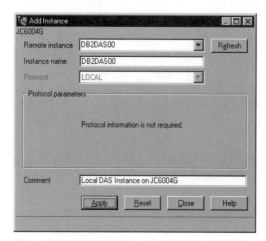

Figure 85. Control Center - Add DAS Instance

To change the DAS instance communications settings:

1. On the entry for your DAS instance (usually DB2DAS00) click the right mouse button, select **Setup Communications** and you will be presented with the Setup Communications panel.

2. From the Setup Communications panel you can either:

   - Alter the settings for the communications protocols on your system. To do this, click on the **Properties** button.

   - Select the protocols that are to be used. To do this, select a protocol for use by clicking the tick box next to the protocol.

   Figure 86 on page 145 shows the Setup Communications panel and the associated properties panels for the communications protocols.

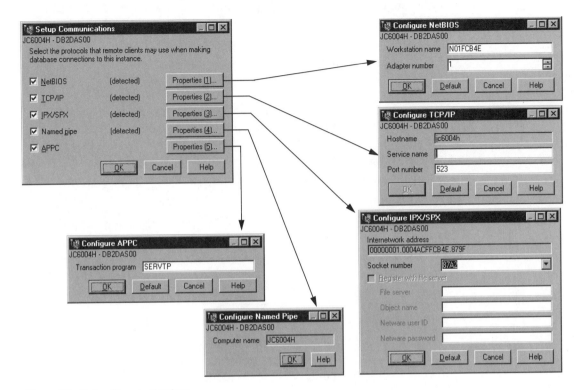

Figure 86. Setup Communications

In the *Setup Communications* panel, a protocol marked *(detected)* shows that the DAS instance has detected the communications protocol on your machine.

We assume here that the communications protocol you wish to use has not been configured for the DAS instance, because it has been added after the installation process. If this is the case you can setup communications for the protocol by selecting **Properties** against the protocol from the *Setup Communications* panel, and click the **Default** button. This will choose default values for the communications settings which are usually acceptable. However this is not the case for all the protocols. Let's briefly look at the settings of the each of the protocols:

- **NetBIOS**:
  - *Workstation name* - This is the name that the DAS instance uses on the network for NetBIOS. This is the name you would specify when using Known Discovery in the CCA to connect to this DAS instance. The workstation name must be unique within the network and for the

instance. Workstation name is the *NNAME* stored in the DAS instance configuration file.

- *Adapter number* - The Adapter number is the logical LAN adapter that the DAS instance will use for transport.

- **TCP/IP:**

  - *Hostname* - This is the name associated with your computer in a TCP/IP network and is used to identify your computer to other computers. This can also be set to the IP address of your system. This is held in the TCP/IP configuration on your machine.

  - *Service name* - This is the service name that is configured in the TCP/IP services file. For the DAS instance this should always be 523.

  - *Port Number* - This is the port number that the DAS listens to for Discovery messages from remote clients. IBM has registered port number 523 to be used for Discovery messages. This value should not be changed.

- **IPX/SPX:**

  1. Direct Addressing:

     - *Internetworking Address* - This is the address assigned to your computer to identify it on the network. It includes the socket number that is unique to each DB2 instance using IPX/SPX.

     - *Socket Number* - Represents a connection point in the computers internetwork address. The socket number needs to be unique for each DB2 instance and unique within the computer to ensure the DAS instance can listen for incoming client requests. The default value is 87A2. You should not change this value.

  2. FileServer Addressing: This is not supported by DB2 UDB for Windows NT.

- **Named Pipes:**

  - *Computer Name* - Corresponds to the Windows NT computer name as set during Windows NT installation. This parameter cannot be changed using the DAS instance, only by using the Identification panel in the Network settings from the Windows NT Control Panel. The Computer Name and DB2 instance name are used to identify an instance. Windows NT is the only operating system that supports the use of Named Pipes.

- **APPC:**

- *Transaction program* - If a client connects to the DAS instance using the APPC protocol, then the Transaction Program name is the name of the transaction program that will be executed when the client connects.

Any time that you make changes to the configuration of the DAS instance you must stop and restart it for the changes to take effect.

4.3.4.2 Updating the DAS Instance Using a Command Window

As well as using the Control Center to change the DAS instance communications configuration you can also use a DB2 Command Window.

To update the DAS instance configuration from a DB2 Command Window, use the UPDATE ADMIN CFG command (see "Configuring the DAS Instance" on page 141).

- **NetBIOS:**

  The parameter that controls the NetBIOS Workstation name in the DAS instance configuration is *NNAME*. To change this, use the following command:

  ```
  DB2 UPDATE ADMIN CFG USING NNAME <wsname>
  ```

  where <wsname> is the value you wish to use for *NNAME*.

- **TCP/IP:**

  The parameter that controls the TCP/IP service to be used by the DAS instance is *SVCENAME*. This is set to the port number 523 which is reserved for the DAS instance. This parameter cannot be changed using the DB2 UPDATE ADMIN command.

- **IPX/SPX:**

  The parameter in the DAS instance configuration that control the IPX/SPX settings is *IPX_SOCKET*:

  - *IPX_SOCKET* - Represents a connection point in the computers internetwork address. The socket number needs to be unique for each DB2 instance and unique within the computer to ensure the DAS instance can listen for incoming remote client requests. To alter this, use:

    ```
    DB2 UPDATE ADMIN CFG USING IPX_SOCKET <socname>
    ```

    where <socname> is the value you wish to use for *IPX_SOCKET*. The default value is 87A2. You should not change this value.

  FileServer Addressing is not supported by DB2 UDB for Windows NT.

- **Named Pipes:**

You cannot alter the Computer Name from a Command Window as it is not held in the DAS instance configuration. To change this parameter you must use the Network settings from the Windows NT control panel.

- **APPC:**

  The parameter that controls the transaction program name for the DAS instance is TPNAME. To change this parameter:

  ```
  DB2 UPDATE ADMIN CFG USING TPNAME <tpname>
  ```

  where `<tpname>` is the value you wish to use for *TPNAME*.

Figure 87 on page 148 shows a comparison of the panels used in the Control Center and the parameters used in the DAS instance configuration file:

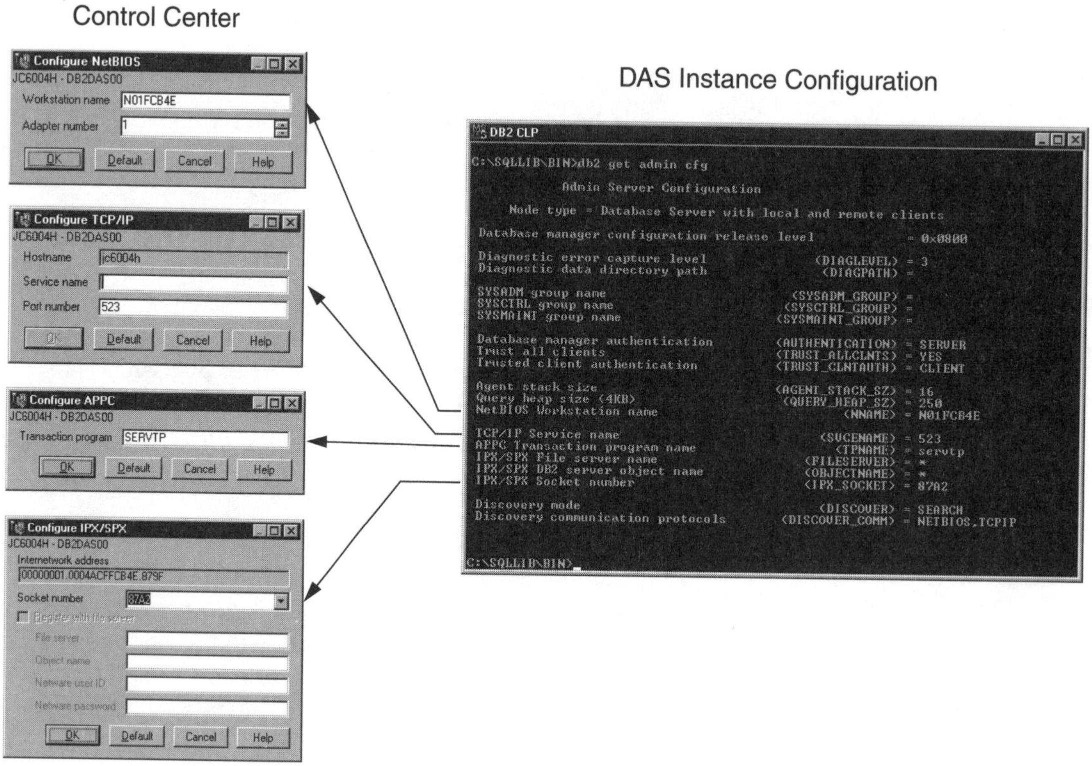

Control Center

DAS Instance Configuration

Figure 87. Comparison of Communications Settings for the DAS Instance

4.4 Client Configuration Assistant

The Client Configuration Assistant (CCA) is one of the GUI tools introduced in DB2 UDB Version 5. It is used on a DB2 UDB client machine to configure connections to remote DB2 databases. The CCA allows you to catalog databases, catalog nodes and alter communications settings, among other tasks. By using the CCA, you are able to add a new database connection without having to know all the communications and database information you might normally need if you cataloged a database from the Command Line Processor. The CCA uses DB2 Discovery to automate the connection to remote DB2 databases. It can search the network for database servers and then find out the necessary information from these servers to setup database connections.

On Windows NT the CCA may be started in one of 2 ways:

1. From the Windows NT taskbar:

   - Click the **Start** icon on the taskbar.

   - Choose **Programs**, then **DB2 for Windows NT**, then **Client Configuration Assistant**.

2. From a command prompt:

   - Enter db2cca.

When the CCA starts you will be presented with the main CCA panel as shown in Figure 88. If this is the first time you have started the CCA then you will be presented with an initial welcome screen.

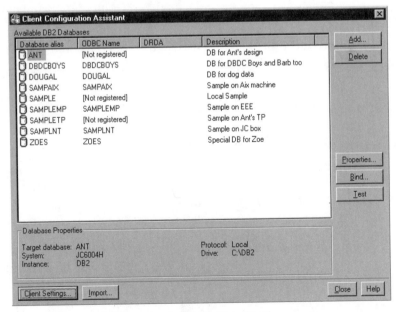

Figure 88. Client Configuration Assistant, Main Panel

This is the main panel of the CCA. In the *Available DB2 Databases* window, you can see the databases cataloged on your DB2 system. These databases may be local or remote. We will now briefly look at each option from this panel before describing how to catalog a new database.

- **Add** - Used to start the Add Database Smartguide, which assists in the configuration and cataloging of a new database connection. Using this option will add entries in the DB2 directories (for example, the node and database directories).

- **Delete** - Used to remove a database entry from your DB2 system. This option will not remove the database itself, just the catalog entries which allow us to connect to it from this system.

- **Properties** - Used to alter any existing database entries on your system, such as the alias, description, CLI/ODBC registration and connection information.

- **Bind** - Used to bind DB2 utilities and user applications to a database. This option will cause the necessary packages to be created on the target database system.

- **Test** - Used to attempt a test connection to a database. If the connection is successful the user is notified; if not, the relevant error message is displayed.

- **Import** - Used to import a Client Access Profile file. This option will read the settings in the supplied file and configure database connections (see "Access Profiles" on page 165).

- **Client Settings** - Used to modify the Database Manager configuration parameters for the local instance.

We will now look at using the CCA to add database connections, using both the Search and Known Discovery methods.

4.4.1 Search Discovery Using the CCA

Search Discovery was introduced in "Search Discovery" on page 126. You use Search Discovery to a catalog a remote database when you want to find a DB2 Server on the network and configure a connection to it. You do not need to know any communications-related information about the DB2 server.

To catalog a new database using Search Discovery, select the **Add** option from the main panel (Figure 88 on page 149). The Add Database Smartguide is displayed (Figure 89):

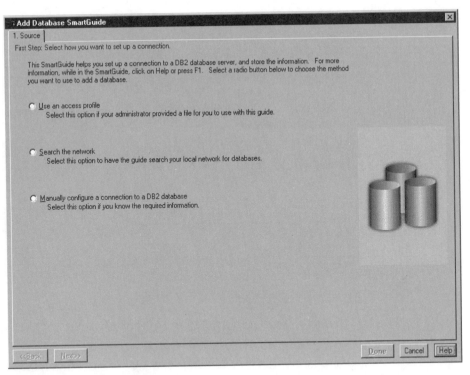

Figure 89. Add Database Smartguide

Note

If the `DISCOVER` parameter in the Database Manager configuration on the local system is set to `DISABLE` then you will not see the option to *Search the network*.

To use Search Discovery, first start the CCA, and select the **Add** option. Select **Search the network** from the Add Database Smartguide then click **Next**.

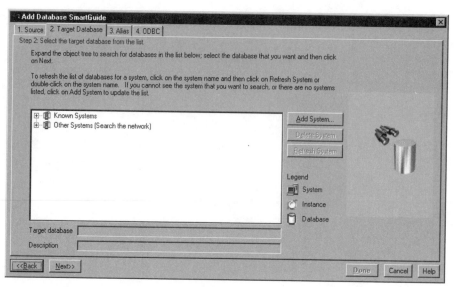

Figure 90. Add Database Using Search Discovery

1. To search the local network for DB2 servers, click on the **[+]** next to *Other Systems (Search the network)*.

2. Once the search has completed, a list of DB2 servers that were found is displayed (Figure 91). Only servers not already listed under Known Systems are shown.

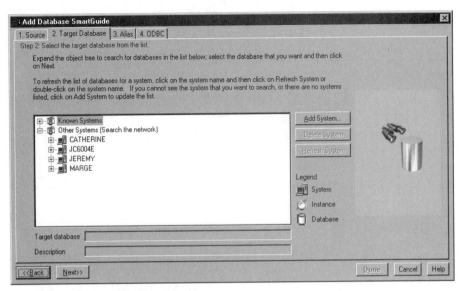

Figure 91. Add Database Search Results

3. To see the available instances and databases on a system, expand the view by clicking on the **[+]** next to the system. This will show you all the instances and databases that are enabled for discovery (Figure 92). This list is generated using the Known Discovery function.

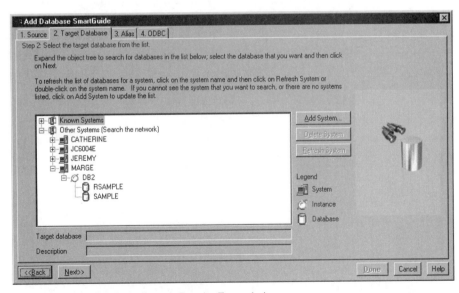

Figure 92. Add Database Search Results Expanded

4. If, for example, we wish to catalog the database RSAMPLE on the system MARGE, we select **RSAMPLE** and click **Next**.

5. On the next screen, choose an alias for the database and optionally add a description. Click **Next**.

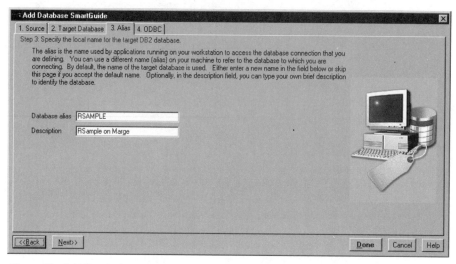

Figure 93. Add Database, Alias Page

6. The final screen allows you to register the database as an ODBC data source. By default the *Register this database for ODBC* check box is ticked. You can choose an application from the **Application** selection box to optimize the ODBC settings for that application. If the application you are using is not shown then choose **Default**. Click **Done** when finished.

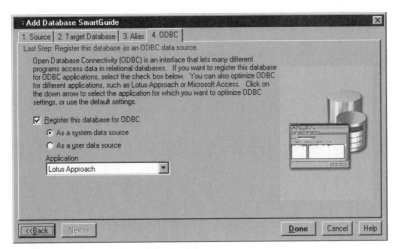

Figure 94. Add Database, ODBC Page

7. Once you have finished entering the details, you can test a connection to this database, catalog another remote database or close the Add Database Smartguide (Figure 95).

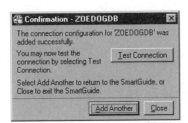

Figure 95. Database Connection Test

8. If you choose **Test Connection**, then the CCA will try to connect to the database. When you test the connection you are required to supply a userid and password to be authenticated at the remote server (Figure 96).

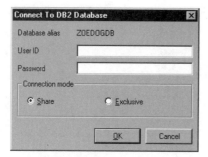

Figure 96. Test Connection

9. If the userid and password are validated successfully and the connection is completed, you will be informed of the details of the established connection (Figure 97). If the connection fails, you are supplied with an error message containing specific details as to why the connection failed. In this case, you should refer to the DB2 UDB Troubleshooting Guide and the DB2 UDB Message Reference for diagnostic information.

Figure 97. Successful Connection

4.4.2 Known Discovery Using the CCA

The Known Discovery method was introduced in "Known Discovery" on page 128. You use Known Discovery to a catalog a remote database when you know which DB2 server you wish to configure a connection to. You must know some basic information about the DB2 server, such as how it is identified on the network (for example, the hostname when using TCP/IP).

To catalog a new database using Known Discovery, select the **Add** option from the main panel (Figure 88 on page 149). The Add Database Smartguide is displayed (Figure 98):

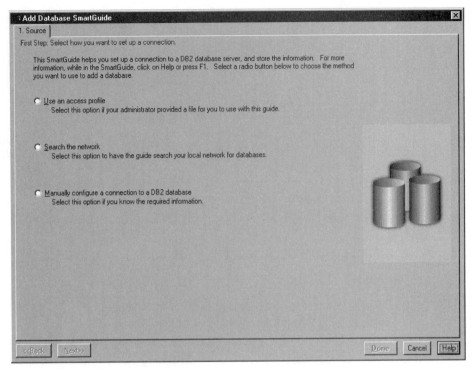

Figure 98. Add Database Smartguide

You should be aware that even though the second option is called *Search the network*, you should choose this option not only if you want to use Search Discovery, but Known Discovery also.

Note ───

If the DISCOVER parameter in the Database Manager configuration on the local system is set to DISABLE then you will not see the option to *Search the Network.*

Select **Search the network** and then click on **Next**. The next panel (Figure 99) allows you to locate a DB2 server using Known Discovery:

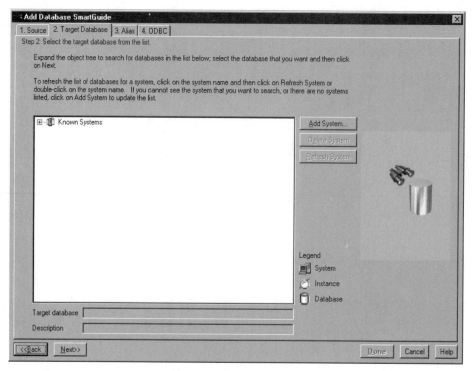

Figure 99. Add Database Using Known Discovery

If the DISCOVER parameter in the local DB2 instance configuration file is set to
SEARCH, you will see both *Known Systems* and *Other Systems (Search the
network)* in the Target Database panel. If DISCOVER is set to KNOWN, you will
only see *Known Systems*.

To locate a DB2 server and list its instances and databases:

1. Click on the **[+]** next to **Known Systems**. This shows the systems that are
   known to your DB2 client. This list of systems has been generated by an
   earlier invocation of Discovery. If the system you wish to connect to is
   shown here then you should go to step 6.

2. If the system is not shown then click on **Add System** to display the Add
   System panel. The contents of this panel changes according to the
   Protocol you select. Figure 100 shows all the possible variants of this
   panel:

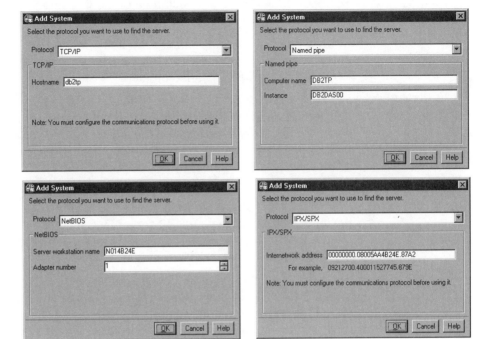

Figure 100. Add System for the Different Protocols

3. From the Protocol selection box, select the protocol you wish to use to establish the connection to the DAS instance on the DB2 server.

   This protocol must be installed and configured on both the DB2 client and the DB2 server. Also, the DB2 server must be listening to requests on this protocol. As long as DB2 UDB was installed on the DB2 server after the protocols were configured, then the necessary registry variables and configuration parameters should be set to enable the DB2 server to listen to requests on the installed protocols. However, if this was not the case, or you wish to check the registry variables and/or the configuration parameters, you should check:

   - The DB2COMM registry variable for the DAS instance at the DB2 server. This is set to a comma-separated list of protocols. The protocol you wish to use must be included in this list.

   - The DISCOVER_COMM parameter for the DAS instance at the DB2 server. This is set to a comma-separated list of protocols. The protocol you wish to use must be included in this list.

4. Once you have specified the protocol to use, enter the protocol specific details for the DB2 server you wish to contact:

- **TCP/IP** - *Hostname* is the hostname or the IP address of the DB2 server.

- **Named Pipe** - *Computer name* is the name of the DB2 server as specified in the network settings on the DB2 server system. *Instance* is the name of the DAS instance on the DB2 Server.

- **NetBIOS** - *Server workstation name* identifies the DAS instance on the DB2 server as set in the NNAME parameter in the server DAS instance configuration. *Adapter number* is the logical network adapter in your DB2 client to be used for the connection. The CCA will detect and provide an adapter number that is mapped to the NBF network in Windows NT.

- **IPX/SPX** - *Internetwork address* specifies the network address used by IPX/SPX to connect to your DB2 server DAS instance. The format is *netid.nodeid.socket_number*. The socket number should always be 87A2 for the DAS instance.

5. Once you have selected the protocol and entered the protocol specific data click **OK**. The CCA then tries to contact the DAS instance on the DB2 server and retrieve the required information to enable the databases on the DB2 server to be cataloged on the client system. If this is successful, then the DB2 server and its instances and databases are displayed:

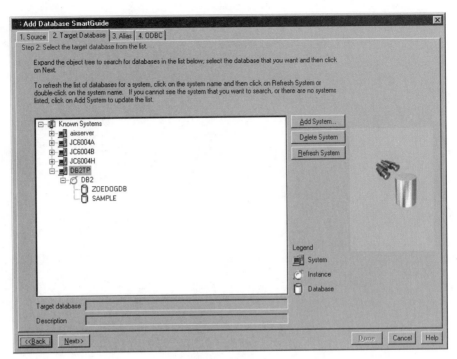

Figure 101. Add Database, Target Database Page

6. You then select the database you wish to add and click the **Next** button.

7. On the screen that follows, choose an alias for the database and optionally a description (Figure 102), then click **Next** to proceed.

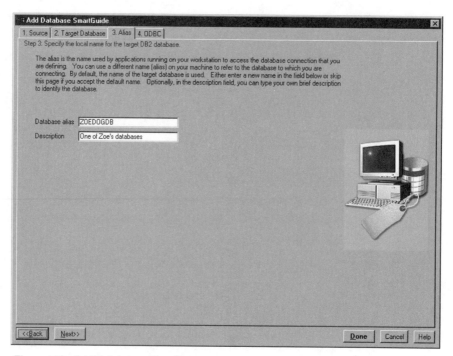

Figure 102. Add Database, Alias Page

8. The final screen allows you to register the database as an ODBC data source. By default the *Register this database for ODBC* check box is ticked. You can choose an application from the **Application** selection box to optimize the ODBC settings for that application. If the application you are using is not shown then choose **Default**. Click **Done** when finished.

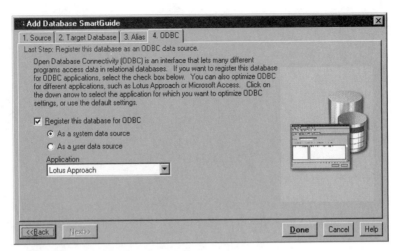

Figure 103. Add Database, ODBC Page

9. Once you have finished entering the details, you can test a connection to this database, catalog another remote database or close the Add Database Smartguide (Figure 104).

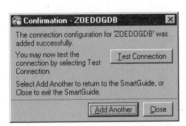

Figure 104. Database Connection Test

10.If you choose **Test Connection**, then the CCA will try to connect to the database. When you test the connection you are required to supply a userid and password to be authenticated at the remote server (Figure 105).

Figure 105. Test Connection

11.If the userid and password are validated successfully and the connection is completed, you will be informed of the details of the established connection (Figure 106). If the connection fails, you are supplied with an error message containing specific details as to why the connection failed. In this case, you should refer to the DB2 UDB Troubleshooting Guide and the DB2 UDB Message Reference for diagnostic information.

Figure 106. Successful Connection

You can repeat this procedure to catalog other remote databases using Known Discovery. Your DB2 system keeps track of the remote DB2 servers and their instances and databases. To catalog other remote databases on a DB2 server known to your CCA, you need only to start the CCA, locate the required DB2 server and then follow this procedure. You are not required to add the same system a second time.

Note

If you do have problems setting up client/server communications, try using the DB2 UDB Protocol Tester. This utility allows users to isolate DB2 and network setup problems. Details are given in the readme.pct file in \sqllib\misc.

4.5 Access Profiles

Access profiles are another automated method to configure a DB2 client to access remote DB2 servers and their databases. An access profile contains the information that a client needs to catalog databases on a DB2 server. Two types of access profiles exist, client and server. *Server access profiles* are created from DB2 servers and contain information about all the instances and databases the DB2 server has cataloged. *Client access profiles* are used for duplicating the cataloged databases and/or the client settings (dbm cfg, CLI/ODBC) from one client to another. Both types of profiles are held in text files and can be imported to another DB2 system.

4.5.1 Server Access Profiles

As you would expect, a server access profile is created from a DB2 server. This profile contains information about the server and includes data about the DB2 server type, the DB2 instances, the DAS instance and databases cataloged at the server.

4.5.1.1 Generating a Server Access Profile

To generate a server access profile, use the Control Center:

- Start the Control Center. Select **Start**, then **Programs**, then **DB2 for Windows NT**, then **Administration Tools**, and then **Control Center.**

- Click on the **[+]** next to Systems to expand the list of known systems.

- From the Control Center, right click on the DB2 server that you wish to generate a server profile for.

- Select the **Generate access profile..** option (Figure 107):

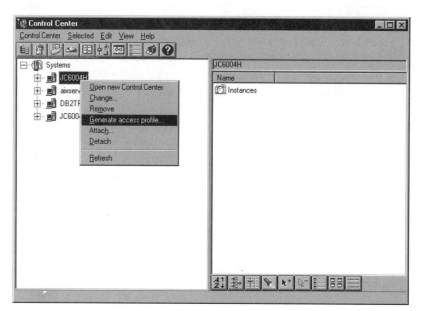

Figure 107. Generate Server Access Profile

- Choose the path and filename for the profile and click **Generate** to create the profile.

The generated server access profile is a text file and can be viewed, but you should not change its contents. The following is a sample server access profile:

```
;DB2 Server Database Access Profile
;Comment lines start with a ";"
;Other lines must be one of the following two types:
;Type A: [section_name]
;Type B: keyword=value

[File_Description]
Application=DB2/NT 5.0.0
Platform=5
File_Content=DB2 Server Definitions
File_Type=CommonServer
File_Format_Version=1.0
DB2System=JC6004H

[inst>INST1]
NodeType=1
Authentication=SERVER
QuietMode=No

[adminst>DB2DAS00]
NodeType=1
DB2Comm=TCPIP
Authentication=SERVER
HostName=jc6004h
PortNumber=523
IpAddress=9.3.1.117
QuietMode=No

[inst>DB2]
NodeType=1
DB2Comm=TCPIP
Authentication=SERVER
HostName=jc6004h
ServiceName=db2cdb20
PortNumber=50002
IpAddress=9.3.1.117
QuietMode=No

[db>DB2:ANT]
DBAlias=ANT
DBName=ANT
Drive=C:\DB2
Comment=DB for Ant's design
Dir_entry_type=INDIRECT

[db>DB2:SAMPLEMP]
DBAlias=SAMPLEMP
DBName=SAMPLE
Comment=Sample on EEE
Dir_entry_type=REMOTE
NodeName=JC600400
```

Figure 108. Sample Extract from a Server Access Profile

The following parameters affect the contents of the server access profile:

- **DISCOVER** - The DISCOVER parameter in the DAS instance must be set to either to KNOWN or SEARCH to allow profile generation. If DISCOVER is set to DISABLE you will be warned that a server profile cannot be currently generated.

- **DISCOVER_INST** - The DISCOVER_INST instance parameter must be set to ENABLE for each instance you wish to include in the server profile. If DISCOVER_INST is set to DISABLE the instance, its databases will not appear in the server profile.

- **DISCOVER_DB** - The DISCOVER_DB database parameter must be set to ENABLE if you wish to include a database in the server profile. If DISCOVER_DB is set to DISABLE for a database then it will not appear in the server profile. This parameter is only effective if DISCOVER_INST is enabled for the instance the database resides in.

4.5.1.2 Importing a Server Access Profile

Once a server access profile file has been generated, it can be copied to a DB2 client (or a server acting as a client) and can be used to catalog remote databases. To import a server access profile on a client, use the Client Configuration Assistant (CCA).

1. Start the CCA. Select **Start**, then **Programs**, then **DB2 for Windows NT**, then **Client Configuration Assistant.**

2. Click either the **Add** or the **Import** button:

   - If you click **Add** then you must select the **Use an access profile** radio button and then the **Next** button.

   - If you click **Import** you must locate the server access profile file on your machine in the directory panel and select **OK**.

3. The next panel is nearly identical whether you selected Add or Import. The only difference being that if you chose Add you now have to use the **Browse** button to find the server access profile file to use.

4. Next, you will see a list of databases you may add to your local system. Select the database you wish to add and follow the panels using the **Next** button and then the **Done** button to finish.

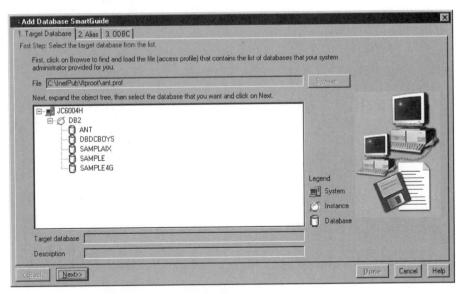

Figure 109. Importing a Server Access Profile

5. Once you have finished you can test the connection by using the **Test Connection button**, add another database from the profile using the **Add Another** button or close the Add Database Smartguide and return to the CCA main panel using the **Close** button.

There is an important consideration to be aware of when importing server access profiles in this way. This can be best explained by using an example:

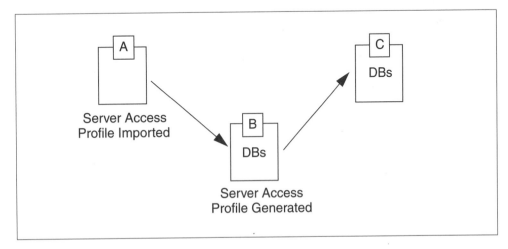

Figure 110. Server Access Profile, Three Tiers

As shown in Figure 110, if you have remote databases (on machine C) cataloged on the DB2 server you generated the server access profile from (machine B), then they are included in the profile. If you then catalog one of these remote databases (located on machine C) on your client machine (machine A), it catalogs the entry to point to the server the profile was taken from (machine B). Therefore you can only connect to this database if the DB2 server the profile was taken from (machine B) is available, as well as the DB2 server the database resides on (machine C).

4.5.2 Client Access Profiles

Client access profiles are used to copy the catalog information from one client machine to another. They are used to configure multiple clients with the same remote database connections. A client access profile is exported from one DB2 client and then imported to other DB2 clients in a similar way as server access profiles. The information contained in a client profile is generated during the export process, and can include:

- Database and node connection information

- Local client settings

- CLI/ODBC parameters

- APPC stack configuration

The information that is exported can be determined by the user during the export process depending on the settings that are chosen.

4.5.2.1 Exporting a Client Access Profile

A client access profile is generated from a DB2 client (or a DB2 server acting as a client) using the Export option of the DB2 Client Configuration Assistant. Export is only available if the CCA is started in administration mode.

To start the CCA in administration mode you can use one of the following methods:

- Enter `db2cca admin` from a command prompt.

- Create a shortcut from the CCA program icon and edit the shortcut properties so that the Target entry is `x:\sqllib\bin\db2cca.exe admin` where x is the drive that DB2 is installed on.

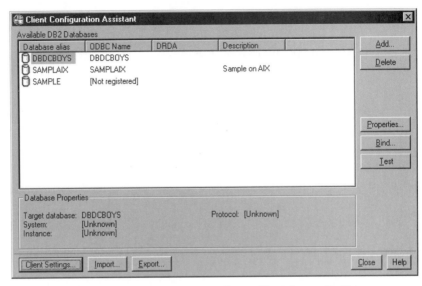

Figure 111. Client Configuration Assistant, Export Client Access Profile

Once the CCA is started (Figure 111), to export a client profile:

1. Click the **Export** button.

2. From the Export Client Profile window, choose the databases you wish to export by moving them from the *Available DB2 Databases* window to the *Databases to be exported* window (Figure 112).

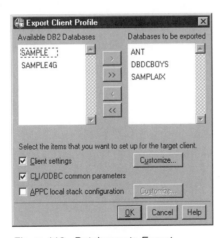

Figure 112. Databases to Export

3. Once you have selected the databases to export, you can modify which other settings are included in the profile by selecting the check boxes next

to the items to include. You can modify the settings to customize different client access profiles for different users or you can export a generic profile to be used by all users.

- Click on **OK**, then enter the directory and filename for the client access profile file.

> **Note**
>
> When customizing the client settings and the APPC local stack, this only affects the contents of the client access profile and does not alter the settings on your local DB2 system. Also be careful if customizing multiple settings for multiple users since if you specify identical communications parameters, for example NNAME, you may encounter network problems.

The client access profile is a text file and can be viewed, but you should not change its contents. The following is a sample client access profile:

```
[FILE_DESCRIPTION]
APPLICATION=DB2/NT 5.0.0
FILE_CONTENT=DB2 CCA Exported Data Sources
FILE_TYPE=CommonServer
FILE_FORMAT_VERSION=1.0
Platform=5
DB2System=JC6004H
Instance=DB2

[DBM_CONFIG]
DiagLevel=4
RqrIoBlk=32767
DrdaHeapSize=128
DirCache=1
Discover=2
TpMonName=
DiagPath=
SysadmGroup=
SysctrlGroup=
SysmaintGroup=
TmDatabase=1ST_CONN
Nname=
DftAccountStr=
DiscoverComm=TCPIP,NETBIOS

[inst>DB2]
instance_name=DB2
NodeType=1
ServerType=DB2NT
Authentication=SERVER
HostName=jc6004h
IpAddress=9.3.1.117
DB2COMM=tcpip

[db>!LOCAL:ANT]
Dir_entry_type=INDIRECT
Drive=C:\DB2
DBName=ANT
Comment=

[Node>AIXSER00]
DB2System=aixserver
Instance=db2inst1
Comment=aixserver:db2inst1
ServerType=DB26000
Protocol=TCPIP
Hostname=cj6006a.itsc.austin.ibm.com
Portnumber=50000

[db>AIXSER00:SAMPLAIX]
Dir_entry_type=REMOTE
Authentication=Server
DBName=SAMPLAIX
Comment=Sampl on AIX
DataSourceName=SAMPLAIX
DataSourceType=System
DESCRIPTION=Sampl on AIX
ODBCParameters=YES
```

Figure 113. Sample Extract from a Client Access Profile

The parameters that affect server access profile generation do not apply when exporting a client profile.

4.5.2.2 Importing a Client Access Profile

After a client access profile has been exported it can be used to add new databases to a DB2 client (or a server acting as a client). In addition, it can update the client settings, CLI/ODBC parameters and the local APPC communications. To import a client access profile, you use the Client Configuration Assistant (CCA).

- Start the CCA. Select **Start**, then **Programs**, then **DB2 for Windows NT**, then **Client Configuration Assistant.**

- Click the **Import** button.

- From the file selection window choose the client access profile you wish to import and click **OK.**

- From the Import Client Profile window (Figure 114) select the options you wish to import and then click on **OK**. Options that are grayed-out are not included in the client access profile and so cannot be imported.

Figure 114. Import Client Access Profile

- When you import databases you are presented with the Add Database Smartguide (for more details, see "Client Configuration Assistant" on page 148).

As well as adding the databases found in the client profile, you can also import:

- **Client Settings** - The client configuration parameters found in the client access profile will be used to set or update the settings on the system you import to.

- **CLI/ODBC Common Parameters** - The values in the client access profile will be used to replace those on the system you import to.

- **APPC configuration** - If you have an APPC stack the values in the client access profile are used to configure the APPC stack on the system you import to.

4.6 Manual Configuration Using the CCA

So far we have looked at two automated methods of cataloging databases using the CCA, DB2 Discovery and Access Profiles. It is also possible to use the CCA to manually configure a database connection. This is the only option (via the CCA) to catalog DRDA databases, usually located on OS/390 or OS/400 platforms. When using the manual option from the CCA to configure a database connection you need to know the details of the communications setup between the client and the server (unlike the automated methods).

DB2 UDB on Windows NT allows you to use the TCP/IP, NetBIOS, Named Pipes, IPX/SPX and APPC communications protocols for communications between a DB2 UDB client and a DB2 UDB server. To use any of these communications protocols for DB2 client/server communications, the protocols must first be installed and configured on both the client and the server. In this section we will not cover the installation and configuration of the communications protocols as we assume this has been completed.

4.6.1 Using TCP/IP

To use the CCA to manually catalog a database using TCP/IP:

1. Start the CCA. Select **Start**, then **Programs**, then **DB2 for Windows NT**, then **Client Configuration Assistant.**

2. Select the **Add** button.

3. Next select **Manually configure a connection to a DB2 database**, then click **Next**.

4. From the protocol tab (Figure 115), select the **TCP/IP** radio button and choose **LAN-based** as the target operating system. Click **Next**. Note that if you only see the *Target Operating system* radio buttons if you have the DB2 Connect component installed.

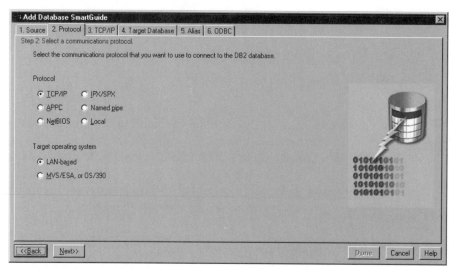

Figure 115. Add Database - Protocol

5. On the TCP/IP tab (Figure 116), enter the **hostname** (or the IP address) of the DB2 server and the **port number** being used. Optionally, enter the service name if you wish an entry to be made to your local services file; normally you should not require this. The hostname or IP address of the DB2 server can be found by typing `ipconfig` from a command prompt at the server, or by checking the TCP/IP protocol settings in the Network settings of the Windows NT Control Panel. The port number and the service name can be found by checking the SERVICES file in the \winnt\system32\drivers\etc directory on the DB2 server.

6. Click **Next**.

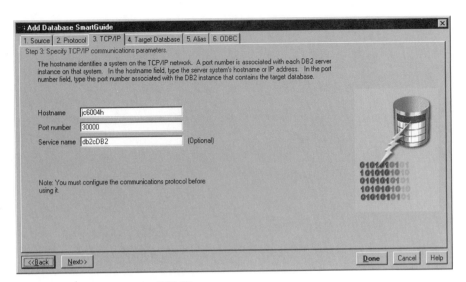

Figure 116. Add Database - TCP/IP

7. On the Target Database tab (Figure 117), enter the database alias of the database on the server. Click **Next**.

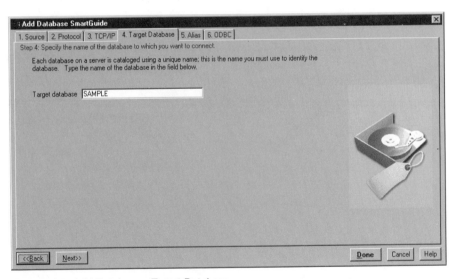

Figure 117. Add Database - Target Database

8. On the Alias tab (Figure 118), enter the **database alias** as it will be known on your client system, and optionally add a description. Click **Next**.

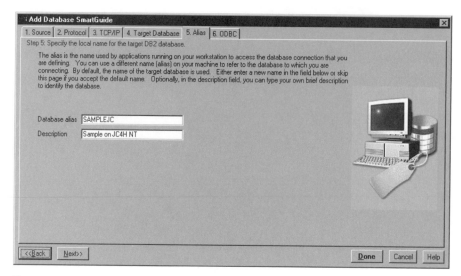

Figure 118. Add Database - Alias

9. On the ODBC tab (Figure 119), optionally register the database for use with ODBC applications. You can turn this option off by deselecting the radio button *Register this database for ODBC*; the default setting is enabled. Click **Done**.

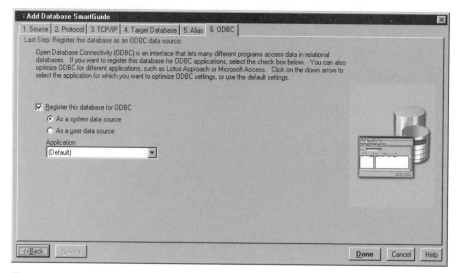

Figure 119. Add Database - ODBC

10. Using the confirmation window, you can either Test the connection, Add another database or Close the Add Database SmartGuide and return to the CCA main panel.

11. If the connection was successful the database will be shown in the CCA.

4.6.2 Using NetBIOS

To use the CCA to manually catalog a database using NetBIOS:

1. Start the CCA. Select **Start**, then **Programs**, then **DB2 for Windows NT**, then **Client Configuration Assistant.**

2. Select the **Add** button.

3. Next select **Manually configure a connection to a DB2 database**, then click **Next**.

4. From the protocol tab (Figure 120), select the **NetBIOS** radio button. Click **Next**.

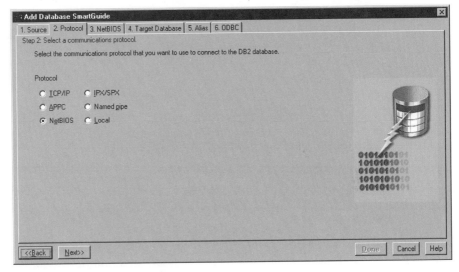

Figure 120. Add Database - Protocol

5. On the NetBIOS tab (Figure 121), in the *Server workstation name* field, enter the **workstation name** (nname) of the DB2 server instance where the database is located. If your local DB2 instance has already been configured with a workstation name, it will appear in the *Local workstation name*. If you have not configured it yet then a default value will be generated and used to update the client instance configuration. The Adapter number is detected from the NetBIOS configuration and is the

adapter used for the Nbf binding. You should not need to alter the adapter number.

6. Click **Next**.

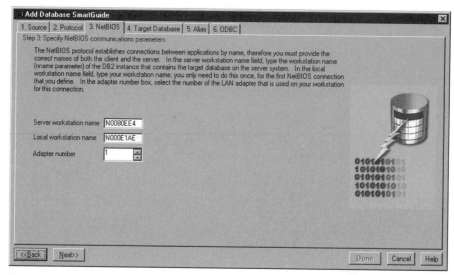

Figure 121. Add Database - NetBIOS

7. On the Target Database tab enter the **database alias** of the database on the server. Click **Next**.

8. On the Alias tab enter the **database alias** as it will be known on your client system, and if you require optionally add a description. Click **Next**.

9. On the ODBC tab, optionally register the database for use with ODBC applications. You can turn this option off by deselecting the radio button *Register this database for ODBC*; the default setting is enabled. Click **Done**.

10. Using the confirmation window, you can either Test the connection, Add another database or Close the Add Database SmartGuide and return to the CCA main panel.

11. If the connection was successful the database will be shown in the CCA.

4.6.3 Named Pipes

To use the CCA to manually catalog a database using Named Pipes:

1. Start the CCA. Select **Start**, then **Programs**, then **DB2 for Windows NT**, then **Client Configuration Assistant.**

2. Select the **Add** button.

3. Next select **Manually configure a connection to a DB2 database**, then click **Next**.

4. From the protocol tab (Figure 122), select the **Named Pipe** radio button. Click **Next**.

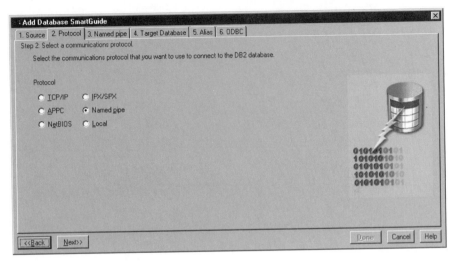

Figure 122. Add Database - Protocol

- On the Named Pipe tab (Figure 123), enter the **Computer name** of the Windows NT system where the database resides. The computer name can be found by typing NET NAME on a command line or by checking the Network configuration in the Windows NT Control Panel. In the *Instance* field, enter the **instance** defined on the DB2 server that contains the database you wish to add.

- Click **Next**.

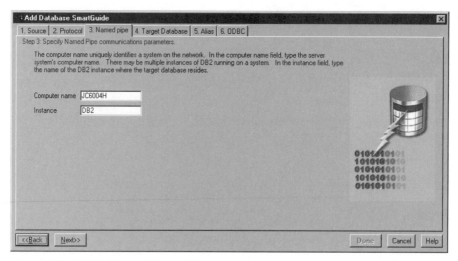

Figure 123. Add Database - Named Pipe

5. On the Target Database tab enter the **database alias** of the database on the server. Click **Next**.

6. On the Alias tab enter the **database alias** as it will be known on your client system, and if you require optionally add a description. Click **Next**.

7. On the ODBC tab, optionally register the database for use with ODBC applications. You can turn this option off by deselecting the radio button *Register this database for ODBC*; the default setting is enabled. Click **Done**.

8. Using the confirmation window, you can either Test the connection, Add another database or Close the Add Database SmartGuide and return to the CCA main panel.

9. If the connection was successful the database will be shown in the CCA.

4.6.4 Using IPX/SPX

To use the CCA to manually catalog a database using IPX/SPX:

1. Start the CCA. Select **Start**, then **Programs**, then **DB2 for Windows NT**, then **Client Configuration Assistant.**

2. Select the **Add** button.

3. Next select **Manually configure a connection to a DB2 database**, then click **Next**.

4. From the protocol tab (Figure 124), select the **IPX/SPX** radio button. Click **Next**.

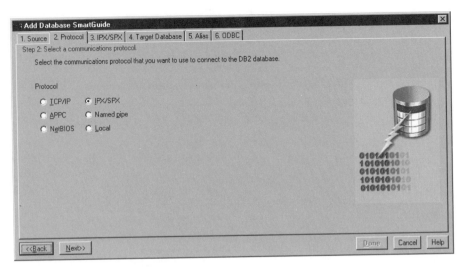

Figure 124. Add Database - Protocol

- From the IPX/SPX tab (Figure 125), enter the **internetwork address** of the instance where the database you wish to add is located. You can find the internetwork address of the instance by using one of these two methods:

  - Start the Control Center and expand the tree view by clicking the **[+]** next to the required system, right-button click on the required instance, and then select **Setup Communications**. In the next panel select the **properties** for IPX/SPX, and you will see the Internetwork address used by the instance.

  - The db2ipxad.exe utility at the DB2 server. This utility is found in the \sqllib\misc directory.

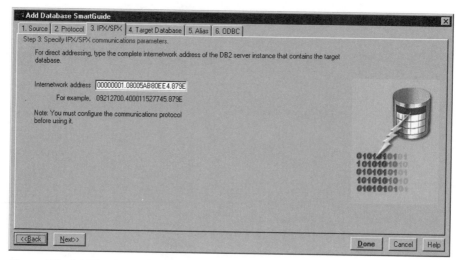

Figure 125. Add Database - IPX/SPX

5. On the Target Database tab enter the **database alias** of the database on the server. Click **Next**.

6. On the Alias tab enter the **database alias** as it will be known on your client system, and if you require optionally add a description. Click **Next**.

7. On the ODBC tab, optionally register the database for use with ODBC applications. You can turn this option off by deselecting the radio button *Register this database for ODBC*; the default setting is enabled. Click **Done**.

8. Using the confirmation window, you can either Test the connection, Add another database or Close the Add Database SmartGuide and return to the CCA main panel.

9. If the connection was successful the database will be shown in the CCA.

4.6.5 Using APPC

To use the CCA to manually catalog a database using APPC:

1. Start the CCA. Select **Start**, then **Programs**, then **DB2 for Windows NT**, then **Client Configuration Assistant.**

2. Select the **Add** button.

3. Next select **Manually configure a connection to a DB2database**, then click **Next**.

4. From the protocol tab (Figure 126), select the **APPC** radio button and select **Lan-based** as the target operating system. Click **Next**. Note that if

you only see the *Target Operating system* radio buttons if you have the DB2 Connect component installed.

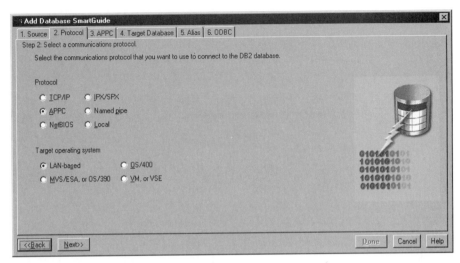

Figure 126. Add Database - Protocol

- On the APPC tab (Figure 127), enter the **symbolic destination name** of the DB2 server as defined at the server in the SNA communications software you are using. The symbolic destination name of the server can be determined by examining the configuration of your SNA software.

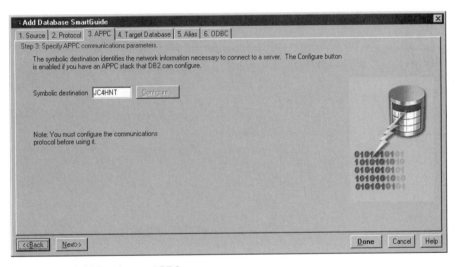

Figure 127. Add Database - APPC

5. On the Target Database tab enter the **database alias** of the database on the server. Click **Next**.

6. On the Alias tab enter the **database alias** as it will be known on your client system, and if you require optionally add a description. Click **Next**.

7. On the ODBC tab, optionally register the database for use with ODBC applications. You can turn this option off by deselecting the radio button *Register this database for ODBC*; the default setting is enabled. Click **Done**.

8. Using the confirmation window, you can either Test the connection, Add another database or Close the Add Database SmartGuide and return to the CCA main panel.

9. If the connection was successful the database will be shown in the CCA.

4.7 Configuration Using the Control Center

The Control Center, one of the DB2 UDB graphical tools, is used to perform a variety of local and remote administrative tasks. "DB2 UDB Graphical Tools" on page 191gives more details about the tasks you perform from the DB2 Control Center. In this section, we will look at using the Control Center to configure communications and add remote DB2 databases.

4.7.1 Adding Databases to the Control Center

Follow these steps:

1. Start the Control Center. Select **Start**, then **Programs**, then **DB2 for Windows NT**, then **Administration Tools**, then **Control Center.**

2. Right mouse button click on **Systems** and select **Add** (Figure 128).

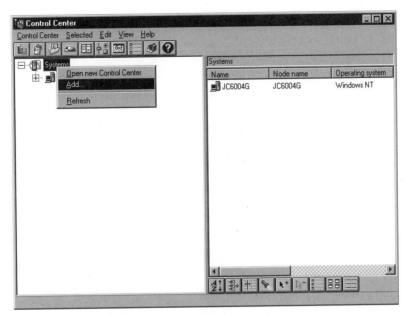

Figure 128. Control Center - Systems Menu

3. In the Add System window (Figure 129), you have two choices:

   - If you click the **Refresh** button, a search for DB2 servers will be started.

   - Alternately, you can specify a protocol and protocol specific data in the Protocol pane and associated panes and then click **Retrieve** to fetch information on the remote DB2 server.

4. Whichever method you choose, once you have the details for the system you require, click the **Apply** button to add the system to the Control Center.

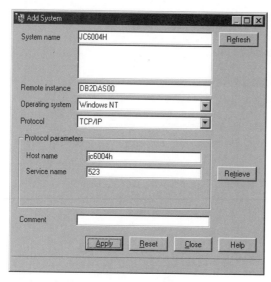

Figure 129. Control Center - Add system

5. Now that the system is known to the Control Center, you can add instances and databases from that system. To add an instance, click on the **[+]** next to the newly added system to expand the view. Then right mouse button click on **Instances**, and then **Add**.

6. In the Add Instance window (Figure 130), click on **Refresh** to retrieve the instances found on server. Select the instance you wish to add and then click on **Apply**.

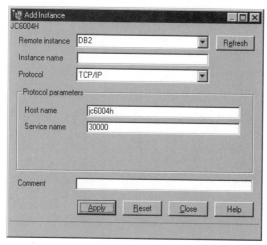

Figure 130. Add Instance

7. Close the Add Instance window and return to Control Center.

8. To add a database from the newly added instance, click on the **[+]** next to instance name to expand the view. Then right mouse button click on **Databases** and select **Add**.

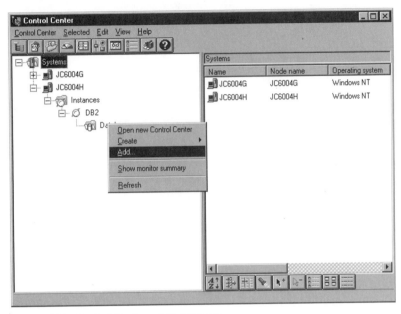

Figure 131. Control Center - Add database

9. From the **Add Database** window, click **Refresh** to retrieve a list of database in the instance.

10. Select a database from the **Database name** list and optionally an **Alias** and **Comment**. Then click **Apply**.

11. The database is now added to the Control Center.

4.7.2 Changing the Communications Settings for an Instance

Another function available from the Control Center is the ability to alter the communications settings of a local or remote instance. To do this:

1. From the Control Center, locate the required instance.

2. Right mouse button click on the instance and then select **Setup Communications**.

3. If you are changing the settings on a remote instance, then enter the **userid** and **password** of the remote DAS instance owner when prompted.

4. If the userid is validated, you are presented with the Setup Communications window as shown in Figure 86 on page 145.

5. After altering the communications settings, the instance will need be restarted. This can be achieved by clicking the right mouse button on the instance and choosing **Stop**. When the instance has stopped, reselect it choose **Start**.

4.8 Summary

In this chapter we have looked at the different methods available in DB2 UDB to enable you to setup client/server configurations. The diagram shown in Figure 132 aims to help you choose which configuration method is best suited to your particular requirements:

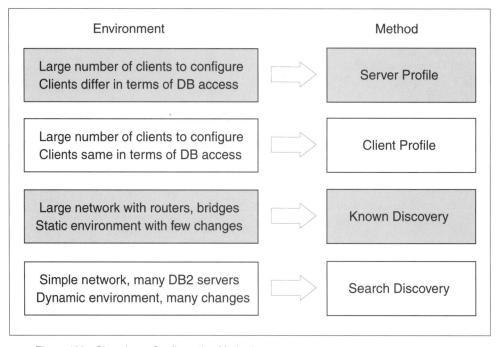

Figure 132. Choosing a Configuration Method

Chapter 5. DB2 UDB Graphical Tools

This chapter presents the DB2 Universal Database graphical (GUI) tools in the Windows NT environment. We describe how to use these graphical tools to:

- Perform DB2 systems and database administration
- Manipulate and access data
- Perform various complex tasks with the SmartGuides

5.1 Overview of the Graphical Tools

DB2 Universal Database Version 5.0 on Windows NT includes a set of integrated graphical tools. These tools allow the user to manage DB2 systems and access DB2 databases in a very intuitive, user-friendly way.

This section gives a brief description of the various GUI tools available in DB2 Universal Database and lists the features and functions that makes DB2 UDB easy to use for end-users, developers and administrators.

Figure 133 on page 192 shows the DB2 folder as it appears in the Programs group on the Windows NT desktop. From the DB2 for Windows NT desktop folder the user can access any tool by clicking on the item that represents the function to be performed. The Administration Tools folder can be opened to access more administration tools.

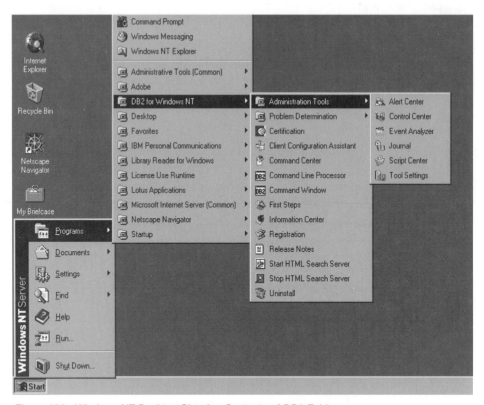

Figure 133. Windows NT Desktop Showing Contents of DB2 Folders

Figure 134 on page 193 provides a roadmap to the DB2 GUI tools available from the DB2 for Windows NT folder:

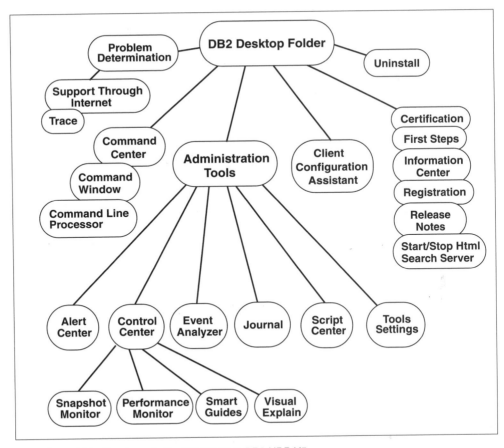

Figure 134. Roadmap to the GUI Tools in DB2 UDB V5

The tools and programs available in the DB2 folder are:

- **Problem Determination Folder -** Contains DB2 Support Information through Internet and the DB2 UDB trace utility. Selecting DB2 Support Information opens a URL page in your web browser containing links to these addresses:

  - The DB2 Universal Database Home Page at http://service.software.ibm.com/db2/support/dbssup.html.

  - The DB2 Universal Database Service and Support Information Page provides additional links and information on Electronic and Voice Support options, IBM Support in your own country, and also a link to the DB2 Product and Service Technical Library.

  - The IBM Software Servers Home Page at http://www.software.ibm.com/is/sw-servers/index.html.

The Trace utility allows you to easily gather DB2 diagnostic information to be sent to IBM for analysis upon direction from an IBM Support Center.

- **Administration Tools Folder** - Contains icons for the administration tools. With these tools you can perform administration tasks on DB2 instances, servers and databases:

  - **Alert Center** - A tool to monitor your system for early warnings of potential problems.

  - **Control Center** - The principal tool for administration of DB2 UDB.

  - **Event Analyzer** - A tool that helps to analyze the event monitor files generated for a database.

  - **Journal** - A tool which displays executing, pending or completed jobs, recovery history, alerts, and DB2 messages.

  - **Script Center** - Allows you to create mini-applications called scripts which can be stored and invoked at a later time of your choosing.

  - **Tools Settings** - A notebook used to change the settings for Control Center, Alert Center, and Replication.

- **Command Window and Command Line Processor** - Intended to support the processing of both interactive and non-interactive of DB2 commands and SQL statements on Windows NT.

- **Command Center** - The preferred graphical version of the Command Line Processor. Allows you to easily recall previous commands, scroll through output and more.

- **Client Configuration Assistant** - The tool enabling easy configuration of access to remote databases.

- **Certification** - Takes you to the web location providing you with detailed information on the IBM and DB2 UDB certification programs.

- **First Steps** - A program configured to be run automatically the first time after DB2 installation. It allows the user to create a sample database, view data easily in that database, and more.

- **Information Center** - A notebook that allows the user to search information by topics, view the DB2 Universal Database List of Books as well as code examples and other documentation.

- **Registration** - For registering as a DB2 UDB V5 customer.

- **Release Notes** - Displays the release notes issued with your version of DB2 UDB.

- **Start/Stop HTML Search Server** - Start or stop the HTML Search Server. When active, it enables searches to be performed on the DB2 UDB books which are in HTML format.
- **Uninstall** - A utility used to safely remove the DB2 software.

Other utilities, such as **Performance Monitor**, **Snapshot Monitor** and **Visual Explain** are invoked from the **Control Center**.

Some of the administration functions are available via **SmartGuides**, which are step-by-step notebooks that prompt the user to fill in the information necessary for the task to be performed. For example, a SmartGuide is available to tune the performance of your system. You will find the SmartGuides excellent sources of information allowing DB2 to determine the best settings for your environment, based on your input.

In the following pages we provide details on how to manipulate DB2 UDB using the main GUI tools (including the SmartGuides) on Windows NT.

5.1.1 Enabling Remote Administration

The remote administration of DB2 UDB servers and databases using the graphical tools is enabled by the DB2 Administration Server. "DB2 UDB Client/Server Communications" on page 123, covers the DB2 Administration Server in detail. In this section we present a brief overview.

The DB2 Administration Server (DAS) is a special DB2 instance that provides a remote client the ability to administer DB2 Universal Database instances and databases. All the remote administration tasks will be sent to DB2 Administration Server for local execution.

On Windows NT, the DAS is implemented as a Windows NT service. Some examples of the administration tasks enabled by the DAS are: starting/stopping DB2 instances, and attaching to DB2 instances to perform administration at the database level, such as updating the database configuration parameters, creating/dropping databases, backing up/restoring databases, and so on.

In addition, the DB2 Administration Server enables automation for enabling communication between remote DB2 UDB clients and DB2 UDB servers, the monitoring of performance and scheduling of jobs. See "DB2 UDB Client/Server Communications" on page 123 for details on how to enable this method of setting up client/server communications. The job scheduler allows a Database Administrator (DBA) to run tasks such as backups at regular intervals. The scheduled jobs may include both DB2 UDB commands and operating system commands.

5.1.2 Control Center

The Control Center provides the database administrator with the necessary tools to perform common DB2 system and database administration tasks. It is designed to be the central point of administration for DB2 Universal Database. The Control Center provides a seamless integration of the administration tools, gives a clear overview of the entire system, enables remote database management and provides step-by-step assistance for complex tasks via the SmartGuides.

Figure 135 shows a example of the information available using the Control Center:

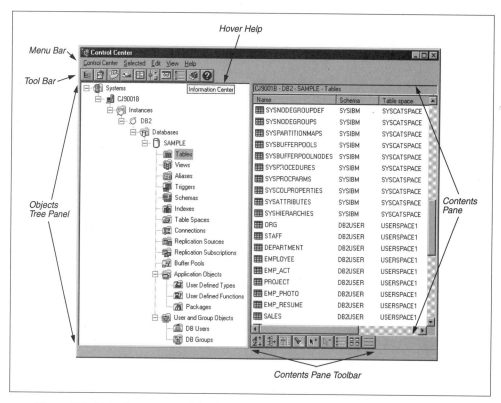

Figure 135. Main Components of the Control Center

The Systems object represents both local and remote machines. To display all the DB2 systems that your system has cataloged, expand the object tree by clicking on the plus sign (+) on Systems. The left portion of the screen lists available systems (local and remote) with DB2 UDB installed. We can see from the figure that the system CJ9001B contains a DB2 instance, in which the database SAMPLE is located. We can also see all the objects within the database that can be administered on the Control Center. On the right portion of the screen is the list of the tables in the SAMPLE database.

The main components of the Control Center are listed below:

- Menu Bar - To access Control Center functions and online help.
- Tool Bar - Icons used to access the other GUI tools, such as Journal, Script Center and so on.
- Object Tree - Contains all the objects that can be managed from the Control Center as well as their inter-relationships.
- Content Pane - Contains the objects that correspond to the object selected in the Objects tree.
- Contents Pane Toolbar - Icons used to tailor the view of objects and information in the Contents pane. These functions can also be selected in the View menu.
- Hover Help is also available in the Control Center, providing a short description for each icon on the tool bar as you move the mouse pointer over the icon.

The Control Center enables the user to graphically manage both local and remote database servers and the database objects within them, all from a single point of control. By database servers, we mean database manager environments known as DB2 instances. You can use the Control Center to perform server administrative tasks such as configuring, backing up and recovering databases, managing directories, scheduling jobs, and managing media.

5.1.2.1 DB2 Instance Level

At the DB2 instance level, in the object tree of the Control Center, the following server administrative tasks can be performed:

- Start/Stop DB2 instances both locally and remotely
- Attach/Detach to instances for performing administrative tasks
- Configure DB2 UDB Database Manager parameters
- Setup Communications Protocols
- List/Force applications running against the Instance

- Invoke the Snapshot Monitoring function of DB2 UDB

The Control Center is designed to make administrative tasks simple to perform. For example, selecting the **Configure Instance** option opens a notebook where you can view and change database manager configuration parameters values. As shown in Figure 136 on page 198, the Configure Instance notebook has the database manager parameter values grouped by function. Each notebook page has the Parameters controls, a Value field to change the value of the selected configuration parameter and a hint box which gives a brief description of what the configuration parameter is used for. Note that for each configuration parameter, you are presented with the values possible for the parameter.

Figure 136 shows the Performance page which contains the database manager configuration parameters that affect the performance of the database manager instance.

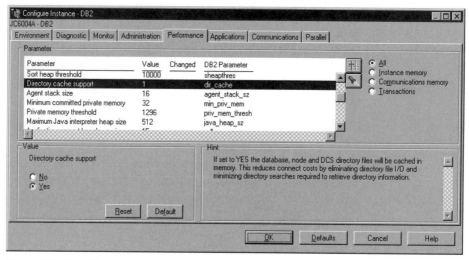

Figure 136. The Database Manager Configuration Notebook

To view the database manager configuration parameters using the DB2 Command Line Processor (CLP) or a DB2 Command Window, you have to type the command:

```
db2 get database manager configuration
```

As you can see in Figure 137 on page 199, the output of this command is an ungrouped list with all the configuration parameters and their values. Looking at this command output, you cannot tell what the limits and possible values are for each parameter. In other words, less information is presented by using the GET DATABASE MANAGER CONFIGURATION command compared to the Configure Instance notebook in the Control Center. (Please note that all commands that can be issued from the DB2 Command Line Processor or DB2 Command Window can also easily be executed from the graphical DB2 Command Center which provides the ability to easily retrieve previous commands and to scroll through output of commands.)

```
$ db2 get database manager configuration

         Database Manager Configuration

    Node type = Database Server with local and remote clients

Database manager configuration release level            = 0x0800

...
   SYSADM group name                    (SYSADM_GROUP) = DB2GADM
   SYSCTRL group name                    (SYSCTRL_GROUP) =
   SYSMAINT group name                  (SYSMAINT_GROUP) =

   Database manager authentication       (AUTHENTICATION) = SERVER
   Trust all clients                     (TRUST_ALLCLNTS) = YES
   Trusted client authentication         (TRUST_CLNTAUTH) = CLIENT

   Default database path                    (DFTDBPATH) = C:

   Database monitor heap size (4KB)        (MON_HEAP_SZ) = 24
   UDB shared memory set size (4KB)        (UDF_MEM_SZ) = 256

   Backup buffer default size (4KB)         (BACKBUFSZ) = 1024
   Restore buffer default size (4KB)        (RESTBUFSZ) = 1024

   Agent stack size                    (AGENT_STACK_SZ) = 16
   Minimum committed private memory (4KB)   (MIN_PRIV_MEM) = 32
...
```

Figure 137. Get Database Manager Configuration Command Output

Another example of an instance level administration task would be using the **list applications** command to display information about the applications executing within local or remote instances. The type of information you receive includes the name of the application, the Authorization Id, the Agent Id, the Application Id and the name of the database that the application is accessing. This option is a very useful as you can determine which users are using which applications and databases, and if necessary, force applications from your database.

In Figure 138, we use the **list applications** command option from the Control Center. We can see that there are four applications using the SAMPLE database and that user AUSRES04 (Agent ID 14) is one of the users. To remove this application from executing against our database we can force the Agent Id of the application.

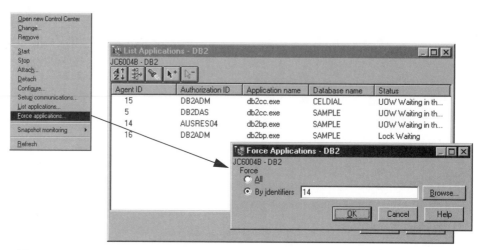

Figure 138. List and Force Application Options

5.1.2.2 DB2 Database Level

Now let's look at using the Control Center to administer DB2 databases themselves. For the database level administrative tasks, select the database you want to administer with the right mouse button. You will be presented a pop-up menu of administrative tasks, including:

- Alter, Drop, Connect and Disconnect to a Database.

- Database Authorities - grant/revoke authorities to/from users or groups.

- Configure Database parameters option and the Configure Database Performance SmartGuide option.

- Database Recovery tasks - restart, restore (version), and roll-forward recovery.

- Visual Explain and Performance Monitoring - snapshot and event monitor.

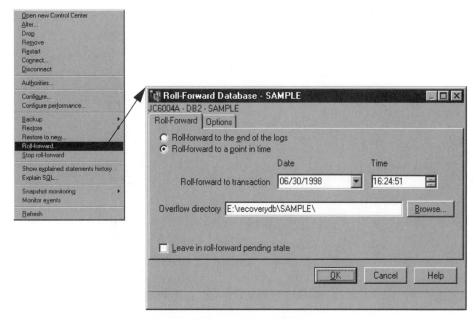

Figure 139. Database Administrative Tasks, Roll-Forward Recovery

For example, the roll-forward of a database's log files can be performed after the restore of a table space backup or a database backup (assuming archival logging is enabled). A roll-forward operation applies transactions recorded in the database log files. Figure 139 shows how to perform the roll-forward to a point-in-time for the SAMPLE database. The Options Panel allows you to choose between performing the roll-forward on-line or off-line if you are doing a table space restore and roll-forward.

The ability to perform administrative tasks such as roll-forward from the Control Center means that the DBA does not have to remember the complex syntax of these types of commands. For instance, the following is the syntax of the ROLLFORWARD DATABASE command, which can be run from the DB2 Command Center or DB2 CLP/DB2 Command Window:

```
$ db2 ? rollforward database

ROLLFORWARD DATABASE database-alias [USER username [USING password]]
[TO {isotime | END OF LOGS [On-Node-Clause]} [AND {COMPLETE | STOP}] |
{COMPLETE | STOP} [On-Node-Clause] | CANCEL [On-Node-Clause] |
QUERY STATUS [On-Node-Clause]] [TABLESPACE ONLINE |
TABLESPACE (tblspace-name [ {,tblspace-name} ... ]) [ONLINE]]
[OVERFLOW LOG PATH (log-directory [{,log-directory ON NODE node-number}
... ])]

On-Node-Clause:
  ON {{NODE | NODES} (node-number [TO node-number] , ... ) |
  ALL NODES [EXCEPT {NODE | NODES} (node-number [TO node-number] , ...)]}
```

Figure 140. Syntax of the Rollforward Command

5.1.2.3 Creating and Working with DB2 Database Objects

In Figure 135 on page 196, in the left portion of the screen in the Objects Tree panel, you can see the objects within the database that can be administered from the Control Center. To create database objects such as databases, table spaces, tables, views and triggers, follow these steps:

- Expand the Object Tree to display an icon for the type of object that you want to create.

- Click the right mouse button on the icon. A pop-up menu of all of the available actions for the object opens.

- Select the **Create** menu choice. A window or notebook opens to guide you through the process for creating the object.

Note that the database, table and table space objects have the additional option using SmartGuide... to create the object. We will discuss the "DB2 UDB SmartGuides" on page 217.

From the Object Tree, you can click on a folder icon such as Tables. If any tables exist, they are displayed in the contents pane. In Figure 135 on page 196, on the right portion of the screen, you can see a list of all the existing tables in SAMPLE database. You can then select a table in the contents pane and invoke an action for it.

For example, we want to perform a load into a table. We right-click on the **EMPLOYEE** table and click on **Load** in the pop-up menu (Figure 141):

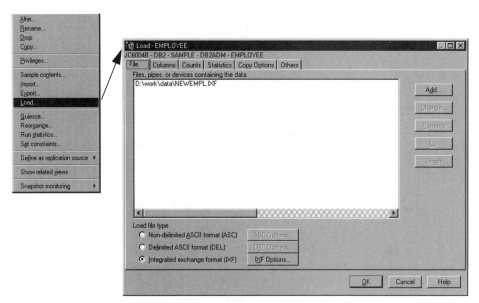

Figure 141. Loading a Table Using the Control Center

In the File Panel, we specify the name and type of the load file. You can configure the different options for the selected load file type (here IXF). You can also select a subset of columns in the table, which can be useful if you only want to load into a few columns in the table. Figure 142 shows how the columns are chosen using this graphical interface to the LOAD utility, and how to specify the column position:

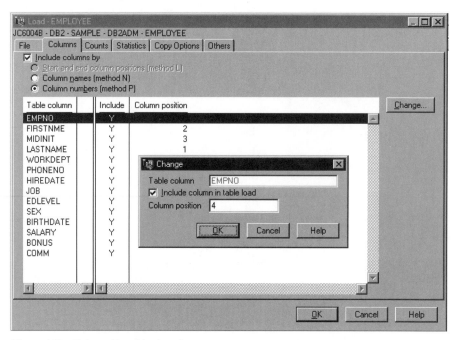

Figure 142. Column Panel for Loading

You can set up the table copy option using the graphical interface, as well as gather statistics during the load. In addition, you specify the Save Count, Row Count, the Restart Options and so on, by using the Counts panel as shown in Figure 143:

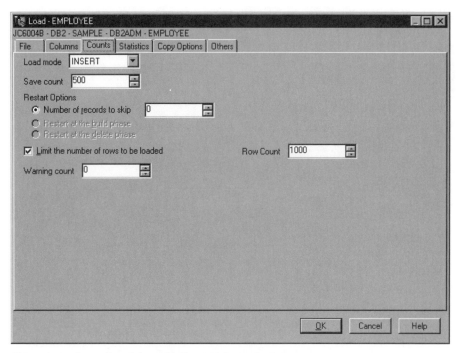

Figure 143. Count Panel, Load Modes and Count Options

In the Others panel, you specify temporary directories used during index creation, data and sort buffers, exception tables, and more.

As you can see, loading tables through the Control Center allows the DBA to easily select the options required for a given load operation. Context-sensitive help is available for each option, if required. In contrast, if we look at the syntax of the LOAD command run from the DB2 Command Center, DB2 CLP or a DB2 Command Window (shown in Figure 144 on page 206), it becomes apparent that a certain amount of prior knowledge is assumed:

```
$ db2 ? load
...
LOAD FROM file/pipe/dev [ {,file/pipe/dev} ... ]
OF {ASC | DEL | IXF}
[LOBS FROM lob-path [ {,lob-path} ... ] ]
[MODIFIED BY filetype-mod [ {filetype-mod} ... ] ]]
[METHOD {L ( col-start col-end [ {,col-start col-end} ... ] )
        [NULL INDICATORS (col-position [ {,col-position} ... ] )]
    | N ( col-name [ {,col-name} ... ] )
    | P ( col-position  [ {,col-position} ... ] )}]
[SAVECOUNT n] [RESTARTCOUNT {n | B | D}]
[ROWCOUNT n] [WARNINGCOUNT n] [MESSAGES msg-file]
[REMOTE FILE remote-file]
{INSERT | REPLACE | RESTART | TERMINATE}
INTO table-name [( insert-column [ {,insert-column} ... ] )]
[FOR EXCEPTION table-name]
[STATISTICS {YES [WITH DISTRIBUTION [AND [DETAILED] INDEXES ALL]
                | {AND | FOR} [DETAILED] INDEXES ALL]
           | NO}]
[ {COPY {NO | YES [USE ADSM [OPEN num-sess SESSIONS]
                | TO dir/dev [ {,dir/dev} ... ]
                | LOAD lib-name [OPEN num-sess SESSIONS]]}
 | NONRECOVERABLE} ]
[USING directory [ {,directory} ... ] ]
[HOLD QUIESCE] [WITHOUT PROMPTING] [DATA BUFFER buffer-size]
[SORT BUFFER buffer-size] [CPU_PARALLELISM n] [DISK_PARALLELISM n]
```

Figure 144. Syntax of the Load Command

5.1.3 Command Center

The DB2 UDB Command Center provides the ability to access and manipulate database instances and databases themselves from a graphical interface. It is a GUI version of Command Line Processor with additional ability to manipulate scripts, scroll through output and so on.

It uses the same options as the traditional CLP for autocommit, SQLCA and SQLCODE display, output file, stop on error, and so on. You can start the Command Center tool from the Control Center toolbar or from the DB2 folder.

The Command Center allows the user to interactively process SQL statements, DB2 commands and run operating system commands. Figure 145 shows the interactive execution of a sequence of SQL statements. As you may have noticed, when using the Command Center, it is not necessary to prefix DB2 commands with the keyword db2 as is required with the DB2 CLP or DB2 Command Window.

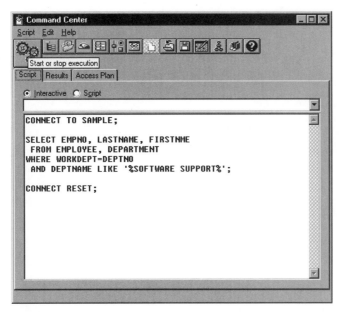

Figure 145. Command Center

After execution, the output is displayed (Figure 146 on page 208) and can be saved to an output file. The DB2 Command Center can also display the access plan and statistics associated with an SQL statement before or after its execution. To do this you can highlight your SQL statement and then choose **Script->Create Access Plan**. This will create the access plan for the SQL statement you are interested in and will put you in the Access Plan panel from which you can view additional information in a Visual Explain format. Please note that by setting the Options in the Command Center appropriately you can choose to always have the access plan generated and available.

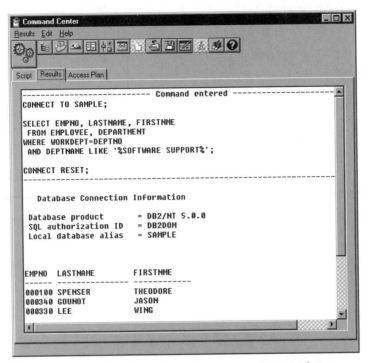

Figure 146. Command Center Showing Results on Scrollable Window

An important feature that the Command Center provides is the ability to save a sequence of SQL statements or DB2 commands to a script file. You can schedule the script to run as a job using the Script Center (see "Script Center" on page 209) and monitor the job in the Journal (see "Journal" on page 213).

From the Command Center, a script file can contain logic in a supported operating system script language, if the operating system commands are proceed by an exclamation mark (!).

Another way of creating scripts is using the Script Center, described in the next section. The benefit of creating a script in the Command Center instead of the Script Center is that you can execute the script first before saving it into the Script Center.

If you choose the Script Mode of the Command Center, the entry area acts like an editor. Script Mode is intended for you to create and edit a script. The following steps are required to create and save a command script using the Command Center:

6. Select the **Script** radio button in the Script Page.

7. Enter your commands in the Script page of the Command Center. (To execute a set of commands immediately, either click on the **Gears** icon, select **Execute** from the Script menu, or press **Ctrl-Enter**.)

8. From the Script menu, select **Save as**. The Save window opens.

9. Complete the fields and select **To Script Center**. The command script is saved and will be accessible through the Script Center.

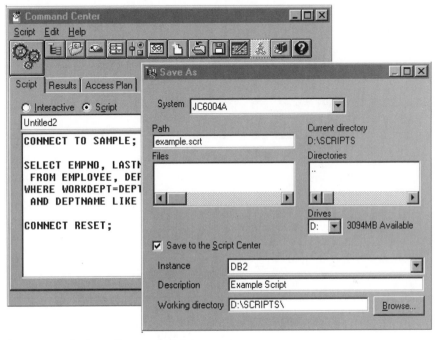

Figure 147. Saving a Command Script

Figure 147 shows the Save As window of the Command Center. To schedule a script to run at a later date, select **Schedule** from the Script Menu. Note that the command script to be scheduled needs first to be saved to the Script Center.

5.1.4 Script Center

The DB2 UDB Script Center is a graphical administration tool that you can use to create, execute and schedule scripts. These scripts can contain a sequence of SQL statements, DB2 commands or operating system commands. You can also import previously created scripts, even those not created with the Script Center (for example, those created in the Command Center).

There are certain advantages to using scripts to perform tasks with DB2 UDB. Database operations can be written once and repeated many times; or scheduled for certain times.

Once the script is created, it is registered in the script list. This registration includes a script ID number, the instance where the script was defined, the script name and description, the command type (OS or DB2) and the last modification timestamp. Figure 148 shows the script which was registered when we saved the example script created in the Command Center:

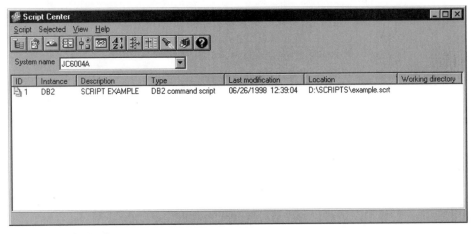

Figure 148. Script Center

The user can select a script from the list and edit its contents, copy the script to a new file or remove it (see Figure 149). A script can also be run immediately or scheduled to run later by specifying the job description, execution frequency and actions to be taken when the job succeeds or fails. The Show pending jobs, Show running jobs and Show job history options open the Journal tool to display the status of scheduled jobs.

Figure 149. Script Center Options

To demonstrate how the Script Center works, we create an example script, schedule it to run later as a job, and then monitor the execution of the job. This script collects statistics against the user tables in the SAMPLE database.

5.1.4.1 Creating a Script

To create a script from the Script Center, click on the **File** menu and click on **New**. You can then start typing your script text in the **New Command Script** panel (or import a previously written text file into the Script Center). You have the choice of writing a script containing DB2 commands or SQL statements (known as a DB2 script) or writing a script containing operating system commands (known as an OS script).

Note

DB2 scripts are the same as input files passed to the Command Line Processor (CLP). You can add comments to the file by prefixing them with two dashes (--) and delimit the commands with a semicolon (;).

The format of OS scripts is, of course, operating system specific. For example in Windows NT, you can write an operating system script as you would write a batch file. Figure 150 on page 212 shows a DB2 script which performs a REORG and a RUNSTATS against the SALES table in the SAMPLE database.

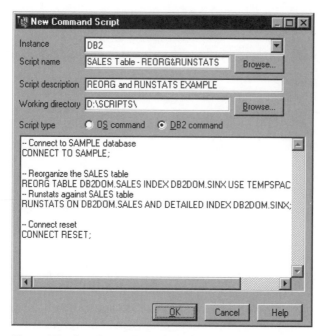

Figure 150. Creating an Example Script in the Script Center

Now that we have created an entry for this script, we will schedule the script for execution. Note that you can also select to run the script immediately.

5.1.4.2 Scheduling a Script

To use the scheduling capabilities of the Script Center we have to specify whether we want to run the script once, or repeat the execution of the script at regular intervals. We can also choose a time for the execution. In our example, we want to reorganize the SALES and then collect statistics for this table at regular intervals during the last three months in the year.

To do this, right-click on our DB2 script from the Script Center view and click on **Schedule**. Then enter a job description for the scheduled script. After this, specify the frequency of the script's execution. You can run the script:

- Once.
- Every x number of days.
- One or more times a week.
- One or more times a month.

You then specify a start and end date for the execution of the script. The start date is mandatory. If the end date is not specified, the execution of the script will be repeated indefinitely. You can also specify scripts to be executed upon the success or failure of the scheduled script. For example, you might want to update an audit table if the script fails. Finally, you specify a userid and password. You must specify a job description, a userid and password to schedule a script.

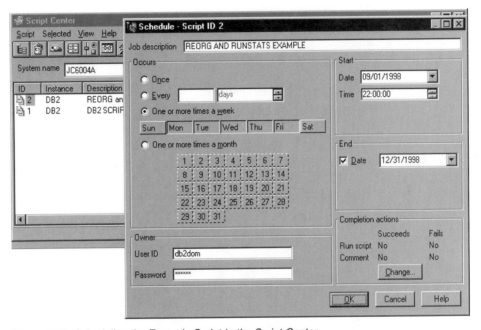

Figure 151. Scheduling the Example Script in the Script Center

In Figure 151, we schedule the script to run at 10 p.m. every weeknight during the the last three months of 1998.

Once we click on **OK**, DB2 UDB creates a job entry for the script. We are informed that the job has been created, and that a job number has been associated with the script. This allows us to later identify messages related to this script. In order to look at the status of the job and to check that it actually runs at the appointed time and completes successfully, we need to use the DB2 Journal.

5.1.5 Journal

The DB2 Journal is an both an auditing tool and a monitoring tool. It allows you to review the results of jobs that are running unattended. Like the Script Center, it can also be used to schedule jobs to run unattended. It also displays the Recovery History, Alert Messages and DB2 Messages. The Journal notebook presents the information in four pages:

- Job Monitor - To see a list of jobs, all the information about the job and to perform actions on each job. You can remove a script, show other scripts associated with it or run it immediately.

- Recovery History File - Displays the recovery history. For example, details from a restore operation.

- Alert Log - Shows the log of all alert messages.

- Messages Log - Shows the log of all DB2 messages.

Let's look at an example of monitoring jobs using the Journal.

5.1.5.1 Monitoring Jobs

You can verify that job entries have been successfully created by using the Jobs Panel. You can also view scheduled jobs, jobs that are currently executing, and jobs have completed execution. You can look at the jobs on the local DB2 UDB system, or on a remote DB2 UDB system. This is all viewed through the Jobs panel of the Journal. In the Jobs panel, you can look at the three types of jobs:

- Pending Jobs

- Running Jobs

- Job History

If we want to look at our scheduled job entry for our example script which performs a REORG and RUNSTATS, we look at the Pending Jobs. The job entry is listed with the job number, job description, userid and so on.

When you right-click on a pending job entry, you can reschedule the job, run the job immediately, remove the pending job or disable the job.

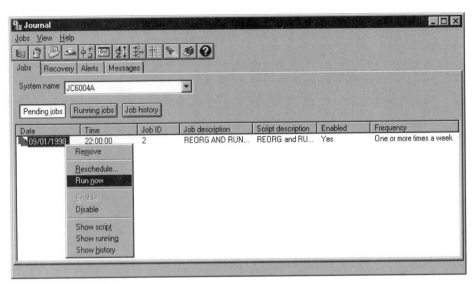

Figure 152. Journal Tool Showing the Pending Job

When the scheduled time for the job arrives, you can switch to the Running Jobs screen to look at the job while it is executing. When it has finished, the results are displayed in Job History. In our example, we executed the job immediately, as shown in Figure 152.

In Figure 153 on page 216, we can see our example job, as well as another job that was a backup of the SAMPLE database.

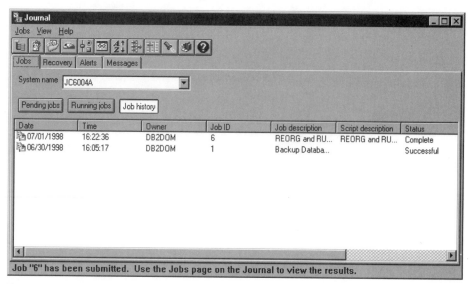

Figure 153. Journal Tool Showing Job History

Note that because our job is going to run every weeknight, it stays in the Pending Jobs list.

In our example, the status of the job is marked Complete. To get more information on the status of each command in the script, double-click on the job entry to display the full output from the job (Figure 154):

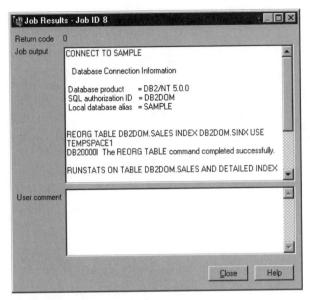

Figure 154. Job Results in Journal

5.1.6 DB2 UDB SmartGuides

The DB2 UDB SmartGuides are tutors that guide a user in creating objects and other database operations. They are integrated into the administration tools, and assist you in completing administration tasks. For each step of a particular task, detailed information is available to help you. This section gives the information about the SmartGuides that you can find in DB2 Universal Database on Windows NT.

As an example of the usage of a SmartGuide, let's look at the Client Configuration Assistant or CCA (see Figure 155). This SmartGuide is used for setting up communications from a remote client to a database server.

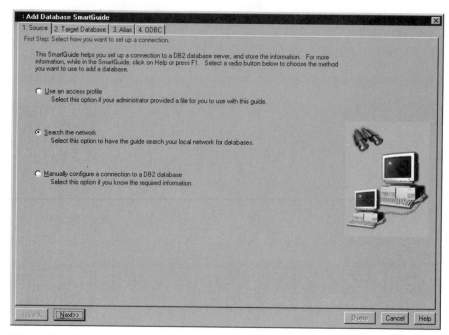

Figure 155. Client Configuration Assistant, Add Database SmartGuide

The CCA uses the Add Database SmartGuide to enable the user to add a database to their configuration. The user does not have to know the syntax of DB2 commands used to perform the actual connection configuration, or even the location of the database server. See "DB2 UDB Client/Server Communications" on page 123.

Another example is the SmartGuide that assists you in database and database manager performance tuning. It is called the Performance Configuration SmartGuide (Figure 156) and is integrated into the Control Center.

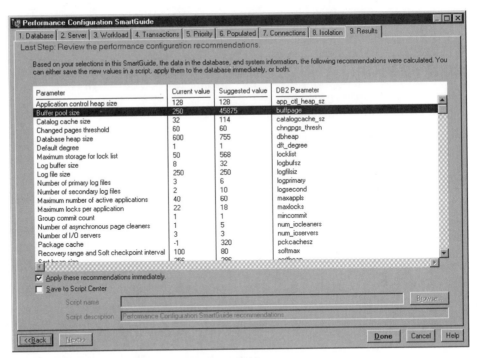

Figure 156. Performance Configuration SmartGuide

By extracting information from the system and asking questions about the use of the database system, this tool will run a series of calculations designed to determine an appropriate set of values for the database configuration parameters.

To run this SmartGuide from the Control Center, right-click on your database and select the **Configure Performance** item from the pop-up menu.

When using this tool, it is recommended that each instance of the database manager has only one production database. If you have more than one active production database at the same time, move one to a new instance before running this tool.

The Performance Configuration SmartGuide prompts you to answer some questions related to:

- The amount of server memory your database can use.
- The type of workload run against your database, choosing between queries (for example, decision support) or transactions (for example, order entry) or mixed.

- The typical database transaction, an estimate of the number of transactions per minute and also the number of SQL statements in a single unit of work.

- The database administration priority for recovering after disk drive failure.

- Whether the database is already populated. (It is recommended to run this tool each time the size of the database increases or decreases significantly.)

- The number of applications connected at the same time. This is used to allocate enough connections, by taking into consideration the number of users waiting for a connection and the available memory resources.

- The isolation level that best reflects your applications needs.

Finally, you will be provided with a list of recommended parameters values as shown in Figure 156 on page 219. Be aware that this tool should be used as a starting point upon which further adjustments can be made to obtain optimized performance.

The parameter value changes recommended can be applied immediately or saved into a script file to be run later. Bear in mind that the database administrator is responsible for stopping and starting the database to make these changes effective. It is also recommended to rebind all packages after changing database parameters.

The Configure Performance SmartGuide can be invoked at any time to adjust the configuration parameters, for example:

- Before a change in estimated workload

- After adding some additional memory to the server

- Each time database size changes significantly

Table 5 presents a list of the SmartGuides available in DB2 Universal Database on Windows NT.

Table 5. List of SmartGuides

SmartGuide	Description
Add Database	Catalog remote databases.
Create Database	Create a database. Tailor some database settings.
Performance Configuration	Tune database performance.
Backup Database	Create a backup plan in case of media and application failure. Displays recommendations for database settings and backup scheduling.
Restore Database	Recover a database.
Create Table	Create new tables.
Create Tablespace	Create new table spaces.

The use of the Backup Database and Restore Database SmartGuides is covered in "Backup and Recovery" on page 223.

Chapter 6. Backup and Recovery

In this chapter, we will discuss how backup and recovery is implemented in DB2 Universal Database. The backup and restore utilities are explained in detail to enable you to choose the best strategy to implement for your business environment. We will also describe the some of the concepts involved in making a database recoverable, so that you can deal with hardware or software related failures and prevent loss of critical data. It is very important to be prepared and test the procedures involved in database recovery before a failure actually occurs.

DB2 Universal Database provides the BACKUP, RESTORE and ROLLFORWARD utilities to enable database recoverability. Before discussing these utilities in detail, we will explain the different methods of recovery used by DB2 Universal Database.

6.1 Overview of Database Recovery

In general, a RDBMS must be able to deal with two types of problems: hardware and software. If a media failure, storage problem, power interruption or applications failure occurs, you need to be able to reconstruct the database into a consistent usable state. This process is called *database recovery.* There are three methods of recovery: crash, restore and roll-forward recovery.

6.1.1 Crash Recovery

Crash recovery is managed by the DB2 UDB database manager itself. When an unexpected event such as power or application failure occurs, the database can be placed into an inconsistent state. In this case, some transactions or units of work that were running against the database could not be committed or were committed but not written to disk. When DB2 UDB is restarted after the failure, for example the machine power failed, you can check the database status in the database configuration file. Figure 157 shows the status of the SAMPLE database. This screen is displayed by selecting **Configure...** against the SAMPLE database in the Control Center:

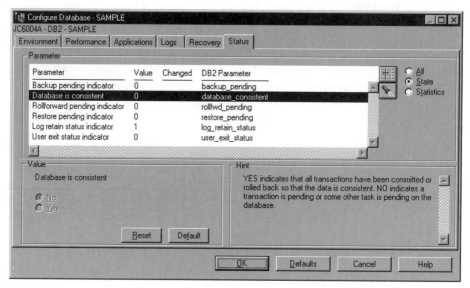

Figure 157. Database Status from the Control Center

A database is placed into an usable or consistent state in one of the following ways:

- If the database configuration parameter AUTORESTART is set to ON (the default setting), the first connection to the database will cause the database to be restarted (or placed into a consistent state).

- If the AUTORESTART parameter is set to OFF, you must manually execute the `RESTART DATABASE` command.

For example, Figure 158 shows the effect of a power failure:

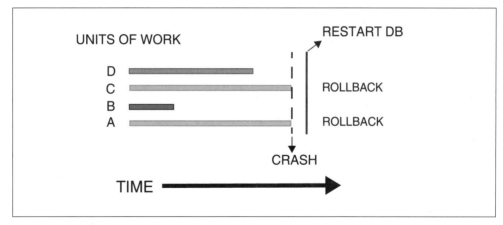

Figure 158. Crash Recovery

At the time of the crash, units of work in applications A and C were in progress (but not yet committed) and units of work in applications B and D had already been committed. The changes made by application D had been committed but the modified data pages had not yet been written back to the database on disk. When the database is restarted, application D's changes are written to disk and the units of work in applications A and C are rolled back. After these events are completed, the database is placed into a consistent state.

6.1.2 Restore Recovery

This method of recovery involves restoring a database backup taken at an earlier date. All the modifications made in the database (inserts, updates, creation of database objects and so on) after the time of the backup are lost.

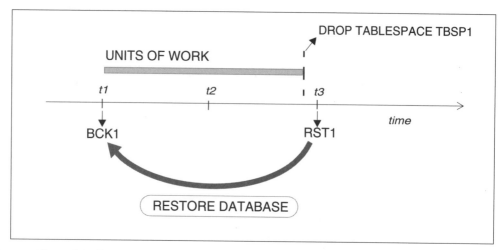

Figure 159. Restore Recovery

Figure 159 shows an example of restore recovery. A database backup was taken at time *t1*. Between *t1* and *t3*, some database tables were loaded. Just before time *t3*, the TBSP1 table space is dropped by mistake. To recover the tables in TBSP1 (at time *t1*), the BCK1 backup could be restored.

If you plan to use the restore recovery method, you should take or schedule regular backups. The `RESTORE` command or the Control Center **Restore...** database option can be used to restore a database backup.

6.1.3 Roll-forward Recovery

If you cannot afford to risk losing changes made after a database backup, you should plan to use roll-forward recovery. This recovery method allows you to recover from a database failure by first performing a restore of a database backup and then applying log files to the end of the logs (or a given point in time).

You might use point-in-time roll-forward recovery if your database gets into an inconsistent state because of a errant transaction. To recover, you first restore a backup and then roll-forward to a point in time just before the time that the errant transaction started.

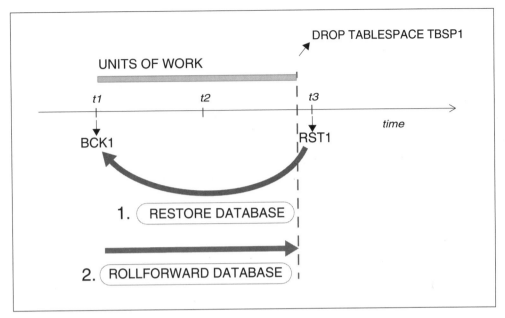

Figure 160. Roll-Forward Recovery

Figure 160 shows an example of roll-forward recovery. We can restore the TBSP1 table space and all the changes since the BCK1 backup was taken by first restoring the BCK1 backup and then performing a roll-forward to a point in time just before the DROP TABLESPACE command was issued.

A roll-forward may be performed either by using the ROLLFORWARD command or by using the Control Center.

6.2 Recovery Concepts and Issues

To help you better understand the task of recovering a damaged database, we will describe some of the concepts with which you must be familiar.

6.2.1 Unit of Work or Transaction

In DB2 UDB terminology, a unit of work (UOW) and a transaction correspond to the same concept; namely a series of operations that the database manager uses to control the consistency of the data in a database. A UOW represents a sequence of operations performed against a database that is always recoverable. By recoverable we mean that when a point of consistency or commit point occurs, data is consistent in the database. This point of consistency is achieved by either the COMMIT or ROLLBACK SQL statements.

6.2.2 Point of Recovery

You should be aware that if you choose to use restore recovery (and not roll-forward recovery), then you can only perform a full off-line database-level backup. The default values of the relevant database configuration parameters are set to use this method of recovery: LOGRETAIN=OFF and USEREXIT=OFF. An off-line backup is performed when the only process connected to the database is the backup process itself. When performing an on-line backup, other applications can be connected to the database during the backup. An on-line backup can only be performed if roll-forward recovery is enabled.

When using roll-forward recovery, you can take advantage of database level and table space level backup and restore. A table space level backup consists of one or a set of table spaces in the database. After a database or table space restore, a roll-forward can be performed to the end of logs or to a point-in-time. Point-in-time recovery may be used to assist you in minimizing damage caused by application logic failures.

To perform a database level or table space level recovery to a point-in-time you must specify the time in Coordinated Universal Time (CUT). The format is yyyy-mm-dd-hh.mm.ss.nnnnnn (year, month, day, hour, minutes, seconds, microseconds). The timestamp used on the backup is based on the local time that the BACKUP started.

Note

The special register, CURRENT TIMEZONE, holds the difference between CUT and the local time. Local time is the CUT plus the value of CURRENT TIMEZONE.

6.2.3 Database Logs

In DB2 UDB databases, log files are used to keep records of all data changes. There are two types of logging: circular and archival.

When DB2 UDB uses circular logging, the log files are used in a round-robin way. The data changes are recorded in the log files and when all the units of work are committed or rolled back in a particular log file, the file can be reused. The number of log files used by circular logging is defined by the

LOGPRIMARY and LOGSECOND database configuration parameters. If
there are UOWs running in a database using all the primary log files that have
not reached a point of consistency, then a secondary log file is allocated. The
secondary log files are allocated one at the time. Only the crash recovery and
restore recovery methods can be performed when using this type of logging.
Figure 161 shows how log files are used in circular logging:

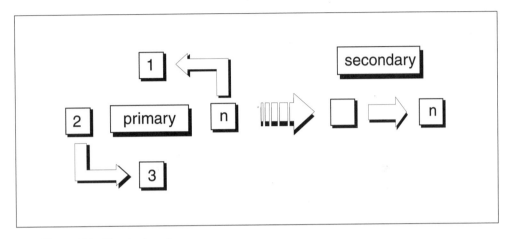

Figure 161. Circular Logging

When using archival logging, roll-forward recovery can be performed.
Roll-forward recovery uses three types of log files to re-apply changes at the
database or table space level (Figure 162):

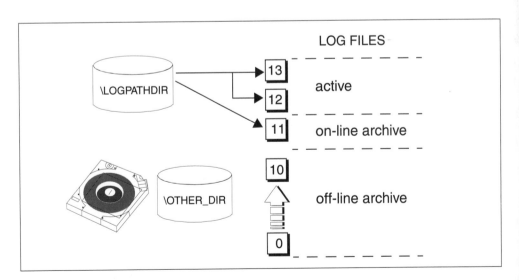

Figure 162. Archival Logging

- Active logs. These are used by crash recovery to place a database into a consistent state. They contain transaction records that have not been committed and also the committed transaction information that has not been written to the database on disk. The active files are located in the database log path directory.

- On-line archived logs. These log files contain the records of data changes that have been committed and written to the database on disk. They are in a closed state and are not needed for normal processing. These file are said to be on-line as they are in the same directory as the active logs.

- Off-line archived logs. This term is used for the on-line archived log files after they have been moved from the database log path directory to another location. This can be done manually or automatically using a userexit program.

6.2.4 Database Configuration Parameters

In this section, we will present the database configuration parameters that are related with database logging. You must have SYSADM, SYSCTRL or SYSMAINT authorization to update them. To enable roll-forward recovery, set either one (or both) of the database configuration parameters, LOGRETAIN or USEREXIT from OFF to ON. As we mentioned before, the default values for those parameters are OFF, which enables restore recovery only.

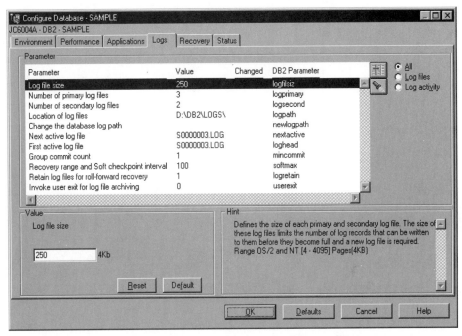

Figure 163. Database Configuration Parameters Related to Database Logging

For example, as shown in Figure 163, you can use the Control Center Configure... database option to display the Logs page. This shows all the database configuration parameters related to database logging:

- LOGPRIMARY. The number of primary logs pre-allocated for database logging.

- SECONDLOG. The number of secondary log files. These file logs are only allocated when they are needed and one at a time. They are created when the primary logs are full of uncommitted transactions.

- LOGFILSZ. The log file size determines the number of pages to allocate for each of the log files. A page is 4 KB in size.

- LOGBUFSZ. The amount of memory to be used as a buffer for log records before writing them to disk.

- NEWLOGPATH. Using this parameter, you can change the location for the active and future archived log files.

- MINCOMMIT. This parameter allows you to group a number of commits before write log records to disk.

- LOGRETAIN. Setting this parameter to ON means that roll-forward recovery can be performed and the archival logging will be used.

- USEREXIT. With USEREXIT=ON, roll-forward recovery is also enabled. In addition, DB2 calls a userexit program to automatically retrieve or archive log files.
- OVERFLOWPATH. This parameter specifies an alternative path to search for archived logs.

The parameters described above can be updated using the Control Center. The same task can also be performed from a Command Window or Command Center by using the DB2 command:

> **UPDATE DATABASE CONFIGURATION FOR** *db* **USING** *parameter*

Table 6 shows the relationship between the values of the LOGRETAIN and USEREXIT parameters, the mode of database logging, the type of backup that you can choose, and the mode of roll-forward. We will explain these relationships in more detail in the following two sections.

Table 6. USEREXIT and LOGRETAIN Parameters

LOGRETAIN	USEREXIT	Logging	Backup	Roll-forward	Description
OFF	OFF	Circular logging	Database off-line	No	Default (LOGRETAIN and USEREXIT=OFF)
ON	OFF	Archive logging	Database or table space on-line or off-line	Point in time or to end of logs	Log files stored in SQLOGDIR
OFF	ON	Archive logging	Database or table space on-line or off-line	Point in time or to end of logs	Log files in SQLOGDIR directory erased by db2uexit
ON	ON	Archive logging	Database or table space on-line or off-line	Point in time or to end of logs	Log files in SQLOGDIR directory erased by db2uexit

> **Note**
>
> When using DB2 UDB Enterprise-Extended Edition (EEE), a table space can only be rolled forward to end of logs (not point in time). See "DB2 UDB Enterprise-Extended Edition" on page 263 for more details about DB2 UDB EEE.

6.2.5 Database and Table Space Backup

In this section, we will discuss the backup utility in DB2 UDB at database and table space levels. To perform a database or table space backup, SYSADM, SYSCTRL or SYSMAINT authorization is required. The database may be located on the local machine or on a remote server. You can backup a database or table space to a fixed disk, a tape, a diskette or a location managed by ADSM or another vendor storage management product.

An off-line database backup implies that other applications cannot access the database during the backup. The backup utility makes an exclusive connection to the database. For an off-line backup, the two database configuration parameters LOGRETAIN and USEREXIT can be either set to ON or OFF. If these parameters are both set to OFF, a restore recovery can be performed and a backup is only possible at the database level. Initially when a database is created these two parameters are set to OFF. To enable roll-forward recovery, either (or both) of the database parameters LOGRETAIN or USEREXIT must be set to ON. The first time this is done for a database, the database is put in a backup pending state. To make the database available, a full off-line backup must be taken.

During an on-line database backup, in contrast with an off-line database backup, the database can be accessed by other applications or processes. An on-line database backup reduces the time during which the database is unavailable. An on-line database backup can to be taken only if roll-forward recovery is enabled. When roll-forward is enabled, the database can be recovered to a point-in-time or to the end of the log files.

In addition to database backups, with LOGRETAIN or USEREXIT set to ON, an on-line or off-line table space backup can be performed. A table space backup contains one or more table spaces in a database, specified when the BACKUP DATABASE utility is executed. A table space backup can be used to recover from problems that only affect specific table spaces. During an off-line table space backup, other applications cannot access the database. In contrast, while an on-line table space backup is taking place, the database is available to other applications. A table space backup can be recovered to a point-in-time or to end of the logs. In addition, a table space backup decreases the time required for the backup operation. For example, you may choose to backup certain key table spaces more often then other less important table spaces.

> **Note**
>
> When you perform a backup of a remote database, whether using the DB2 GUI tools or DB2 Command Window, the backup image is placed on the remote DB2 server machine.

6.2.6 Using the Control Center Backup Database Notebook

Let's look at how to perform a database backup using the Control Center. In Figure 164, you can see the backup options shown when you right-click against a particular database in the Control Center. In this section, we will cover the **Backup Database...** option. See "Database Backup and Recovery Using the SmartGuides" on page 249 for details on how to use the Backup Smartguide.

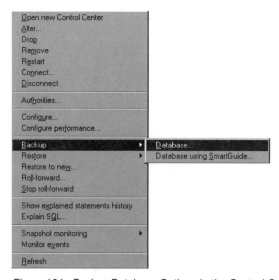

Figure 164. Backup Database Options in the Control Center

Figure 165 on page 235 shows the Backup page in the Backup Database notebook. Here you can choose the media type for the backup image. In our example, the SAMPLE database image will be placed in a directory. In the 'Specify directories or tape' entry box, you can select more than one path and backup the database to more than one location. A backup image which is split over multiple locations will use the same timestamp.

> **Note**
>
> You cannot use a shared drive from a remote machine to store your database backup image. Conversely, you cannot use a remote shared drive to restore a database image to the local machine.

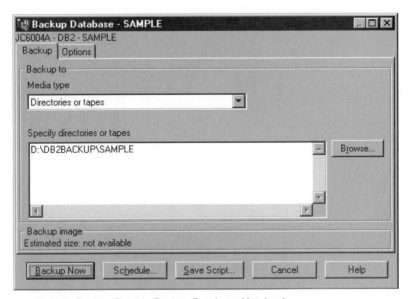

Figure 165. Backup Page in Backup Database Notebook

In the Options page of the Backup Database notebook you can specify whether the backup is to be on-line or off-line. You can also specify performance options for the backup operation, as shown in Figure 166.

As already stated, when a database is first enabled for roll-forward recovery, you are required to perform a full off-line backup. If the Backup Database notebook is used to perform the first backup, you will notice that in the Options page (Figure 166), the on-line mode is grayed-out and only the off-line backup mode is allowed.

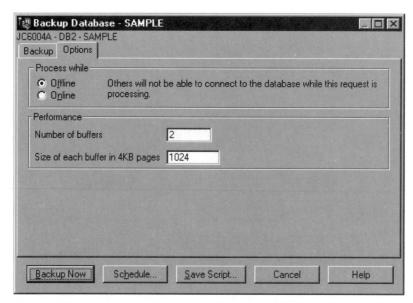

Figure 166. Options Page in the Backup Database Notebook

You can choose to perform the backup immediately, or schedule it for a later time. You can also save the backup command as script file to the Script Center.

For example, we saved a backup database command in a script along with a backup command for the most accessed table space. Figure 167 on page 237 shows the Script Center with the two scripts. Note that the command script is system generated and the content cannot be edited.

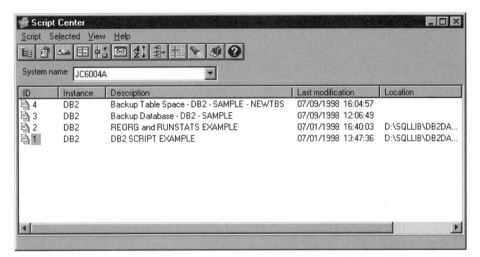

Figure 167. Script Center Showing the Backup Database and Table Space Scripts

Using the Control Center, a table space backup operation is performed in a similar way to the database backup operation. You just click on the **Table Space** folder within the database and select in the contents pane the table space that you want to backup. The backup operation can be selected from the pop-up menu. The Backup Table Space notebook has the same options as the Backup Database notebook.

Alternatively, you can use the BACKUP DATABASE command from a Command Window or the Command Center to perform the backup. For example, the following command takes an on-line table space backup:

```
BACKUP DATABASE SAMPLE TABLESPACE (userspace1,
accounttbs) ONLINE TO C:\db2backup WITH 2 BUFFERS
BUFFER 2048 WITHOUT PROMPTING
```

6.2.7 Backup File Format

If you store a database or table space backup on the Windows NT file system, the backup image file is placed in a multi-level subdirectory tree as follows:

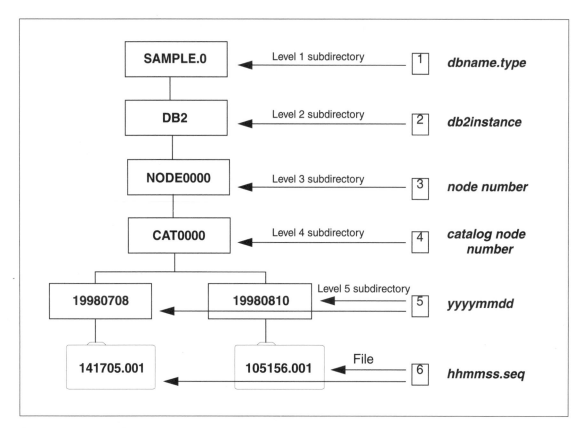

Figure 168. Backup File Format Example

The format of the backup file shown in Figure 168 is as follows:

1. ***dbname.*** 1 to 8 character database alias, followed by:

   - ***type.*** Type of backup taken. **0** for full database backup, **3** for table space level backup, **4** for copy from a table load, and **5** for table unload.

2. ***db2instance.*** 1 to 8 character database instance name.

3. ***nodexxxx.*** The number of the node. In non-partitioned database systems, this is always zero (NODE0000). In a partitioned database system, it is NODExxxx, where xxxx is the number assigned to the node (partition) in the db2nodes.cfg file.

4. ***catnxxxx.*** The number of the catalog node for the database. In non-partitioned database systems, this is always zero (CATN0000). In a partitioned database system, it is CATNxxxx, where xxxx is the number assigned to the node (partition) in the db2nodes.cfg file.

5. **yyyymmdd.** Date (year, month, day), followed by:

- **seq.** A file extension consisting of a 3-digit sequence number.

Note that tape images for backups are not named, but contain the same information in the backup header for verification purposes.

In Figure 168, there are two database backup files for the database alias SAMPLE in the instance DB2. One of them is taken at 14:17:05 on Aug 7, 1998, which is placed in SAMPLE.0\DB2.0\19980807\141705.001. Another one is done at 10:51:56 on Aug 10, 1998, which is placed in SAMPLE.0\DB2.0\19980810\105156.001.

6.2.8 Database and Table Space Restore

In this section, we will discuss the RESTORE utility at both database and table space level as provided by DB2 UDB. We also will explain the use of the ROLLFORWARD utility in the case that the database is recoverable. To perform a database or table space restore, SYSADM, SYSCTRL or SYSMAINT authorization is required. This level of authorization is required for an existing database. If a database restore is performed into a new database, SYSADM or SYSCTRL authorization is required. Figure 169 shows the option to restore a database backup image to a new database. As for backup, you can choose to use the SmartGuide for the restore operation or the simple Restore Notebook.

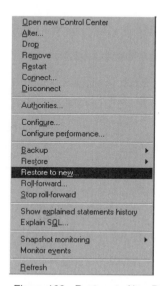

Figure 169. Restore to New Database

If you are restoring a table space backup, you must restore into the same database from which the backup image was taken. In other words, you cannot perform a table space restore into a new database. The database to restore into can be on the local machine or on a remote server. DB2 Universal Database allows you to restore a database or table space from a fixed disk, a tape, a diskette or a location managed by ADSM or another vendor storage management product.

Figure 170 shows the Restore Database notebook pages. On the Backup Image page, you specify the backup image that you want to restore the database from. For example, for our SAMPLE database, we have already created two database backups and a table space backup. If you click on **Select an entry from the list**, the recovery history file for the SAMPLE database is displayed. To select a backup image that is not displayed, you must click on **Manually enter the backup image information**. Once you have selected a backup, the media type and the location for the backup image is displayed.

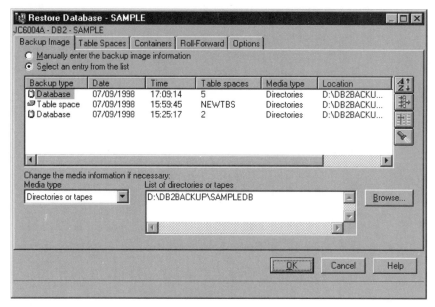

Figure 170. The Restore Database Notebook

A database restore must be done in off-line mode, that is, you require an exclusive connection to the database. When performing a database restore, you can choose which type of restore to perform: either a full restore, partial (a set of table spaces) restore or just the recovery history file. When doing a partial restore, you choose one or more table spaces from the backup image to restore. To do a partial restore, roll-forward recovery must be enabled for the database.

As an example, Figure 171 shows that we have chosen to restore the NEWTBS and ACCTBS table spaces from the SAMPLE database backup image.

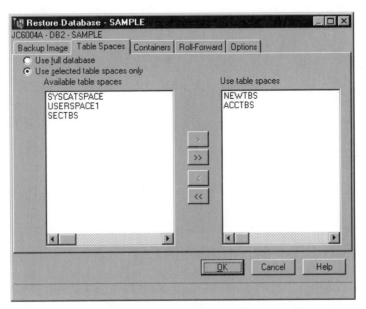

Figure 171. Table Spaces Page on the Restore Database Notebook

As previously stated, the restore operation is the first phase of roll-forward recovery. The second phase is a roll-forward operation. This can be done to the end of logs or to a point-in-time. For example, when an application failure places a database in an inconsistent state, you must first perform a RESTORE DATABASE, followed by a ROLLFORWARD DATABASE to apply the changes held in the log files up to just before the time the corruption occurred. Restore and roll-forward are independent operations.

Using the Control Center Restore Database option, you can also specify that you want to perform roll-forward recovery on the database as part of the restore operation. Figure 172 on page 242 shows the Roll-Forward page. On the Roll-Forward page, click on **Roll-Forward** to indicate that you want to perform roll-forward recovery. Then specify the type of roll-forward recovery that you want: end-of-log or point-in-time recovery. On the Roll-Forward page, clear the **Leave in roll-forward pending state** check box to make the database usable immediately after the restore operation. By default, this check box is on.

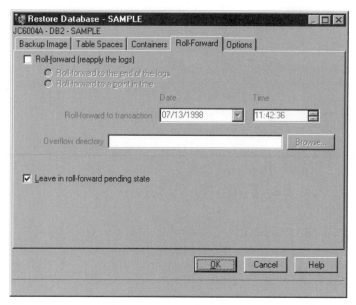

Figure 172. Roll-Forward Page on the Restore Database Notebook

If an off-line database backup is done and roll-forward recovery is enabled for the database, then any subsequent restore can be optionally followed by a roll-forward operation. After the restore, the database is left in a roll-forward pending state and to make the database usable you can just unselect the **Leave in roll-forward pending state** check. In contrast, if an on-line database backup image is restored, then to make the database usable, a roll-forward operation must be performed after the restore (the database will be left in roll-forward pending state after the restore).

When restoring a database level image, as shown in Figure 173, the on-line mode is grayed-out, so only a off-line database restore can be done.

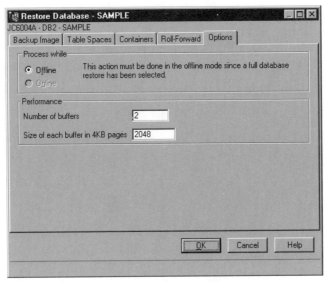

Figure 173. Options Page in Recover Database Notebook

Taking backups at the table space level can help reduce the time during which the database is unavailable. You may want to implement a recovery strategy for individual table spaces because this can save time: it takes less time to recover a portion of the database than it does to recover the entire database.

For example, if a disk is corrupt and it only contains one table space, the table space can be restored and rolled forward without having to recover the entire database (and without impacting user access to the rest of the database). Also, table space backups allow you to back up critical portions of the database more frequently than other portions, which requires less time than backing up the entire database. A table space will be placed in roll-forward pending state after it is restored, or following an I/O error.

For example in Figure 174 on page 244, you can see the state of the NEWTBS table space after the manual deletion of a table space container. The NEWTBS table space had only one file container and the file was accidently deleted.

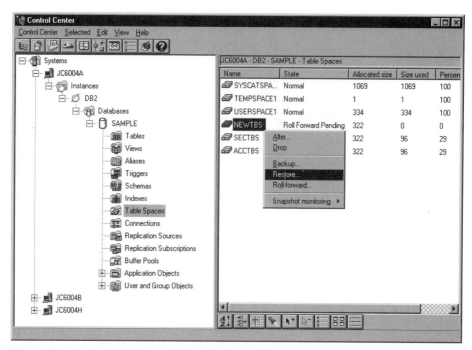

Figure 174. Restore Table Space Using the Control Center

A table space restore can be done either off-line or on-line. During an off-line table space restore, other applications cannot access the database. On the other hand, during an on-line table space restore, other applications can access data in other table spaces within the database. The table space being restored is not accessible. In either of the modes, the table spaces being restored are placed into a roll-forward pending state. All the logs files associated with those table spaces must exist from the time the backup image was created. At the table space level, the recovery process can be performed to the end of logs or to a point-in-time.

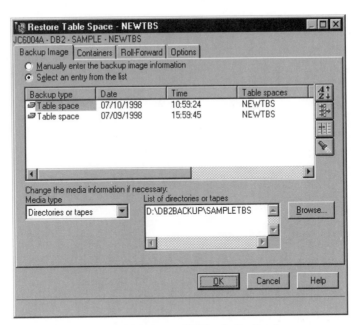

Figure 175. Restore Table Space Notebook, Backup Image

Figure 175 shows the Restore Table Space notebook. It has the same options as the Restore Database notebook, except for the Table Space page. You can see the table space backup images for the NEWTBS table space.

As shown in Figure 176 on page 246, we also will perform a roll-forward to apply the log files to the point-in-time before the I/O error. The roll-forward operation checks for logs in the location specified by the LOGPATH database configuration parameter. If you have moved any logs from the location specified by the LOGPATH parameter, use the **Overflow directory** field to specify the path to the logs that you have moved.

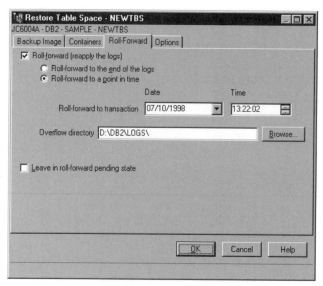

Figure 176. Restore Table Space Notebook, Roll-Forward Page

There are some considerations to be aware of if you want to roll-forward a table space to a point in time:

- You cannot roll-forward system catalog tables to a point in time. These must be rolled forward to the end of the logs to ensure that all table spaces in the database remain consistent.

- If a table is contained in multiple table spaces, all table spaces that contain the table must be rolled forward simultaneously.

- Because the recovered table space must be consistent with the system catalog tables, you cannot perform a table space roll-forward to recover a dropped table space or table, because the catalog table will indicate that the object was previously dropped.

- To roll-forward a table space to a point in time which contains a table participating in a referential integrity relationship with another table from another table space, you should roll-forward both table spaces simultaneously to the same point in time. If you do not, both table spaces will be in the check pending state at the end of the point-in-time roll-forward operation.

- Before rolling forward a table space, use the LIST TABLESPACES SHOW DETAIL command. This command returns information on the Minimum Recover Time, which is the earliest point in time to which the table space can be rolled forward.

6.2.9 Redefining Table Space Containers During Restore

There are certain times when you may need to change the definition of the table space containers in your database. For example, imagine that a media error occurs in a disk device containing one or more database table spaces. During a backup of the database (or one or more of the table spaces), a record is kept of all the table space containers used by the table spaces that are backed up. During a restore, all containers listed in the backup are checked to see if they currently exist and are accessible. If one or more of the containers is inaccessible for any reason, the restore will not complete successfully. A redirect option for table space containers is provided in the RESTORE command. Redirecting table space containers means that the definition of the containers can be changed, and also that containers can be added or removed during the restore of a database.

Continuing the previous example, we will restore from a database backup even though the container listed in the backup does not exist on the system. We will also add a new container to the table space. Figure 177 shows the redirect table space containers option. A second file container, ACCTBS.DMS, will be added to the NEWTBS table space. You can also perform changes to the container listed in the backup image; for instance, increase the space allocated for the container or change the file path.

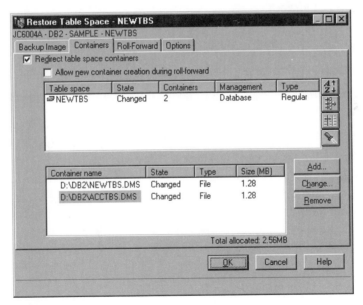

Figure 177. Restore Table Space Using the Redirect Option

If you need to add more disk resource to a DB2 UDB database server machine and you have a disk array, you can use a redirected restore to redistribute table spaces among the newly available disks. You can use the Control Center or the command line to perform a redirected restore.

Note

Redirected restore is not allowed when a user exit program is used to perform the restore.

6.2.10 Recovery History File

A recovery history file (RHF) keeps a history of all recovery-related events for a database. It is created when the database is created. The recovery history file resides in the same directory as the database configuration file and is automatically updated whenever there is a:

- Database or table space backup

- Database or table space restore

- Database or table space roll-forward

- Table space quiesce

- Load of a table

The file contains a summary of the backup information that can be used in the event that all or part of the database must be recovered to a given point in time. The information in the file includes:

- The part of the database that was copied and how it was copied

- The time the copy was made

- The location of the copy (stating both the device information and the logical way to access the copy)

- The last time a restore was done

Every backup operation (both table space and full database) includes a copy of the recovery history file. The recovery history file is linked to the database. Dropping a database deletes the recovery history file.

If the current database is unusable or not available and the associated recovery history file is damaged or deleted, an option on the RESTORE command allows only the recovery history file to be restored. The recovery history file can then be reviewed to provide information on which backup to use to restore the database.

6.3 Database Backup and Recovery Using the SmartGuides

In "DB2 UDB Graphical Tools" on page 191, we discussed the SmartGuides role of performing complex administrative tasks in a very user-friendly way and their integration into the DB2 GUI tools. In this section, we will go through the most important features of the Backup and Restore Database SmartGuides and show you how they can make life easier for a database administrator (DBA). SmartGuides simplify the task of database recovery from database failure or corruption.

6.3.1 Backup Database SmartGuide

The Backup Database SmartGuide helps the DBA to define a database backup plan. The backup strategy is extremely important because it will give the DBA the ability to deal with database recovery in case of critical data loss. The Database Backup SmartGuide will help to define a backup strategy tailored to your business needs. The Database Backup SmartGuide is presented in five pages:

1. *Database*. In the Database page, you select the database you want to backup, either on the local system or on one of the remote systems you are administering.

2. *Availability*. In this page, you enter information about how your database is used. Based on this information, the Backup Database SmartGuide will determine what type of backup you should perform and how often your database should be backed up. Figure 178 on page 250 shows an example of a database that can only be stopped during the weekends. During the week, the database must be available 24 hours per day.

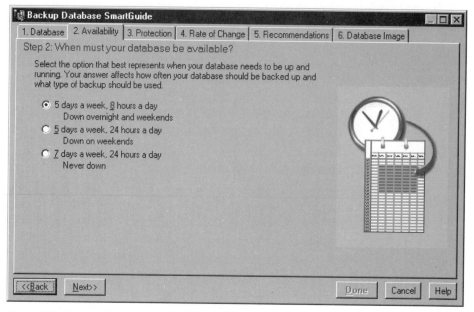

Figure 178. Backup Database SmartGuide, Availability Panel

3. **Protection**. In the Protection page, you select which level of protection you want for your database: fast or complete database recovery. Fast recovery represents circular logging. If you choose this option, you will not be able to perform roll-forward recovery. Complete recovery represents archival logging, which requires more database maintenance. In this example, we chose complete recovery.

4. **Rate of Change**. In this page, you can indicate how much your database is modified per day. The Rate of Change information determines how often the database should be backed up. Note the backup frequency recommended for our example in Figure 179 on page 251.

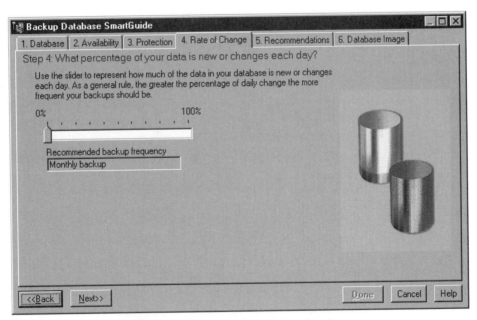

Figure 179. Backup Database SmartGuide, Rate of Change Panel

The decision of when to schedule a backup is a trade off between the time it takes to backup or recover the database and all the amount of data that you can recover after a database failure. In our example, we chose archival logging for the SAMPLE database in the Protection page. If circular logging (fast recovery) had been selected, the Backup Database SmartGuide would have recommended an hourly backup frequency as there are too many data modifications that would be lost in case of failure.

5. ***Recommendations***. The Recommendations page gives a summary of the Database Backup SmartGuide recommendations. You can review the recommendations and override them if necessary. The Backup Database SmartGuide automatically schedules a job for the backup database operation using a script created in the Script Center. By default the scheduled time set is 23:59:59 (you can change this if required). In Figure 180, you can see the recommendations made by the Database Backup SmartGuide tool. Archival logging and on-line backups are recommended.

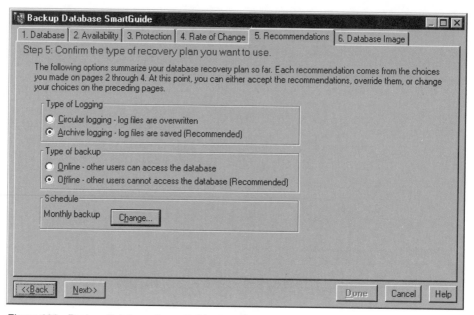

Figure 180. Backup Database SmartGuide, Recommendations Panel

6.3.2 Restore Database SmartGuide

The Restore Database SmartGuide leads you through a number of steps to recover your database. In "Database and Table Space Restore" on page 239, we described how to recover a database using the Restore Database notebook, which requires more knowledge and can be used for more complex recovery database tasks. The Restore Database SmartGuide has three pages:

1. ***Restore Status***. As shown in Figure 181 on page 253, on the Restore Status page, you can select the database you want to restore. This may be a database on the local system or on a remote system that you are administering.

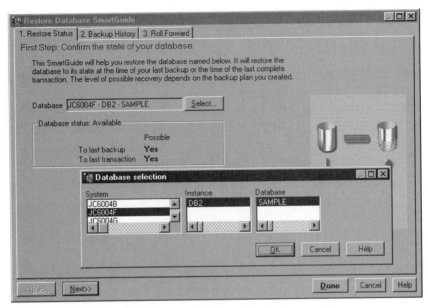

Figure 181. Restore Database SmartGuide, Restore Status Panel

The database status box helps you to understand the current state of the database you want to restore. The database state can be:

- Available. Indicates that the database is available for use.

- Inconsistent. Indicates that a transaction is pending or some other task is pending on the database and the data is not consistent at this point.

- Backup Pending. This state indicates that a full backup of the database must be done before accessing it.

- Roll-Forward Pending. The database is being or has to be rolled forward from the contents of the database log files.

- Table Space Roll-Forward Pending. Changes to a single table space are being or has to be rolled forward from the contents of the database log files.

- Unknown. Indicates that a connection cannot be established to the database. The connection may be faulty, or the database may not be started.

2. ***Backup History***. In this page, you select the database backup image you want to use for the restore operation. All the database backup images shown are read from the database recovery history file.

3. **Roll Forward**. Figure 182 shows this page. Here you can apply the log files to redo all the changes made in the database since the database backup image was taken.

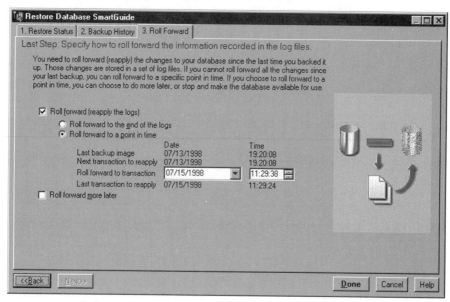

Figure 182. Restore Database SmartGuide, Roll Forward Panel

6.4 DB2 UDB for Windows NT Tape Support

DB2 UDB for Windows NT supports backup and restore to streaming tape devices. The tape media to be used for database backup and restore must be available through the standard operating system interface. Figure 183 on page 255, shows the SCSI adapter tape device type in the Control Panel of Windows NT.

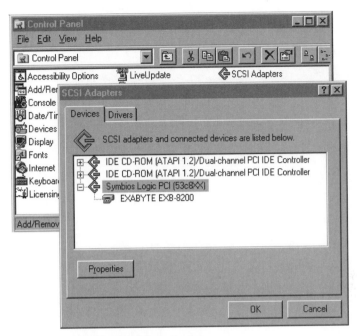

Figure 183. SCSI Adapter Tape Devices

Clicking on the **Tape Device** icon in the Control Panel, you can see the properties for the tape devices in your Windows NT system. Figure 184 on page 256 shows the Device Mapping and the Status.

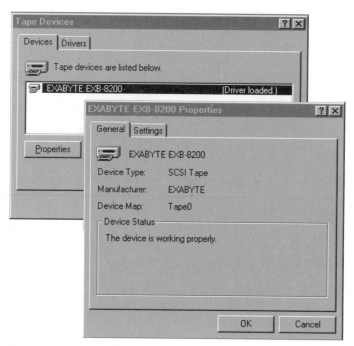

Figure 184. Tape Device Properties

When performing a backup operation to tape, information about the database is stored in the backup header for verification purposes at restore time. The DB2 UDB database image created using the backup has a format that can only be restored using a DB2 UDB restore. Other applications will not recognize the format used by DB2. For example, Figure 185 on page 257 shows the message given by the NTBACKUP tool when trying to read a tape which holds a DB2 backup image.

Figure 185. Windows NT Backup Tool

DB2 UDB provides commands for performing tape preparation before using the BACKUP or RESTORE commands. You can use the Command Center or a Command Window to perform these steps. The following DB2 UDB commands are available for tape initialization and positioning:

```
REWIND TAPE [ON device]
SET TAPE POSITION [ON device] TO position
INITIALIZE TAPE [ON device] [USING blocksize]
```

For these tape management commands:

device This must be a valid Windows NT tape device name. This parameter is optional and defaults to the first device, TAPE0. For example, "\\.\TAPE0" is the first tape device.

position This is the tape mark position. DB2 for Windows NT supports the writing of TAPEMARKS and SETMARKS. It writes a tape mark after every backup. Thus, position 1 is the tape mark after the first archive. Position 2 is the tape mark after the second archive, and so forth. If the tape is positioned at tape mark 1, archive 2 is positioned to be restored.

block size This is the block size to be used for the device. It is checked against the range of blocking sizes valid for the device. It must also be a proper factor, or a multiple of 4096. This parameter is optional and defaults to the default blocking factor for the hardware you are using.

When the tape media is being accessed by another application or tape is in a open state, any access by DB2 UDB will result in an error message. For example, Figure 186 shows the error message displayed if you try to initialize the tape using the DB2 UDB INITIALIZE TAPE command while the NTBACKUP tool is already using the tape drive:

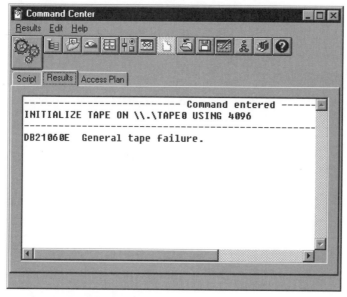

Figure 186. Initialize Tape Command

The following considerations and recommendations should be noted when using tapes with DB2 UDB for Windows NT:

1. It is recommended to use a blocking factor of 4096 and a buffer of 16 for both backup and restore.

2. If your data is absolutely critical, you should consider using duplicate tape media.

3. The tape media for database backup and restore operations must be available through the standard operating system interface. On a large partitioned database system, however, it may not be practical to have a tape device dedicated to each database partition server.

4. If your database is enabled for roll-forward recovery and you are using a tape system that does not support the ability to uniquely reference a

backup, it is recommended that you do not keep multiple backup copies of the same database on the same tape.

5. If you are using the BACKUP command for concurrent backup processes to tape, ensure that the processes do not target the same tape.

6.4.1 Backing Up To Tape

Let's go through a sample scenario for backing up a DB2 UDB database to tape. We created a DB2 UDB command script in the Script Center to perform the backup operations, as shown in Figure 187. See "Script Center" on page 209 for information how to create a command script.

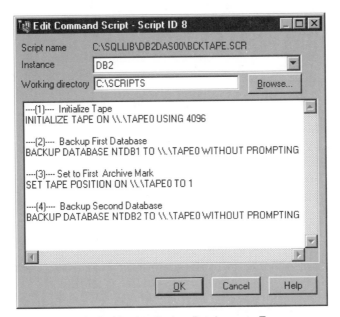

Figure 187. Script Used to Backup Databases to Tape

In the script shown in Figure 187:

1. Before backing up the first database, the first DB2 command shown initializes a tape with a block size of 4096 bytes.

   DB2 UDB opens the tape, rewinds it, and queries the device to see if the blocking factor is acceptable. If the blocking factor had not been specified, DB2 UDB would have queried the default block size of the device and used that.

2. The second step shows the DB2 UDB command used to perform a backup of the NTDB1 database. The backup is performed to tape device 0. When the backup is finished, a tape mark is written and the tape will not be

rewound automatically (you can use the REWIND TAPE command to do this).

3. In backing up the NTDB2 database, the DB2 command shown in step 3 positions the tape to the mark after the first archive. DB2 UDB first determines whether the device supports direct positioning. If it does not, the tape will be rewound first and then positioned.

4. The last command takes the backup of the second database, NTDB2.

The following considerations should be noted when backing up DB2 UDB databases (or table spaces) to tape on Windows NT:

- It is recommended to put only one backup image on a tape cartridge. In this way, if a backup fails for any reason, you can erase the entire tape and start again.

- If the backup image needs to span over multiple tapes, DB2 will prompt for a new tape unless you specify the WITHOUT PROMPTING option of the BACKUP DATABASE command.

- After changing the tape during backup or restore operations, allow enough time for the tape device to re-initialize before entering c to continue the backup or restore. This time varies by tape device. This hardware initialization may take as long as three to five minutes. If this is not done properly, the backup or restore will not complete successfully.

- You can not partially erase a tape if you have multiple backup images on a tape. If you want to reuse the tape at all, the entire tape must be erased.

6.4.2 Restoring From Tape

Now let's look at how to restore DB2 database backups from tape. We created a DB2 UDB command script in the Script Center to perform the restore operations. Figure 188 on page 261 shows the DB2 UDB command script we used:

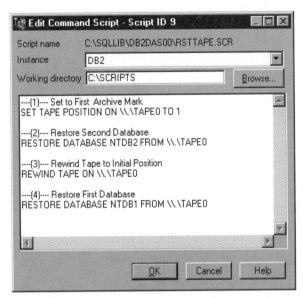

```
Edit Command Script - Script ID 9                    _ □ X

Script name      C:\SQLLIB\DB2DAS00\RSTTAPE.SCR
Instance         DB2                                        ▼
Working directory C:\SCRIPTS                          Browse...

----(1)---- Set to First Archive Mark
SET TAPE POSITION ON \\.\TAPE0 TO 1

----(2)---- Restore Second Database
RESTORE DATABASE NTDB2 FROM \\.\TAPE0

----(3)---- Rewind Tape to Initial Position
REWIND TAPE ON \\.\TAPE0

----(4)---- Restore First Database
RESTORE DATABASE NTDB1 FROM \\.\TAPE0


              OK        Cancel        Help
```

Figure 188. Script Used to Restore Databases from Tape

In the script shown in Figure 188:

1. Before restoring the NTDB2 database in the second archive, step 1 positions the tape to the second archive.

2. The restore command is performed for the second database, NTDB2.

3. To restore the first archive, the DB2 command in step 3 rewinds the tape to position 0, where the NTDB1 backup is stored.

4. This step restores first database, NTDB1.

The following considerations should be noted when performing a restore from tape using DB2 UDB on Windows NT:

1. The tape is assumed to be positioned. If it is not, you will receive a warning reporting an I/O error. The device is opened and read until the end of file (the next tapemark) is detected. The tape is rewound and ejected if the tape device supports it.

2. If the backup image spans over multiple tapes, DB2 will prompt you for a new tape unless you specify the WITHOUT PROMPTING option of the RESTORE DATABASE command.

6.4.3 Disaster Recovery Considerations

The term disaster recovery is used to describe the activities that need to be performed to restore the database in the event of a fire, earthquake, vandalism, or another catastrophic event. A plan for disaster recovery can include one or more of the following:

- A site to be used in the event of an emergency

- A different machine on which to recover the database

- Off-site storage of database backups and archived logs

If your plan for disaster recovery is to recover the entire database on another machine, you require at least one full database backup and all the archived logs for the database. When operating your business with this consideration, you may choose to keep a standby database up-to-date by applying the logs to it as they are archived. Or, you may choose to keep the database backup and log archives in the standby site, and perform a restore/roll-forward only after a disaster has occurred. (In this case, a recent database backup is clearly desirable). With a disaster, however, it is generally not possible to recover all of the transactions up to the time of the disaster.

The usefulness of a table space backup for disaster recovery depends on the scope of the failure. When a major disaster occurs, a full database backup is needed on a standby site. If the disaster is a damaged disk, then a table space backup (for each table space using that disk) can be used to recover. If you have lost access to a container because of a disk failure (or for any other reason), you can restore the container to a different location.

With critical business data being stored in your database, you should plan for the possibility of a natural or man-made disaster affecting your database. Both table space backups and full database backups can have a role to play in any disaster recovery plan. The DB2 facilities available for backing up, restoring, and rolling forward data changes provide a foundation for a disaster recovery plan. You should ensure that you have tested the recovery procedures in place to protect your business.

Chapter 7. DB2 UDB Enterprise-Extended Edition

DB2 UDB Enterprise-Extended Edition (EEE) is an implementation of a *partitioned* database management system. This means that a DB2 UDB EEE system typically includes multiple machines, with data spread across these machines. This chapter will discuss the concepts involved in such a system, such as nodegroups, partitioning, and manipulation of the DB2 objects. We also cover the installation of DB2 UDB EEE including a step-by-step example.

7.1 DB2 UDB EEE Concepts

Let's start by introducing some of the basic concepts of DB2 UDB Enterprise-Extended Edition:

- A *database* is simply a collection of data.

- A *database manager* is the software that allows users to store and access data in a database. It achieves this function by using system resources, including CPU, memory, disk, and communications.

  In a partitioned database system, a single database manager and the collection of data and system resources that it manages are referred to collectively as a *database partition server*. A database partition server is also known as a *node*.

- A *partitioned database system* consists of one or more database partition servers.

  In a partitioned database system, multiple database partition servers can be assigned per machine (or across machines), and each database manager is responsible for a portion of a database's total data (each database partition server houses a portion of a database). This portion of a database is known as a *database partition*. The fact that databases are partitioned across database partition servers is transparent to general users.

- In DB2 UDB EEE, an *instance* contains all the database partition servers (nodes) that have been defined to take part in a given partitioned database system. An instance has its own databases and instance directory. The instance directory contains the database manager configuration file, system database directories, node directories, etc.

- You can have multiple instances on the same machine, with each configured differently:

  - To have distinct test and production environments
  - To restrict access to specific databases

- To exploit different database configurations

Each instance is owned by the machine where the instance was first created (known as the instance-owning machine). The instance-owning machine stores information that is common to all of the database partition servers involved in that instance.

We illustrate the preceding concepts as follows:

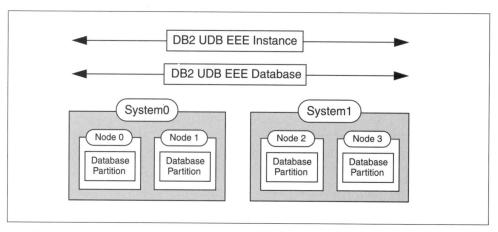

Figure 189. DB2 UDB EEE Concepts

Figure 189 shows four database partition servers (or nodes), labelled Node 0, Node 1, Node 2, and Node 3, that are all defined in the DB2 UDB EEE instance. There are two database partition servers per system (or machine). Each database partition server manages its portion (or database partition) of any databases created in the instance.

7.1.1 Database Partition Servers per Machine

DB2 UDB EEE is a *shared nothing* architecture, in which machines do not have to compete for resources and each machine has exclusive access to its own disks and memory, and the machines communicate with each other through the use of messages. A single database partition server is typically assigned to each machine. Because a database can be partitioned across multiple machines, you can use multiple CPUs to satisfy requests for information. The retrieval and update requests are decomposed automatically into sub-requests and executed in parallel on each database partition server on each machine.

There are times, however, when it is advantageous to have several database partition servers running per machine. In this case, the machine is said to be configured with *multiple logical nodes.*

Multiple logical nodes should be considered when:

- You are using symmetric multiprocessor (SMP) machines. The processing of each database partition server can be shared across the multiple CPUs on each machine.

- You need to support failover. If a machine fails (causing the database partition server or servers on it to fail), you can restart the database partition server (or servers) on another machine. This ensures that user data remains available.

The DB2NODE environment variable is used to indicate to which target partition to route local requests to (see "Connecting to a Logical Node" on page 281). This variable is set in the session in which the application or command is issued. If this variable is not set, the target logical node defaults to the logical node which is defined with port 0 on the machine (or what is set in the DB2NODE registry variable). It is also important to note that in a multiple logical node environment, remote clients can only connect into the node associated with port 0. (We discuss the concept of a port later in this chapter.)

See also "Managing DB2 Database Partitions" on page 281 for more information about commands for managing DB2 database partitions.

7.1.2 Coordinator Node

A user's or application's interaction with a database in a DB2 UDB EEE instance is handled through one database partition server (node). This database partition server is known as the *coordinator node* and is the partition to which the user or application connect to the database. Any physical database partition server can be used as a coordinator node (in an MLN environment, only logical node 0 may be used as the coordinating node). If you have a large number of users, you may wish to consider spreading users across database partitions servers to distribute the coordinator function (i.e., having more than one coordinator partition).

7.1.3 Nodegroups

You can define named subsets of one or more database partitions in a database. Each subset you define is known as a *nodegroup.*

Each subset that contains more than one database partition is known as a *multipartition nodegroup*. Multipartition nodegroups can only be defined with database partitions that belong to the same database.

Three default nodegroups are created when you create a database: IBMDEFAULTGROUP, IBMCATGROUP and IBMTEMPGROUP.

- The IBMDEFAULTGROUP nodegroup contains all the database partitions for the database. When you create a database, a database partition is created at each database partition server (node) in the instance.

- The IBMCATGROUP nodegroup for the database is created at the database partition server where you issued the create database command. This nodegroup only contains one database partition server, the local machine where the command was issued. This database partition server is referred to as the catalog node of the database as it contains the catalog tables for the database.

- IBMTEMPGROUP, like IBMDEFAULTGROUP, contains all database partitions in your database. You cannot however directly manipulate this nodegroup. This nodegroup is used to contain temporary tables spaces (and hence temporary tables) used by DB2.

When you want to create table spaces in a database, you first create the nodegroup where the table spaces will be stored (or use the default nodegroup IBMDEFAULTGROUP), then create a table space in the nodegroup. Finally, you create the tables in the table space.

You can remove database partitions from a nodegroup, or if new partitions have been defined, add them to a nodegroup in the database.

As your database increases in size, you may choose to add database partition servers to the database system. This may provide you with improved performance. When you add a database partition server, a database partition is created for each database that already exists in the database system. To be able to take advantage of this new partition in a database, you add the new database partition to an existing nodegroup that belongs to that database. Finally you want to move some of your data to this new partition by redistributing your data across your nodegroup.

Figure 190 on page 267, illustrates the nodegroup, database and system relationships as follows:

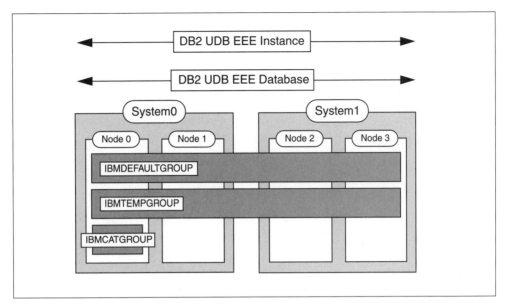

Figure 190. Default Nodegroups

Remember that when a database is created in the DB2 UDB EEE instance shown in Figure 190, the IBMDEFAULTGROUP and IBMTEMPGROUP nodegroups are created and include all the nodes (database partition servers). The IBMCATGROUP is created and includes only the node at which the database was created (in this case Node 0).

7.1.4 The DB2 Node Configuration File

The definition of database partition servers in a DB2 instance is contained in the *node configuration file*. This file contains configuration information for all database partitions in an instance, and is shared by all database partitions for that instance. It is created for you when you create the DB2 for Windows NT EEE instance and is accessed and manipulated using DB2 commands on the DB2 UDB for Windows NT system.

When you install DB2 UDB EEE for Windows NT, an instance with multipartition support is created and the node configuration file configured automatically. Any manipulation of database partitions also updates this file.

The node configuration file (when listed using the db2nlist command) contains one line for each database partition server that belongs to an instance. Each line has the following format:

```
Node: "nn" Host: "hhhh"  Machine: "mmmm"  Port: "n"
```

The values are as follows:

- **Node** specifies the node number, which identifies the database partition server. This number can be from 0 to 999 and uniquely defines a node. The node/partition numbers will be listed in ascending sequence. There can be gaps in the sequence.

  Once a node number is assigned, it cannot be changed. If a partition is removed from your instance configuration, its number can be reused for any new partition that is added.

  The node number will also be used to generate a node name in the database directory path. The name has the format "NODE*nnnn*" where nnnn is the node number, which is left-padded with zeros. This node number can also be used in the CREATE DATABASE and DROP DATABASE commands.

  For example, if you have an instance named DB2, with two partitions (0 and 1), running on the same server, the directory DB2 on that server will have subdirectories NODE0000 and NODE0001.

- **Host** specifies the default hostname associated with the IP address for inter-partition communications.

- **Machine** is the computer name of the Windows NT workstation on which the partition resides.

- **Port** specifies the logical port number used for the database partition server. On every machine, there must be a database partition server that has a logical port 0. The port number will not exceed the port range reserved for FCM communications in the services file in the x:\winnt\system32\drivers\etc\ directory. For example, if you reserve a range of 4 ports for the current instance, then the maximum port number would be 3 (ports 1, 2, and 3; port 0 is for the default logical node)

The following example shows a possible node configuration (using the db2nlist command) for a Windows NT DB2 UDB EEE partitioned database system, consisting of three machines, TOR, SAN and AUS. Machine SAN has two logical partitions on it as we see the Port 0 and Port 1 values. The other two machines have only one logical partition currently defined on them.

```
Node: "0" Host: "HOST1" Machine: "TOR" Port: "0"
Node: "1" Host: "HOST2" Machine: "SAN" Port: "0"
Node: "2" Host: "HOST2" Machine: "SAN" Port: "1"
Node: "3" Host: "HOST3" Machine: "AUS" Port: "0"
```

For a complete list and description of the DB2 UDB EEE for Windows NT commands you must use to list, and manipulate the node configuration file, please refer to the Quick Beginnings for DB2 Enterprise-Extended Edition documentation.

7.1.5 Partitioning

Each table defined in a multipartition nodegroup has a *partitioning key* associated with it. The partitioning key is an ordered set of columns whose values are used in conjunction with a *partitioning map* to determine the database partition on which a row of a given table resides. The partitioning map is an array of 4096 database partition numbers.

See Figure 191 on page 270 for an example of how the partitioning key is used to determine which database partition a row is located.

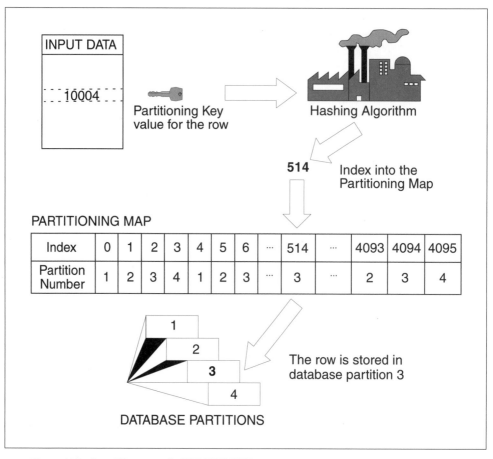

Figure 191. Data Placement in DB2 UDB EEE

In this example, in order to find out in which database partition a given row is stored in, DB2 performs the following steps:

- The partitioning key value of the row (in this example, 10004) is used as input for a hashing algorithm. This algorithm transforms the partition key value into a number between 0 and 4095 that is an index into the partitioning map.

- The partitioning map contains a value at that index that indicates the database partition where the row is to be stored/found.

Columns of any data type (except long or large object data types) can be used in the partitioning key. A table defined in a single-partition nodegroup may or may not have a partitioning key. Tables with only long-field columns can be defined only in single-partition nodegroups, and they cannot have a partitioning key.

The use of nodegroups and partitioning keys means that:

- Data can be distributed across multiple database partitions to reduce I/O and processing bottlenecks.
- Data can be redistributed when large volumes of system activity or increases in table size require the addition of more machines.

7.2 Managing DB2 UDB EEE Instances

This section covers several common tasks used to manage DB2 UDB EEE instances. Note that many of the commands and utilities used are virtually identical to their counterpart in a single partition environment. However there are often additional parameters which are required for a multipartition environment.

The tasks to be covered include:

- Creating a multipartition instance
- Listing instances
- Starting/stopping instances
- Removing instances

7.2.1 Creating a Multipartition Instance

By default, the DB2MPP instance is created as part of the instance owning server installation. If you need to create another DB2 multipartition instance you use the `db2icrt` command, much as you would for a single partition DB2 instance, but with additional parameters. The machine that you run the `db2icrt` command on will become the instance-owning machine (node 0). It is recommended that you always create instances on a machine where a DB2 Administration Server resides.

Note

You can choose to update an existing single partition instance to a multipartition format using the `db2iupdt` command. See "Updating a DB2 instance to a Multipartition System" on page 274.

To create an instance, perform the following steps:

1. You must be logged on as a domain user. You will use this account to not only install the instance owning partition, but all other partitions in this configuration. It is recommended that this account be part of the Domain Administrator's group. If it is not, it must have local administrator authority for each machine in the partitioned database system (this scenario creates more administrative work). If it is, it automatically has local administrator authority on any of the machines within the domain.

2. From any command prompt, run the `db2icrt` command as follows:

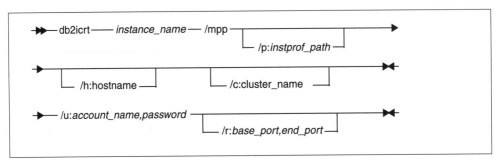

Figure 192. Syntax of the db2icrt Command

where:

- ***instance_name*** is the name of the instance.

- **/mpp** specifies that this is a partitioned database system.

- **/p: *instprof_path*** specifies the instance profile path. This parameter is optional. If you do not specify the instance profile path, the instance directory is created under the \sqllib directory, and given the shared name "DB2-*instance_name*". Read and write permissions will automatically be granted to everyone in the domain.

  To specify a different instance profile path, you must create a Windows NT shared drive or directory first. The instprof_path parameter must use the universal naming convention (UNC), and include both the network name and the share name that were created: /p:\\network_name\share_name. For example, to use a file share DB2-DB2MPP on server server0, specify:

  ```
  /p:\\server0\DB2-DB2MPP
  ```

- **/h:host_name** to override the default TCP/IP hostname if the there is more than one TCP/IP hostname for the current machine. The TCP/IP hostname is used when creating the default node (node 0).

- **/c:cluster_name** to specify the MSCS cluster name. This option is specified to create a DB2 instance that supports MSCS.

- **/u:*account_name, password*** specifies the domain account used as the logon account name of the DB2 Service. For example, to use a domain account of db2admin in the JCEEEDOM domain, password db2admin, specify:

  ```
  /u:jceeedom\db2admin,db2admin
  ```

- **/r: *base_port, end_port*** specifies the TCP/IP port range used for inter-node communications; for example, to use a range of 10013 to 10017, specify:

  ```
  /r:10013,10017
  ```

  This parameter is optional. The services file of the local machine will be updated with the following entries if this option is specified

  ```
  DB2_instance_name            base_port/tcp
  DB2_instance_name_END        end_port/tcp
  ```

  The port range you specify must be at least equal to the number of logical nodes running on the machine. To select a port range that is available on the machine, check the services file which is located in the x:\winnt\system32\drivers\etc directory, where x: is the drive on which you installed Windows NT. It is important to note that this port range must be available on machines which will participate in this partitioned database system.

  If this option is not specified, the db2icrt command will select a port range that is available on your system.

3. Optionally, you may also wish to perform the following tasks after creating the instance:

   1. Create a DB2 Administration Server, if one does not already exist on this physical machine.

   2. Update the database manager configuration for the newly created DB2 instance, to allow DB2 clients to access the databases that will be created in this instance. For example:

      - Use db2set to update the DB2COMM registry variable.

      - Use db2 update dbm cfg to update the SVCENAME parameter for TCP/IP support, or NNAME for NETBIOS support.

      See "DB2 UDB Client/Server Communications" on page 123 for more details about setting up communications for DB2.

   3. Add the instance to the DB2 Control Center. See "Adding the DB2 Instance to the Control Center" on page 277.

> **Note**
>
> The `db2icrt` command grants the username used to create the instance
> the following Windows NT rights:
>
> - Act as a part of the operating system
> - Create a token object
> - Increase quota
> - Logon as a service
> - Replace a process level token.
>
> The instance requires these user rights to access the shared drive,
> authenticate the user account, and run DB2 as a Windows NT service.

7.2.2 Updating a DB2 instance to a Multipartition System

To update a single partition instance to a partitioned instance, you use the
`db2iupdt` command. DB2 UDB EEE for Windows NT must have been already
installed on the system. The syntax of the db2iupdt command is:

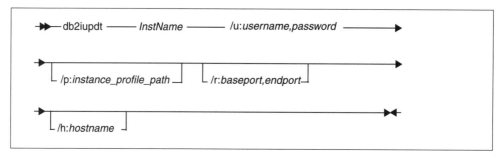

Figure 193. Syntax of the db2iupdt Command

where the parameters are the same as for the `db2icrt` command with the
exception of:

- *InstName* is the name of the instance to be updated.

- */h:hostname* specifies a hostname to override the default TCP/IP
  hostname, if there is more than one TCP/IP hostname for the current
  machine.

Refer to the DB2 UDB EEE Quick Beginnings for further tasks to be
performed before and after the updating of a DB2 instance to a partitioned
database system.

7.2.3 Listing Instances

Listing instances in a multipartition database system is similar to that for a single partition database system. To get a list of all the instances that are available on a system,

- From the Control Center, click against the **[+]** on the required system to display the instances defined on that system (see Figure 194 on page 276).

- Alternately, in any command window, enter:

```
db2ilist
```

7.2.4 Starting a DB2 Instance

You must start an instance before you can perform the following tasks:

- Connect to a database on the instance
- Precompile an application
- Bind a package to a database
- Access host databases

To start an instance manually, you can either log on as a Windows NT Administrator or log in with a username that has SYSADM, SYSMAINT, or SYSCTRL authority on the instance (and also has the right to start a Windows NT Service by being a member of the Administrators, Server Operators or Power Users group in Windows NT), and use one of these methods to start the instance:

- From the Control Center, click with the right mouse button on the instance that you want to start, and select the **Start** option from the pop-up menu (Figure 194).

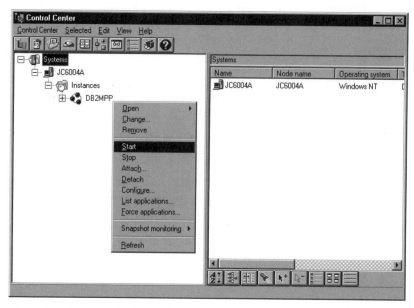

Figure 194. Starting a Database Instance from the DB2 UDB Control Center

- Alternately, from a command line, enter the `db2start` command as follows:

```
db2start
```

The `db2start` command will start the instance as defined by the value of the DB2INSTANCE environment variable in that command line session.

7.2.5 Stopping a DB2 Instance

To stop an instance, log in with a username that has SYSADM, SYSMAINT, or SYSCTRL authority on the instance, ensure there are no applications and users attached to the database, and use one of these methods:

- From the Control Center, click with the right mouse button on the instance that you want to stop and select the **Stop** option from the pop-up menu. See Figure 194 on page 276 (except this time choose "Stop" as the action to perform on the instance selected).

- From a command line, enter the `db2stop` command as follows:

```
db2stop
```

The `db2stop` command will stop the instance defined by the DB2INSTANCE environment variable. It can be run as an operating system command or as a Command Line Processor command. This command can only be run at the server. No database connections are allowed when running this command; however, if there are any instance attachments, they are forced off before DB2 is stopped.

7.2.6 Adding the DB2 Instance to the Control Center

By default, the DB2MPP instance that is created as part of the instance owning node installation is cataloged in the DB2 UDB Control Center, under the Instances subtree for that system. However, new instances created with the `db2icrt` command (see "Creating a Multipartition Instance" on page 271) will not be displayed unless they are added manually.

To add a newly created DB2 instance to the Control Center list of instances, perform the following steps:

1. Start the DB2 UDB Control Center.

2. Expand the subtree for the system where the instance has been created.

3. Select the Instances object, then click on the right mouse button and select **Add** (Figure 195):

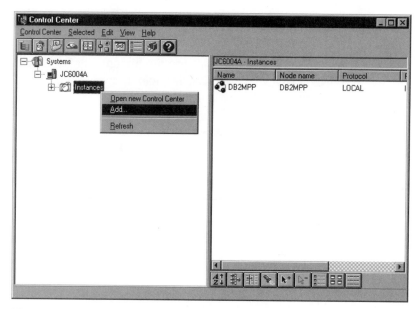

Figure 195. Adding an Instance to the Control Center List

4. Click on **Refresh** button in the *Add Instance* window to refresh the list of instances shown.

5. Once this is done, you will see a list of instances for the *Remote instance* choice (See Figure 196 on page 279, where we have two instances, the default DB2MPP, and a second newly created instance called ANT). From this pulldown list, choose the appropriate one to be added, and click on the **Apply** button.

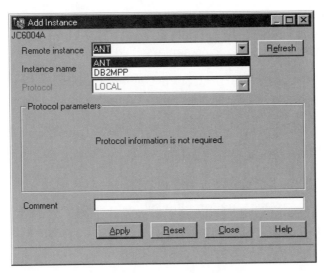

Figure 196. Choosing an Instance to be Added.

6. Click on the **Close** button to close the *Add Instance* window.

7. You will notice that the list of instances in the right hand panel has been updated to show the newly added instance (see Figure 197, where it now shows two instances, DB2MPP and ANT)

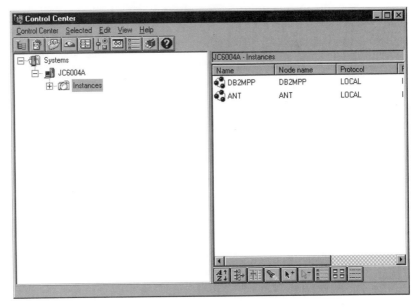

Figure 197. New List of Instances

By default, the DB2 UDB Control Center runs in the default instance environment. You can also start the Control Center within a different instance, by setting the DB2INSTANCE environment variable, and running `db2cc` (the DB2 UDB Control Center executable) within that session.

If so, note that the DB2 UDB Control Center may display a different set of instances and databases compared to the default instance. For example, using our previous example, if you start the Control Center from a session with a DB2INSTANCE of ANT, you will see ANT listed as an instance, and have to manually add DB2MPP.

7.2.7 Removing a DB2 Instance

To remove an instance, perform the following steps:

1. Quit all applications that are currently using the instance.

2. Stop the Command Line Processor by running `db2 terminate` command in each DB2 command window, as follows:

```
db2 terminate
```

3. Stop the instance by running the `db2stop` command. Remember to set the DB2INSTANCE environment variable to the appropriate DB2 instance.

4. Back up the instance directory indicated by the DB2INSTPROF registry value. For example, you might want to save the database manager configuration file, which is kept in the db2systm file.

5. Issue the `db2idrop` command as follows:

```
db2idrop InstName
```

where **InstName** is the name of the instance being dropped.

This command removes the instance entry from the list of instances and removes the instance directory.

6. If you manually added the instance just dropped to any DB2 Control Center window, you will now want to go back and remove this instance from that window following similar steps as before, but this time choosing the remove option from the pulldown when you right mouse button click on the instance to be removed.

7.3 Managing DB2 Database Partitions

This section covers some common tasks for manipulating DB2 database partition servers (also called nodes) in a multipartition database environment. The tasks to be covered include:

- Listing database partition servers
- Connecting to a logical node

7.3.1 Listing Database Partition Servers

Use the `db2nlist` command to obtain a list of database partition servers that participate in an instance. The syntax of the command is as follows:

Figure 198. Syntax of the db2nlist command

where:

- **/i:*instance_name*** specifies the instance name; the default is the current instance (set by the DB2INSTANCE environment variable.

- **/s** displays the status of each node. The status of each node can be one of the following:

  - Starting
  - Running
  - Stopping
  - Stopped

For example, to run a `db2nlist` command against the two node DB2MPP instance:

```
C:\>db2nlist /s
List of nodes for instance "DB2MPP" is as follows:
Node: "0" Host: "jc6004a" Machine: "JC6004A" Port: "0" - "running"
Node: "1" Host: "jc6004f" Machine: "JC6004F" Port: "0" - "running"
```

7.3.2 Connecting to a Logical Node

The default logical node is the one that has a value of 0 for the logical_port. By default, a local client connects to the default logical node unless the DB2NODE environment variable is set to another node number (remote clients will only be able to connect to the partition server associated with logical port value 0). For all commands and applications that connect to a database, you must ensure that the DB2NODE environment variable is set to reference the node number of the logical node that you want the operation to run on. You can find this node number by running the db2nlist command. If the database partition server being connected to is not started on the machine, the application returns an error. In DB2 UDB EEE, the set client command can also be used to target a specific node within a partitioned database system. For more information, refer to the DB2 UDB Command Reference.

As an example, assume that you want to update the configuration of a database partition server that belongs to a database called SAMPLE, and that database partition server is on a machine called SERVER1. Also assume that you defined nodes 0 and 1 on SERVER1.

Because database configuration is defined at the database partition level, you would connect to each logical node on the machine and change the database configuration. You could do the following in two sessions on SERVER1:

1. In session 1:

    1. Set DB2NODE=0 using the following command:

    ```
    set db2node=0
    ```

    2. Connect to the database partition server on logical node 0. Issue the following statement:

    ```
    db2 connect to sample
    ```

    3. Update the database configuration file for the particular server.

    4. End the connection by issuing the following statements:

    ```
    db2 connect reset
    db2 terminate
    ```

2. In session 2:

    1. Set DB2NODE=1 using the following command:

```
set db2node=1
```

2. Connect to the database partition server on logical node 1. Issue the following statement:

```
db2 connect to sample
```

3. Update the database configuration file for the particular server.
4. End the connection by issuing the following statement:

```
db2 connect reset
db2 terminate
```

If you want, you can run session 1 and 2 one after the other.

When you are connected to a database, you can list the local database directory by issuing the `list database directory on path` command. The output will show the catalog node number for the database and the current node number where you are connected.

7.4 Installing DB2 UDB EEE

This section covers the installation of the Enterprise-Extended Edition of DB2 UDB for Windows NT.

7.4.1 Installation Pre-Requisites

There are things to check before installation begins.

1. What other software products need to be installed first?

DB2 UDB Enterprise-Extended Edition can be installed on a Windows NT system at version 3.51 or version 4.0 or higher. If you need to use APPC communications, you will need an SNA product installed on your system, like:

- IBM Communications Server for NT Version 5.0 or
- Microsoft SNA Server Version 2.11 or later

The Windows NT base operating system provides NetBIOS, IPX/SPX, Named Pipes, and TCP/IP protocol stacks.

2. How much memory and disk are required?

The amount of memory you require depends on the number of concurrent users you will have, and also the complexity of the applications you will run. For a simple static SQL application, you will need at least 32 MB of memory to accommodate 5 concurrent clients. For 25 concurrent clients, 48 MB of memory is required, and for 50 concurrent clients, you will need 64 MB of memory. Bear in mind that these are minimum requirements, and that installing more memory than these recommendations may improve the performance of your DB2 UDB server.

The disk space required by the DB2 UDB EEE product depends on the options you choose during the installation. The maximum total size of all the files included in Enterprise-Extended Edition at Version 5.0 is about 125 MB, of which around 35 MB is the online documentation. The maximum total size of all the graphical tools files is around 35 MB. The amount of disk actually allocated to the DB2 UDB files depends on the type of file system (FAT or NTFS) you use. As the online documentation consists of a large number of small files, using a FAT partition with a large (16/32 KB) cluster size is not recommended.

7.4.2 Pre-Installation Tasks

There are a number of tasks to do before actually stating the installation program. These include creating required users, deciding the role of each machine in the partitioned database system, and reserving ports in the TCP/IP services file.

7.4.2.1 Required Users

The following users are required before you can run the installation program:

The Installation User

You need to have a username that will be used to install DB2. This username must meet the following requirements:

- It must be a domain user.

- If the domain user is not part of the Domain Administrators account then it must belong to the local Administrators group on all of the machines that will make up the partitioned database system. The local Administrators group must have the "Act as part of the operating system" advanced user right.

Use the same domain user account to install each database partition server that will participate in the partitioned database system.

The Domain Username

You need to have a domain username that will be used to create a database partition server. DB2 will use this domain username to log on when DB2 is started as a Windows NT service. This username must meet the following requirements:

- It must be an existing domain username.
- It must be a valid DB2 username. A valid DB2 username is eight characters or less, and complies with DB2's naming rules (see "User ID and Group ID Limitations" on page 67).

The User Account for DAS Instance Owner

By default, the setup program will suggest db2admin as the DAS instance owner, with the password db2admin. For minimal security, you should at least change the password during the installation process (see Figure 205 on page 293). If you need better security, then you should add a new user, following the required rules (again, these rules are given "User ID and Group ID Limitations" on page 67). You can do this before the installation, or let the installation program create this new user for you. If you choose a different user, that user must belong to the Administrator's group as this userid will be used by the DAS to logon to the system and start itself as a Windows NT service.

7.4.2.2 Decide How Each of the Machines will be Used

When you are creating a partitioned database system, the installation of DB2 Universal Database Enterprise-Extended Edition differs between the first machine and subsequent machines. When you install on the first machine, you create the instance-owning database partition server. When you perform each subsequent install, you will choose to add a new node to an existing partitioned database system.

When you run the installation program, you will be presented with the following choices:

- If there is no previous version of DB2 on the machine, you have two installation options:

    1. This machine will be the instance-owning database partition server.

       The setup program creates the default instance on this machine which now becomes the instance-owning database partition server. The default instance is named DB2MPP.

    2. This machine will be a new node on an existing partitioned database system.

The setup program adds this machine as a node in an existing partitioned database system. Part of the installation will allow you to specify a system and configure the new node.

- If there is a previous version of DB2 on the machine, you have three installation options:

  1. This machine will be the instance-owning database partition server.

     If you choose this option, the setup program will ask you if you want to use the existing default instance as the default instance in the partitioned database system. You can choose one of the following options:

     - Yes, use the instance

       If you choose to use the existing default instance, the setup program migrates the existing instance to the DB2 Version 5 multipartition format (the default instance retains its name). This machine becomes the instance-owning database partition server. All other existing DB2 instances will be migrated to the DB2 Version 5 single-partition format.

     - No, create a new default instance

       If you choose to create a new default instance, the setup program creates a default instance, called DB2MPP. All existing DB2 instances will be migrated to the DB2 Version 5 single-partition format.

  2. This machine will be a new node on an existing partitioned database system.

     The setup program adds the machine as a node in an existing partitioned database system. All existing DB2 instances will be migrated to the DB2 Version 5 single-partition format. Part of the installation will allow you to specify a system and configure the new node.

  3. This machine will be a single-partition database server.

     This option does not allow you to exploit the scalability and power of a multipartition database system. All existing DB2 instances are migrated to the DB2 Version 5 single-partition format.

These choices are summarized in Figure 199 on page 287.

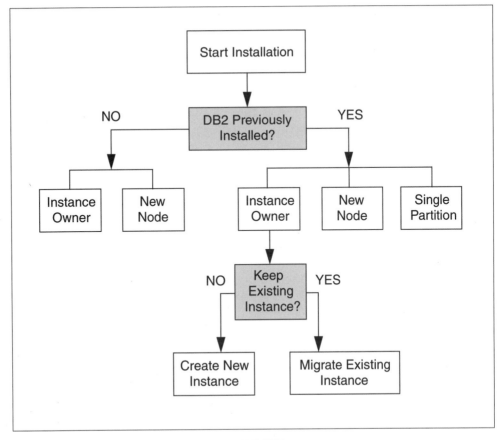

Figure 199. Installation Choices for DB2 UDB EEE

7.4.2.3 Other Pre-Installation Tasks

Before you install DB2 Enterprise-Extended Edition, for each of the machines that will make up your partitioned database system, you need to:

1. Ensure that all machines are connected to a LAN with TCP/IP configured, so that the machines can connect to each other using TCP/IP.

2. Ensure that all machines belong to the same Windows NT domain.

3. Ensure that all machines are set to a consistent data and time.

   In order to be considered consistent, the difference in GMT time between the machines must not exceed the value configured for the **max_time_diff** parameter in the database manager configuration file. The default time for max_time_diff is 1 hour.

4. Reserve a TCP/IP port range on each machine, to be used by the Fast Communications Manager (FCM). FCM is a feature of DB2 that handles communications between database partition servers.

To determine the port range, check the services file on each of the machines on which the database will reside. The services file is located in the directory:

```
x:\winnt\system32\drivers\etc
```

where *x:* is the drive on which you installed Windows NT. This file lists the port numbers that are already in use. Determine a port range that is available on all the machines. You will need to specify this port range during installation.

Note

If any of the machines that will make up your partitioned database system will be running multiple logical nodes, then the port range you set must be equal to or greater than the number of logical nodes on the machine running the most multiple logical nodes.

If you are not planning to run multiple logical nodes, the port range you specify only needs to span two ports.

By default, the port range is defined as the following service name, port number and protocol:

- Start of port range

```
DB2_<instance_name>        10013/tcp
```

- End of port range

```
DB2_<instance_name>_END    10017/tcp
```

5. Reserve a TCP/IP port on each machine, to be used by the DB2 Performance Monitor component of the Control Center. Use the instructions above to determine a port that is available on all machines. The same port must be reserved on all machines that will make up the partitioned database system.

The service name used for the DB2 Performance Monitor is db2ccmsv.

6. Check the existing PATH environment variable

The setup program does not support PATH environment variables with a length exceeding 512 bytes. A typical installation will add these directories to PATH:

```
C:\IMNNQ_NT;C:\ifor\WIN\BIN;C:\ifor\WIN\BIN\EN_US;C:\SQLLIB\BIN;
C:\SQLLIB\FUNCTION;C:\SQLLIB\SAMPLES\REPL;C:\SQLLIB\HELP
```

Check the current setting for PATH to determine whether the total length
might exceed 512 bytes after installation.

7.4.3 Run the Installation Program

We will show two examples here. The first covers the installation of the
instance-owning database partition server. The second will cover the
installation of a new node on the existing partitioned database system
previously created (see "Installing as a New Node" on page 294).

7.4.3.1 Installing the Instance Owning Database Partition Server

To install DB2 UDB EEE on a Windows NT machine as the instance owning
database partition server:

1. Log on as a user that meets the requirements for installing DB2, as
   described in "Required Users" on page 284. In our example, we will log on
   to machine JC6004A, and we will be using a domain user db2dom that
   belongs to the domain administrators group in the domain JCEEEDM.

2. Shut down any other programs so that the setup program can update files
   as required. This includes any previous versions of DB2, and any remote
   connections to DB2.

3. Insert the CD-ROM into the drive. The autorun feature automatically starts
   the setup program. The setup program will determine the system
   language, and launch the setup program for that language. If autorun is
   disabled, you can also launch the DB2 installation program by running the
   setup command, located in the root directory of the CD-ROM.

4. The *Welcome* window opens. Click on the **Next** button, and after space
   requirements are calculated, the *Select Products* window is displayed
   (Figure 200 on page 290):

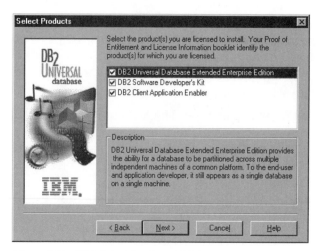

Figure 200. DB2 Select Products Window

Select the product that you want to install and click on the **Next** button. Here, we are installing DB2 UDB EEE, as well as the SDK and CAE code.

5. The *Select an Installation Option* window opens.

   The setup program allows you to choose different installation options. All of the options cause the setup program to install DB2 UDB EEE. Because this is a new install, we will install DB2 UDB EEE on this system as the instance owning partition server (Figure 201):

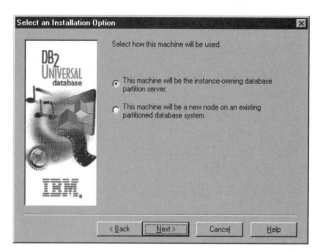

Figure 201. Select an Installation Option

6. Click on the **Next** button to continue, and choose an installation type. In our example, we chose a custom installation.

7. Since we have chosen the custom installation process, the next window is the *Select Components* window, which allows us to customize the DB2 components to be installed, as well as the path and drive where DB2 will be installed. Click on the **Next** button to continue.

8. We now fill in the required information for configuring the instance-owning database partition server. In our example, we will be using the default TCP/IP port range for FCM, of 10013 to 10017. We will also use the username db2dom, and associated password (see Figure 202). Click on the **Next** button to continue.

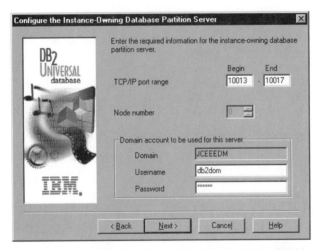

Figure 202. Configure the Instance Owning Database Partition Server

9. The next window allows us to configure a TCP/IP port number for the DB2 performance monitor. We will accept the default of 10018 (Figure 203):

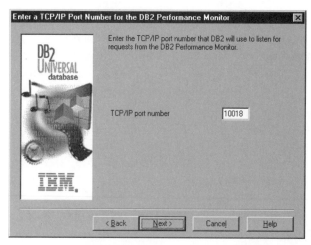

Figure 203. Enter a TCP/IP Port Number for the DB2 Performance Monitor

10. Click on the **Next** button. You will now be asked if you wish the DB2 Control Center to automatically start on at boot time. Make your selection, and click on the **Next** button to continue.

11. ,You can now customize the protocols used by the DB2 default instance, and the DAS instance (see Figure 204). After you have finished any customization, click on the **Next** button to continue.

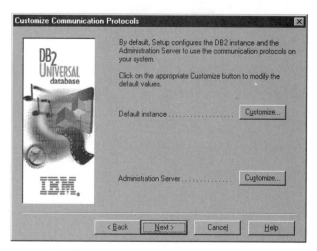

Figure 204. Customize Communications Protocols

12. You now enter the username and password to be used for the Windows NT service which runs the DAS instance (see Figure 205). Refer to

"Required Users" on page 284 for more information about this username (also known as the DAS instance owner).

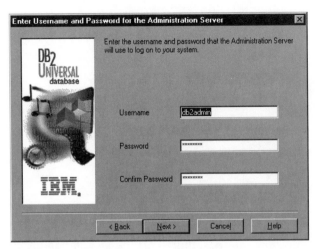

Figure 205. Enter Username and Password for the Administration Server

13. Click on the **Next** button, which will bring you to the final installation panel. Here, you should review the current settings. If the settings are OK, click on the **Install** button to start copying the DB2 UDB EEE files to your hard disk.

14. Finally, once the installation process is complete, you can choose to restart the system now or later (see Figure 206). You must restart the Windows NT system before using DB2 on this system for the first time, and before installation of any new nodes on this newly created instance-owning database partition server.

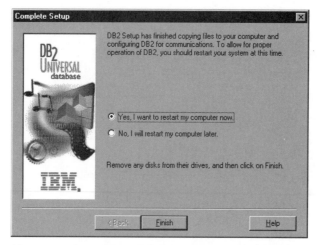

Figure 206. Completion of the DB2 Installation Procedure

We choose to reboot now and then start the installation for a new node on this newly created existing partitioned database system.

7.4.3.2 Installing as a New Node

To install DB2 Enterprise-Extended Edition on a Windows NT machine as a new node on an existing partitioned database system:

1. Log on as a user that meets the requirements for installing DB2. In our previous example, we used a domain user db2dom, that belonged to the domain administrators group, of the domain JCEEEDM. We will use this user again.

2. Shut down any other programs so that the setup program can update files as required. This includes any previous versions of DB2, and any remote connections to DB2.

3. Insert the CD-ROM into the drive. The autorun feature automatically starts the setup program. The setup program will determine the system language, and launch the setup program for that language. If autorun is disabled, you can also launch the DB2 installation program by running the `setup` command, located in the root directory of the CD-ROM.

4. The *Welcome* window opens. Click on the **Next** button, and after space requirements are calculated, the installation program will open the *Select Products* window (see Figure 207 on page 295). Select the product that you want to install and click on the **Next** button. Here, we are installing DB2 UDB EEE, as well as the SDK and CAE code.

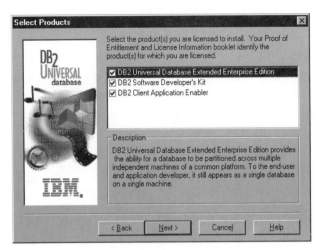

Figure 207. Select Products Window

5. The *Select an Installation Option* window is displayed.

The setup program allows you to choose different installation options. All of the options cause the setup program to install DB2 UDB EEE. This time, we install DB2 UDB EEE on this system as a new node on an existing partitioned database system (see Figure 208):

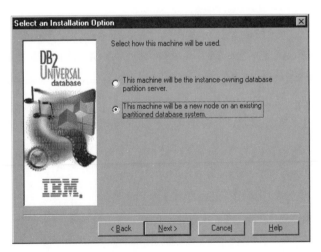

Figure 208. Select an Installation Option

6. Click on the **Next** button to continue, and choose an installation type. In our example, we chose a custom installation.

7. Since we have chosen the custom installation process, the next window is the *Select Components* window, which allows us to customize the DB2 components to be installed, as well as the path and drive where DB2 will be installed to. Click on the **Next** button to continue.

8. As part of the new node configuration, you will now have to select the system which this node will belong to. As shown in Figure 209, we select JC6004A as our instance owning machine, and click on the **OK** button.

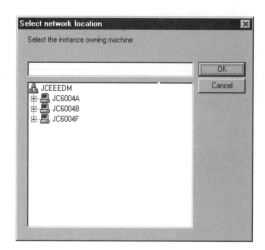

Figure 209. Select the Instance Owning Machine

9. The next window, Figure 210 on page 297, is a continuation of the new node configuration window. Note that most of the information has been filled in automatically (it is derived from the instance-owning machine). The only field left to fill in is the password for the domain administrator user that we have chosen to use (in our example, db2dom). Enter the password information and click on the **Next** button to continue.

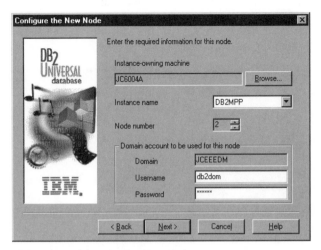

Figure 210. Configure the New Node

10. Click on the **Next** button. You will now be asked if you wish the DB2 Control Center to automatically start on at boot time. Make your selection, and click on the **Next** button to continue.

11. The final installation panel is displayed. Here, you should review the current settings. If you agree with the settings you have chosen, click on the **Install** button to start copying the DB2 UDB EEE files to your hard disk.

12. Finally, once the installation process is complete, you can choose to restart the system now or later. Once the system is restarted, the new partitioned database system DB2MPP, consisting of two DB2 nodes, is ready to be used.

7.4.3.3 Post Installation
You have completed all the installation steps. If you have finished installing all the machines that will make up your partitioned database system, you can now verify the installation.

Verifying the Installation
This section describes how you can create a sample database to verify that DB2 is properly installed. You should do this after you have added all of the machines that will make up your partitioned database system.

If you installed the DB2 tools, you can verify the installation as follows:

1. Log on to the instance-owning machine with a valid DB2 username that has System Administrative (SYSADM) authority.

2. To invoke First Steps, click on **Start** and select **Programs**, then **DB2 for Windows NT**, and finally **First Steps**. This will bring up the following panel:

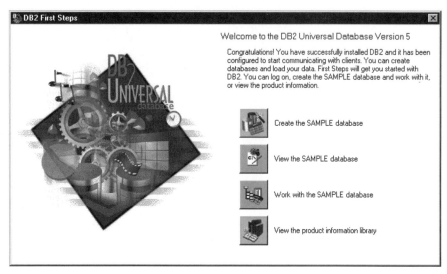

Figure 211. DB2 First Steps

3. Click on the **Create the SAMPLE Database** button on the main panel of First Steps.

4. Once the database is created, click on the **View the SAMPLE Database** button on the main panel of First Steps to select data from the SAMPLE database. This starts the Command Center and enables you to use the supplied script to select some of the data from the database. Click on the **Execute** icon to begin the query.

5. Click on the **Work with the SAMPLE Database** button on the main panel of First Steps to start the Control Center. This allows you to see the tables that are in the SAMPLE database and enables you to perform actions on them.

If you did not install the DB2 tools, you can verify the installation as follows:

1. Log on to the instance-owning machine with a valid DB2 username that has System Administrative (SYSADM) authority.

2. If the it is not started, start the database manager by issuing the `db2start` command in the command line processor. Type:

```
db2start
```

3. Create the sample database using the `db2sampl` command at the operating system command prompt. Type:

```
db2sampl
```

4. Once the database is created, enter the following commands in a DB2 command line processor window or the DB2 Command Center to connect to the sample database and retrieve a list of all the employees that work in department 20.

```
db2 connect to sample
db2 "select * from staff where dept = 20"
```

After you have verified the installation, you can remove the sample database to free up disk space. You can use the Command Center to drop the sample database. Alternatively, you can issue the **drop database** sample command from the DB2 command line processor window.

Chapter 8. Failover Support with DB2 UDB EEE

In a clustered environment of multiple computer systems, failover refers to the event when a system takes over responsibilities for resources and tasks from another system, when that system has failed. In the past this was only available for high-end servers and workstations. Today however, with the availability of high speed processors, fast networks, etc. this solution is feasible for today's low-cost PC servers.

This chapter discusses the clustering solution available from Microsoft, known as Microsoft Cluster Server or MSCS, in conjunction with Windows NT Server Enterprise Edition. We discuss the possible configurations available using MSCS for implementing failover support for DB2 UDB Enterprise-Extended Edition (EEE). We then present a detailed implementation scenario.

This chapter covers configuring DB2 UDB EEE, a partitioned database system, in an MSCS environment. For details on how to configure a single-partition database system (such as DB2 UDB Enterprise Edition) for failover in an MSCS environment, see the DB2 UDB Administration Guide Version 5.2.

8.1 Microsoft Cluster Server

The first phase of Microsoft Cluster Server (MSCS), also known as Wolfpack, links two servers and a shared disk subsystem to form a single, two-node cluster. This allows for system redundancy by allowing one server to fail, and client access to server resources (for example, disks) is largely unaffected. MSCS also allows for software failures at the:

- Operating system level, where all applications and services will be restarted on the other server in the cluster.

- Application level, where the application that fails can be managed individually by MSCS to run on the other server in the cluster.

Applications will only run on one MSCS node at a time. MSCS currently does not offer any facility to extend the running of an application across the two servers simultaneously in the MSCS cluster.

We discuss some important MSCS concepts and terminology, followed by a short description of the failover configurations that are implementable with the current phase 1 release of MSCS.

Note

It is a mandatory requirement of MSCS that these two servers have access to a shared disk subsystem (using SCSI or SSA adapters). This is required for the MSCS quorum resource, which MUST reside on a disk on the shared disk subsystem. MSCS resources are defined in the following pages.

8.1.1 MSCS Concepts

A MSCS phase 1 *cluster* consists of two *nodes*, which host and provide *resources* of a *resource type*. Each resource may depend on other resources, forming a *dependency*, and hence require the grouping of these resources into a *resource group*. Each resource and resource group can be in a particular *resource* or *group* *state* at any point in time.

TCP/IP is the network protocol used for all network and resource communications. In the event of communications failure between nodes, MSCS's use of a *shared nothing* model for resource ownership requires that a *quorum resource* be used to arbitrate resource ownership.

MSCS determines when to initiate *failover* and *failback*, with the use of one or more *resource monitors*. These resource monitors determine when to failover or failback with the *Looks Alive/Is Alive polling* strategy of the *resource modules*.

These concepts are explained in further detail in the following sections.

8.1.2 Clusters of Nodes

A cluster, as defined in phase 1 of MSCS, consists of two systems or nodes. These two systems are connected by one or more networks, and share one or more disks. Each node, as well as the entire cluster, is accessible via LAN connections to client workstations. An independent, internal network is often used to provide monitoring within the cluster. This is illustrated in Figure 212 on page 303.

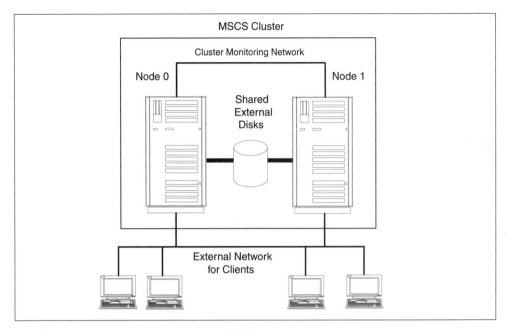

Figure 212. Basic Configuration of an MSCS Cluster

8.1.3 Resources in MSCS

A resource is an application, service or component running on a node. Communications between a resource and the Resource Monitor is provided by the resource modules. These resource modules are polled at regular intervals by the resource monitor to determine their state.

8.1.3.1 Resource Monitor

The Resource Monitor is responsible for watching its assigned resources, and notifying the Cluster Service if there is any change in resource state. The Cluster Service oversees the MSCS related activities on each node in the MSCS cluster.

By default, each cluster has one Resource Monitor to service all resource modules in the cluster environment. This can be changed by choosing to run the resource in a separate Resource Monitor. This choice is made at the creation of the resource. Resources that will have to be tested or resource modules that may conflict with other resource modules should have a separate Resource Monitor.

The Resource Monitor is separate from the Cluster Service and as such provides an extra level of security. The resource DLLs are running in the address space of the applications themselves. If the applications fail, the resource DLLs may malfunction causing the resource monitor to fail as well. The Cluster Service, however, should remain available to the cluster.

8.1.3.2 Looks Alive/Is Alive

You adjust how often the Resource Monitor attempts to verify if a resource is available and running. These actions are called polls. There are the two levels of polling and the polling type performed depends on how the resource module was written.

1. Looks Alive polling

    With Looks Alive polling, the resource monitor makes a high-level check to determine resource availability.

    If a resource fails to respond to a Looks Alive poll, the resource monitor will notify the Cluster Service. When you create a new resource, you define the length of the interval (in milliseconds) between polling attempts.

2. Is Alive polling

    With Is Alive polling, the Resource Monitor performs a complete check of the resource to verify it is fully operational. If it gets a failed response, the Cluster Service is immediately notified and depending on the configuration defined for the resource, the Resource Monitor can terminate the resource or try to bring it back on-line on the same node or on the other node.

8.1.3.3 Resource Types

There are 12 resource types for which Resources can be defined:

1. DHCP Server
2. Distributed Transaction Server
3. File Share
4. Generic Application
5. Generic Service
6. IIS Root
7. IP Address
8. Microsoft Message Queue Server
9. Network Name
10. Physical Disk
11. Print Spooler
12. Time Service

Other types of resources can be offered by software vendors using the application programming interface (API) in the Microsoft Platform Software Development Kit (SDK). We discuss in more detail the four resources types provided by MSCS which are used in a DB2 UDB EEE environment. We also describe the DB2 resource type provided by DB2 UDB.

- DB2

   This resource is provided by DB2 UDB. It represents a DB2 database partition server (also known as a DB2 node). You defined a resource of type "DB2" for each node that requires fail-over support. The instance owning DB2 node should have dependencies on the instance directory file share (with associated disk resource) and the DB2 network name (with associated cluster IP address for DB2). Optionally, each DB2 node may also have dependencies on disk resources which will be required to store user data. For example, each DB2 node may be assigned a disk resource for the creation and storage of databases. In the event of fail-over, this shared disk (and therefore the user data on it) will be accessible to the fail-over server.

- File Share

   This resource type lets you share a directory on one of the shared disks in your configuration and allows you to configure the permissions to give access to that directory to clients. You are asked to enter the name of the share, the network path, a comment and the maximum number of users that can connect to the share at one time. The configuration of a file share of this resource type is identical to the configuration of a file share in Windows NT Explorer. This resource requires the physical disk resource and the network name resource. For example, you can store files in a shared directory on the server and give access only to a group of clients.

- IP Address

   The IP address resource is used to assign an IP address. You need to obtain a static IP address and subnet mask from your network administrator. This new IP address will be bound to the network interface chosen at the 'Network to use' option during the creation of the resource. This resource does not have any dependencies.

- Network Name

   The resource gives identity to the group. With a Network Name resource, the group can become a virtual server. Clients can access the group remotely by using the Universal Naming Convention (UNC) name. For example, if you create a network name resource DB2WOLF0 and you have a file share resource DB2MPP in the same group, you can access it from a client desktop by entering the path \\DB2WOLF0\DB2MPP. This will give access to the directory on the shared disk regardless of which node actually owns the disk at the time.

- Physical Disk

   When you first install MSCS on servers, you select the available disks on the shared storage. Each disk will be configured as a physical disk resource. If it becomes necessary to add more disk after the installation, you would use the physical disk resource. This resource does is not dependent on any other resources.

8.1.3.4 Resource States

Resources can be in one of five states:

1. **Offline**: The resource is unavailable for use by any other resource or client.

2. **Offline Pending**: This is a transitional state. The resource is being take offline.

3. **Online**: The resource is available.

4. **Online Pending**: The resource is being brought online.

5. **Failed**: If a resource cannot be brought on-line or off-line within a configured amount of time (see below), the resource will go into the failed state. (If you have a resource on-line it means it's available for use. If it is off-line, then it is unavailable for use. The off-line pending and on-line pending shows that the resource is going off-line or on-line by the Cluster Service. You can specify the amount of time that MSCS allows for a resource to go on-line or off-line.)

8.1.3.5 Dependencies

During a failover, MSCS brings each resource on-line in a specific sequence that is defined when the resources are created. For example, if you want to create a file share resource, then the file share will require a disk drive. In order for MSCS to know what the sequence order is, you need to define a physical disk resource first; then when you define the file share resource, you specify that the physical disk resource is a dependency.

As described in "Resource Groups and Group States" on page 306, all dependent resources must be placed together in a single resource group.

8.1.3.6 Resource Groups and Group States

Some resources need other resources to run successfully and so have resource dependencies, as described in "Dependencies" on page 306. MSCS requires dependent resources to be kept together in Resource Groups. When one resource is listed as a dependency for another resource, the two resources must be placed in the same group.

If all resources are ultimately dependent on a single resource (for example a physical disk resource) then all resources must be in the same group. It is quite possible that all your cluster resources will need to be in a single group.

Any cluster operation on a group is performed on all resources that are present within that group. For example, if a resource needs to be moved from one MSCS node to another, all the resources defined in that resource's group will be moved.

A resource group can be in any one of the following states:

1. **Online**: when all resources of the group are online.
2. **Offline**: when all resources of the group are offline.
3. **Partially Online**: when some resources are offline and some are online.

8.1.3.7 Quorum Resource

There is a special resource, called a quorum resource, which is specified during the initial install of the first node of the MSCS cluster. This resource creates and logs data that is critical to recovery when MSCS nodes fail to communicate with each other. This data can be owned by only one node. It is used to determine which node will take ownership of the resources if they cannot communicate with each other.

In phase 1 of MSCS, only the physical disk resource type can be used as a quorum resource. The quorum disk must reside in the shared disk subsystem.

8.1.4 Virtual Server

Groups that contain at least an IP address resource and a network name resource appear on the network as virtual servers. A virtual server allows clients to connect to the cluster instead of connecting to the individual nodes. From a client perspective, the MSCS application runs within this virtual server and not on one node or another in that cluster.

It is very important to always connect to the virtual server to take advantage of the failover policy. For example, if you create a group that has the network name resource DB2WOLF0, then browse your network, you will see a server called DB2WOLF0 under the same domain of the physical servers. You will also see both physical servers that are under the same domain, but you should not connect to them. (The name of the network resource makes it a virtual server.)

8.1.4.1 TCP/IP

MSCS uses TCP/IP to communicate with network applications and to all resources. MSCS cannot have an IP address assigned from a Dynamic Host Configuration Protocol (DHCP) server for any IP Address resource or for the cluster administration address (registered during the installation of MSCS). You must use a static IP address for both nodes and for the IP address resources.

Note

You must have TCP/IP installed on both servers in order to use MSCS. Applications that use only NetBEUI or IPX will not work within the failover ability of MSCS. NetBIOS over TCP/IP will work, however.

8.1.5 Failover

Failover is the relocation of tasks and resources in a group from the failed node to the surviving node. The detection of a failure is made by the resource monitor responsible for the resource. When a resource fails, the resource monitor will notify the Cluster Service, which triggers the actions defined in the failover policy for that resource. Failover can occur either manually (at the request of an administrator) or automatically when the *group failover threshold* is reached within the *group failover period*. It can also have a scheduled failover using IBM Cluster Systems Management.

Failover generally consists of three phases:

1. Failure detection
2. Resource relocation
3. Application restart

Application restart usually takes the longest time to complete.

You can configure when MSCS performs failover by setting two variables, Failover Threshold and Failover Period.

Both groups and resources have failover threshold and period properties with the same name. However, the functions perform different actions as described below.

- For **resources**:

    Failover Threshold defines:

- The number of times in the specified period that MSCS allows the resource to be restarted on the same node. If the threshold count is exceeded, the resource and all other resources in that group will failover to another node in the cluster.

Failover Period defines:

- The failure threshold number of restart attempts must occur within this period of time (in seconds) before the group fails over.

After exceeding the threshold count of restart attempts, MSCS fails over the group that contains the failing resource. Every resource will be brought on-line according to the startup sequence defined by the dependencies.

- For **groups**:

Failover Threshold defines:

- The maximum number of times that the group is allowed to fail over within the specified failover period. If the group fails over more often than specified, MSCS will leave it off-line or partially on-line depending on the state of the resources in the group.

Failover Period defines:

- This defines the time period (in hours) over which the group will be allowed to fail over. The number of times it is allowed to fail over is defined by the failover threshold.

8.1.5.1 Failback
Failback is a special case of failover. It is the process of moving back some or all groups to the preferred owner after a failover has occurred.

Note

The preferred owner is the node in the cluster on which you prefer each group of resources to run. If the preferred owner fails, its resources will be transferred to another node. When the preferred owner comes back on-line and failback is enabled, the resources will automatically transfer back to that node.

You may choose not to set a preferred owner, if it does not matter where the resources reside.

When you create a group, the default failback policy is set to prevent failback. You can allow failback in one of two cases:

1. Immediately after the preferred node is available.

2. To occur between specific hours, once the preferred node is available. This second option is very useful, as you may want the failback to occur only after business hours.

8.1.6 Shared Disk versus Shared Nothing

There are two main clustering models used today: shared disk and shared nothing. As mentioned before, MSCS is based on the shared nothing model.

1. Shared Disk

   Applications running on one node may access any data on disks connected to any other node in the cluster. If two nodes want to read the same data, each node must read the data separately, or one node must transfer the data to the other. If two nodes want to write data to the disk, the writes must be coordinated to ensure data integrity. This model allows for multiple readers at any one time, but only one write operation can be performed at a given time.

   The shared disk model is useful in load-balancing. Data on any disk can be obtained by any node at any time. There is a drawback to this scenario, however and it is that the software required to manage this type of environment is significantly more complex than in the shared nothing model.

2. Shared Nothing

   In a shared nothing environment, each node in the cluster owns some of the resources of the cluster. No resource is owned by more than one node at any given point-in-time. Only one node owns and is allowed to use each disk at any one time. If another node needs to access data on a disk owned by another node, a request is sent to the owning node, which performs the request on its behalf. If a failure occurs, the resource can automatically be transferred to another node and any requests for that resource are automatically re-routed to the new owner. This ensures that all client requests are fulfilled regardless of the status of individual nodes.

   This model can be extended so that when a client request is made of the cluster, the request can be divided up and given to each of the nodes in the cluster. The nodes then process their part of the request and the results are then assembled and returned to the client.

Even though most MSCS hardware implementations are based on a shared SCSI bus, MSCS is considered a shared-nothing clustering architecture as every server has its own system disk. No concurrent access to data on the physically shared disk is allowed.

8.2 DB2 UDB EEE Failover Support

DB2 UDB EEE for Windows NT provides support for MSCS, allowing DB2 to be defined and managed as an MSCS aware server application, using the following:

- A resource module, DB2WOLF.DLL, which allows a DB2 instance to be defined and managed as an MSCS resource. This allows MSCS to start and stop DB2 UDB for Windows NT.

- Pre and post on-line script support, allowing additional configuration, before and after DB2 is brought on-line in a clustering scenario.

- Utilities to manage DB2 instances defined in MSCS clusters.

Client application behavior is unchanged in a clustered environment except for the following (see "Application Support Considerations" on page 340):

- During DB2 UDB failover, client applications will receive a communications failure.

- DB2 UDB will be brought online on the other node of the cluster, at which point in time client applications can reconnect to DB2.

- In-flight transactions that were not completed during the failover are rolled back by DB2. The application must resubmit the transaction.

We discuss possible failover configurations for DB2 UDB EEE, and present a step-by-step approach to implementing DB2 UDB with MSCS in these configurations in the following sections. We then present a detailed implementation of a two node DB2 instance configured for mutual failover.

Please see the section entitled "Limitations and Restrictions" on page 351, for limitations and restrictions regarding DB2 in an MSCS environment.

8.2.1 DB2 UDB EEE Failover Configurations

There are two possible configurations for DB2 UDB EEE in an MSCS environment:

1. Hot Standby:

   Also known as Active-Passive, in this configuration an MSCS-enabled (or clustered) DB2 instance is defined with one or more database partition servers running on one server, while the other server is inactive. Upon failover, DB2 will be started on the inactive server, the failover system. The failover system is simply used to provide high availability, and acts as a standby system.

Figure 213 shows a hot standby failover configuration, where two DB2 database partition servers (logical partitions or nodes) run on server 0, with server 1 providing standby support for both logical partitions.

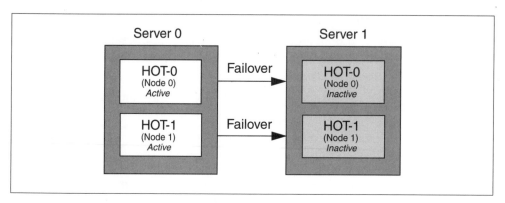

Figure 213. Hot-Standby Failover Configuration

2. Mutual Takeover:

This is also known as Active-Active. Within the MSCS-enabled DB2 instance, database partition servers (logical partitions) are defined on the two servers in the MSCS cluster, each with their own set of MSCS resources. During failover, database partition servers from the failed system will be started on the remaining server.

Figure 214 shows a mutual takeover scenario, where two DB2 database partition servers (MUTUAL-0 and MUTUAL-2) of the MUTUAL instance are running on server 0, while another DB2 database partition server (MUTUAL-1) runs on server 1. In the event server 0 fails, MUTUAL-0 and MUTUAL-2 will become active on server 1. In the event of failover of server 1, MUTUAL-1 will become active on server 0.

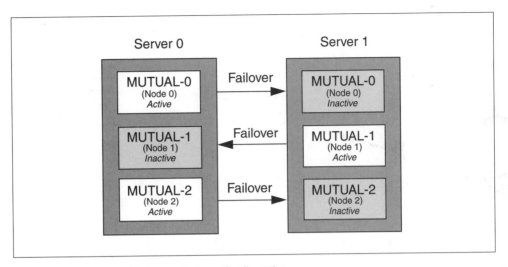

Figure 214. Mutual Takeover Failover Configuration

Note that because of the ability of DB2 UDB EEE instances to be defined over more than 2 machines, you may have a mix of hot-standby and mutual takeover MSCS clusters (pairs of machines) within the same DB2 instance.

8.2.2 Implementing a DB2 UDB EEE Instance with Failover Support

Before you enable a DB2 UDB EEE instance for failover support, ensure that you are familiar with either the DB2MSCS utility or the Cluster Administrator tool and how to work with MSCS resources. The following steps should be performed in the planning phase:

1. Decide on the number of database partition servers that you want in the instance.

2. Decide which disks to use for data storage. Each database partition server should be assigned at least one disk for its own use. The disk that you use to store data must be attached to a shared disk subsystem, and must be configured as an MSCS disk resource.

3. Decide which database partition servers you want to enable to fail over. You should enable the database partition server that runs on the instance-owning machine for failover. If you use a database partition server as a dedicated catalog node, this would also be a good candidate for failover support.

4. Ensure that you have one IP address for each database partition server that you want to use as a coordinator node.

Once you have an operational MSCS cluster, to enable DB2 for failover support you have the choice of two tools: the DB2MSCS command line utility provided with DB2 UDB for Windows NT V5.2 (available on the CD-ROM provided with this book) or the Cluster Administrator graphical tool provided with MSCS. The DB2MSCS utility is very useful if you need to automate the configuration of the MSCS-enabled DB2 UDB environment and make it an easily repeatable task. It should be your utility of choice since it automates the configuration process and verifies all input data for correctness for you.

> **Note**
>
> The DB2MSCS tool can only be used to migrate an existing DB2 instance.

The DB2MSCS utility can only be used to migrate an existing MSCS-enabled DB2 instance, based on parameters supplied with a user-written input file. Regardless of your failover configuration, you must:

1. Create an input file for DB2MSCS (see "Using DB2MSCS to Enable MSCS Support" on page 315).

2. Run the DB2MSCS utility (see "Running the DB2MSCS utility" on page 320).

After implementation, there are several issues to consider:

- You should register database drive mappings with the DB2DRVMP utility, so that databases can be created on the clustered disks (see "Registering Database Drive Mappings" on page 333).

- You may also need to use the DB2NCHG utility (see "Changing DB2 Node Configuration Information" on page 337), as well as set up additional MSCS IP resources, to enable successful DB2 UDB EEE failover.

- To understand some of the DB2 UDB EEE general concepts related to DB2 UDB EEE in an MSCS-enabled system, please refer to "Miscellaneous DB2 UDB EEE Concepts" on page 341.

- Finally for considerations when administering DB2 in an MSCS environment. refer to "Administering DB2 in an MSCS Environment" on page 342

The Cluster Administrator tool is used to create and manipulate MSCS groups and resources. It can be used to enable a DB2 instance to participate in an MSCS environment.

Regardless of your failover configuration, you must:

1. Register the DB2 resource type with MSCS (see "Registering the DB2 Resource Type With MSCS" on page 322).

2. Set up MSCS groups and resources for DB2 (see "Setting up MSCS Groups and Resources for DB2" on page 322).

3. Create a new DB2 instance and enable it for MSCS support (see "Creating an MSCS-Enabled DB2 Instance" on page 329) or migrate an existing DB2 instance, and enable it for MSCS support (see "Migrating to an MSCS-Enabled DB2 Instance" on page 330).

4. Enable the instance for failover support on the second MSCS node in the cluster (see "Enabling the DB2 Resource to Fail Over" on page 331). If you need to disable this instance for failover support, see "Disabling DB2 Resource Failover to the second MSCS node" on page 338.

   Refer to "Failback Considerations" on page 339 for additional DB2 failback considerations.

5. If you have a DB2 instance already enabled for MSCS, you may add additional database partition servers to the DB2 instance (see "Adding a DB Partition Server to the DB2 Instance" on page 332).

See "Using the Cluster Administrator to Enable MSCS Support" on page 321 for details on how to use the Cluster Administrator tool.

8.2.3 Using DB2MSCS to Enable MSCS Support

The recommended approach is to use the DB2MSCS utility to enable MSCS support for a DB2 instance. This utility is run from a command line and takes an input file as its parameter. It performs the following tasks:

- Registers the DB2 Resource Type With MSCS.

- Creates the MSCS Groups and Resources required by DB2.

- Converts an existing DB2 instance to an MSCS-enabled DB2 instance.

- Brings the DB2 resources online.

A DB2 instance must already exist before you can use the DB2MSCS utility. You can either use the default instance, DB2MPP, created during the installation process, or you can create a new DB2 instance (see "Creating a DB2 Instance" on page 364).

8.2.3.1 Creating a DB2MSCS input file

The DB2MSCS input file is an ASCII text file that contains parameters to be used by the DB2MSCS utility. You specify each parameter on a separate line using the following format:

```
PARAMETER_KEYWORD=parameter_value
```

For example:

```
CLUSTER_NAME=DB2CLUS
GROUP_NAME=DB2 Node 0
IP_ADDRESS=10.10.10.13
```

A more complete example configuration file is provided in Figure 240 on page 367. Also, a complete sample file is provided with DB2 UDB Version 5.2. We recommend that you use that sample file as a starting point and modify it for your needs. See also the example file in "An Example DB2MSCS input configuration file" on page 319.

The parameters for the DB2MSCS input configuration file are:

- DB2_INSTANCE: The name of the DB2 instance. If the instance name is not specified, the default instance (the value of the DB2INSTANCE environment variable) is used.

  This parameter has a global scope, and you specify it only once in the configuration file.

  This parameter is optional.

> **Note**
>
> The DB2MSCS utility can only be used to migrate an already existing DB2 instance, to a clustered DB2 instance. Hence, the DB2 instance must already exist, before the DB2MSCS utility is run.

- DB2_LOGON_USERNAME: The name of the logon account for the DB2 service.

  This parameter has a global scope, and you specify it only once in the configuration file.

- DB2_LOGON_PASSWORD: The password of the logon account for the DB2 service. If the DB2_LOGON_USERNAME parameter is provided, but this parameter is not, the DB2MSCS utility will prompt for a password. This password is not displayed when typed at the command line.

  This parameter has a global scope, and you specify it only once in the configuration file.

- CLUSTER_NAME: The name of the MSCS cluster. All the resources specified following this line are created in this cluster until another CLUSTER_NAME tag is specified.

Specify this parameter once for each cluster.

This parameter is optional. If not specified, the name of the MSCS cluster on the local machine is used.

- GROUP_NAME: The name of the MSCS group. If this parameter is specified, a new MSCS group is created if it does not exist. If it does exist, it is used as the target group. Any MSCS resource created following this line is created in this group until another GROUP_NAME tag is specified.

Specify this parameter once for each group.

This parameter is required.

- DB2_NODE: The node number of the database partition server (node) to be included in the current MSCS group. If multiple logical nodes exist on the same machine, each node requires a separate DB2_NODE tag.

You specify this parameter after the GROUP_NAME parameter so that DB2 resources are created in the correct MSCS group.

- IP_NAME: The name of the IP Address resource. The value for IP_NAME is arbitrary, but must be unique. When this parameter is specified, an MSCS resource of type IP Address is created.

This parameter is required for remote TCP/IP connections. You must specify this parameter for the instance-owning machine in a partitioned database environment. This parameter is optional in single-partition database environments.

The attributes of the IP resource are as follows:

  - IP_ADDRESS: The TCP/IP address of the IP resource. Specify this keyword to set the TCP/IP address for the preceding IP resource.

  This parameter is required if the IP_NAME parameter is specified.

  - IP_SUBNET: The subnet mask for the preceding IP resource.

  This parameter is required if the IP_NAME parameter is specified.

  - IP_NETWORK: The name of the MSCS network that the preceding IP resource belongs to. If this parameter is not specified, the first MSCS network detected by the system is used.

  This parameter is optional.

> **Note**
>
> DB2 clients should use the TCP/IP address of this IP resource to catalog the TCP/IP node entry. By using the MSCS IP address, when the database server fails over to the other system, DB2 clients can still connect to the database server because the IP address is available on the failover system.

- NETWORK_NAME: The name of the Network Name resource. Specify this parameter to create the Network Name resource.

  This parameter is optional for single-partition database environments. It is required for multi-partitioned database environments.

  The attributes of the Network Name resource are as follows:

  - NETNAME_VALUE: The value of the preceding Network Name resource.

    This parameter is required if the NETNAME_NAME parameter is specified.

  - NETNAME_DEPENDENCY: The dependency list for the Network Name resource. Each Network Name resource must have a dependency on an IP Address resource. If this parameter is not specified, the Network Name resource has a dependency on the first IP Address resource in the group.

    This parameter is optional.

- DISK_NAME: The name of the physical disk resources to be moved to the current groups. Specify as many disk resources as you need.

> **Note**
>
> - The disk resource must already exist.
>
> - When the DB2 MSCS utilities configures the DB2 instance for MSCS support, the instance directory is copied to the first MSCS disk in the group. To specify a different MSCS disk for the instance directory, use the INSTPROF_DISK parameter.

- INSTPROF_DISK: An optional parameter to specify an MSCS disk to contain the DB2 instance directory.

  The DB2 instance directory is created on the MSCS disk under the X:\DB2PROFS directory (where X is the MSCS disk drive letter).

> **Note**
>
> Before running the DB2MSCS utility, check the comments in the parameter descriptions for the parameters you are using. You may need to ensure that certain resources are available and on-line in the MSCS Cluster Administrator tool. For example, you must ensure the directory "\DB2PROFS" already exists in the disk resource you have specified for the INSTPROF_DISK parameter.

8.2.3.2 An Example DB2MSCS input configuration file

We present here an example of a DB2MSCS input configuration file for a partitioned database system using multiple MSCS clusters.

When you run the DB2MSCS utility against a multi-partition database system, one MSCS group is created for each physical machine that participates in the system. The DB2MSCS.CFG file must contain multiple sections, where each section has a different value for the GROUP_NAME parameter, and for all the required dependent resources for that group.

In addition, you must specify the DB2_NODE parameter for each database partition server in each MSCS group. If you have multiple logical partitions on a physical machine, each logical partition requires a separate DB2_NODE keyword.

For example, assume that you have a multiple partition database system that consists of four database partition servers on four machines, and you want to configure two MSCS clusters using mutual takeover configuration. You would set up the DB2MSCS.CFG configuration file as follows:

```
DB2_INSTANCE=DB2MPP
DB2_LOGON_USERNAME=...
DB2_LOGON_PASSWORD=...
    # First Cluster
CLUSTER_NAME=DB2CLUS0
    # First MSCS Group
GROUP_NAME=DB2 Node 0
DB2_NODE=0
IP_NAME=...
...
    # Second MSCS Group
GROUP_NAME=DB2 Node 1
DB2_NODE=1
IP_NAME=...
...
    # Next Cluster
CLUSTER_NAME=DB2CLUS1
    # Third MSCS Group
GROUP_NAME=DB2 Node 2
DB2_NODE=2
IP_NAME=...
...
    # Fourth MSCS Group
GROUP_NAME=DB2 Node 3
DB2_NODE=3
IP_NAME=...
...
```

Here, the instance name for the multi-partition database system is DB2MPP.
It consists of four DB2 nodes, which will reside in four MSCS groups, called
DB2 Node 0 through to DB2 Node 3. Within each MSCS group, you also have
to specify and define all dependent resources, for example, IP address,
network name, disk.

For a full example, see "DB2 UDB EEE Two-Node Mutual Takeover Example"
on page 351.

For more information about using DB2MSCS in other failover scenarios,
including single partition database systems, see the DB2 UDB Administration
Guide Version 5.2.

8.2.3.3 Running the DB2MSCS utility

You run the DB2MSCS utility once for each instance on its instance-owning
system. You can run the DB2MSCS utility from a command window.

The DB2MSCS utility performs the following steps:

1. Reads all required MSCS and DB2 parameters from an input file.

2. Validates the parameters in the input file.

3. Registers the DB2 resource type.

4. Creates the MSCS group (or groups) to contain the MSCS and DB2 resources.

5. Creates the IP resource.

6. Creates the Network Name resource.

7. Moves MSCS disks to the group.

8. Creates the DB2 resource (or resources).

9. Adds all required dependencies for the DB2 resource.

10.Converts the DB2 instance into an MSCS-enabled instance.

11.Brings all resources online.

The syntax of the DB2MSCS utility is as follows:

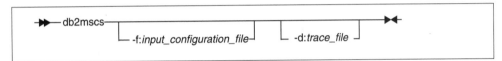

Figure 215. Syntax of the DB2MSCS utility

Where:

- **-f:*input_configuration_file*** specifies the DB2MSCS input configuration file to be used. If this parameter is not specified, the DB2MSCS utility reads the file named DB2MSCS.CFG that is in the current directory.

- **-d:*trace_file*** specifies an output file to place a debugging trace produced by the DB2MSCS utility. By default, no trace is produced.

The next sections cover the use of the Cluster Administrator to enable a DB2 instance for MSCS support, which is an alternative to using the DB2MSCS tool to configure the MSCS groups and resources to enable MSCS support for the DB2 instance. The next step in this process is "Registering Database Drive Mappings" on page 333.

8.2.4 Using the Cluster Administrator to Enable MSCS Support

This section takes you through the manual steps using the Cluster Administration tool. For an automated approach, please refer to earlier discussions in this chapter on the DB2MSCS utility.

8.2.4.1 Registering the DB2 Resource Type With MSCS

Before you can set up your MSCS groups and resources for DB2, you must register a resource of type DB2 by issuing the **db2wolfi** command. Each MSCS resource that you register with a type of DB2 maps to a database partition server. Issue the following command from a command window after DB2 is installed. You run this command only once for each MSCS cluster:

```
db2wolfi i
```

You can verify that the resource has been installed by starting the Cluster Administrator tool, if it is not already active, and selecting **Resource Types**, as shown in Figure 216. You should see a DB2 resource type listed under Display Name. Associated with the DB2 resource type is the Resource DLL db2wolf.dll.

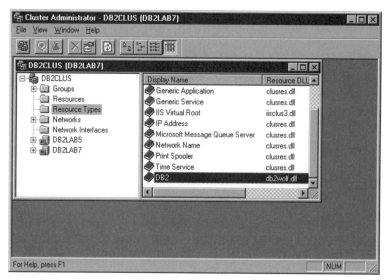

Figure 216. Verifying Installation of DB2 Resource Type

To uninstall the DB2 resource type, run:

```
db2wolfi u
```

8.2.4.2 Setting up MSCS Groups and Resources for DB2

The following two sections outline the steps required to set up the MSCS groups and resources for DB2. These are required for hot-standby and mutual takeover configurations respectively. For a more detailed example, refer to "DB2 UDB EEE Two-Node Mutual Takeover Example" on page 351.

Hot Standby Configuration

1. Create an MSCS group for DB2.

   You must fill in a group name (for example, DB2 Node 0), optional description, and then specify the preferred nodes this group will run in.

   The preferred node is the node that the group will run in during normal operation. If failback is enabled, this group will automatically failback to the preferred node when available.

2. Set up a disk resource to store the user data.

   MSCS's shared nothing disk model requires the DB2 instance directory be placed on an MSCS disk resource. On failover, this directory is made available to the standby system.

   When you create the disk resource, you are required to fill in a name (for example, Disk J:), optional description, indicate it is of resource type Physical Disk, belonging to the appropriate group. Accept the defaults for possible owners (which should be both nodes), defaults for dependencies (which should be none), and select the appropriate shared disk for this disk resource.

   If you choose to use an existing disk resource, move that disk resource to the appropriate group.

Note

- If you wish to have user data made available during failover, you must also set up MSCS disk resources for each disk that will be used.

- Only the shared disks can be used for creating MSCS disk resources.

---

3. Set up an MSCS File Share resource for the instance directory.

   This allows the instance directory to be accessed via a Windows NT Universal Naming Convention (UNC) name, for example, \\DB2WOLF0\DB2MPP. On failover, this disk will still be accessible regardless of which cluster node owns it.

   You are required to fill in a file share name (for example, Instance Directory), optional description, indicate that it is of resource type File

Share, belonging to the appropriate group. Accept the defaults for possible owners (which should be none).

Make sure the disk resource that is to be used for the file share is on-line, then choose that disk resource as a dependency. Fill in a share name for the file share (for example, DB2MPP), and a path of the form <drive letter>:\<subdirectory name> (for example, J:\PROFILE). The comment is optional.

> **Note**
>
> - The path must exist on the shared drive before the file share is brought on-line.
>
> - Make sure you do not specify a file share which has the same name as the file share for your existing DB2 instance directory (this is represented by the DB2 registry variable DB2INSTPROF). Otherwise, the file share will be replaced when this file share is brought on-line.

Bring this file share online.

4. Create the IP resource for TCP/IP connections.

   This enables remote client connections to attach to the MSCS virtual server for the DB2 instance, rather than connecting to a particular system within the cluster. This IP address, rather than a particular system's IP address, should be used when cataloging TCP/IP node entries.

   You are required to fill in a name (for example, IP Address for DB2 HOT), optional description, indicate it is of resource type IP Address, belonging to the appropriate group. Accept the defaults for possible owners (which should be both nodes) and dependencies (which should be none).

   Fill in the IP address, subnet mask and the appropriate network which this IP address belongs to.

> **Note**
>
> This IP address should not already exist.

Bring this IP Address resource online.

5. Create a network name resource.

This completes the UNC name for the instance directory file share (see "Set up an MSCS File Share resource for the instance directory." on page 323).

You are required to fill in a name (for example, Network Name for DB2), optional description, indicate it is of resource type Network Name, belonging to the appropriate group. Accept the defaults for possible owners (which should be both nodes). Then add the IP address, previously defined, as a dependency, and fill in the network name (for example, DB2WOLF0).

Bring this network name resource online.

6. Create a DB2 resource for each database partition server in the cluster.

   The name must be of the form <instance name>-<node number>. The instance name and DB2 node number must be separated by a hyphen.

   You are required to fill in the name (for example, DB2MPP-0), optional description, indicate it is of resource type DB2, belonging to the appropriate group. Accept the defaults for possible owners (which should be both nodes), then add all the resources you have defined in the current group as dependencies for the DB2 instance resource.

Note

- The instance name must be the name of the DB2 instance you intend to migrate (or enable) for MSCS support.

- If the instance does not yet exist, you must use this instance name when creating the instance with the DB2ICRT utility. Also, the DB2 node number is the number you must specify when creating the DB2 node with the DB2NCRT utility.

Do not bring the DB2 instance resource online yet.

Mutual Takeover Configuration

1. Create an MSCS group for each database partition server in the partitioned database system. For example, in a four-node DB2 partitioned database system, you must create four groups.

   You are required to fill in a group name (for example, DB2 Node 0, DB2 Node 1, and so on), optional description, and then specify the preferred nodes this group will run in.

The preferred node is the node that the group will run in during normal operations. If failback is enabled, this group will automatically failback to the preferred node when available.

2. Set up a disk resource to store the user data.

   MSCS's shared nothing disk model requires the DB2 instance directory be placed on an MSCS disk resource. On failover, this directory will be made available to the remaining system in the cluster.

   When you create a disk resource, you will be required to fill in a name (for example, Disk J:), optional description, indicate it is of resource type Physical Disk, belonging to the appropriate group. Accept the defaults for possible owners (which should be both nodes), defaults for dependencies (which should be none), and select the appropriate shared disk for this disk resource.

   If you choose to use an existing disk resource, move that disk resource to the appropriate group.

Note

- If you wish to have user data made available during failover, you must also set up MSCS disk resources for each disk that will be used.

- Only the shared disks can be used for creating MSCS disk resources.

   Bring this disk resource online (and any others if required).

3. Set up an MSCS File Share resource for the instance directory.

   This allows the instance directory to be accessed via a Windows NT UNC name, for example, \\DB2WOLF0\DB2MPP. On failover, this disk will still be accessible regardless of which cluster node owns it.

   You will be required to fill in a file share name (for example, Instance Directory), optional description, indicate it is of resource type File Share, belonging to the appropriate group. Accept the defaults for possible owners (which should be none).

   Make sure the disk resource that is to be used for the file share is on-line, then choose that disk resource as a dependency. Fill in a share name for the file share (for example, DB2MPP), and a path of the form <drive letter>:\<subdirectory name> (for example, J:\PROFILE). The comment is optional.

> **Note**
>
> On the instance owning node (node 0), the path must exist on the shared drive, before the file share is brought on-line. Make sure you do not specify a file share which has the same name as the file share for your existing DB2 instance directory (this is represented by the DB2 registry variable DB2INSTPROF). Otherwise, the file share will be replaced when this file share is brought on-line.

Bring this file share on-line.

4. Create the IP resource for TCP/IP connections.

   This enables remote client connections to attach to the MSCS virtual server for the DB2 instance, rather than connecting to a particular system within the cluster. This IP address, rather than a particular system's IP address, should be used when cataloging TCP/IP node entries.

   You are required to fill in a name (for example, IP Address for DB2 MUTUAL), optional description, indicate it is of resource type IP Address, belonging to the appropriate group. Accept the defaults for possible owners (which should be both nodes) and dependencies (which should be none).

   Then fill in the IP address, subnet mask and the appropriate network which this IP address belongs to.

> **Note**
>
> This IP address should not already exist.

   Bring this IP Address resource online.

5. Create a network name resource.

   This completes the UNC name for the instance directory file share (see "Set up an MSCS File Share resource for the instance directory." on page 323).

   You are required to fill in a name (for example, Network Name for DB2), optional description, indicate it is of resource type Network Name, belonging to the appropriate group. Accept the defaults for possible owners (which should be both nodes). Then add the IP address, previously defined, as a dependency, and fill in the network name (for example, DB2WOLF0).

Bring this network name resource on-line.

Note

You only need to create a network name resource for Node 0 (or the instance owning node).

---

6. Create one DB2 resource for the database partition server in this group.

   The name must be of the form <instance name>-<node number>. The instance name and DB2 node number must be separated by a hyphen.

   You are required to fill in the name (for example, DB2MPP-0), optional description, indicate it is of resource type DB2, belonging to the appropriate group. Accept the defaults for possible owners (which should be both nodes), then add all the resources you have defined in the current group as dependencies for the DB2 instance resource.

Note

- The instance name must be the name of the DB2 instance you intend to migrate to a MSCS-enabled DB2 instance.

- If the instance does not yet exist, you must use this instance name when creating the instance using the DB2ICRT utility. Also, the DB2 node number is the number you must specify when creating the DB2 node with the DB2NCRT utility.

Do not bring the DB2 instance resource online yet.

For each database partition server on each machine, repeat the procedures to create a MSCS group, set up a disk resource for user data, IP Address and create a DB2 resource. You do not have to repeat the steps to create an MSCS File Share resource for the instance directory, nor do you have to create another network name resource. Remember to specify a different node number for each DB2 resource that you create, and to use the same node number when you issue the DB2NCRT command to add a database partition server to the instance.

8.2.4.3 Adding MSCS Support to a DB2 Instance

To add MSCS support to a DB2 instance, you have two choices:

- Create a new instance with DB2ICRT and use the /c flag. You should use this command if you do not wish to use the default instance, DB2MPP, or this instance does not exist.

- Migrate an existing instance with DB2ICLUS. You should use this command if you want to migrate the existing default instance, DB2MPP.

Creating an MSCS-Enabled DB2 Instance

To create an MSCS-enabled DB2 Instance, use the DB2ICRT command from a command window. Be sure that you run the command from the machine which you previously assigned as the instance-owning machine. The command syntax is:

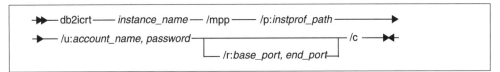

Figure 217. Syntax of the db2icrt Command

where:

- ***instance_name*** is the name of the instance.

- /mpp specifies that this is a partitioned database system.

- **/p:*instprof_path*** specifies the instance profile path. The path must use the Universal Naming Convention (UNC), and include both the network name and the share name that were created as MSCS resources for node 0. The form is as follows: /p:\\network_name\share_name. For example:

  ```
  /p:\\DB2WOLF0\DB2MPP
  ```

- **/u:*account_name, password*** specifies the domain account used as the logon account name of the DB2 Service. For example:

  ```
  /u:db2dom\db2team,db2team
  ```

- **/r:*base_port, end_port*** specifies the TCP/IP port range for the FCM. For example:

  ```
  /r:10013,10017
  ```

- **/c** specifies that DB2 will use MSCS support.

The instance profile path must reside on an MSCS cluster disk, so that when the machine fails and its resources fail over to the other machine, the MSCS cluster disk also fails over and the instance can still access the instance directory. To achieve this, specify the MSCS network name (instead of the machine name) and the MSCS file share (instead of a normal network share) for the /p: parameter. See "Setting up MSCS Groups and Resources for DB2" on page 322 for more information.

> **Note**
>
> - An MSCS DB2 resource must be created before creating the corresponding DB2 instance. This instance must then be named the same as the DB2 resource that has been created.
>
> - DB2 Instance Profile variables will be stored in the Cluster Registry under the DB2 Resource Key. This allows all cluster nodes to see the same set of DB2 profile variables. See "DB2 Registry Variables for MSCS" on page 342.

Migrating to an MSCS-Enabled DB2 Instance

Use the db2iclus migrate command, from a command window, to migrate a partitioned database instance for MSCS support. The instance must have been created with the /mpp parameter of the db2icrt command. You must run this command on the machine that runs node 0 (that is, the instance-owning machine). The command syntax is as follows:

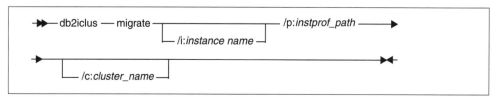

Figure 218. Syntax of the db2iclus migrate Command

Where:

- **/i:*instance_name*** specifies the name of the instance.

- **/p:*instprof_path*** specifies the instance profile path. The path must use the Universal Naming Convention (UNC), and include both the network name and the share name that were created as MSCS resources for node 0. The form is as follows: /p:\\network_name\share_name. For example:

      /p:\\DB2WOLF\DB2-DB2MPP

- **/c:*cluster_name*** specifies the name of the MSCS cluster as it is known on the LAN. This name is specified when the MSCS cluster is first created.

If a database already exists in the instance and you want it to be available if the instance fails over, you must migrate it to an MSCS shared disk. If you do not migrate the database to a shared disk, it will not be available if the instance fails over. To migrate a database:

- Take an offline backup of all database partitions for the database.
- Uncatalog the database.
- Migrate the instance to use MSCS support.
- Set up database drive mapping. See "Registering Database Drive Mappings" on page 333 for details.
- Restore the database partitions to the shared disk.
- Catalog the database that you restored.
- Verify that the instance is working correctly.
- Using a different alias, recatalog the original database.
- Drop the original database.

For information about database recovery, refer to the DB2 UDB Administration Guide.

8.2.4.4 Enabling the DB2 Resource to Fail Over
After the DB2 instance is created, configure the second MSCS node in the cluster to support the DB2 resource (database partition server) that fails over.

To enable the DB2 resource to fail over to the second node, use the db2iclus add command from any command window. The command syntax is as follows:

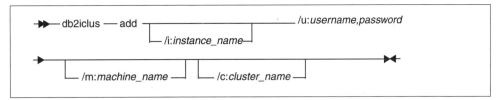

Figure 219. Syntax of the db2iclus add Command

Where:

- **/i:*instance_name*** specifies the name of the instance. (This parameter overrides the setting of the DB2INSTANCE environment variable.)
- **/u:*username,password*** specifies the domain account used as the logon account name of the DB2 Service. For example:

    ```
    /u:db2dom\db2team,db2team
    ```

- **/m:*machine_name*** specifies the computer name of the machine where the database partition server is to fail over to. You must specify this option if you run the command from a machine other than the one that is to support the database partition server that fails over.

- **/c:*cluster_name*** specifies the name of the MSCS cluster as it is known on the LAN. This name is specified when the MSCS cluster is first created.

After you run the db2iclus add command, both machines in the MSCS cluster will be configured to run DB2 resources.

8.2.4.5 Adding a DB Partition Server to the DB2 Instance

To add a database partition server to an existing instance, use the db2ncrt command from a command window. The command syntax is as follows:

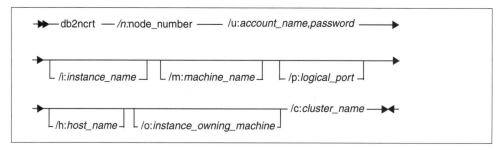

Figure 220. Syntax of the db2ncrt Command

Where:

- **/n:*node_number*** specifies the unique node number to identify the database partition server. The number can be from 0 to 999 in ascending sequence.

- **/u:*account_name,password*** specifies the domain account used as the logon account name of the DB2 service.

- **/i:*instance_name*** specifies the instance name; the default is the current instance. (This parameter overrides the setting of the DB2INSTANCE environment variable.)

- **/m:*machine_name*** specifies the computer name of the machine on which the node resides; the default name is the computer name of the local machine.

- **/p:*logical_port*** specifies the logical port number used for the database partition server, if the logical port number is not 0.

- **/h:*host_name*** specifies the TCP/IP host name of the IP address that is used by FCM for internal communications, if the host name is not the local host name.

- **/o:*instance_owning_machine*** specifies the computer name of the machine that is the instance-owning machine; the default is the local machine. This parameter is required when the db2ncrt command is invoked on any machine that is not the instance-owning machine.

- **/c:*cluster_name*** specifies the name of the MSCS cluster as it is known on the LAN. This name is specified when the MSCS cluster is first created.

You can run the db2ncrt command from either the machine on which you installed DB2, or from the instance-owning machine.

Note

If a user account is associated with the DB2 service on the node where the DB2 instance was created, the same user account should be associated with the DB2 service on the other MSCS node that will support the DB2 instance. This can be configured using the Services option from the Windows NT Control Panel. When associating a user account with a DB2 clustered service, a domain account is recommended to ensure that DB2 behaves identically on either MSCS node.

8.2.5 Registering Database Drive Mappings

Whether you use the DB2MSCS utility or the Cluster Administrator tool to enable the DB2 instance for MSCS support, before you create a partitioned database, you must register drive mappings.

When you create a database in a partitioned database environment, you specify a drive letter for the create database command to indicate where the database is to be created. When the command runs, it expects that the drive that you specify will be simultaneously available to all the machines that participate in the instance. Because this is not possible, DB2 uses database drive mapping to assign the same drive letter a different name (and so use a different disk) for each machine.

For example, assume that a DB2 instance called DB2MPP contains two database partition servers, where:

- DB2MPP-0 is active on machine WOLFNODE0
- DB2MPP-1 is active on machine WOLFNODE1

Also assume that the shared disk J: belongs to the same group as DB2MPP-0, and that the shared disk K: belongs to the same group as DB2MPP-1.

From server WOLFNODE0, to create a database on the share disk J:, the create database command, from a DB2 command window, would be as follows:

```
db2 create database mppdb on J:
```

For the create database command to be successful, drive J: must be available to both machines. In this example, each database partition server is active on a different machine, and the cluster disk J: is only available to one machine at a time. In this situation, the create database command will always fail.

To resolve this problem, the database drive should be mapped as follows:

- For DB2MPP-0, map drive K: to drive J:
- For DB2MPP-1, map drive J: to drive K:

Any database access for DB2MPP-0 to drive K: is then mapped to drive J:, and any database access for DB2MPP-1 to drive J: is mapped to drive K:. Using drive mapping, the preceding create database command will create database files on drive J: for DB2MPP-0 and drive K: for DB2MPP-1.

Use the db2drvmp command, from any command window, to set up the drive mapping. The syntax of the db2drvmp command on the instance owning machine is:

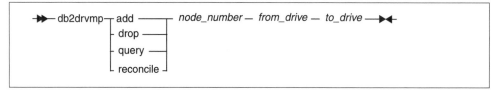

Figure 221. Syntax of the db2ncrt Command

The parameters are:

- **add** assigns a new database drive map.
- **drop** removes an existing database drive map.
- **query** queries a database map

- **reconcile** repairs a database map drive when the registry contents are damaged. See "Reconciling Database Drive Mapping" on page 336" for more information.
- *node_number* is the node number. This parameter is required for add and drop operations.
- *from_drive* is the drive letter to map from. This parameter is required for add and drop operations.
- *to_drive* is the drive letter to map to. This parameter is required for add operations. It is not applicable to other operations.

For example, if you wanted to set up a database drive mapping from K: to J: for DB2MPP-0 (WOLFNODE0), on the instance owning machine you would use the following command :

```
C:\>db2drvmp add 0 k j
SQL2813I  The drive mapping from drive "k" to drive "j" was added
for node "0".
```

Note that database drive mappings do not apply to table spaces, containers, or any other database storage objects.

Similarly, to set up a database drive mapping from drive J: to drive K: for DB2MPP-1 (WOLFNODE1), on the instance owning machine you would issue the following command:

```
C:\>db2drvmp add 1 j k
SQL2813I  The drive mapping from drive "j" to drive "k" was added
for node "1".
```

You can check your drive mappings by issuing a db2drvmp query command on the MSCS node where you issued the initial db2drvmp commands (the instance owning machine).

Any setup of, or changes to, database drive mapping do not take effect immediately. To activate the database drive mapping, use the Cluster Administrator tool to bring the DB2 resource offline, then online.

If you attempt to do a drive mapping for the second node and fail, you may receive the following error message:

```
C:\>db2drvmp add 1 j k
DBI1965N The node "<node number> was not found in the node list.
Cause: The specified node was not found in the node list.
Action: Verify that the node exists by displaying the list of
nodes using the DB2NLIST command.
```

Check that the DB2NLIST command shows node 1 in the DB2 node list. If
not, then the second node may not have been enabled for failover support
(via the db2iclus add command; see "Enabling the DB2 Resource to Fail
Over" on page 331), before adding the second DB2 node as an additional
DB2 partition server to the DB2 instance.

To resolve this, perform the following steps:

1. Remove the second DB2 node with the db2ndrop command.

2. Enable it for MSCS support.

3. Add the DB2 node to the instance again.

4. Finally, retry the drive mapping for the second DB2 node (node 1).

8.2.5.1 Reconciling Database Drive Mapping

When a database is created on a machine that has database drive mapping
in effect, the map is saved on the drive in a hidden file. By doing this, we
prevent the database drive from being removed after the database has been
created. We need to reconcile the mapping. This is done using the db2drvmp
reconcile command for each database partition server that contains the
database. (As an example of why you would want to or need to do this
reconciliation, is if you accidentally dropped the database drive map.) The
command syntax is:

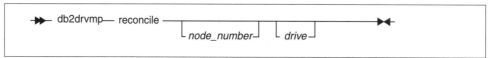

Figure 222. Syntax of the db2drvmp reconcile Command

where:

- **node_number** is the node number of the node to be repaired. If this is not
  specified, then mapping reconciliation is done for all nodes.

- **drive** is the drive to reconcile. If you choose not to specify this value, then
  the reconciliation is done for all drives.

The db2drvmp command scans all drives on the machine for database partitions that are managed by the database partition server. It reapplies the database drive mapping to the registry as required. You can run the db2drvmp command from a command window.

8.2.6 Changing DB2 Node Configuration Information

In an MSCS cluster configuration, it is common for each system in the MSCS cluster to use two or more network adapters, where one network adapter from each machine will be used as an internal network for cluster monitoring. This adds further complexity, in terms of DB2 FCM communications, to the DB2 node configuration.

FCM, for security reasons, only checks for FCM related communication on a specific network adapter. If both DB2 nodes of the DB2 instance are defined and available (for example, using db2nlist /s shows the status for both nodes), but you find that FCM cannot communicate with the other node (for example, you cannot create a partitioned database due to FCM communications failure), you may have to explicitly specify which network adapter to use via the db2nchg command.

The DB2NCHG utility changes or updates node configuration for a given node in a partitioned database system. This utility is run from a command window and the command syntax is:

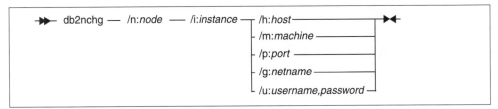

Figure 223. Syntax of the db2nchg Command

where:

- **/h:***host* specifies a change in the TCP/IP host name
- **/m:***machine* specifies a change in the server name
- **/p:***port* specifies a change in the logical port number
- **/i:***instance* specifies the instance if different from the default/current instance
- **/g:***netname* used to specify a specific IP address for FCM to use when communicating to another node

- **/u:*username,password*** specifies a change in the Logon Account name and password

For example, to change the DB2 nodes (system name WOLFNODE0 has DB2 node 0, while system name WOLFNODE1 has DB2 node 1) to use a specific network IP address (10.10.10.8 and 10.10.10.9 respectively) on the 10.10.10 network, use the following commands:

```
C:>db2nchg /n:0 /g:10.10.10.8
SQL281W Node "0" changed in instance: "DB2MPP" (Host: "wolfnode0"
Machine: "WOLFNODE0" Port: "0")
C:>db2nchg /n:1 /g:10.10.10.9
SQL281W Node "1" changed in instance: "DB2MPP" (Host: "wolfnode1"
Machine: "WOLFNODE1" Port: "0")
```

To verify this, use the db2nlist command. The above example would yield the following result:

```
C:>db2nlist
Node: "0" Host: "wolfnode0" Machine: "WOLFNODE0" Port: 0 Netname:
"10.10.10.8"
Node: "0" Host: "wolfnode1" Machine: "WOLFNODE1" Port: 0 Netname:
"10.10.10.9"
```

Note

You have to configure these new IP addresses as MSCS resources, enabled for failover on the respective MSCS nodes in the cluster. See "Failover of FCM IP Address" on page 394 for a detailed example.

8.2.7 Disabling DB2 Resource Failover to the second MSCS node

To disable an MSCS DB2 resource (database partition server) from failing over to the second MSCS node, use the db2iclus drop command, from any command window. The command syntax is:

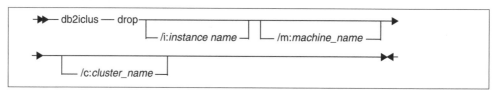

Figure 224. Syntax of the db2iclus drop Command

where:

- **/i:*instance_name*** specifies the instance name. The default is the current instance. This parameter overrides the setting of the DB2INSTANCE environment variable.

- **/m:*machine_name*** specifies the computer name of the machine where the DB2 resource can currently failover to. You must specify this option if you run the command from a machine other than the one that the DB2 resource can failover to.

- **/c:*cluster_name*** specifies the name of the MSCS cluster as it is known on the LAN. This name is specified when the MSCS cluster is first created.

8.2.8 Failback Considerations

By default, MSCS groups are set to not failback to the original (failed) system. Unless you manually configure a DB2 group to failback after failing over, it continues to run on the alternative MSCS node after the cause of the failover has been resolved.

If you configure a DB2 group to automatically failback to the original machine, all the resources in the DB2 group, including the DB2 resource (database partition server), will failback as soon as the original machine is available. If, during the failback, a database connection exists, the DB2 resource cannot be brought offline, and failback processing will fail.

To force all database connections during failback processing, set the DB2_FALLBACK registry variable to ON. This variable is set in any command window as follows:

```
db2set DB2_FALLBACK=ON
```

You do not have to reboot or restart the cluster service after setting this registry variable.

8.2.9 Application Support Considerations

DB2 UDB in an MSCS environment is a high availability solution providing
online recovery in the time it takes for MSCS to restart the clustered
resources and for DB2 to perform recovery. DB2 will rollback any
uncommitted transactions after it is restarted.

DB2 clients should have a TCP/IP entry in the DB2 node directory to
reference the DB2 IP address resource, the IP resource defined in the MSCS
resource group that contains the DB2 resource.

Applications running in this environment will experience a communication
failure as the communications layer is moved from one MSCS node to
another. Applications can exploit this environment by caching
connection/transaction information. In the event of a communications failure,
the application can automatically reconnect and retry the transaction.

Any application UDFs or Stored Procedures that are installed at the server
must be made available on all MSCS nodes that will participate in the failover.
Typically, UDF DLLs and Stored Procedures are located in the DB2 install
path subdirectories FUNCTION or FUNCTION\UNFENCED. The
Administrator should ensure these are mirrored on all clustered nodes to

ensure consistent application behavior, regardless of which node DB2 is active on.

8.2.10 Miscellaneous DB2 UDB EEE Concepts

In this section, we cover some DB2 UDB EEE concepts that you should be aware of when configuring DB2 UDB EEE in a MSCS environment.

8.2.10.1 Dropping DB2 instance with db2idrop

The db2idrop command is used to drop DB2 instances. The db2idrop command is run from a command window as follows:

```
db2idrop instance_name
```

Where

- *instance_name* is the name of the DB2 instance to be dropped.

This command will drop the specified instance. It will also remove the DB2 instance infrastructure from all clustered nodes. For example, if a DB2 resource was configured to run on systems WOLFNODE0 and WOLFNODE1, db2idrop would remove the instance from both systems.

8.2.10.2 Listing DB2 Instances with db2ilist

The db2ilist is used to list all DB2 instances on the current system. The db2ilist command is run from a command window as follows:

```
db2ilist
```

The db2ilist utility will differentiate an MSCS-enabled DB2 instance from a normal DB2 instance by displaying the letter C against the instance, followed by the name of the MSCS cluster. For example, if we have a clustered DB2 instance called DB2MPP, in the MSCS cluster DB2CLUS, if we run the db2ilist command in a command window, we receive the following:

```
C:\>db2ilist
DB2MPP      C : DB2CLUS
```

8.2.10.3 Dropping Nodes from a DB2 Instance

Use db2ndrop to remove a DB2 node from an instance. The command is run in a command window as follows:

```
db2ndrop /n:node /i:instance_name
```

where:

- /n:*node* specifies the node to be dropped from the instance

- /i:**instance_name** optionally specifies the instance to drop the node from if it is different from the current instance

8.2.10.4 DB2 Registry Variables for MSCS

Profile variables for an MSCS-enabled DB2 instance will be stored in the MSCS Cluster Registry. This registry is a single image that is visible to all clustered MSCS nodes. The DB2 instance will see the same set of instance profile variables regardless of which clustered MSCS node DB2 is active on.

The db2set command, run in a command window to view and set DB2 registry variables, is unchanged in command syntax in a DB2 MSCS environment. When db2set is used, DB2 will detect whether or not the DB2 instance is MSCS-enabled, and will use either the local system registry or the MSCS clustered registry as appropriate.

Two new registry variables have been introduced for MSCS support:

- DB2CLUSTER is the name of the cluster that the DB2 instance is a member of.

- DB2CLUSTERLIST is a list of servers (the machine names) in the cluster that support the DB2 instance.

These registry variables should not be altered by a user.

8.3 Administering DB2 in an MSCS Environment

Having your DB2 instance participate as part of an MSCS cluster requires you to think about a number of other issues regarding administration. This includes how you configure your database, issues relating to day-to-day operation of your system, etc. The goal of course is for DB2 UDB to execute seamlessly on any MSCS node. To accomplish this end, you must take some additional administrative steps. Possibly the most important step is ensuring that all DB2 dependent operating system resources be available on all MSCS nodes. Since some of the resources required by DB2 do not fall under MSCS (cannot be defined as a resource) you must ensure that each system is configured such that the same operating system resources are available on all MSCS nodes. The additional administrative tasks to accomplish this are discussed in the sections that follow.

8.3.1 Starting and Stopping DB2 Resources

It is important to know that DB2 resources should **only** be started and stopped from the Cluster Administration utility. You must ensure that DB2 is started from the Cluster Administrator since if you do not, the MSCS software will not be able to be aware of the state of the DB2 instance. As such, the standard mechanisms available to start a DB2 instance such as the db2start command, and the Services option from the Control Panel are insufficient. If a DB2 instance is started using the Cluster Administrator and stopped using the db2stop command, the MSCS software will interpret the db2stop command as a software failure and attempt to restart DB2.

Conversely, if you use db2start to start a DB2 instance, MSCS cannot detect that the resource is on-line and as a result would not attempt to bring the DB2 resource on-line on the failover machine in the event that the partition server fails.

Three operations can be applied to a DB2 instance from the Cluster Administration tool:

- **Online**: This operation is equivalent to using the db2start command. If DB2 is already active, this operation can be used simply to notify MSCS that DB2 is active. Any errors during this operation will be written to the Windows NT Event Log.

- **Offline**: This operation is equivalent to using the db2stop command. You cannot have active connections to the instance as this will cause the off-line action to fail.

- **Fail resource**: This operation is equivalent to using the db2stop command with the force option specified.

8.3.2 Running Scripts

You may find it useful to execute certain DB2 related commands before or after (or both) the DB2 resource is brought on-line. This is accomplished through the use of scripts which must reside in the instance profile directory that is specified by the DB2INSTPROF registry variable. If you wish to determine the current setting of this variable issue the following command from any command window:

```
db2set -i:instance_name DB2INSTPROF
```

where

- **-i:*instance_name*** specifies the instance name for which you want the D2INSTPROF profile variable. If this is not specified, the default instance indicated by the DB2 environment variable DB2INSTANCE is used.

Remember that since you are now dealing with a clustered environment, this file path must be on a clustered disk so that the instance directory is available on all cluster nodes.

The script files will only be executed by the MSCS Cluster Server if they are found in the instance directory. They are optional.

The same script will be used by every database partition server in the instance. As a result, if you need to distinguish among the different database partition servers in the script file itself, you need to make use of the DB2NODE value to distinguish the partition you are on.

8.3.2.1 Running Scripts Before Bringing DB2 Resources Online

If you want to run a script before you bring a DB2 resource on-line, the script must be named DB2CPRE.BAT. DB2 calls functions that will launch this batch file from the Windows NT command line processor and wait for the command line processor to complete execution before the DB2 resource is brought on-line. You can use this batch file for tasks such as modifying the DB2 database manager configuration.

The commands placed in the DB2CPRE.BAT script should execute synchronously. You need to ensure this happens otherwise the DB2 resource may be brought on-line before all tasks in the script are completed. Depending on the statements in the script file, this may result in unexpected behavior. As an example, do not initiate a DB2 command window from within the script since anything executed in that command window will be asynchronous to the running of the script.

If you want to use DB2 commands in the DB2CPRE.BAT script, the commands should be placed in a file and executed as a CLP batch file from within a program that initializes the DB2 environment for the DB2 command line processor, then waits for the completion of the DB2 command line processor. For example, one such program could be coded in C as follows:

```
#include <windows.h>

int WINAPI DB2SetCLPEnv_api(DWORD pid);

void main (int argc, char *argv [ ] )
{
    STARTUPINFO         startInfo = {0};
    PROCESS_INFORMATION pidInfo = {0};
    char                title  [32] = "Run Synchronously";
    char                runCmd [64] = "DB2 -z c:\\run.out -tvf c:\\run.clp";

/* Invoke API to setup a CLP Environment */
    if ( DB2SetCLPEnv_api (GetCurrentProcessId ()) == 0 )(1)
    {
        startInfo.cb          = sizeof(STARTUPINFO);
        startInfo.lpReserved  = NULL;
        startInfo.lpTitle     = title;
        startInfo.lpDesktop   = NULL;
        startInfo.dwX         = 0;
        startInfo.dwY         = 0;
        startInfo.dwXSize     = 0;
        startInfo.dwYSize     = 0;
        startInfo.dwFlags     = 0L;
        startInfo.wShowWindow = SW_HIDE;
        startInfo.lpReserved2 = NULL;
        startInfo.cbReserved2 = 0;

        if ( CreateProcessA( NULL,
                             runCmd, (2)
                             NULL,
                             NULL,
                             FALSE,
                             NORMAL_PRIORITY_CLASS | CREATE_NEW_CONSOLE,
                             NULL,
                             NULL,
                             &startInfo,
                             &pidInfo))
        {
            WaitForSingleObject (pidInfo.hProcess, INFINITE);
            CloseHandle (pidInfo.hProcess);
            CloseHandle (pidInfo.hThread);
        }
    }
    return;
}
```

Notes:

1. The API DB2SetCLPEnv_api is resolved by the import library DB2API.LIB.
   This API sets an environment that allows CLP commands to be invoked. If
   this program is invoked from the DB2CPRE.BAT script, the command
   processor will wait for the CLP commands to complete.

2. runCmd is the name of the script file that contains the DB2 CLP
   commands.

A sample program called db2clpex.exe can be found in the MISC subdirectory of SQLLIB (where DB2 is installed). It is similar to the example provided, but accepts the DB2 CLP command as a command line argument. If you want to use this sample program, copy it to the BIN subdirectory or SQLLIB and use it in the db2cpre.bat script as follows:

```
db2clpex "DB2 -Z \\network_name\share_name\wolfinst\pre.log
-tvf \\cluster_name\share_name\wolfinst\pre.clp"
```

Unless specifically provided, the user account used with the DB2 attach command or connect statement will be that account associated with the cluster service. Finally, DB2 CLP scripts should also complete with the terminate command to end the DB2 CLP background process.

The following is an example of a DB2CPRE.BAT file using the DB2 CLP executable db2clpex:

```
db2cpre.bat : (1)
-----------------------
set DB2INSTANCE=WOLFINST  (2)
dir \\network_name\share_name\wolfinst > \\network_name\share_name\wolfinst.log (3)
db2clpex "db2 -z \\network_name\share_name\wolfinst\pre-%DB2NODE%.log (4)
   -tvf \\network_name\share_name\wolfinst\pre.clp" (5)
-----------------------
PRE.CLP (6)
-----------------------
update dbm cfg using MAXAGENTS 200;
get dbm cfg;
terminate;
-----------------------
```

Notes:

1. The DB2CPRE.BAT script executes under the user account associated with the Cluster Server service.

2. Ensure that the DB2INSTANCE environment variable is set so that the script executes under the correct DB2 instance

3. The directory must use the universal naming convention, and include both the network name and the share name (that is, the name of the MSCS shared disk resource that is used for the instance directory).

4. The name of the log file must be different for each node to avoid file contention when both logical nodes are brought on-line at the same time.

5. The db2clpex.exe sample program must be made available on all MSCS cluster nodes.

6. The CLP commands in this example set a limit on the number of agents.

8.3.2.2 Running Scripts After Bringing DB2 Resources Online

If you want to run a script after you bring a DB2 resource on-line, it must be named DB2CPOST.BAT. All statements in this script file will be run after the DB2 resource has been successfully brought on-line. Since the statements are executed after the resource is on-line, we do not have the worry about the synchronization of the statements and as such we can use the db2cmd command to execute DB2 CLP script files. Use the -c parameter of the db2cmd command to specify that the utility should close all windows on completion of the task. For example, in a command window:

```
db2cmd -c db2 -tvf mycmds.clp
```

The -c parameter must be the first argument to the db2cmd command, as it prevents orphaned command processors in the background.

The DB2CPOST.BAT script is useful if you want to perform database activities immediately after the DB2 resource fails over and becomes active.

The following is an example of a DB2CPOST.BAT script:

```
db2cpost.bat (1)
-----------------------
SET DB2INSTANCE=WOLFINST (2)
db2cmd -c db2 -z \\network_name\share_name\wolfinst\post-%DB2NODE%.log (3)
   -tvf \\network_name\share_name\wolfinst\post.clp (4)
-----------------------
POST.CLP (5)
-----------------------
restart database SAMPLE;
connect reset;
activate database SAMPLE;
terminate;
-----------------------
```

Notes:

1. The DB2CPOST.BAT script executes under the user account associated with the Cluster Service.

2. Ensure that the DB2INSTANCE environment variable is set so that the script executes under the correct DB2 instance

3. The name of the log file must be different for each node to avoid file contention when both logical nodes are brought online at the same time.

4. The directory must use the universal naming convention, and include both the cluster name and the share name (that is, the name of the MSCS shared disk resource that is used for the instance directory).

5. The CLP script in this example contains commands to restart and activate the database. This script returns the database to an active state immediately after the database manager is started. If multiple DB2 resources are brought online on the same machine at the same time, the restart database command may fail because another logical node is activating the database. If this occurs, rerun the script to ensure that the database is restarted correctly.

8.3.3 Database Considerations

An instance with MSCS support can support both databases that will fail over, and databases that are local to a specific system. To ensure that a database will fail over, define all its dependent resources as cluster resources, and place them in the same resource group so that the Cluster Administrator tool can treat the resources as a single unit (for example the DB2 log files). In addition, you should configure a dependency using the Cluster Administrator to ensure that all dependent resources are brought on-line and available before the DB2 resource is started.

When you create a database, you must make sure that certain steps are taken to ensure that files can be seen across all MSCS nodes and that files are setup such that DB2 can failover successfully. Specifically ensure that the database path refers to a share disk. This allows the database to be seen on all MSCS nodes. All logs and other database files must also refer to clustered disks for DB2 to failover successfully.

Finally you need to make sure that you have enough system resources on each MSCS node to support the database and database manager configuration parameters and the resources they require. In addition, you want to ensure that the database is consistent as quickly as possible after a successful failover. To ensure consistency you need to restart the database(s). There are two ways to do this. The preferred method to bring the database to a ready state is to use the DB2CPOST.BAT script to restart and activate the database. This method is preferred, because there will be no dependency on autorestart, and you do not need to have a user connection or activation occur. The alternate method is to enable AUTORESTART in the database which will cause a database restart to occur on first connect or activation.

8.3.4 Windows NT User and Group Support

DB2 UDB relies on Windows NT for user authentication and group support. For a DB2 instance to fail over from one MSCS node to another, each MSCS node must have access to the same Windows NT security databases. To achieve this end, you need to use Windows NT Domain Security. (Define all DB2 users and groups in a Domain Security database. The MSCS nodes must be members of this Domain or the Domain must be a Trusted Domain.) DB2 will then use the Domain Security database for authentication and group support, independent of which MSCS node DB2 is executing on.

You can choose not to use Domain Security, however if you do this then you must have the local accounts replicated on each MSCS node. This approach would be more work and since more administration is required, prone to more errors.

Since the MSCS service runs under a particular user account, and that user account may be used (by default) for any DB2 commands in either the pre or post script files, you need also to make sure that this user account meets all DB2 naming standards.

8.3.5 Communications Considerations

DB2 supports the TCP/IP and NetBIOS LAN protocols in an MSCS Environment.

TCP/IP is inherently supported as it is a supported cluster resource type. The steps you need to take to enable DB2 in this configuration to be able to use TCP/IP as a communications protocol are:

1. create an IP Address resource
2. place the created IP Address in the same group as the DB2 resource that represents the database partition server that you want to use as a coordinator partition for remote applications.
3. create a dependency using the Cluster Administrator tool to ensure that the IP resource is on-line before the DB2 resource is started.

When the above has been completed, DB2 clients can then catalog TCP/IP node directory entries to use this TCP/IP address and will be able to continue accessing the DB2 data in the event of a failover.

Although NetBIOS is not a supported cluster resource, you can use NetBIOS as a LAN protocol because the protocol ensures that NetBIOS names are unique on the LAN. When DB2 registers a NetBIOS name, NetBIOS ensures the name is not in use on the LAN. In a failover scenario, when DB2 is moved from one system to another, the NNAME used by DB2 will be deregistered from one partner machine in the MSCS cluster and registered on the other machine.

8.3.6 System Time Considerations

DB2 uses the system time to timestamp certain operations. All MSCS nodes that participate in DB2 failover must have the system time zone and system time synchronized to ensure DB2 behaves consistently on all machines.

Set the system time zone using the Date/Time option from the Control Panel dialog. MSCS has a time service that synchronizes the date and time when the MSCS nodes join to form a cluster. The time service, however, only synchronizes the time every 12 hours, which may result in problems if the time is changed on one system and DB2 fails over before the time is synchronized.

If the date/time is changed on one of the MSCS cluster nodes, the time should be manually synchronized on the other cluster nodes using the command (in any command window):

```
net time /set /y \\remote_node
```

Where

- ***remote_node*** is the machine name of the cluster node.

8.3.7 Administration Server and Control Center Considerations

The DB2 Administration Server or DAS is optionally created during the installation of DB2 Universal Database. The Control Center uses the services provided by the Administration Server to administer DB2 instances and databases.

In an MSCS environment, a DB2 instance can reside on multiple MSCS nodes. This implies that a DB2 instance must be cataloged on multiple systems under the Control Center so that the instance remains accessible, regardless of which MSCS node the DB2 instance is active on.

The DB2 Administration Server instance directory is not shared. You must mirror all user-defined files in the Administration Server directory to all MSCS nodes to provide the same level of administration to all MSCS nodes. Specifically, you must make user scripts and scheduled executables available on all nodes. You must also ensure that scheduled activities are scheduled on both machines in an MSCS cluster.

Another consideration is to have the DB2 Administration Server fail over. For more information on setting up the DB2 Administration Server for fail over, please see the DB2 Universal Database Version 5.2 Administration Guide.

8.3.8 Limitations and Restrictions

When you run DB2 in an MSCS environment:

- You cannot use physical I/O on shared disks, unless the shared disks have the same physical disk number across both MSCS nodes. You can use logical I/O because the disk is accessed using a partition identifier.

- To uninstall DB2, you must first stop MSCS. This also applies to installing fixpacks, which require all DB2 processes be stopped.

> **Note**
>
> Do not use the Windows NT Task Manager to kill the db2start process in a high availability environment. This may invalidate failover recovery in your environment.

8.4 DB2 UDB EEE Two-Node Mutual Takeover Example

Let's look at a detailed example of an MSCS cluster setup, supporting a two-node DB2 UDB EEE instance configured in mutual takeover mode. We will also discuss some considerations when using the FCM (Fast Communications Manager) in an MSCS environment.

This section is presented as follows:

- Creating the MSCS Cluster.
- Setting up DB2 UDB for failover support in one of two ways:
  4. Using the DB2MSCS tool included with DB2 UDB.
  5. Using the MSCS Cluster Administrator tool.
- Registering database drive mappings for DB2 UDB.
- Configuring the DB2 UDB Administration Server for Failover.
- Performing additional configuration to support FCM communications.
- Verifying failover and failback.

8.4.1 Creating the MSCS Cluster

Windows NT 4.0 Enterprise Edition, with Service Pack 3, is installed on the two systems, and TCP/IP is installed and configured as follows:

Server 1:

- Machine name: DB2LAB7
- TCP/IP hostname: db2lab7
- Adapter 1 (IBMFE1) IP Address: 10.10.10.8
- Adapter 2 (AMDPCN2) IP Address 20.20.20.20

Server 2:

- Machine name: DB2LAB5
- TCP/IP hostname: db2lab5
- Adapter 1 (IBMFE1) IP Address: 10.10.10.9
- Adapter 2 (AMDPCN2) IP Address 20.20.20.21

Note that adapter 1 of each system is connected directly to the other system via the crossover connection. Hence, this network will be used for internal cluster communications only.The hosts file on both systems contain the following entries:

```
10.10.10.8      db2lab7
10.10.10.9      db2lab5
10.10.10.12     db2clus
```

The extra definition of IP address 10.10.10.12, hostname db2clus, will be used as the IP address of the MSCS cluster (for cluster administration).

- For the purposes of this example, we created a domain administrator account with account name: db2team and password: db2team.
- We also assume that all shared disks in the shared disk subsystem have been assigned drive letters, on both systems. In this example, we are using an SSA array, with five disks defined, starting from I: through to M:.
- Finally, both systems are members of the Windows NT domain DB2DOM, and the PDC for this domain is up and running (the Primary Domain Controller is required for authentication purposes).

Figure 225 shows this configuration:

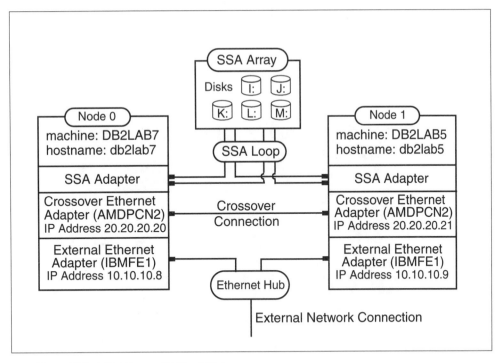

Figure 225. Initial Server Configuration

8.4.1.1 Configuring MSCS on the First Server

The steps to install MSCS on the first server (DB2LAB7 in our example) are as follows:

1. Reboot the system to start Windows NT.

   Log on with a user ID that has domain administrator privileges. You can log on with the administrator account that was created during Windows NT Server installation. The user must have a password.

Note

The second server must be powered off at this stage.

---

2. Run **SETUP** from the MSCS CD-ROM to start the installation process.

3. You should stop any other applications that are running on the machine. This will ensure a clean installation. Continue the installation by clicking on the **Next** button.

4. You will now see an information panel telling you that you should check if the hardware you are using is supported by the MSCS software. Read the information and click on the **I Agree** button. This will then allow you to click on then **Next** button.

5. Select **Form a new cluster** in the next panel (see Figure 226), and click on the **Next** button.

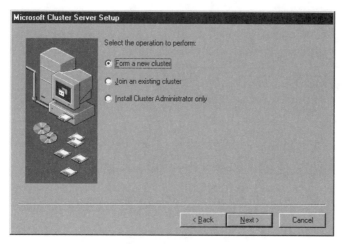

Figure 226. Forming a New MSCS Cluster

6. In our example, we named the cluster DB2CLUS (see Figure 227 below). Click on the **Next** button to continue.

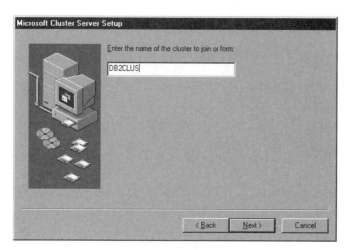

Figure 227. Naming the New MSCS Cluster

7. You now have to define the directory in which the cluster files will be stored. This directory must be on a local drive. We accepted the default: `C:\WINNT\CLUSTER`. You can also use the Browse button to see the available drives. All drives will be listed, but you can only use the local ones. Click on the **Next** button to continue.

8. You are then asked to fill in a user name and password. We chose the same administrator account we used to log on to Windows NT Server. The domain is the NT domain in which this system is defined. In this example (see Figure 228), we used:

   • user name: db2team

   • password: db2team

   • domain: db2dom (the domain name should already be filled in)

Note

• The password is only asked for once. Be sure you enter the right characters.

• You must install the cluster using a domain administrator account.

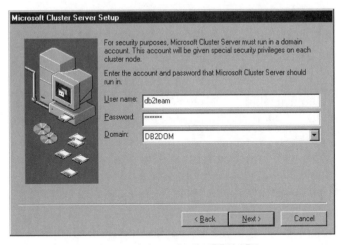

Figure 228. User Account Information for DB2LAB7

9. Click on the **Next** button. On the right side in the Shared cluster disks panel, all external drives that are shared by the SCSI buses are listed. If you want a particular drive to be not shared by the cluster, simply select the drive and click on **Remove**. You should see this drive now on the left side in the Available unshared disks panel.

Click on the **Next** button to continue.

10. Select the disk where the cluster log files will be stored. The log files are also called quorum files. They enable the failover management.

The quorum files must be stored on a shared drive as both nodes must be able to access these files. Therefore only shared drives are listed in the pull-down menu (see Figure 229). If you have previously defined any shared drives to be not shared, they will not be listed here.

We accepted the default drive (drive I:). Click on the **Next** button.

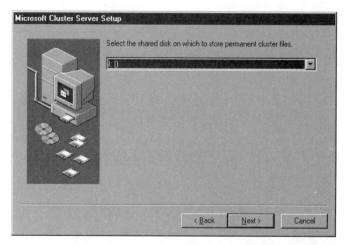

Figure 229. Shared Drive for the DB2CLUS MSCS Cluster Quorum Files

11. The installation procedure will now identify network resources that are to be made available to the cluster. Click on the **Next** button, and then fill in the information for each network adapter identified by the MSCS installation procedure.

We have two network adapters in each system. Hence, one will be configured for all communications, while the other will be configured for internal communications only.

1. Network adapter IBMFE1 (see Figure 230) is to be used for all communications. We will call this network IBMFE.

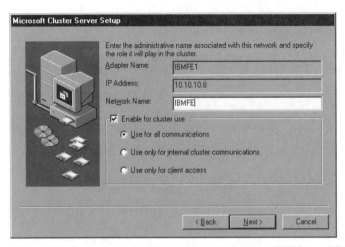

Figure 230. Network Information for Network Adapter IBMFE1 on DB2LAB7

2. Click on the **Next** button to continue. Now we fill in network information for the second network adapter, AMDPCN2. This network adapter is using the crossover network connection. Hence, we will use it for internal cluster communications only, and call this network AMDPCN7(see Figure 231). The 7 at the end of AMDPCN7 relates to DB2LAB7. Then click on the **Next** button.

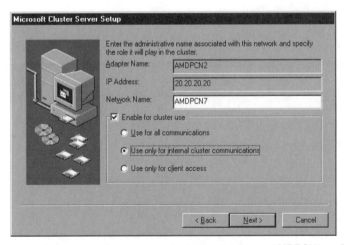

Figure 231. Network Information for Network Adapter AMDPCN2 on DB2LAB7

12.The next panel allows you to prioritize the networks to be used for internal cluster communications. Since we are using network adapter AMDPCN2 on DB2LAB7 for internal cluster communications, we will select the

AMDPCN7 network as first priority, followed by the IBMFE network (see Figure 232). Click on the **Next** button.

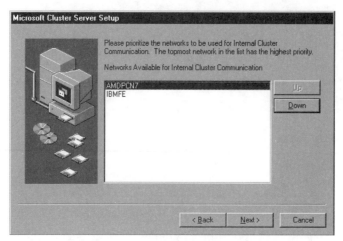

Figure 232. Prioritizing Internal Network Communications on DB2LAB7

13.We now define the cluster IP Address as 10.10.10.12, and fill in the appropriate subnet mask for the network IBMFE, as shown in Figure 233.

This is the IP address that other machines in the network use to access the cluster. This address can be used for both client access and cluster administration from a remote system.

Note that this is the IP address for the whole cluster, not one of the machines in the cluster. If you connect through the server-specific IP address, you will lose your connection if that server fails. However, if you connect through the cluster IP address, you will continue to have access to defined cluster resources, regardless of which node they may be running on.

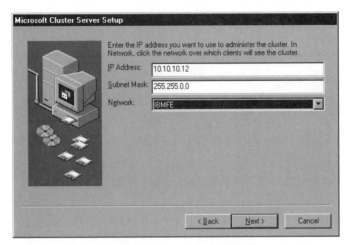

Figure 233. Defining the IP Address for the DB2CLUS cluster

14.Click on the **Next** button to continue, then click on **Finish**.

15.You should then receive a status window indicating success of the MSCS install. Click on the **OK** button, and the system will automatically reboot.

This finalizes the MSCS installation on the first server, and creates the first MSCS node in the DB2CLUS cluster. To verify that Cluster Server is installed and successfully running after the system has rebooted, log in with the domain administrator account again, and check in the Services panel of the Windows NT Control Panel. You should see that the Cluster Server is started (see Figure 234).

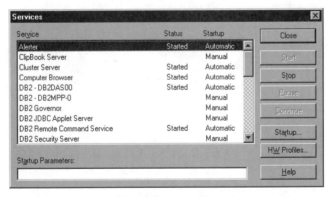

Figure 234. Verifying Cluster Server is Started

8.4.1.2 Configuring MSCS on the Second Server

Once you have completed the installation of MSCS on the first server, make sure that this machine is running with the Cluster Server started. Then install MSCS on the second server (in this example DB2LAB5) as follows:

1. Power on the second server.

   Log on to Windows NT with the same domain administrator account as you did before on the first machine.

2. Run **SETUP** from the MSCS CD-ROM to start the installation process.

3. You should stop any other applications that are running on the machine. This will ensure a clean installation. Continue the installation by clicking on the **Next** button.

4. You will now see an information panel telling you that you should check if the hardware you are using is supported by the MSCS software. Read the information and click on the **I Agree** button. You can then click on the **Next** button.

5. Select **Join an existing cluster** in the next panel (see Figure 235), and click on the **Next** button.

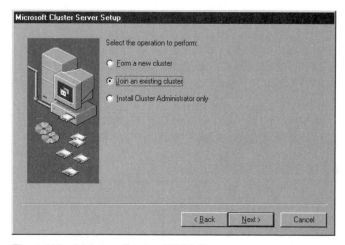

Figure 235. Joining an Existing MSCS Cluster

6. You are prompted for the name of the cluster you want to join (see Figure 236).

   Fill in the name of the cluster you previously defined (here DB2CLUS). Then click on the **Next** button to continue.

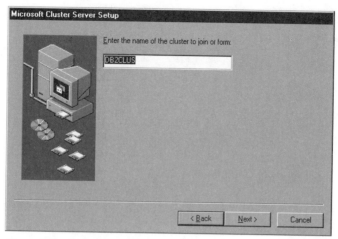

Figure 236. Name of the Cluster to Join

> If you receive an error message indicating that the MSCS installation program cannot find the cluster DB2CLUS, try using the server name instead (for example, DB2LAB7).

7. You now have to define the directory in which the cluster files will be stored. This directory must be on a local drive. We accepted the default: `C:\WINNT\CLUSTER`. You can also use Browse to see the available drives. All drives will be listed, but you can only use the local ones. Click on the **Next** button to continue.

8. In the next panel, the user name and the domain name should already be filled in. Type in the password for the specified user name. This is the user name you logged on with before. The domain is the NT domain in which the system is defined. In this example (see Figure 237), we once again used:

   - user name: db2team
   - password: db2team
   - domain: db2dom

Note

The password is only asked for once. Be sure you enter the right characters.

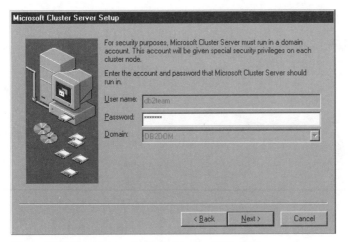

Figure 237. User Account Information for DB2LAB5

9. Click on the **Next** button. The installation will now identify network resources that were not previously defined in the setup for the first MSCS node. Click on the **Next** button. Since the network for the first network adapter has already been configured (IBMFE), we will only need to fill in the information for the second network adapter in the second server, AMDPCN2.

This network adapter is connected to the other server using the crossover network connection. Hence, we enable it for internal cluster communications only, and call this network AMDPCN5 (see Figure 238). The 5 at the end of AMDPCN5 relates to DB2LAB5. Then, click on the **Next** button.

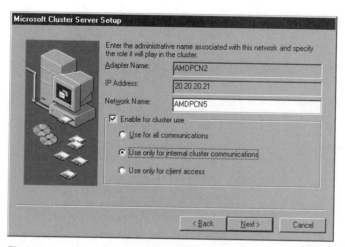

Figure 238. Network Information for Network Adapter AMDPCN2 on DB2LAB5

10. Finally, click on the **Finish** button to finalize the installation of the second server (DB2LAB5) in the cluster.

11. After the install has finished, you should receive a status window indicating the success of the MSCS install. Click on the **OK** button, and the system will automatically reboot.

Once the system has rebooted, you should verify the installation of MSCS on the second server. To do this, check that the Cluster Server is started in the Services panel of the Windows NT Control Panel (see Figure 234 on page 359).

8.4.1.3 Verifying the MSCS Cluster

To verify that the DB2CLUS cluster is operational, on each system in the cluster, start the Cluster Administrator tool. To do this, click on the Windows NT **Start** button, select **Programs**, **Administration Tools**, and finally **Cluster Administrator**.

When prompted for a cluster or server name in the Open Connection to Cluster panel, type in the name of the server, not the cluster (here DB2CLUS). For example, on the first server, type DB2LAB7, and on the second server, type DB2LAB5. In the Cluster Administrator tool on each server, you should see both nodes of the cluster (see Figure 239 for an example of the Cluster Administrator tool panel on DB2LAB7).

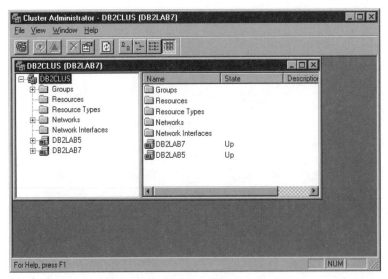

Figure 239. Cluster Administrator Tool on DB2LAB7

This completes the installation and configuration of MSCS on both servers in the cluster. The DB2CLUS MSCS cluster is now available for use.

8.4.2 Configuring DB2 UDB EEE and MSCS for Failover Support

DB2 UDB EEE should be already installed on both MSCS nodes of the cluster, with the first MSCS node (DB2LAB7) running the instance owning DB2 node or partition server, and the second MSCS node (DB2LAB5) being an additional DB2 node on an existing partitioned database system. In our example, this instance is called DB2MPP (the default). See "DB2 UDB Enterprise-Extended Edition" on page 263 if you need more information about installing DB2 UDB EEE.

8.4.2.1 Creating a DB2 Instance

If DB2 UDB EEE is already installed on both nodes, and you need create (or re-create) the instance, you can do so by issuing the following commands on DB2LAB7:

- To create the initial instance (DB2LAB7 is the instance owning server), run the following command from a command window:

```
db2icrt DB2MPP /mpp /u:db2team,db2team /r:10013,10017
```

- To add the second server (DB2LAB5) as the second partition server (node) of the DB2MPP instance, run the following command from a command window:

```
db2ncrt /i:DB2MPP /n:1 /u:db2team,db2team /h:db2lab5
/m:DB2LAB5 /o:DB2LAB7
```

Note that the db2ncrt command has been split for formatting purposes.

We now present the two methods to enable (or migrate) the DB2MPP instance for MSCS support.

The first method uses the DB2MSCS tool (included in DB2 UDB). It is the easiest and recommended approach and requires the following steps:

1. Creating a DB2MSCS.CFG input file
2. Running the DB2MSCS tool

The second method is the more manual step-by-step method using the MSCS Cluster Administrator tool. It is provided for interest and completeness and requires the following steps:

1. Registering the DB2 resource type
2. Configuring the MSCS resource groups and resources for each server.
3. Migrating (or enabling) the DB2 instance for MSCS failover support
4. Enabling failover support on the second DB2 node

See "Enabling MSCS Support Using Cluster Administrator" on page 368 for an example of the use of the Cluster Administrator tool.

8.4.2.2 Enabling MSCS Support Using DB2MSCS

To enable the DB2MPP instance for MSCS support using the DB2MSCS tool provided with DB2 UDB, requires the following steps.

1. Creating the DB2MSCS.CFG Input File

Following the rules presented in "Using DB2MSCS to Enable MSCS Support" on page 315, create a configuration file for DB2MSCS. Using a text editor, we created a file called cluster.cfg, shown Figure 240 on page 367.

Please note that DB2 ships a sample configuration file. We suggest you use this file as a template and modify its contents to suit your needs.

The values in the cluster.cfg file are as follows:

- Global values:
  - The DB2 instance to be migrated is DB2MPP.
  - The domain userid to be used for the migration process is db2team.
  - The password for the db2team domain user is db2team.

    If you do not include this line, you will be prompted for a password for the db2team userid when the DB2MSCS utility is run.
  - The MSCS cluster name is DB2CLUS.
- Two MSCS groups, one for each DB2 node:
  - For the first DB2 node, an MSCS group called DB2 Node 0
  - The virtual IP address for DB2 is called IP Address for DB2. We use an IP address of 10.10.10.12, subnet mask 255.255.0.0, in network IBMFE.
  - The network name for the virtual DB2 server is DB2WOLF0. It has dependencies as follows:
    - The virtual IP address for DB2, called IP Address for DB2.
  - We use Disk J: for the instance directory. Note that if we had not included this line in the configuration file, the first disk name specified as a dependency for the DB2 Node 0 group would be used for the instance directory.
  - For the second DB2 node, an MSCS group called DB2 Node 1.
  - Because user data will be placed on a shared disk, we include disk resource Disk K: in group DB2 Node 1.

```
DB2_INSTANCE=DB2MPP
DB2_LOGON_USERNAME=db2team
DB2_LOGON_PASSWORD=db2team
CLUSTER_NAME=DB2CLUS
######## DB2 NODE 0 ########
GROUP_NAME=DB2 Node 0
DB2_NODE=0
IP_NAME=IP Address for DB2
IP_ADDRESS=10.10.10.12
IP_SUBNET=255.255.0.0
IP_NETWORK=IBMFE
NETNAME_NAME=Network Name for DB2
NETNAME_VALUE=DB2WOLF0
NETNAME_DEPENDENCY=IP Address for DB2
DISK_NAME=Disk J:
INSTPROF_DISK=Disk J:
######## DB2 NODE 1 ########
GROUP_NAME=DB2 Node 1
DB2_NODE=1
DISK_NAME=Disk K:
```

Figure 240. The DB2MSCS Input File, cluster.cfg

Note that any dependencies not created in the DB2MSCS configuration file must already be displayed in the MSCS Cluster Administrator tool. For example, ensure that there are disk resources named Disk J: and Disk K:.

Note also that the instance directory will be placed on the specified disk, under the subdirectory \db2profs. The DB2MSCS utility will create this directory if it does not already exist.

2. Running DB2MSCS

To run the DB2MSCS utility using the cluster.cfg configuration file, use the following command, in a command window, on the instance-owning server (here DB2LAB7):

```
db2mscs -f:cluster.cfg
```

DB2MSCS will read the cluster.cfg file, and verify the parameters. After a successful verification, the following sequence of events occurs on DB2LAB7:

1. The DB2 resource type is registered, and is displayed in the Resource Types subtree of the Cluster Administrator tool (see Figure 216 on page 322 for an example).

2. The first MSCS group is created (DB2 Node 0). This is displayed in the Groups subtree of the Cluster Administrator tool.

   In this first MSCS group, the following resources are created:

   - The DB2 IP address resource, IP Address for DB2, is created, and brought online.

   - The DB2 network name resource, DB2WOLF0, is created, and brought online.

   - The Disk resource Disk J: is moved to this group. It should be already online.

   - The file share for the instance directory, DB2MSCS-DB2MPP, is created, and brought online.

   - The DB2 resource, DB2MPP-0, is created.

3. The second MSCS group is created (DB2 Node 1).

   In this second MSCS group, the following resources are created:

   - The disk resource Disk K: is moved to this group. It should already be online.

   - The DB2 resource, DB2MPP-1, is created.

4. At this stage, if all the previous steps have completed successfully, DB2MSCS will then convert the DB2MPP DB2 instance into an MSCS-enabled DB2 instance.

   You will not see this conversion process in the Cluster Administrator tool.

5. Finally, if the conversion is successful, both DB2 resources DB2MPP-0 and DB2MPP-1 will be brought on-line.

At this point, to continue with our example we need to register the database drive mappings as shown in "Registering Database Drive Mappings for DB2" on page 390.

8.4.2.3 Enabling MSCS Support Using Cluster Administrator

To enable the DB2MPP instance for MSCS support using the MSCS Cluster Administrator tool, requires the following steps.

1. Registering the DB2 Resource Type

We register the DB2 resource type with MSCS, by running the db2wolfi command on the first node of the cluster (DB2LAB7), in a command window as follows:

```
db2wolfi i
```

You can verify that the resource has been installed by starting the Cluster Administrator tool on the first node, if it is not already active, and selecting Resource Types, as shown in Figure 241. You should see a resource type listed under Display Name of DB2, with a Resource DLL of db2wolf.dll.

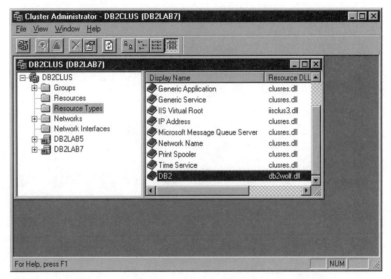

Figure 241. Verifying the Installation of the DB2 Resource Type

2. Configuring the MSCS Resource Groups and Resources

On DB2LAB7 (the first MSCS node of the DB2CLUS cluster), we use the Cluster Administrator tool to create the two MSCS groups (one for each DB2 node in the DB2MPP DB2 instance), and the required resources in each group.

We will create:

- A MSCS group called DB2 Node 0 (relating to DB2LAB7) containing:
  - A disk resource called Disk J:
  - A file share resource called 'Instance Directory' using J:\PROFILE.

- An IP resource called 'IP Address for DB2' using IP address 10.10.10.12.

- A Network Name resource called 'Network Name for DB2' using DB2WOLF0.

- A DB2 resource called DB2MPP-0.

- A MSCS group called DB2 Node 1 (relating to DB2LAB5) containing:

  - A disk resource called Disk K:

  - A DB2 resource called DB2MPP-1.

The first step is to create the first MSCS group for the cluster using the Cluster Administrator tool.

1. Create an MSCS group, DB2 Node 0. You can either create a new group or rename an existing one.

   - To create a new group:

     1. Select the **Groups** object with the right mouse button, choose menu item **New**, and then **Group**, as shown in Figure 242.

Figure 242. Creating a New MSCS Group

     2. Then fill in the new cluster group name, and an optional description (our example, using DB2 Node 0, is shown in Figure 243). Click on the **Next** button to continue.

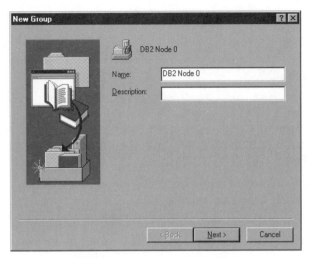

Figure 243. Creating the DB2 Node 0 Cluster Group

3. Finally, nominate the preferred owner(s) for this cluster group, as shown in Figure 244. In our case, DB2LAB7 is the preferred owner for failback of the DB2 Node 0 cluster group.

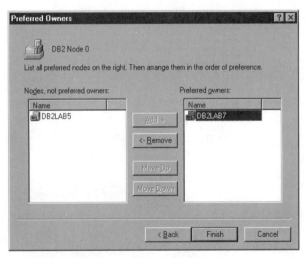

Figure 244. Nominating Preferred Owners

4. Click on the **Finish** button to finish creating the group. You should receive a status message on successful creation of the cluster group, as shown in Figure 245.

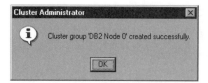

Figure 245. Successful Creation of the Cluster Group

- To rename an existing group, expand the **Groups** subtree, select the cluster group to be renamed with the right mouse button, and select **Rename**.

2. Set up an MSCS disk resource for the physical disks that will store the user data. You have two options:

- If you already have a disk resource that was created for the physical disk, then move it to the DB2 Node 0 group as follows:

    1. Expand the DB2LAB7 object, and select **Active Resources**. From the list, select the disk resource to be moved, click on the right mouse button, and choose **Change Group** to assign it to a new group (see Figure 246, where we assign disk resource Disk J: to the DB2 Node 0 cluster group).

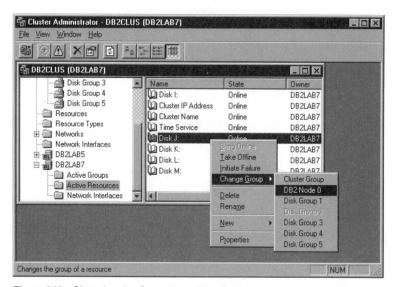

Figure 246. Changing the Group for a Disk Resource

2. Confirm the change by clicking the **Yes** button on the next panel, as shown in Figure 247.

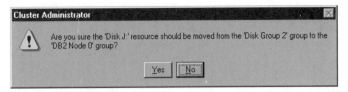

Figure 247. Confirming Resource Group Changes

3. Click on the **Yes** button to finalize the changes, as shown in Figure 248.

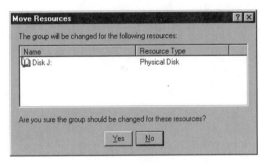

Figure 248. Moving Disk Resources

- If you do not have a disk resource for the physical disk, create one in the DB2 Node 0 group as follows:

  1. Select the **Resource Types** object, then select **Physical Disk** with the right mouse button, choose **New**, and then **Resource**.

  2. Fill in the Name, Description (which is optional), leave the Resource type as Physical Disk, and DB2 Node 0 as the group for the new disk resource. In our example shown in Figure 249, we create a new disk resource for disk M:, a Physical Disk, in the DB2 Node 0 group.

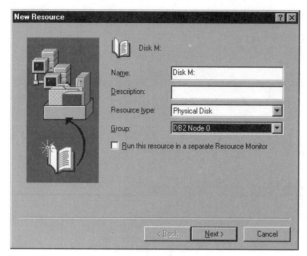

Figure 249. Creating a New Disk Resource

Click on the **Next** button to continue.

3. On the Possible Owners window, click on the **Next** button to accept the default settings.

4. On the Dependencies window, click on the **Next** button. This action accepts the default resource dependencies.

5. Finally, on the Disk Parameters window, select the disk for the disk resource. Our example, Figure 250, shows we are mapping our disk resource Disk M: to Disk M:.

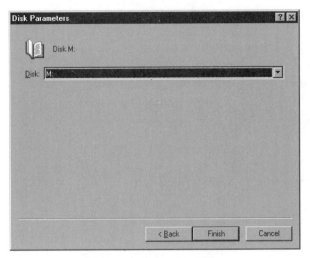

Figure 250. Assigning a Disk to a Disk Resource

Click on the **Finish** button to create this disk resource.

6. When the resource is created successfully, you will receive a status message.

> **Note**
>
> You should set up all disk resources that are to be used in the DB2 Node 0 group before continuing. In our example, for simplicity, the instance directory will be kept on Disk J:, together with user data.

3. Set up an MSCS File Share for the instance directory. You perform this step on the machine that will run DB2 UDB EEE partition server (node) 0, the instance-owning machine. This step enables the instance directory to fail over, which ensures that the instance remains available:

1. Select the DB2 Node 0 group and click the right mouse button, choose the **New** menu item, and then **Resource**.

2. On the New Resource window, in our example (see Figure 251), we create a file share called Instance Directory, of resource type File Share, belonging to the DB2 Node 0 group. Note that the description in the Description field is optional.

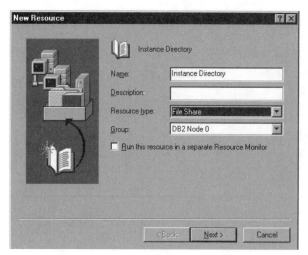

Figure 251. Creating a File Share for the Instance Directory

Click on the **Next** button to continue.

3. On the Possible Owners window, click on the **Next** button. This action accepts the default settings.

4. On the Dependencies window, select the disk resource (or resources) associated with the instance directory, and click on the **Add** button. This action adds the resource dependency to the File Share resource.

> **Note**
>
> The disk must be on-line before the File Share resource can be brought on-line.

In our example, Disk J: will be used as the instance directory, as shown in Figure 252.

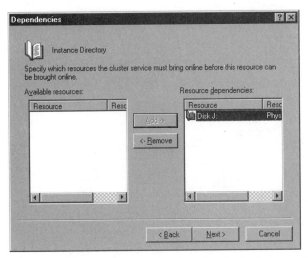

Figure 252. Assigning a Drive Dependency for the Instance Directory

Click on the **Next** button to continue.

5. On the File Share Parameters window, enter a name in the Share name field. For our example (see Figure 253), we use DB2MPP.

> **Note**
>
> Make sure the Share Name is not the same as your current share name, by default, DB2-DB2MPP. Otherwise, when this file share is brought on-line, it will redefine the current share, and the db2iclus migrate command (used to migrate the DB2 instance for MSCS support) will fail as it will not be able to find the current instance directory.

Enter a path that exists on the cluster disk in the Path field. For our example, we use J:\profile. Make sure this directory exists on the disk. The comment in the Comment Field is optional.

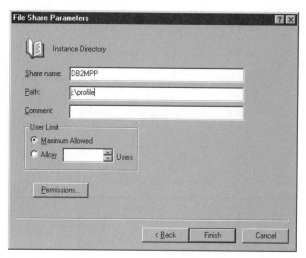

Figure 253. File Share Parameters for the Instance Directory

Click on the **Finish** button to create the file share. When the File Share has been created successfully, you will receive a status message.

Make sure you have already created the directory you enter in Path (in this example, J:\profile). Bring the instance directory on-line, by selecting it with the right mouse button, and selecting **Bring Online** from the pop-up menu. Wait for the state to change from Online Pending to Online.

If you receive any errors, ensure the directory has been created on the disk drive, and that the domain user has appropriate permissions on the drive and directory.

4. Create the IP resource for TCP/IP connections. Only perform this step if you want the database partition server on the machine to function as a coordinator partition for remote applications. This step also helps ensure that the instance directory can fail over.

   1. Select the DB2 Node 0 group with the right mouse button, choose menu item **New**, and then **Resource**.

   2. On the New Resource window, create the IP resource for the TCP/IP connection in DB2 Node 0. Our example, shown in Figure 254, uses a name of IP Address for DB2, belonging to the DB2 Node 0 group. Select **IP Address** from the list for the Resource Type field. The description in the Description Field is optional.

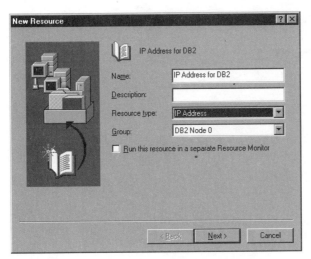

Figure 254. Creating the IP Address Resource for DB2

Click on the **Next** button to continue.

3. On The Possible Owners window, click on the **Next** button This action accepts the default settings for possible owners.

4. On the Dependencies window, click on the **Next** button. This action accepts the default resource dependencies.

5. On the TCP/IP Address Parameters window, use a new IP address on the external network of the cluster group, with an appropriate subnet mask. Our example, shown in Figure 255, uses IP address 10.10.10.12 on the IBMFE network, with subnet mask 255.255.0.0.

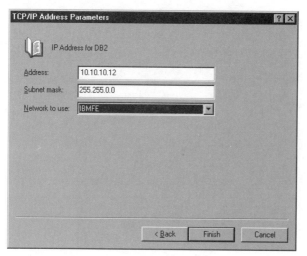

Figure 255. Parameters for the IP Address Resource for DB2

Click on the **Finish** button to create the IP resource. Successful creation is indicated by a status message.

> **Note**
>
> The IP Address parameter for the IP Resource should be used when cataloging the TCP/IP node on the client machine.

6. To bring the IP resource online, and verify the parameters settings, select the **DB2 Node 0** group with the right mouse button, select **IP Address for DB2** with the right mouse button, and select **Bring Online**. Wait for the state to change from Online Pending to Online.

> **Note**
>
> If an error occurs, select the **IP Address for DB2** resource with the right mouse button. Select **Properties**, and on the Parameters tab, verify the values in the Address and Subnet mask fields.

5. Create a network name. You perform this step on the machine that is the instance-owning machine (in our example, DB2LAB7). This step, combined with the step to create the File Share (as performed in Step 3 on page 375) allows DB2 to access the instance directory when the instance directory fails over:

1. Select **DB2 Node 0** with the right mouse button, choose **New** and then select **Resource**.

2. On the New Resource window, create a network name resource. In our example, we create a network name of Network Name for DB2, with a Resource Type of Network Name, belonging to the DB2 Node 0 group. Note that the Description field is optional. This screen is shown in Figure 256.

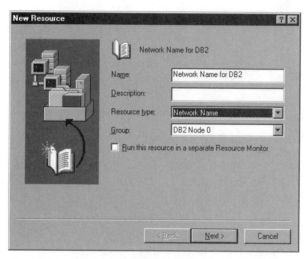

Figure 256. Creating a New Network Name for DB2

Click on the **Next** button to continue.

3. On the Possible Owners window, click on the **Next** button. This action accepts the default settings for possible owners.

4. On the Dependencies window, select IP Address for DB2 into the Resource Dependencies list (as shown in Figure 257) by using the **Add** button, then click on the **Next** button to continue.

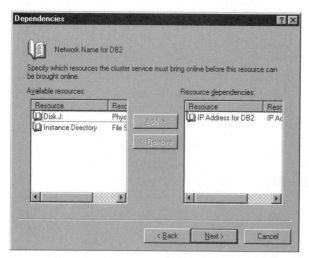

Figure 257. Dependencies for the Network Name for DB2

5. In the Network Name Parameters window, enter a name in the Name field to use for the network. In our example, we use DB2WOLF0, as shown in Figure 258.

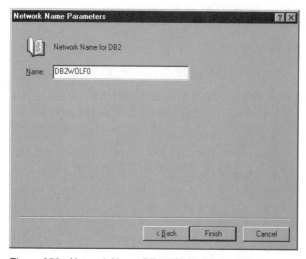

Figure 258. Network Name DB2WOLF0 for the DB2 Instance

Click on the **Finish** button to finish creating the network name. You will receive a status message on successful creation of the network name.

6. Bring the network name resource online. Select **DB2 Node 0** from the Groups subtree. Select **Network Name for DB2** with the right mouse

button, then select **Bring Online**. Wait for the state to change from Online Pending to Online.

6. Create a DB2 resource for this database partition server.

   1. Select **DB2 Node 0** with the right mouse button, then choose **New**, and then **Resource**.

   2. On the New Resource window, type a two-part name in the form <instance_name>-<node_number> in the Name field. Our example uses DB2MPP-0.

      The two-part name is made up of the instance name (DB2MPP) and the DB2 node or partition server number (0). Ensure you include the hyphen (-). If the instance does not already exist, you must use the same name when you create it with the db2icrt command. In addition, the DB2 node number that you specify for the resource must be the same number that you specify for the db2ncrt command.

      Note

      The DB2 node number for each database partition server must be unique.

      Select a Resource Type of **DB2** and leave the Group as DB2 Node 0. You can fill in an optional description in the Description field. This is shown in Figure 259.

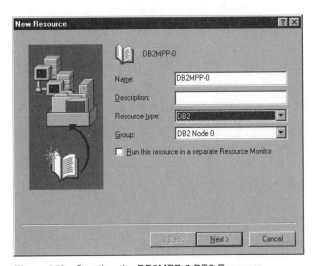

Figure 259. Creating the DB2MPP-0 DB2 Resource

Click on the **Next** button to continue.

3. On the Possible Owners window, click on the **Next** button. This action accepts the default settings for possible owners.

4. On the Dependencies window, select the available disk resources and IP resources into the Resources dependencies list by using the **Add** push button. Add all the resources to the dependencies list. This is shown in Figure 260.

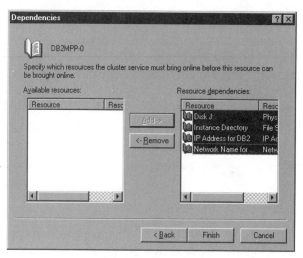

Figure 260. Dependencies for the DB2MPP-0 DB2 Resource

Click on the **Finish** button to create the DB2 resource. You will receive a status message on creation of the DB2 resource.

Note

1. Do not bring the resource for the database partition server (DB2MPP-0) on-line yet, as DB2 is not yet fully configured.

2. When creating the DB2 resource, set dependencies on the Disk and IP resources so that it will be started after the other resources are

---

When you finish, the Cluster Administration tool initial panel will resemble Figure 261.

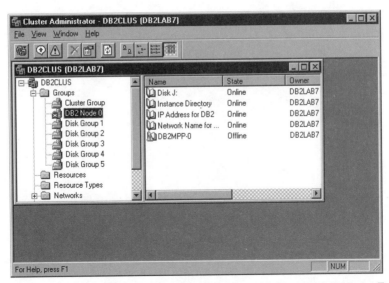

Figure 261. Configuration of DB2 Node 0 Group in the Cluster Administrator Tool

Now we must create the MSCS group and resources for the second DB2 node (partition server) on DB2LAB5 using the Cluster Administrator tool. If you have more than two DB2 nodes, then repeat this step for each extra node, ensuring you name the resources appropriately (for example, for the third DB2 node, use a group called DB2 Node 2, with a DB2 resource of DB2MPP-2 and so on).

1. Create a group, called DB2 Node 1, in the same way that you created the group DB2 Node 0. However, ensure that this time the preferred owner is now the second node, in our example DB2LAB5. This is shown in Figure 262.

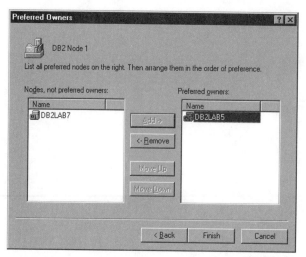

Figure 262. Nominating Preferred Owners for the Second MSCS Group

2. Set up a disk resource for the physical disks that will store the user data. Once again, you can either move an existing disk resource to the DB2 Node 1 group, or create a new physical disk in that MSCS group.

   In our example, we will use Disk K: as the disk resource for the second DB2 node. However, Disk K: is currently owned by DB2LAB7, and it needs to moved to a group owned by DB2LAB5. This process requires two steps:

   1. Change the ownership of the relevant disk resource group to DB2LAB5.

      Select the MSCS group that Disk K: is in (here Disk Group 3) with the right mouse button, and select **Move Group** (Figure 263).

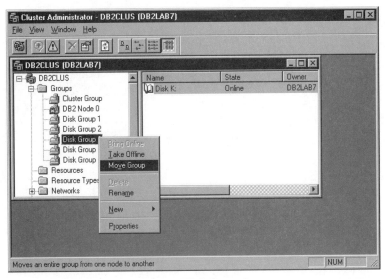

Figure 263. Changing Ownership of Disk Group 3

Disk resource Disk K: will go into online-pending state, as MSCS attempts to change the ownership of all resources in Disk Group 3. Once it is successful, you should then see the change in ownership of "Disk K:" (Figure 264).

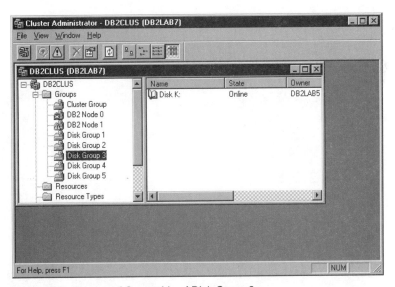

Figure 264. Change of Ownership of Disk Group 3

> **Note**
>
> If MSCS cannot change ownership of the Disk resource group
> (you will notice that the resources in that group, for example, Disk
> K:, will stay online-pending to the other node (here DB2LAB5) for
> a long time, and then change ownership back to the original
> MSCS node), you may have to do a hardware reboot of both
> systems, letting the first MSCS cluster node boot to Windows NT
> first, then powering on the second MSCS cluster node.

2. Move the Disk resource to MSCS group DB2 Node 1.

Now you should be able to move the Disk K: resource to the DB2 Node 1
group. This process is similar to changing the group of Disk J: to DB2
Node 0 shown in Figure 246 on page 372.

3. Finally, create a DB2 resource for this database partition server.

This process is identical to the creation of the DB2MPP-0 resource as
shown in Figure 259 on page 383. However, since we are dealing with the
second DB2 node, DB2MPP-1, we will name the DB2 resource
DB2MPP-1, with a dependency on disk resource Disk K:.

The Cluster Administrator tool now displays the following entries for the DB2
Node 1 group:

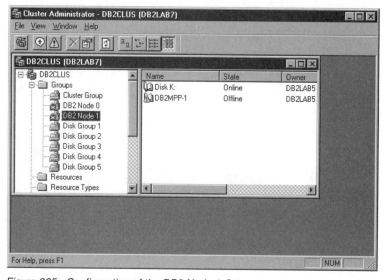

Figure 265. Configuration of the DB2 Node 1 Group

> **Note**
>
> Do not bring the resource for the database partition server (DB2MPP-1) on-line yet, as DB2 is not yet fully configured.

3. Migrating the DB2 Instance for MSCS Failover Support

This step migrates (or enables) the DB2 instance on the instance-owning server for MSCS failover. Use the db2iclus migrate command (see "Migrating to an MSCS-Enabled DB2 Instance" on page 330). In our example, the command is as follows:

```
C:\>db2iclus migrate /i:DB2MPP /c:DB2CLUS /m:DB2LAB7
 /p:\\DB2WOLF0\DB2MPP
 DBI1912I The DB2 Cluster command was successful.

Cause:  The user request was successfully processed.

Action:  No action required.
```

Note that the command has been split for formatting reasons.

You may encounter the following difficulties after an attempted migration of the DB2 instance to a MSCS-enabled DB2 instance.

1. There are no files in the file share of the instance directory (in our example, \\DB2WOLF0\DB2MPP). You may notice this the first time you attempt to start DB2MPP-0, and receive an SQL5005 DB2 error.

   If this is the case, copy the contents (including subdirectories) of the original instance directory on the instance-owning server to the file share directory. In our example, this is the contents of the default \sqllib\DB2MPP directory.

2. If the migration fails, and does not rollback correctly, the DB2 instance may be left in an inaccessible state. You should check the following:

   - db2set -all (in a command window) may show the following two DB2 profile variables set as follows (using our example of cluster DB2CLUS, with a share on \\DB2WOLF0\DB2MPP):

```
DB2CLUSTER=DB2CLUS
DB2INSTPROF=\\DB2WOLF0\DB2MPP
```

If so, the rollback of the migration has failed. Unset the DB2CLUSTER profile with the following command (in a command window):

```
db2set DB2CLUSTER=
```

Then change the DB2INSTPROF profile to point back to the original instance directory for DB2. In our example, where the instance owning server was DB2LAB7, with a file share of the instance directory of DB2-DB2MPP, the command is as follows:

```
db2set DB2INSTPROF=\\DB2LAB7\DB2-DB2MPP
```

- Check the value of the DB2INSTPROF profile variable for each node (partition server) in the partitioned database instance as well.

4. Enabling the Second Node for MSCS Support

Before adding the second DB2 node (which is on the second MSCS node) to the MSCS-enabled DB2 instance, you must first enable the second node for MSCS failover support. This is accomplished by using the db2iclus add command, in a command window, as follows:

```
C:\>db2iclus ADD /i:DB2MPP /u:db2team,db2team /m:DB2LAB5 /c:DB2CLUS
DBI1912I The DB2 Cluster command was successful.

Cause: The user request was successfully processed.

Action: No action required.
```

See "Enabling the DB2 Resource to Fail Over" on page 331 for more details about the db2iclus add command.

This completes the process of setting up DB2 and MSCS for DB2 failover support using the MSCS Cluster Administrator tool. The next step is to register the drive mappings for DB2.

8.4.3 Registering Database Drive Mappings for DB2

When creating a partitioned DB2 database in this environment, we intend to store user data on the shared drive Disk J:. In order to be able to create a DB2 partitioned database on drive J:, we must add drive mappings for drives J: and K:. We used the db2drvmp utility on the first MSCS node (DB2LAB7) as follows:

```
C:\>db2drvmp add 0 k j
SQL2813I  The drive mapping from drive "k" to drive "j" was added for
node "0".
C:\>db2drvmp add 1 j k
SQL2813I  The drive mapping from drive "j" to drive "k" was added for
node "1".
```

Check that the drive mappings have been registered successfully by issuing the db2drvmp query command, in any command window.

8.4.4 Configuring the DB2 Administration Server for MSCS Failover

There are some steps required to enable the DB2 Administration Server for MSCS failover:

1. Stop the Administration Server on both machines by executing the db2admin stop command (in a command window) on each machine.

2. On all administration client machines, uncatalog all references to the Administration Servers on both MSCS nodes using the db2 uncatalog command in a DB2 command window.

3. Determine the name of the Administration Server on MSCS node 1 (server DB2LAB5) by executing the db2admin command. The default is DB2DAS00. Drop the Administration Server on this machine by executing the db2admin drop command.

4. Determine the name of the Administration Server on MSCS node 0 (DB2LAB7) by issuing the db2admin command. The default is DB2DAS00.

5. In the same resource group that you are using for the DB2 resource, create a DB2 resource named DB2DAS00 that has dependencies on the IP and disk resources.

   In our example, we create DB2DAS00 in MSCS group DB2 Node 0, of type DB2 (see Figure 266).

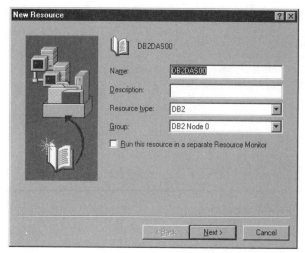

Figure 266. Creating the DB2DAS00 DB2 Resource

This DB2 resource has dependencies on the DB2 IP Address (the virtual IP address for DB2), Disk J: (where the instance directory for DB2DAS00 will reside), and the DB2 instance directory.

6. Assuming that MSCS node 0 owns the cluster disk to be used for the DB2DAS00 instance directory, execute the following command from MSCS node 0 (DB2LAB7):

```
db2iclus migrate -i:DB2DAS00 -c:DB2CLUS -p:\\DB2WOLF0\DB2MPP
```

7. On MSCS node 0 (DB2LAB7), execute the following command to enable the Administration Server to fail over to MSCS node 1:

```
db2iclus add /i:DB2DAS00 /u:db2team,db2team /m:DB2LAB5
```

8. On MSCS node 1 (DB2LAB5), execute the following command to set DB2DAS00 as the Administration Server:

```
db2set -g db2adminserver=DB2DAS00
```

9. On MSCS node 0 (DB2LAB7), using the Services panel of the Windows NT Control Panel, change the startup properties of DB2DAS00 to Manual.

On server DB2LAB7, click on the Windows NT **Start** button, select
Settings, **Control Panel** and then **Services**. Select DB2DAS00 as in
Figure 267:

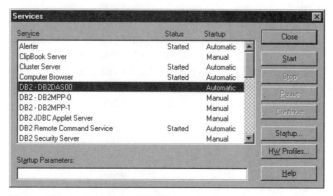

Figure 267. Selecting the DB2DAS00 Service

Click on the **Startup** button, and change the setting from Automatic to
Manual (see Figure 268).

Figure 268. Changing the Startup Type for the DB2DAS00 Service

You should now verify the setup of the DB2DAS00 MSCS Resource, by using
the Cluster Administrator tool to bring it online.

8.4.5 Additional Configuration to Support FCM communications

Our example configuration has been setup using two network adapters. As
explained in "Changing DB2 Node Configuration Information" on page 337,
FCM may encounter problems with inter-node communications. In our

example, this is the case. Hence, we will have to use the db2nchg utility to explicitly specify the IP addresses to be used by each DB2 node for FCM communications.

We also need to make sure these IP addresses are available to the failover MSCS node, in the event of a failover. Bearing this in mind, we will use two new IP addresses, and configure them under MSCS for failover.

8.4.5.1 Failover of FCM IP Address

We will use the TCP/IP address 10.10.10.14 for FCM communications to the first DB2 node (node 0) on DB2LAB7, and TCP/IP address 10.10.10.15 for the second DB2 node (node 1) on DB2LAB5.

To define these new IP addresses, as MSCS IP Address resources, in the appropriate MSCS groups, do the following:

- For the first DB2 node:

  1. Using the Cluster Administrator tool, select the **DB2 Node 0** group with the right mouse button, and select **New**, then **Resource**.

  2. On the New Resource window, fill in a name of 'FCM IP Address for Node 0', resource type 'IP Address', in the DB2 Node 0 group, and click on the **Next** button.

  3. On the Possible Owners window, click on the **Next** button to accept the default settings (which should be both MSCS nodes in the cluster).

  4. On the Dependencies window, click on the **Next** button to accept the default resource dependencies (which should be none).

  5. On the TCP/IP Address Parameters window, use a new address on the external network of the cluster group, IBMFE, with IP address 10.10.10.14, and a subnet mask of 255.255.0.0.

     Click on the **Finish** button to finish creating the IP resource.

  6. Once the status message indicates successful creation, bring the resource online, so we can add this IP address resource as a dependency to the DB2MPP-0 DB2 resource.

  7. Select the **DB2MPP-0** resource with the right mouse button, and select **Properties**. Click on the **Dependencies** tab, and select **Modify**. Add 'FCM IP Address for Node 0' to the dependencies list. Click on the **OK** button. The Dependencies tab will now look like Figure 269:

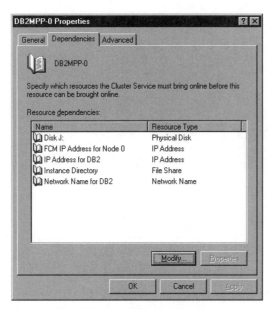

Figure 269. Adding the FCM IP Address as a Dependency to DB2MPP-0

8. Click on the **Apply** button, and then **OK**.

- Repeat the preceding steps for the DB2 Node 1 group. However we will call the IP resource 'FCM IP Address for Node 1', with an IP Address of 10.10.10.15.

  Bring this IP resource on-line, then add this as a dependency for the DB2MPP-1 DB2 resource. The dependencies list for DB2MPP-0 will now look like Figure 270:

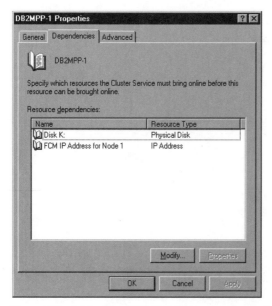

Figure 270. Adding the FCM IP Address as a Dependency to DB2MPP-1

8.4.5.2 Specifying IP Addresses for DB2 FCM Communication

Now that the IP addresses are available for use, we use the db2nchg utility to change the DB2 node configuration as follows:

```
C:\>db2nchg /n:0 /g:10.10.10.14
SQL281W  Node" "0" changed in instance: "DB2MPP" (Host: "db2lab7"
Machine: "DB2LAB7" Port: "0")
C:\>db2nchg /n:1 /g:10.10.10.15
SQL281W  Node" "1" changed in instance: "DB2MPP" (Host: "db2lab5"
Machine: "DB2LAB5" Port: "0")
```

This change in DB2 node configuration will be reflected in the output of the db2nlist command as follows:

```
C:\>db2nlist
Node: "0" Host: "db2lab7" Machine: "DB2LAB7" Port: "0" Netname:
"10.10.10.14"
Node: "1" Host: "db2lab5" Machine: "DB2LAB5" Port: "0" Netname:
"10.10.10.15"
```

8.4.6 Verifying Failover and Failback

Before testing failover, we will enable automatic failback. By default, MSCS groups are not set to failback. If you have set preferred owners, you can enable failback in one of two ways:

1. Manually:

   Select the MSCS group to failback with the right mouse button, and select **Move Group**. This also works if preferred owners are not set. In effect, it can operate as a primitive, manual means of load balancing.

2. Automatically:

   For each MSCS group you wish to failback automatically, select the group with the right mouse button, and select **Properties**.

   Under the **Failback** tab, you must choose the **Allow failback** option. For our testing purposes, we will allow failback to occur immediately (see Figure 271).

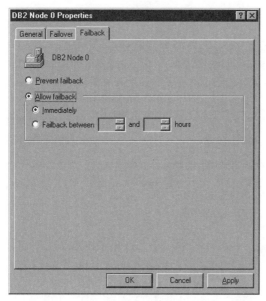

Figure 271. Failback Properties for DB2 Node 0

Click on the **Apply** button, then **OK**.

Once failback is configured, we can proceed with our testing. Note that the immediate failback configuration is not recommended for a production environment (see "Failback Considerations" on page 339).

For our testing purposes, we will test failover and failback gracefully, by stopping and starting the MSCS cluster service, rather than by initiating some form of hardware failure.

8.4.6.1 Failover Verification

Make sure all MSCS groups and resources are on-line. To test failover of the first MSCS node (DB2LAB7) to the second (DB2LAB5), stop the Cluster Server service. You can either do this from the Services panel of the Windows NT Control panel, or from the Windows NT command windows, using the NET STOP command on the Cluster Server service. You can also use the abbreviation CLUSSVC in place of Cluster Server, when using the NET STOP command.

We will stop the Cluster Server service from the command window, using the NET STOP command. In a Windows NT command window, type the following command:

```
net stop clussvc
```

If you have the MSCS Cluster Administrator tool started on the failover node (in our example, server DB2LAB5), you will notice that the DB2CLUS cluster goes offline, then each group goes online pending as they wait for their dependencies to come back online on the failover node. Finally, as all MSCS groups come back online, you will notice that they are now owned by the failover node (DB2LAB5).

8.4.6.2 Failback Verification

To test failback to DB2LAB7 from DB2LAB5, start the Cluster Server service on DB2LAB7 with the NET START command. For example, to start it from the Windows NT Command window on DB2LAB7, use the command:

```
net start clussvc
```

If the Cluster Administrator is started on DB2LAB5, and immediate failback has been enabled, you will see on the Cluster Administrator panel that the DB2 Node 0 group resources will go offline, go online pending as their dependencies come online, and finally become owned by DB2LAB7 again (similarly with any other resources which are in groups with preferred owner set to DB2LAB7).

> **Note**
>
> Any groups which do not have a preferred owner will not failback, since they have been configured to run on any MSCS node which is available.

Finally, you should repeat the failover and failback verification process, this time failing from the second MSCS node (DB2LAB5), to the first (DB2LAB7). Once the failover process has been verified, you can then initiate the failback process from DB2LAB7 to DB2LAB5.

Chapter 9. Performance Monitoring

An essential requirement of a database administrator (DBA) is the ability to perform routine performance checking and tuning to optimize system usage and correct performance issues when they arise. The overall performance of a DB2 system is dependent on efficient tuning of both the Windows NT operating system and DB2. To maintain a high level of service to the users of the system, it is essential to keep Windows NT and DB2 running without bottlenecks or delays.

In this chapter we look at the tools and utilities provided in both Windows NT and DB2 which you can use for performance monitoring and tuning. For these tasks, Windows NT includes the NT Performance Monitor, while DB2 provides snapshot and event monitoring.

In addition, the DB2 Performance SmartGuide can be used as an overall performance tuning tool for your DB2 system parameters. See "DB2 UDB Graphical Tools" on page 191 for an overview of the DB2 Performance SmartGuide.

9.1 Windows NT Performance Monitor

The first tool we cover is the Windows NT Performance Monitor. This provides monitoring functions for features of the Windows NT operating system, such as:

- CPU usage
- Storage - read and write
- Memory utilization - physical and virtual
- Efficiency of networking
- Threads and processes
- Cache

The Windows NT Performance Monitor is a graphical tool and is installed as part of the base Windows NT installation for both Windows NT Server and Windows NT Workstation systems. It can be used locally and also to monitor other Windows NT machines on your network. Some of the abilities of the Windows NT Performance Monitor include:

- System logging
- Ability to chart data
- Setting event alerts
- Exporting captured information
- Report creation

- Local and remote monitoring

The Windows NT Performance monitor works by monitoring counters. A counter is a variable used to measure a distinct feature of the operating system. Counters are grouped into objects, each object covering a specific area of the operating system: processor, memory, physical disk, logical disk or threads etc.

9.1.1 Registering DB2 Performance Counters

When you install DB2 on Windows NT, DB2 performance information is made available to the Windows NT Performance Monitor by adding the DB2 performance objects and counters to it. This is achieved by the installation program copying the DB2 performance counter's Dynamic Linked Library (DLL), db2perf.dll, to the SYSTEM32 directory under Windows NT. The setup program also registers the DLL and updates the Windows NT registry with the new counters.

There is also a program shipped with DB2 that allows you to manually install (or register) and uninstall (or de-register) the DB2 performance counters. This program is called db2perfi and has the following syntax:

- `db2perfi -i` - to install and register the counters
- `db2perfi -u` - to uninstall and de-register the counters

The db2perfi command is executed from a command line.

Once the DB2 performance monitor objects and counters have been installed and registered the following performance objects are available from the Windows NT Performance monitor:

- DB2 NT Database Manager

  This object provides general server information for a single Windows NT server instance. The DB2 instance being monitored appears as the object instance. You can only get performance information from one DB2 server instance at a time. The instance shown in the performance monitor is governed by the DB2INSTANCE registry value. If you have multiple DB2 instances running and you wish to view performance data for more than one, you must start a separate NT Performance Monitor session with DB2INSTANCE set to the relevant value of the DB2 instance to be monitored.

- DB2 NT Databases

  This object provides information for a particular database. Information is available for each currently active database.

- DB2 NT Applications

  This object provides information for a particular DB2 application. Information is available for each currently active DB2 application.

9.1.2 Using the NT Performance Monitor with DB2

In this section, we look at how we can use the Windows NT Performance Monitor to monitor the DB2 performance objects. We also look at the modes offered by the Windows NT Performance Monitor and show an example of using these modes to monitor the number of connections to a database. More information on the Windows NT Performance monitor is available through the online help.

The Windows NT Performance Monitor has the following modes in which data can be monitored:

- Chart mode - to display performance data in a graphical format. Data logged in this mode can also be exported for use in spreadsheet and database applications.

- Alert mode - to raise an alert when the value of a counter is less or greater than an established threshold.

- Log mode - to log object data for future use.

- Report mode - to format performance counters in a readable format; a report can be generated from a log file or in real time.

To start the Windows NT Performance Monitor click **Start**, then **Programs**, then **Administrative Tools (Common)**, then **Performance Monitor**.

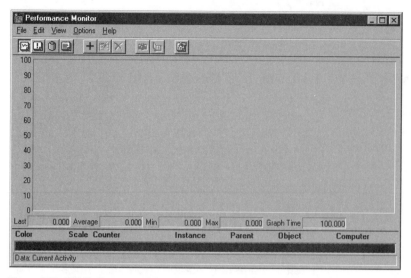

Figure 272. NT Performance Monitor

9.1.2.1 Chart mode

Chart mode is the default mode that is used by the Windows NT Performance Monitor on startup and is shown in Figure 272. Using chart mode, you can display performance data in a graphical format and monitor the counters of your choice. The default plotting style for chart mode is a line graph, although by altering the chart options you can also plot the data using a histogram. Chart data can be gathered in real time, which is the default, or previously logged data can be used to plot performance counters. This mode also allows you to export data to tab or comma delimited files for use in spreadsheets and database applications.

Once the Windows NT Performance monitor is started, you need to add some counters to be charted:

- From the Windows NT Performance Monitor select the **Edit** menu tab, then click **Add to Chart**. Alternately, you can click the **+** icon on the menu tool bar.

- The *Add to Chart* window is displayed. In this example, we chart the number of local database connections to a database.

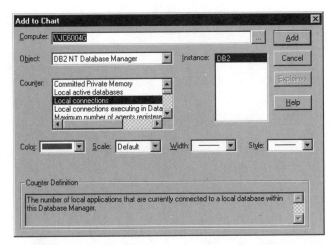

Figure 273. Add to Chart

- In the *Add to Chart* window select **DB2 NT Database Manager** for the Object and select **Local connections** for the counter. The Instance selection should be set to the DB2 instance you wish to monitor. Select the color, scale, width and style of the line you wish to plot. The Explain button can be used to give an explanation of the counter you are plotting. When you have finished, click the **Add** button then the **Done** button.

This will add a line to the chart graph showing the number of local database connections over time.

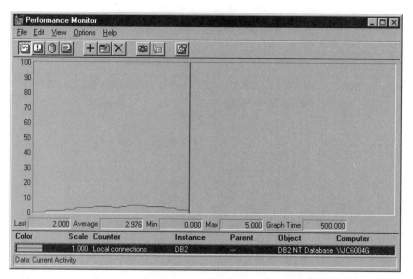

Figure 274. NT Performance Monitor - Local Database Connections

Figure 274 shows how the chart option looks when monitoring local database connections over time. A step-up in the graph represents a new connection to a local database and a step-down represents the reset of a connection to a local database.

To monitor the performance of multiple counters at one time follow the procedure above but choose all the counters you wish to display before clicking **Done**. You can use different colors, line widths, and line styles to represent different counters.

To change the chart mode settings, select **Options** from the menu and then select **Chart**. You can also click on the following icon shown on the tool bar menu:

The following window is displayed:

Figure 275. Chart Options

The *Chart Options* panel allows you to alter some of the aspects of the chart window. Figure 275 shows the features of the chart window you can alter. Figure 276 shows a graph plotted as a histogram:

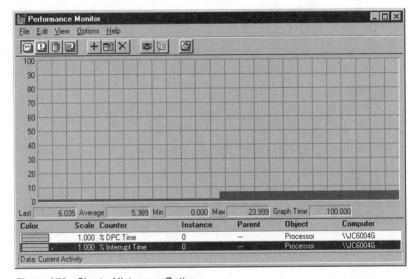

Figure 276. Chart - Histogram Option

It is also possible to choose the input source for the monitoring, which can be either real time data or data from a log file. The default setting is to monitor in real time but you can choose to use the data from a log file. To do this:

- Select the **Options** pull down menu.

- Select the **Data From** option.

- Click the **Log File** radio button and choose the log file, then click **OK.**

Now use the method described in "Log Mode" on page 411 to add the counters to the chart from the log file.

9.1.2.2 Alert mode

The Alert mode of the Windows NT Performance monitor allows you to set up alarms based on configured parameters. You can configure the Alert mode so that if a counter is less than or greater than a predefined value an alert is generated. Once an alert has been generated it can be sent to the Windows NT Performance Monitor Alert window, logged in the application log or sent across the network to another Windows NT machine.

To configure an alert:

- From the Windows NT Performance Monitor, click the **View** menu option and select **Alert**. This will switch you to the Alert window (Figure 277).

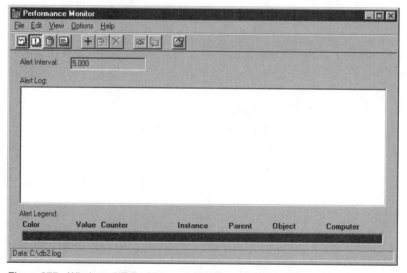

Figure 277. Windows NT Performance Monitor - Alert

- Select the **Edit** menu tab, then click **Add to Alert**. Alternately, you can click the **+** icon on the menu tool bar.

- The *Add to Alert* window is displayed. For this example we create an alert on the number of local applications connected to local databases. If this number exceeds 10, then an alert will be generated.

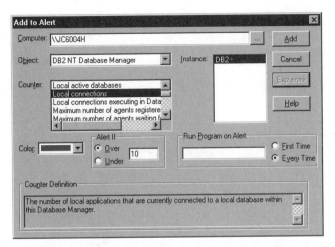

Figure 278. Add to Alert

- In the Add to Alert window (Figure 278), select **DB2 NT Database Manager** for the Object and select **Local connections** for the counter. The **Instance** selection should be set to the DB2 instance you wish to monitor. Select the color, scale, width and style of the line you wish to plot. The Explain button can be used to give an explanation of the counter you are plotting. You choose the thresholds of the alert. In this example, an alert will be generated if the counter is greater than 10. You can also specify if you want a program to be run if the alert is raised. When you have finished, click the **Add** button and then the **Done** button.

- The Alert is added to the Windows NT Performance Monitor alert window (Figure 279):

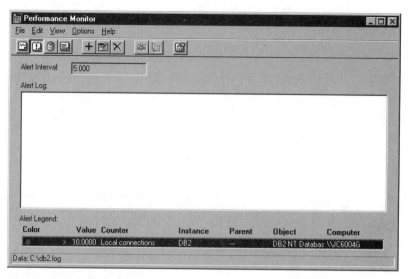

Figure 279. Alert Added

- You can alter the settings of the alert. To do this, select **Options** from the menu and the select **Alert**. You can also click on the following icon shown on the tool bar menu:

The following window will be shown:

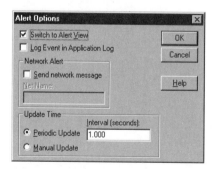

Figure 280. Alert Options

From the *Alert Options* window we can set the following:

- Selecting *Switch to Alert View* will switch focus to the Performance Monitor alert window if an alert is raised.

- Selecting *Log Event in the Application Log* will add an entry in the application log if an alert is raised.

- Select *Generate a Network Alert* to send a message across the network to another machine if an alert is raised. The machine name is specified in the **NetName** entry. The alert pops up in a window on the remote machine. The messenger and NetBIOS services must be running to use this option.

- In the *Update Time* box, the update period can be changed or manual update can be specified.

If the alert conditions are met then an alert is generated in the selected manner.

9.1.2.3 Log Mode

Log mode allows you to record performance data in a log file so that it can be reviewed at a later time for analysis in the chart or report modes. When logging performance data, you must log an object and all its counters, not one specific counter.

To start logging:

- From the Windows NT Performance Monitor, click the **View** menu option and select **Log**. This switches you to the log window:

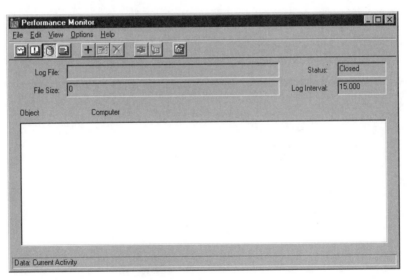

Figure 281. NT Performance Monitor - Log

- Select the **Edit** menu tab, then click **Add to Log**. Alternately, you can click the **+** icon on the menu tool bar.

- The *Add to Log* window is displayed. For this example, we log the DB2 NT Database manager object.

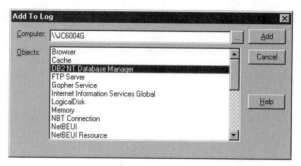

Figure 282. Add to Log

- From the Add to Log window (Figure 282), select the **DB2 NT Database Manager** object. Click **Add**, then **Done**. We have set up to log the DB2 NT Database Manager object.

- Next, you need to start the log. To do this, select **Options** from the menu and the select **Log**. You can also click on the following icon shown on the tool bar menu:

The following window is displayed:

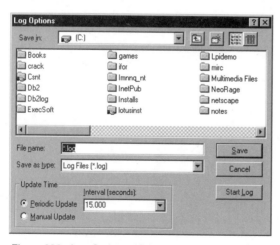

Figure 283. Log Options - Start Logging

- From the *Log Options* window, enter the path and filename for the log file. Enter the logging interval or select manual update (manual update is updated from the Options menu via Update now). Once you have specified the path and logging options, click the **Start** button and logging will commence.

- While logging is in progress, you are returned to the Windows NT Performance Monitor window in log mode. Here you can see the path and name of the log file, the size of the log file as it grows, the status of the logging and the capture interval shown in seconds.

- You can use the bookmark icon on the menu tool bar to add bookmark text to the log. Bookmarks can be used to record an event.

Note

While logging is in progress, the log file grows without limitation other than disk space. You are logging an object and all its counters so if the logging interval is low then the log file can grow rapidly.

- To stop logging, return to the log options as described above and click the **Stop Log** button.

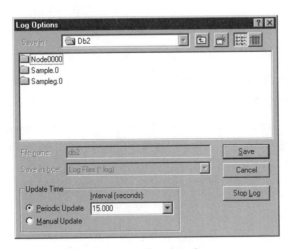

Figure 284. Log Options - Stop Logging

- Once logged data has been captured, it can be used in the other Performance Monitor modes as a data input source. To change the source from real-time to captured log data, use the **Options** menu and select

Data From. Choose the required log file, and instead of capturing real-time data, data from this log file is used.

9.1.2.4 Report Mode

Report mode is used to generate a text representation of performance data. Data can be captured in real-time or used from a log file.

To create a report:

• Click the **View** menu option and select **Report**. This switches you to the Windows NT Performance Report window.

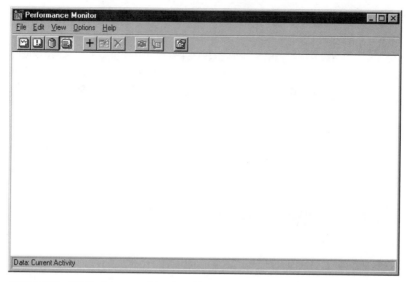

Figure 285. NT Performance Monitor - Report

• To add counters to the report select the **Edit** menu tab, then click **Add to Report**. Alternately, you can click the **+** icon on the menu tool bar.

• The *Add to Report* window is displayed.

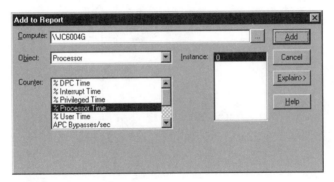

Figure 286. Add to Report

- From the *Add to Report* window, select the object counters to be displayed in the report. If you are using a log file for the data source, you can only select the object and counters that were logged. Once you have selected all the counters you desire, click **Done** to generate the report. An example report is shown in Figure 287:

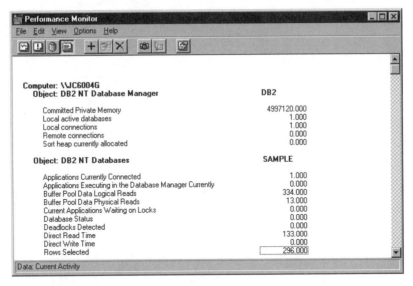

Figure 287. Sample Report

- If you are monitoring in real-time, the report will be constantly updated. If you are using a log file, you can choose the time period over which the report should be generated. This is achieved by using the Log File Timeframe. Select the **Edit** menu tab and then click **Time Window**.

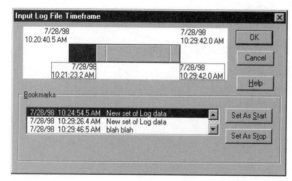

Figure 288. Timeframe of Logged Data

- You can use the slider or the bookmarks (if you set any in the log) to adjust the start and end points for the data you wish to analyse. Only data between the start and end points will be reported.

9.1.2.5 Exporting data

As we have seen, the Windows NT Performance Monitor can display performance data in many ways. In addition, it is also possible to export the performance data for use in other applications. You can export performance data in Comma Separated Variable (CSV) or Tab Separated Variable (TSV) formats to a file; the first having its values separated by commas and the second separated by tabs. Once a file has been exported it can be used by applications that support these file types, such as spreadsheets and databases.

For example, to export data while monitoring in chart mode:

- Select the **File** menu tab and then click **Export Chart.**

- From the *Export As* window choose either **CSV** or **TSV** export file format and then select a destination and filename. Click **Save** to complete the export.

To use Log mode to export the performance data:

- Create a log file as described on page "Log Mode" on page 411.

- Switch to Chart mode by selecting **Chart** from the **View** menu.

- From the *Options* menu select **Data From** and choose the log file you have just created as the data input source.

- Select **Add to Chart** from the **Edit** menu, and add the counters you wish to export. Remember that only the object and its counters you logged will be available. Click **Done** when you have all the counters you require.

- To export, select **Export Chart** from the **File** menu. Choose either **CSV** or **TSV** export file format and select a destination and filename. Click **Save** to complete the export.

The data should now be exported to a file; if required, you can import it into other applications supporting the format chosen.

9.1.2.6 Remote Monitoring
The Windows NT Performance Monitor provides you with the ability to monitor performance data on other Windows NT machines on your network. By default, the local machine is monitored when you add a counter. It is possible to choose another machine on your network to monitor by selecting a remote computer from the *Add to* window.

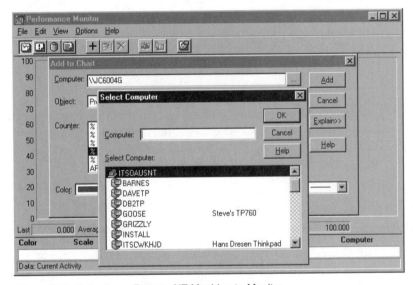

Figure 289. Selecting a Remote NT Machine to Monitor

To be able to view the NT Performance objects and counters on another DB2 for Windows NT machine, you need to register the remote DB2 administrator userid and password on the local machine. The purpose of this is to allow the performance DLL, db2perf.dll, to correctly identify itself to the DB2 database manager on a remote request.

To register the remote DB2 administrator userid and password on the local system (the system you wish to monitor from), use the db2perfr utility shipped with DB2. To register a userid and password:

```
db2perfr -r username password
```

To deregister a userid and password:

```
db2perfr -u
```

> **Note**
>
> The username and password that you register must be kept up to date
> with the userid and password stored in the Windows NT security
> database. If the userid and/or password in the Windows NT security
> database is changed, then you must perform the registration again.

9.1.2.7 Resetting DB2 Performance Values

When an application calls the DB2 monitor APIs, the information returned is
by default the cumulative values since the DB2 server started. You should
reset the performance values between repeated runs of a particular test
scenario.

To reset the performance values, use the db2perfc utility:

```
db2perfc [database_name [databasename]....]
```

The db2perfc command can be used without parameters which resets
performance values for all databases; or it can be used with a list of
databases. Resetting the values also effects anyone remotely accessing the
performance values.

9.2 DB2 UDB Monitoring

DB2 Monitors are used to collect detailed resource usage information.
Monitoring activity may be performed from a DB2 client or a DB2 server. The
monitor interface can be invoked using CLP commands, graphical
Performance Monitors or monitoring APIs. DB2 provides two methods of
monitoring which differ in the way monitoring data is gathered. They are:

- *Snapshot Monitoring* provides information regarding database activity at a
  specific point in time. It shows you the DB2 activity at that time and the
  amount of data returned to the user when a snapshot is taken is
  determined using monitor switches. These switches can be set at instance
  or application level.

- *Event monitoring* records the occurrence of specific milestones of DB2
  events. This allows you to collect information about transient events such
  as deadlocks, connections, and SQL statements.

9.2.1 Snapshot Monitoring

As suggested by its name, snapshot monitoring provides data regarding database activity at a specific moment in time. It is a window into the state of the database system at the time the snapshot is taken.

Monitor switches control the amount of data that is collected. By default, the monitor switches are set to off as there is a small overhead generated by the collection of data. If they are all set to off, a small amount of data is always collected by the snapshot monitor.

The data collected by a given monitor is cumulative. It starts being collected when a monitor switch is turned on or reset.

The monitor switches can be turned on and off at the instance level (DBM configuration) or at an application level. Table 7 shows the available monitor switches and the data their associated monitors collect:

Table 7. Monitor Switches

Group	Data Provided	Monitor Switch	DBM Parameter
Sorts	Number of heaps used, overflows, sorts, performance	SORT	DFT_MON_SORT
Locks	Number of locks held, number of deadlocks	LOCK	DFT_MON_LOCK
Tables	Table activity, rows read, rows written	TABLE	DFT_MON_TABLE
Bufferpools	Number of reads and writes, time taken	BUFFERPOOL	DFT_MON_BUFPOOL
Unit of Work	Start times, end times, completion status	UOW	DFT_MON_UOW
SQL Statements	Start time, stop time, statement identification	STATEMENT	DFT_MON_STMT

When setting the monitor switches at the instance level, all the databases within that instance will be affected and applications that connect to a database will inherit the default switches set at the instance level. For example if the LOCK monitor switch was turned on at the instance level and an application connected to a database in that instance, then the application would also have the LOCK monitor switch enabled.

Note

The state of the monitor switches can be changed by users who have SYSADM, SYSCTRL, or SYSMAINT authority.

9.2.1.1 Altering Monitor Switches Using the Control Center

To alter the monitor switches at the instance level using the Control Center, follow these steps:

- Start the Control Center by clicking on **Start**, then **Programs**, then **DB2 for Windows NT**, then **Administration tools**, then **Control Center ;** or by issuing **db2cc** from a Command Window.

- Once the Control Center is started, expand the system tree and right-button click on the required instance. Click on **Configure** from the pop-up menu and the following window is displayed:

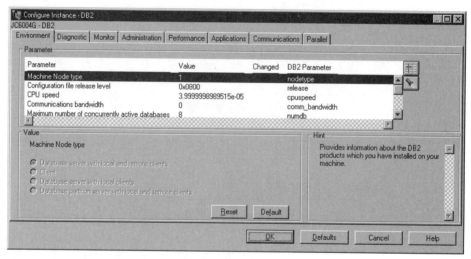

Figure 290. DB2 Control Center - Configure Instance

- From this window, select the *Monitor* tab. This panel shows the monitor switches for the instance and their current state:

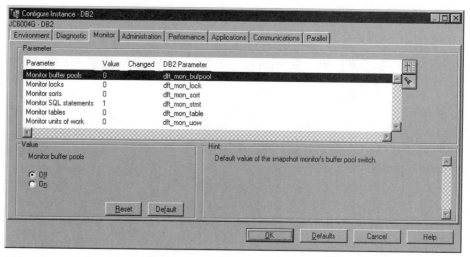

Figure 291. Configure Instance - Monitor Tab

To alter a switch, select the switch from the list you wish to alter and in the value radio boxes choose either On or Off. Click OK when you are finished.

9.2.1.2 Altering Monitor Switches Using a Command Window

To alter the monitor switches at the instance level using a DB2 Command Window (or a Command Line Processor session), you use the UPDATE DBM CONFIGURATION command:

```
UPDATE DBM CFG USING <monitor_switch> ON|OFF
```

where <monitor_switch> is one of the DBM configuration monitor switches as shown in the DBM parameters in Table 7 on page 419.

For example, to enable the monitor switch for SQL statements at the instance level, issue the following command:

```
UPDATE DBM CFG USING DFT_MON_STMT ON
```

You can check that the command was successful by verifying the DBM configuration (note that for any changes to the DBM configuration to take effect you must stop and start the DB2 Database Manager for that instance):

```
GET DBM CFG
```

This shows us the current instance configuration and we should see
something similar to the following, showing that the DFT_MON_STMT switch
has been turned on:

```
Default database monitor switches
   Buffer pool                           (DFT_MON_BUFPOOL) = OFF
   Lock                                     (DFT_MON_LOCK) = OFF
   Sort                                     (DFT_MON_SORT) = OFF
   Statement                                (DFT_MON_STMT) = ON
   Table                                   (DFT_MON_TABLE) = OFF
   Unit of work                              (DFT_MON_UOW) = OFF
```

You can also alter the state of the switches for an application, for example, the
Command Line Processor (CLP). You can alter the CLP monitor switches and
then capture performance data for subsequent commands run from the CLP.
To alter the CLP monitor switches:

```
UPDATE MONITOR SWITCHES USING <switch_name> ON|OFF
```

where <switch_name> is one of the monitor switches shown in Table 7 on
page 419.

To enable the monitor switch for SQL statements for the CLP, issue the
following command:

```
UPDATE MONITOR SWITCHES USING STATEMENT ON
```

This would then capture the SQL statement data for any statements run from
the CLP. You can check the state of the application monitor switches by
issuing the following command:

```
GET MONITOR SWITCHES
```

You should see something similar to the following, showing that the
STATEMENT switch has been turned on and at what time:

```
Monitor Recording Switches

   Buffer Pool Activity Information  (BUFFERPOOL) = OFF
   Lock Information                        (LOCK) = OFF
   Sorting Information                     (SORT) = OFF
   SQL Statement Information          (STATEMENT) = ON  07-30-1998
11:32:26.973488
   Table Activity Information             (TABLE) = OFF
   Unit of Work Information                 (UOW) = OFF
```

9.2.1.3 Displaying Snapshot Monitor Data

Once you have enabled a monitor switch and have started collecting monitor data, you can take a snapshot to view the related data. This displays the monitor data for that point in time.

You can display a snapshot of the monitor data by using the DB2 Control Center, the DB2 Command Center, DB2 CLP or application API's.

When we request a snapshot for the monitor data we can request the level of data we require. This enables us to examine particular areas of the database system. The following snapshot monitor levels exist:

- Database Manager - captures information for an active instance
- Database - database(s) information
- Application - captures application(s) information
- Buffer pool - captures buffer pool information
- Table space - captures information for table spaces
- Table - captures information for tables
- Lock - captures information on locks held by applications

The snapshot level and the monitor switches are related. If we do not have a monitor switch enabled when the request is made, we may not see any data. For example if we had the LOCK monitor switch disabled and yet request a snapshot of locks held, we would not be provided with **all** the relevant data as it would not have been collected.

Snapshot Monitoring Using The Graphical Tools

The *Performance Monitor* can be used to display snapshot information at predefined intervals (default interval is 20 seconds). It can be used to analyze the activity of a specific instance, database, table space, table or connection. The *Performance Monitor* is initiated from the Control Center interface.

Performance monitoring in DB2 UDB can be done using the defaults provided when DB2 is first installed, or can be customized to monitor only the parts of

UDB which are of interest to you. The *Performance Monitor* is customized using *monitor profiles.* You can think of monitor profiles as separate "instances" of the *Performance Monitor.* Within each profile, you specify what part of the system you wish to monitor (such as database) and what activity you wish to monitor (such as buffer pool activity).

You can also set alarms in the *Performance Monitor* to trigger when certain characteristics drop below/rise above set values. You can then choose between different monitor profiles and activate the profile you wish to use.

To start the DB2 Performance Monitor:

- Open the DB2 Control Center by selecting **Start**, then **Programs**, then **DB2 for Windows NT**, then **Administration Tools**, then **Control Center** or type **db2cc** from a command prompt.

- Once the Control Center is started, expand the system tree and right-button click on the required database. Select **Snapshot Monitoring**, then **Show Monitor Profile**. The following window is displayed:

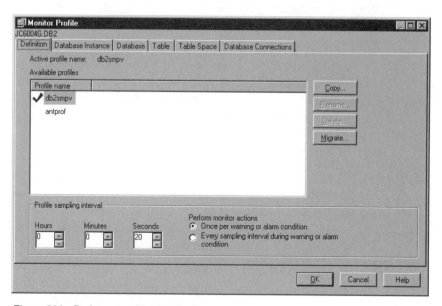

Figure 292. Performance Monitor Profile

This window shows the available profiles, and enables you to copy profiles, migrate profiles from one release to another and alter the sampling rate.

The tabs in this window allow you to select the monitor variables you wish to monitor. For example, if you only want to monitor table activity, you could turn monitoring off for the other selections and only turn monitoring on for tables.

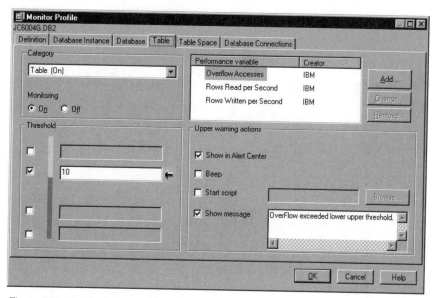

Figure 293. Table Monitoring Enabled

You set upper and lower thresholds for a performance variable. If the value of the variable exceeds the upper threshold or drops below the lower threshold then an alert can be raised. You then choose the actions that are generated when an alert is raised:

- Display it in the Alert Center
- Sound an operating system beep
- Execute a script
- Display a system message window

You can set two values for each of the upper and lower thresholds, a warning and an alarm. In Figure 293, if the lower of the two settings of the upper threshold (warning) is exceeded then an alert is logged in the Alert Center (see Figure 296 on page 427) and a message window is displayed.

Once you have chosen the performance variables you wish to monitor, you can start monitoring. From the Control Center, click the right mouse button on the required database and then click on **Snapshot Monitoring**, followed by **Start Monitoring**. Monitoring is now started for the active monitor profile for the database level. Please note that you may also perform these same steps (setting and starting) from the instance level object in the DB2 Control Center.

To see the results of this performance monitoring, take the same steps as above, but this time click on **Show Monitor Details**. The information displayed will depend on whether you request this from the instance level object (in which case the instance items will be shown) or the database object (in which case the database items will be shown to you). A window similar to the following is displayed if you choose to view the details from the database object level:

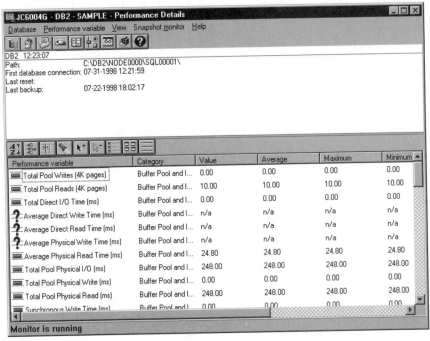

Figure 294. Performance Monitor Details

From this screen, you monitor the variables you chose in the performance profile, alter the threshold settings, graph data and monitor the status of performance. The display will update by default every 20 seconds. To graph a variable, select a variable, right mouse button click on it and choose **Show Performance Graph**.

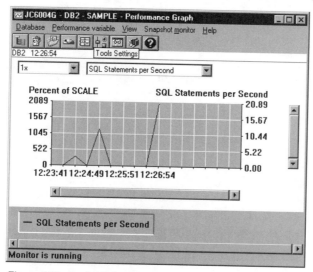

Figure 295. Performance Graph

When you wish to stop monitoring, click the right mouse button on the database/instance from the Control Center and select **Snapshot Monitoring**, then **Stop Monitoring** or use the Snapshot Monitor menu from the Performance Monitor window shown in Figure 294 on page 426.

If an alert is raised, and the option to display it in the Alert Center has been selected, then an icon appears in the *Alert Center* window:

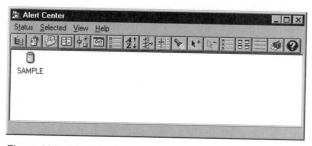

Figure 296. Alert Center

The color of the icon reflects the severity of the raised alert. A red icon indicates an alarm while a yellow icon indicates a warning. Figure 296 shows that a warning alert has been raised in the SAMPLE database. (When this happens, the database icon for SAMPLE in the Control Center turns yellow also). If you double click on the SAMPLE database icon, the Performance Details window is displayed (Figure 294).

Snapshot Monitoring From a Command Line

To request a database snapshot we use the GET SNAPSHOT command. The format for the GET SNAPSHOT command is:

```
GET SNAPSHOT FOR <LEVEL> ON <db_alias>
```

Where <level> is the level of data you require and <db_alias> is the database alias name. For a complete list of the parameters and options for the GET SNAPSHOT command, please refer to the DB2 Command Reference.

When requesting snapshot data it is normally a good idea to save the output to a file. If you are using the CLP you may save the output to a file as follows:

```
GET SNAPSHOT FOR LOCKS ON SAMPLE > OUT.TXT
```

Where OUT.TXT is the name of a file to write the results to. If you are using the DB2 Command Center, you can use the **Results** menu option to save the results to a file.

Let's look at some examples of taking snapshots. For these examples, all the instance level monitor switches have been enabled. To view snapshot data for applications connected to the SAMPLE database, you issue the following command:

```
GET SNAPSHOT FOR APPLICATIONS ON SAMPLE
```

This shows you detailed monitor data concerning the activity of applications on the SAMPLE database. The data shown is the cumulative data collected since the monitor counters had been started or last reset. An extract from the output follows:

```
Application Snapshot

Application handle                           = 1
Application status                           = UOW Waiting
Status change time                           = 07-30-1998 15:58:52.756886
Application code page                        = 1252
Application country code                     = 1
DUOW correlation token                       = *LOCAL.DB2.980730205400
Application name                             = db2bp.exe
Application ID                               = *LOCAL.DB2.980730205730
Sequence number                              = 0001
Connection request start timestamp           = 07-30-1998 15:57:30.984026
Connect request completion timestamp         = 07-30-1998 15:57:32.940270
Application idle time                        = 4 minutes
Authorization ID                             = ADMIN
Execution ID                                 = ADMIN
Configuration NNAME of client                = N000E1AE
Client database manager product ID           = SQL05000
Process ID of client application             = 226
Platform of client application               = NT
Communication protocol of client             = Local Client
Database name                                = SAMPLE
Database path                                = C:\DB2\NODE0000\SQL00001\
Client database alias                        = sample
Input database alias                         = SAMPLE
Last reset timestamp                         =
Snapshot timestamp                           = 07-30-1998 16:02:52.934740
.......................................
Total sorts                                  = 2
Total sort time (ms)                         = 48
Total sort overflows                         = 0
.......................................
Buffer pool data logical reads               = 94
Buffer pool data physical reads              = 14
Buffer pool data writes                      = 0
Buffer pool index logical reads              = 133
Buffer pool index physical reads             = 30
Buffer pool index writes                     = 0
Total buffer pool read time (ms)             = 316
Total buffer pool write time (ms)            = 0
Time waited for prefetch (ms)                = 0
Direct reads                                 = 34
Direct writes                                = 0
Direct read requests                         = 5
Direct write requests                        = 0
Direct reads elapsed time (ms)               = 56
Direct write elapsed time (ms)               = 0
```

You can also request monitor data for tables in the SAMPLE database. To achieve this, you issue:

```
GET SNAPSHOT FOR TABLES ON SAMPLE
```

This command shows you the details of the activity and tables in the SAMPLE database. You see which tables have been accessed or written to the most. For example:

```
Table Snapshot

First database connect timestamp    = 07-30-1998 15:57:30.984026

Last reset timestamp                =
Snapshot timestamp                  = 07-30-1998 16:14:11.300382
Database name                       = SAMPLE
Database path                       = C:\DB2\NODE0000\SQL00001\
Input database alias                = SAMPLE
Number of accessed tables           = 5

Table Schema          Table Name            Table Type          Rows Written  Rows Read  Overflows
--------------------  --------------------  --------------------  ------------ ---------- ----------
ADMIN                 EMPLOYEE              User                           0         64          0
SYSIBM                SYSTABLES            Catalog                        0          2          0
SYSIBM                SYSTABLESPACES       Catalog                        0          3          0
SYSIBM                SYSPLAN              Catalog                        0          1          0
SYSIBM                SYSDBAUTH            Catalog                        0          3          0
```

These two examples show just two of the levels of snapshot data that can be collected. By using the other levels it is possible to get detailed data on all areas of your database system for monitoring performance. See the GET SNAPSHOT command in the DB2 Command Reference manual for more details on taking snapshots.

9.2.2 Event Monitoring

While Snapshot Monitoring records the state of database activity when the snapshot is taken, an Event Monitor records the database activity when an *event* or *transition* occurs. Some database activities that need to be monitored cannot be easily captured using the Snapshot Monitor. These activities include deadlock scenarios. When a deadlock occurs, DB2 resolves the deadlock by issuing a ROLLBACK for one of the transactions. Information regarding the deadlock event cannot be easily captured using the Snapshot Monitor, since the deadlock has probably been resolved before a snapshot can be taken.

Event Monitors, like other database objects, are created using SQL DDL (Data Definition Language). Event Monitors can be turned on or off, much like the Snapshot Monitor switches. SYSADM or DBADM authority is required to create an Event Monitor.

When an Event Monitor is created, the type of event to be monitored must be stated. The Event Monitor can monitor the following events:

- DATABASE — records an event record when the last application disconnects from the database.

- TABLES — records an event record for each active table when the last application disconnects from the database.

- DEADLOCKS — records an event record for each deadlock event.
- TABLESPACES — records an event record for each active table space when the last application disconnects from the database.
- BUFFERPOOLS — records an event record for buffer pools when the last application disconnects from the database.
- CONNECTIONS — records an event record for each database connection event when an application disconnects from a database.
- STATEMENTS — records an event record for every SQL statement issued by an application (dynamic and static).
- TRANSACTIONS — records an event record for every transaction when it completes (COMMIT or ROLLBACK).

The output of an Event Monitor is stored in a directory or in a named pipe. The existence of the pipe or the file will be verified when the Event Monitor is activated. If the target location for an Event Monitor is a named pipe, then it is the responsibility of the application to read the data promptly from the pipe. If the target for an Event Monitor is a directory, then the stream of data will be written to a series of files. The files are sequentially numbered and have a file extension of evt (such as 00000000.evt, 00000001.evt, and so forth.). The maximum size and number of Event Monitor files is specified when the monitor is defined.

Note that an Event Monitor will turn itself off if the defined file space has been exceeded.

9.2.2.1 Creating Event Monitors

Let's create a Event Monitor that will capture SQL statements and will store its event records in the 'd:\eventmonitors\sql\evmon1' directory.

To create an Event Monitor, from the Control Center, click the right mouse on the database you want to monitor and select **Monitor Events** from the pop-up menu. The Event Monitors window opens, then select **Event Monitor**, **Create** from the Menu Bar.

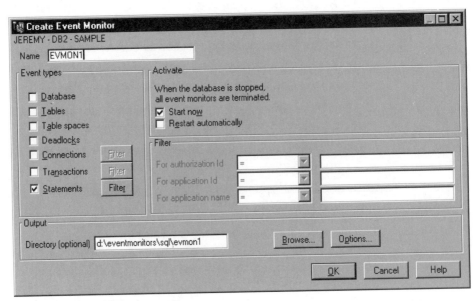

Figure 297. Creating an Event Monitor

In the *Create Event Monitor* window shown in Figure 297 we have specified **EVMON1** as the event monitor name and **Statements** as the event type to be monitored. The event monitor will be started immediately, and the output will be sent to the 'd:\eventmonitors\deadlocks\evmon1' directory.

The number of defined event monitors is unlimited but only 32 can be active at the same time. Remember that the directory specified for the output must exist at event monitor activation and the instance owner must be able to write to the specified directory. Do not specify the same directory for the output of more than one event monitor.

Event Monitors can be defined to monitor many different types of database activities. A filter can also be specified for an Event Monitor. The filter can be based on the application id, authorization id or the application name. Filtering the event monitor output can be used as a form of database auditing.

To specify further details about this Event Monitor, click on **Options**.

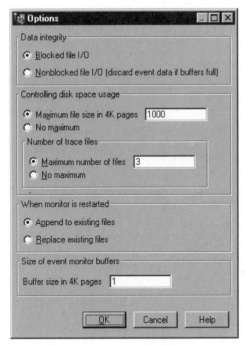

Figure 298. Create Event Monitors - Options

The above monitor is defined to allocate up to 3 files each 4 MB in size, for a total monitor storage area of 12 MB. Other Event Monitor options include specifying the size of the write buffer, synchronous or asynchronous writes, append the Event Monitor data to existing records, or replace the Event Monitor data in the directory when the monitor is activated.

Alternately, the following SQL statement could be used to create this Event Monitor.

```
CREATE EVENT MONITOR EVMON1 FOR STATEMENTS
WRITE TO FILE 'd:\eventmonitors\sql\evmon1' MAXFILES 3
MAXFILESIZE 1000
```

To start the event monitor created by the above SQL statement, the following command needs to be issued:

```
SET EVENT MONITOR EVMON1 STATE = 1
```

Two system catalog tables are used to store Event Monitor definitions:

- SYSCAT.EVENTMONITORS

    Contains a record for each Event Monitor showing details on the definition.

- SYSCAT.EVENTS

    Contains a record for each event being monitored. A single Event Monitor can be defined to monitor multiple events (for example, DEADLOCKS and STATEMENTS).

9.2.2.2 Viewing Event Monitor Records

Event Monitor files are not readable by a text editor. An application must be used. Let's first examine some of the Event Monitor records.

Event monitoring is similar to tracing since each event is recorded as it occurs and it is appended to the event record log files. An Event Monitor file will contain a number of event records. Table 8 shows all of the event record types and when they are used.

Table 8. Event Monitor Records

Record Type	Collected for Event Type
Event Monitor Log Header	All
Event Monitor Start	All
Database Header	All
Database Event	Database
Table Space Event	Table Space
Table Event	Table
Connection Header	Connection
Connection Event	Connection
Connection Header	Transaction
Transaction (Unit of Work) Event	Transaction
Connection Header	Statement
Statement Event	Statement
Dynamic Statement Even	Statement
Connection Header	Deadlock
Deadlock Event	Deadlock

Record Type	Collected for Event Type
Deadlock Connection Even	Deadlock
Event Monitor Overflow	All (if any)

Some event records are created when any application disconnects from the database and others are only created when the *last* application disconnects from the database.

If an Event Monitor is monitoring database, table space, or table events, it will only write event records when the last application using the database disconnects. If database, table space, or table monitoring data is required before the last application disconnects, use the Snapshot Monitor.

To ensure that all of the event records have been written to disk (some may be buffered), simply turn the Event Monitor off by clicking the right mouse button on the event monitor you want to use and select **Stop Event Monitoring** from the pop-up menu as shown in Figure 299. (Please see the DB2 SQL Reference for the commands to use from the Command Window.)

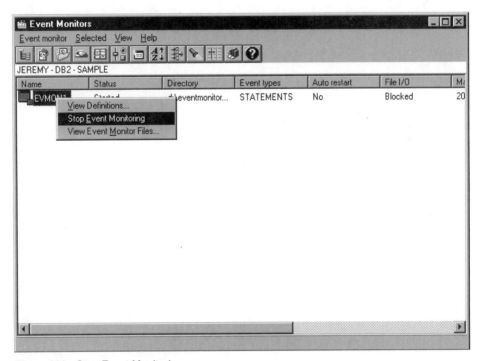

Figure 299. Stop Event Monitoring

To review the files generated, you can either:

- Click the right mouse button on the event monitor just stopped and select **View Event Monitor Files** from the pop-up menu as shown in Figure 299, or:

- From the DB2 for Windows NT Administration Tools folder, double-click on the **Event Analyzer** icon (Figure 300). Complete the information requested, such as Event file path, database name and whether you want to view static SQL text or not and click **OK**.

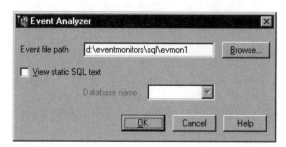

Figure 300. Event Analyzer

The *Monitored Periods View* window is displayed:

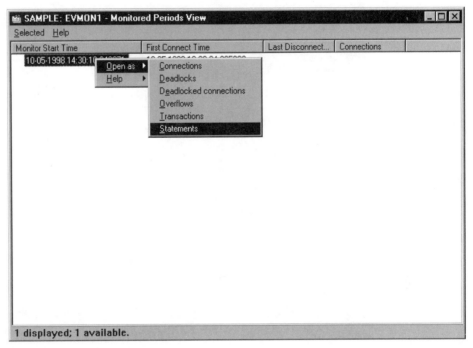

Figure 301. Monitored Periods View

You can view and analyze the information gathered for connections, deadlocks, transactions, statements and so on. In our example, we are interested in the SQL statements, so we select **Open as** and then **Statements**, as shown in Figure 302.

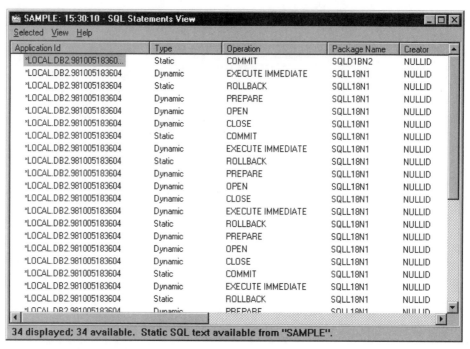

Application Id	Type	Operation	Package Name	Creator
*LOCAL.DB2.98100518360...	Static	COMMIT	SQLD1BN2	NULLID
*LOCAL.DB2.981005183604	Dynamic	EXECUTE IMMEDIATE	SQLL18N1	NULLID
*LOCAL.DB2.981005183604	Static	ROLLBACK	SQLL18N1	NULLID
*LOCAL.DB2.981005183604	Dynamic	PREPARE	SQLL18N1	NULLID
*LOCAL.DB2.981005183604	Dynamic	OPEN	SQLL18N1	NULLID
*LOCAL.DB2.981005183604	Dynamic	CLOSE	SQLL18N1	NULLID
*LOCAL.DB2.981005183604	Static	COMMIT	SQLL18N1	NULLID
*LOCAL.DB2.981005183604	Dynamic	EXECUTE IMMEDIATE	SQLL18N1	NULLID
*LOCAL.DB2.981005183604	Static	ROLLBACK	SQLL18N1	NULLID
*LOCAL.DB2.981005183604	Dynamic	PREPARE	SQLL18N1	NULLID
*LOCAL.DB2.981005183604	Dynamic	OPEN	SQLL18N1	NULLID
*LOCAL.DB2.981005183604	Dynamic	CLOSE	SQLL18N1	NULLID
*LOCAL.DB2.981005183604	Dynamic	EXECUTE IMMEDIATE	SQLL18N1	NULLID
*LOCAL.DB2.981005183604	Static	ROLLBACK	SQLL18N1	NULLID
*LOCAL.DB2.981005183604	Dynamic	PREPARE	SQLL18N1	NULLID
*LOCAL.DB2.981005183604	Dynamic	OPEN	SQLL18N1	NULLID
*LOCAL.DB2.981005183604	Dynamic	CLOSE	SQLL18N1	NULLID
*LOCAL.DB2.981005183604	Static	COMMIT	SQLL18N1	NULLID
*LOCAL.DB2.981005183604	Dynamic	EXECUTE IMMEDIATE	SQLL18N1	NULLID
*LOCAL.DB2.981005183604	Static	ROLLBACK	SQLL18N1	NULLID
*LOCAL.DB2.981005183604	Dynamic	PREPARE	SQLL18N1	NULLID

34 displayed; 34 available. Static SQL text available from "SAMPLE".

Figure 302. SQL Statements View

If we then select one of the entries, we can view more details about the SQL statement. For example, if we choose a PREPARE statement, we can see the associated SQL as shown in Figure 303:

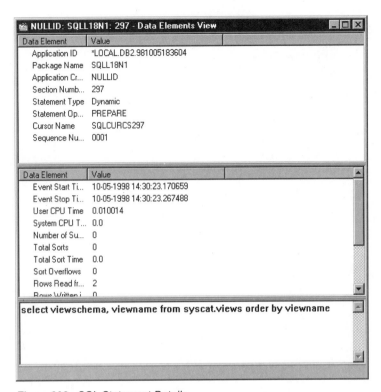

Data Element	Value
Application ID	*LOCAL.DB2.981005183604
Package Name	SQLL18N1
Application Cr...	NULLID
Section Numb...	297
Statement Type	Dynamic
Statement Op...	PREPARE
Cursor Name	SQLCURCS297
Sequence Nu...	0001

Data Element	Value
Event Start Ti...	10-05-1998 14:30:23.170659
Event Stop Ti...	10-05-1998 14:30:23.267488
User CPU Time	0.010014
System CPU T...	0.0
Number of Su...	0
Total Sorts	0
Total Sort Time	0.0
Sort Overflows	0
Rows Read fr...	2
Rows Written i...	0

`select viewschema, viewname from syscat.views order by viewname`

Figure 303. SQL Statement Details

As you can see, the monitoring facilities in DB2 UDB for Windows NT are very rich and can be incorporated into the native Windows NT facilities. The tools provided for you by DB2 will allow you to monitor and analyze your system to better understand what is happening. This allows you to plan a course of action to correct a potential problem situation.

Chapter 10. Problem Determination

In this chapter we discuss the procedures involved in determining the source of DB2 UDB related problems or errors. We list the steps which should be performed if an error occurs to enable the source of the error to be found quickly and efficiently. For each step in the process we discuss which data to gather to help resolve the error. Once gathered, the data must be analyzed to determine the source of the error. After the source of the error has been identified the appropriate changes must be made to resolve the error.

It is good practice to keep a record of all problems you or your users experience, and the actions that were taken to resolve them. This will help in the event that similar errors occur in the future. In the log you should include a complete problem description including all SQL codes and reason codes as well as the cause of the error and the solution to the problem.

In this chapter we'll discuss the following:

- The steps which should be followed when diagnosing a DB2 UDB problem.

- The data to gather to help determine the source of the problem.

- Available online help.

- Diagnostic tools available within DB2 UDB, such as the DB2 diagnostic log file DB2DIAG.LOG.

- Using the Windows NT Event Log to assist in problem determination.

- Performing a DB2 trace.

- Performing a CLI trace.

- Recovering from errors that occur during installation

10.1 Approach to DB2 UDB Problem Determination

To solve DB2 UDB problems as quickly and efficiently as possible there are a number of steps which should be followed. These steps include:

1. Describe the error condition fully: Include the SQL code/state and any associated reason codes. If it is an operating system error, record the system error code.

2. Gather the appropriate diagnostic information: DB2 UDB provides a number of sources of diagnostic information including: the DB2DIAG.LOG file, the DB2 Trace Facility, the operating system error/event log and so on.

It is important to gather the appropriate information when the error occurs so that you can find the source of the problem.

3. Analyze the diagnostic information: Once the data has been gathered it must be examined to find the true source of the error condition. We will discuss methods for analyzing the diagnostic information.

4. Make the appropriate changes: Many times the error is not a DB2 UDB problem. In many cases DB2 UDB is working correctly and the error is a user or application error (that is, running out of disk space). In the event that the problem is a DB2 UDB error you may need to contact IBM DB2 UDB support.

Following these steps simplifies the problem determination process and helps to solve your DB2 UDB related problems more efficiently.

10.2 Describing the Problem

The first step in solving a problem is determining what the problem really is. To help determine what the problem is you need to start with a good problem description. When describing the problem condition it is very important that you include all relevant information.

When describing the error condition always include the SQL code/state and any associated reason code (or the system error code if it is an operating system error). The reason code is required because some SQL codes have many different reason codes associated with them. In this case the SQL code itself will not be sufficient to understand the problem.

It is also important to describe what was happening on the system prior to the error and when the error occurred. This will help to determine the state of the system when the error occurred.

Is the error reproducible? If you can reproduce the error then perform the steps required to make the error reoccur and record each step. It is important that you record the steps in case you need additional information during the course of your investigation.

When using DB2 UDB Enterprise-Extended Edition (DB2 UDB EEE), it is important to note which partition encountered the error. Typically errors are not encountered on all partitions, therefore it is important to know which partition reported the error so you can gather the required information from the correct partition(s).

10.2.1 Example Problem Descriptions

Now let's look at some example problem descriptions:

1. My DB2 application fails every time I run it.

2. Within my DB2 application I receive an SQL1042 error code every time I connect to my database SALESDB.

Which of the above descriptions provides more information? The second gives the SQL code as well as the action being performed when the error occurs. It provides a reproducible scenario as it occurs when connecting to the SALESDB database.

Let's look at another example:

1. When I try to insert data into the personnel table in my SALESDB database using my application I receive an SQL900 error code; however, I can insert records into the table using the Command Center.

2. My DB2 application fails with an SQL900 error.

Which of the above description provides more information? The first description gives the SQL code as well as the action being performed when the error occurs. It provides information which implies there are no problems with the database or the table since an insert into the table using the Command Center works fine. Although the second description provides the SQL code, it does not give the action being performed when the error occurs.

10.3 Gathering the Appropriate Diagnostic Information

DB2 UDB provides a number of sources of diagnostic information. Some of this information is required for all types of DB2 problems while some other information may be specific to the actual error condition. For all error conditions you should gather the following information:

1. The DB2DIAG.LOG file, plus all associated trap and dump files. With DB2 UDB EEE all partitions will write to the same DB2DIAG.LOG file by default, however, this can be changed by the system administrator. Ensure that you gather the DB2DIAG.LOG file from the partition (or partitions) which encounter the error.

2. The database manager (instance) configuration.

3. The database configuration for the problem database. (With a DB2 UDB EEE installation you may need to provide the database configuration for more than one partition if the values differ across partitions).

In the event that you cannot find the source of the problem you may need to call the DB2 UDB Support team. Before doing this it is important to have all of the above information ready and also know what version and level of DB2 you are running. This information is contained in the Windows NT registry:

```
HKEY_LOCAL_MACHINE\SOFTWARE\IBM\DB2\DB2 Universal Database ???
Edition\CurrentVersion
```

In some cases additional diagnostic information may be required to determine the source of the problem. Once we have discussed the required information we will discuss the optional sources of information and indicate when they may be required.

10.3.1 Choosing the Correct Diagnostic Level

The most important piece of DB2 diagnostic information is the DB2DIAG.LOG diagnostic log file. This log file is DB2's error log and is updated whenever an error occurs within DB2. Since the log file is updated when the error occurs it is referred to as a First Failure Data Capture (FFDC) log. The advantage of FFDC logging is that it captures the information as the error is actually happening, many times eliminating the need to reproduce the error.

The DB2DIAG.LOG file is located in the path specified by the database manager configuration parameter DIAGPATH. If this parameter is null (the default value) DB2DIAG.LOG and all the associated dump and trap files will be created in the directory:

```
x:\SQLLIB\<instance name>
```

where `x:` is the drive referenced in the DB2PATH registry variable.

As errors or events occur, information is appended to the end of the DB2DIAG.LOG file. The DB2DIAG.LOG file is not automatically truncated or pruned. If the file becomes too large, you can erase the file and a new file will be created as needed.

10.3.1.1 Choosing the Correct Diagnostic Level

As the DB2 UDB database administrator you control the amount and type of information that is recorded in the DB2DIAG.LOG file using the database manager configuration parameter DIAGLEVEL. The DIAGLEVEL parameter can be set to:

- 0 - NO diagnostic data will be captured
- 1 - SEVERE errors only
- 2 - SEVERE and NON-SEVERE errors
- 3 - SEVERE, NON-SEVERE errors and WARNING messages (Default)

- 4 - SEVERE, NON-SEVERE errors, WARNING and INFORMATION messages

The default DIAGLEVEL setting is 3. A DIAGLEVEL of 4 will allow you to capture additional data that can be very helpful in problem determination. Since DIAGLEVEL 4 records more information, this may slow down the performance of the system. However, this additional information is only logged during the start and stop of DB2 and any first connection to a database or during times of errors. Since the DB2 start and stop and first connections do not occur frequently under normal circumstances, it is better to set the DIAGLEVEL to 4 and record the extra information when the error occurs. In a DB2 UDB EEE environment a DIAGLEVEL of 3 is recommended due to the volume of entries which can be recorded. If you receive an error and the information provided is not detailed enough, increase DIAGLEVEL to 4 and re-create the problem.

10.3.2 The DB2 Trace Facility

If you have a recurring, reproducible problem you may also wish to take a trace of the error. Unlike the DB2DIAG.LOG which captures information as the error is occurring, taking a DB2 trace requires you to reproduce the error. When taking a trace you need to be aware that you may be capturing information on a condition resulting from the original error, not the error itself.

Since the DB2 trace records the flow of control within internal DB2 functions, it cannot be interpreted by a database administrator. The DB2 UDB Support team may request a DB2 trace if the DB2DIAG.LOG file does not provide enough information to determine the source of the problem. In this section we will discuss the methods and considerations for taking DB2 traces.

DB2 trace information can be stored in memory or directly to disk. When DB2 trace collection is activated, the trace information is recorded in chronological order. Each entry in the trace file is called a *trace point* and is recorded sequentially.

The amount of information gathered from the trace will grow rapidly. The goal in performing a DB2 trace is to capture only the error situation. Any other activities, such as starting the database manager instance (NET START <db2instance>) or connecting to a database (DB2 CONNECT) that does not reproduce the error situation should be avoided. The goal in capturing trace information is to reproduce the *smallest, recreatable* scenario and capture it for further analysis.

Since the DB2 trace gathers information for every function within DB2 there will be a degradation in overall performance. How much degradation you experience is dependent on the type of problem and how the trace is being recorded (that is, in memory or on disk).

To perform a trace for DB2 UDB for Windows NT, you may either use the db2trc command or initiate a trace though the Problem Determination Tools Folder. We will examine both of these methods.

10.3.2.1 The db2trc Command

The general syntax of the db2trc command is:

```
db2trc <subcommand> <options>
```

The complete syntax of the db2trc command can be found when the command is issued with the -u option. The following screen shows the subcommands of the db2trc command:

More detail for each of the different subcommands can also be found by issuing a subcommand and using the -u option. Let's have a closer look at the syntax of the db2trc command and its subcommands.

```
DB2 CLP                                                    _ □ ✕
C:\>db2trc on -u
Usage: db2trc on
         [-m <mask>]
                <mask> = <prods>.<events>.<comps>.<fncs>
         [-p <pid>[.<tid>]]
                <trace only this proc/thread>
         [-c <cpid>]
                <trace only this companion proc>
         [-rc <rc>]
                <treat rc as a SysError>
         [-e <maxSysErrors>]
                <stop trace after maxSysErrors>
         [-r <maxRecordSize>]
                <truncate records to maxRecordSize bytes>
         [-s | -n | -f <fileName>]
                <send to shared mem, native trace or file>
         [-l [<bufferSize>] | -i [<bufferSize>]]
                <retain the last or the initial records>
         [-d]
                <check data pointer validity>

C:\>
C:\>
C:\>_
```

Collection of the trace information begins when `db2trc` is executed with the `on` subcommand. This will start the trace function and record the trace entries to a destination which may also be specified as part of the `on` subcommand. By default, trace entries are collected into *shared memory*. However, they can optionally be written directly to a file. Trace collection ends when `db2trc` is executed with the `off` subcommand.

10.3.2.2 Capturing Trace Information into Memory

Since writing to memory is much quicker than writing to disk, it is recommended that you use a memory buffer when taking a DB2 trace unless absolutely necessary. We will now discuss the steps required to take a DB2 trace using a memory buffer.

In this command we will issue the `on` subcommand with the parameters `-e` and `-l`. These parameters are used to control:

- `-e` Specifies the maximum number of system errors allowed before trace collection is automatically terminated. If it is set to `-1`, as in this example, all errors will be collected until trace is manually turned off.

- `-l` (note that it is a lowercase L, not the number one) Indicates you wish to retain the latest entries into the trace buffer. The number specifies the size of the trace buffer in memory. It is expressed in the number of bytes. In this case we used a 4 MB trace buffer (4000000 bytes). Unless you are using DB2 UDB EEE we recommend a trace buffer of 4 MB. With DB2 UDB EEE we recommend an 8 MB trace buffer due to the extra volume of activity being traced. If you want to keep the initial trace entries use the `-i` parameter instead of `-l`.

```
db2trc on -e -1 -l 4000000
```

This will start the trace facility with a 4 MB buffer and the trace will run until manually stopped. The next step should be the recreation of the problem for which the trace is being collected. After you have reproduced the problem the trace information will need to be written to a file for analysis.

The subcommand to write the contents of the memory buffer to disk is `dump`. When dumping the memory buffer to disk you must specify the name of the file to write to. To write the contents of the trace buffer to the file named tracefile.dmp we would issue the command:

```
db2trc dump tracefile.dmp
```

It is very important that as soon as the collection of the trace is completed and the information that is contained in memory is written to a file that you stop the trace facility to eliminate the effect on the performance of the system. The trace can be stopped using the subcommand `off` as follows:

```
db2trc off
```

It is important to note that you must dump the trace buffer to disk prior to turning the trace off as the trace buffer is released when the trace is turned off. This trace dump file is a binary file and must be formatted for analysis by the DB2 UDB Support team. There are two methods of formatting the file for analysis:

You can issue the command

```
db2trc flow tracefile.dmp tracefile.flw
```

to format the events by process and thread, or:

```
db2trc format tracefile.dmp tracefile.fmt
```

to list the events chronologically, independent of process or thread.

10.3.2.3 Capturing Trace Information to a Disk File

In the event that the entire system hangs so that you cannot issue the `db2trc dump` command to write the contents of the memory buffer to disk, you will need to trace directly to a file.

In order to write to a file we need to specify the `-e`, `-l` and `-f` parameters. These parameters are used to control:

- `-e` Specifies the maximum number of system errors allowed before trace collection is automatically terminated. If it is set to `-1`, as in this example, all errors will be collected until trace is manually turned off.

- -l (note that it is a lowercase L, not the number one) Indicates you wish to retain the latest entries into the trace file. The number specifies the size of the file. It is expressed in the number of bytes. In this case we used a 4 MB trace file (4000000 bytes). Unless you are using DB2 UDB EEE we recommend a trace file size of 4 MB. With DB2 UDB EEE we recommend an 8 MB trace file due to the extra volume of activity being traced. If you want to keep the initial trace entries use the -i parameter instead of -l.

- -f Specifies the file name and extension of the file to which trace should be written. This file will be written to the directory from where the command is executed.

```
db2trc on -e -1 -l 4000000 -f tracefile.dmp
```

After the trace is turned on you will need to reproduce the error and then turn the trace off. You can stop the trace facility using the command:

```
db2trc off
```

You will find that there is a significant performance difference between tracing to shared memory and tracing directly to a file. A trace that is activated with the -f option will cause the system to be noticeably slower than the trace that is performed in memory.

The -f option of db2trc

The -f option of the db2trc utility is recommended when the error results in system hang situations such that you can no longer dump the trace file manually.

10.3.2.4 Using the info Subcommand
The info subcommand is used to look at information about the trace while it is occurring. It also gives you information about the environment and settings that were present when the trace was activated. The following screen shows you the syntax of the command and an example of the output of that command when tracing to shared memory.

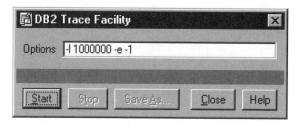

```
┌─────────────────────────────────────────────────────────────┐
│ 🔲 DB2 CLP                                              _□×    │
├─────────────────────────────────────────────────────────────┤
│ C:\>                                                        ▲ │
│ C:\>db2trc info -                                           █ │
│ Trace Version          :     3.01                           █ │
│ Op. System             :       NT                           █ │
│ Op. Sys. Version       :      1.0                           █ │
│ H/W Platform           :    80×86                           █ │
│ Version prod   1        :     3.01   <DB2>                   █ │
│                                                               │
│ Mask                   : *.*.*.*                             █ │
│ pid.tid to trace       : all                                 █ │
│ cpid    to trace       : all                                 █ │
│ Treat this rc as sys err: none                               █ │
│ Max system errors      : infinite                            █ │
│ Max record size        : 32768 bytes                         █ │
│ Trace destination      : SHARED MEMORY                       █ │
│ Records to keep        : LAST                                █ │
│ Trace buffer size      : 2097152 bytes                       █ │
│ Trace data pointer check: NO                                 █ │
│ C:\>                                                        ▼ │
│ ◄                                                         ► │
└─────────────────────────────────────────────────────────────┘
```

10.3.2.5 Starting a DB2 Trace from the Graphical Interface

The task of starting or stopping a trace is made easier in DB2 UDB for
Windows NT through the use of a graphical interface. Select **Start ->
Programs -> DB2 for Windows NT -> Problem Determination ->Trace**.
This sequence will bring up the following window:

```
┌─────────────────────────────────────────────────────────┐
│ 🔳 DB2 Trace Facility                                 ×  │
├─────────────────────────────────────────────────────────┤
│                                                           │
│  Options │-l 1000000 -e -1                             │  │
│                                                           │
│  ┌──────────────────────────────────────────────────┐    │
│  │                                                    │    │
│  └──────────────────────────────────────────────────┘    │
│  ┌──────┐ ┌──────┐ ┌──────────┐ ┌───────┐ ┌──────┐        │
│  │ Start│ │ Stop │ │ Save As..│ │ Close │ │ Help │        │
│  └──────┘ └──────┘ └──────────┘ └───────┘ └──────┘        │
└─────────────────────────────────────────────────────────┘
```

Figure 304. DB2 Trace Facility

You may start, stop, input any applicable parameters, and save to a file, just
as you would if entering db2trc from the command line. Default options are
already entered for you.

When you select the **Save As** push button, you may select a filename for the
binary dump file. You may also select to format the output of your trace to
ASCII files if you wish to verify the output. Select **Generate formatted trace
file** if you want the full trace information, or **Generate control-flow trace file**
if you want only the control flow of the trace information in a nested format.

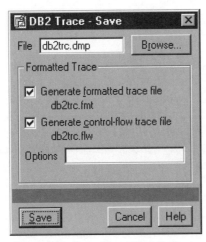

Figure 305. Trace Formatting Options

The following are valid options for trace formatting options:

-m mask	Specifies trace record types. The mask variable consists of four byte-masks that are separated by periods. The byte-masks correspond to products, event types, components, and functions, respectively.
-r	Output trace in reverse-chronological order.
-p process ID[.thread ID}	Format only the trace records that belong to the specified process and thread.
-x single record	Format only the specified record.
--x first record-last record	Format all records between the specified first and last record.

None of these options are mandatory. If omitted, the defaults are:

- Mask is as specified for execution.
- All records are formatted in chronological order.

10.3.3 CLI/ODBC Traces

The DB2 Call Level Interface (DB2 CLI) is an application programming interface for database access that uses function calls to invoke dynamic SQL statements. The DB2 CLI provides a set of database functions that include the core and a subset of the extended functions of Microsoft's Open Database Connectivity interface (ODBC). The CLI interface is very popular with database application vendors because it is an open database standard and an application written to this standard can be used on multiple database platforms.

ODBC applications such as Microsoft Access, Lotus Approach and Powerbuilder are very popular for use with DB2 UDB. If you are experiencing problems with an ODBC or CLI application that you are unable to solve, you may need to trace the ODBC/CLI function calls. The CLI/ODBC trace facility will log the function calls to a file which you specify. This trace is in a regular ASCII format and can be read by a database administrator or application developer to help analyze the problem.

10.3.3.1 Enabling CLI/ODBC Trace (DB2CLI.INI)

In order to activate an ODBC/CLI trace you must modify the DB2CLI.INI file. This is the configuration file for ODBC and CLI functions. Within the DB2CLI.INI file you will need to add the following statements:

```
Trace=1
TraceFileName=<path and file name of the trace file>
TraceFlush=1
```

These statements need to be inserted in the [COMMON] section of the DB2CLI.INI file. The ODBC/CLI trace will then be active for all DB2 databases accessible through ODBC or CLI. The DB2CLI.INI file is located in the SQLLIB directory for the database instance.

Note that the ODBC/CLI trace is activated and deactivated by setting the value of the TRACE= parameter to 1 and 0 respectively. The trace will be placed in the file specified by TRACEFILENAME. When TRACEFLUSH is set to 1, the trace files will be written to disk after every function call. This greatly increases the overhead of the trace, but prevents loss of data in the event of a system crash.

Rather than directly editing the DB2CLI.INI, you may choose to configure the driver by using the DB2 Client Configuration Assistant, accessed on Windows NT by selecting **Start -> Programs -> DB2 for Windows NT -> Client Configuration Assistant**. Follow these steps to configure a CLI/ODBC trace:

1. Select the DB2 database alias you are configuring.
2. Select the **Properties...** push button to bring up the **Database Properties** window.
3. Click on the CLI/ODBC **Settings** push button. You will be prompted to connect to the database.
4. When the CLI/ODBC **Settings** window comes up, select the **Advanced...** push button to bring up the **Advanced Settings** notebook.

5. Select the **Service** tab, and highlight **Trace**. Enter the filename where you wish to save the trace and select **Flush after each entry** if you want TRACEFLUSH set to ON. Click on **OK** to save your settings.

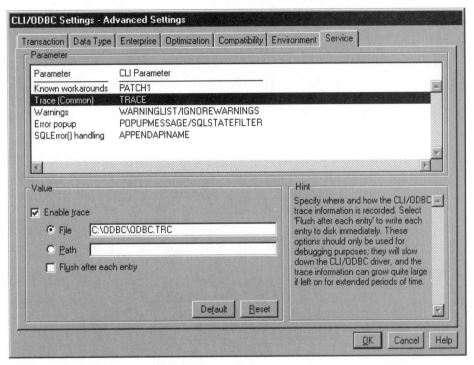

Figure 306. Configuring for a CLI/ODBC Trace

Reverse the procedure to turn tracing off when you have completed your trace

10.3.4 The Windows NT Event Log

DB2 UDB also writes First Failure Data Capture (FFDC) information to the Windows NT Event Log. Error detection and message logging during the operation of DB2 UDB will cause entries in the DB2DIAG.LOG as well as the Windows NT Event Log.

Windows NT maintains separate System, Security and Application Event Logs. DB2 UDB writes information in the System and Application Logs, however, the most relevant error information is contained in the Application Log. When installed, DB2 UDB is automatically configured to use the Windows NT Event Log.

10.3.4.1 Viewing Windows NT Event Logs

To view events from any of the logs, open the **Event Viewer** and select the log (System, Security or Application) from the Log menu. By default, all events for that log are displayed with the most recent event appearing first. These options can be changed in the View menu along with a range of other options. You may change the time range through which you want to view events and the type of events to display.

Five event types can appear in the event log, namely: information, warning, error, successful audit and failure audit. Figure 307 on page 455 shows the Application Event Log with entries written by DB2. In this case there are a number of different events being logged.

If you want to see more details about an occurrence of a specific event, double-click on the event you wish to examine. The Event Detail dialog box for that event will popup. The data pertinent to the event will be displayed, for example:

- The date and time the event occurred
- The source of the event (typically the software that logged the event)

In this example a message has been received that the database cannot be accessed because a backup is pending. For more details the database administrator can refer to the DB2DIAG.LOG.

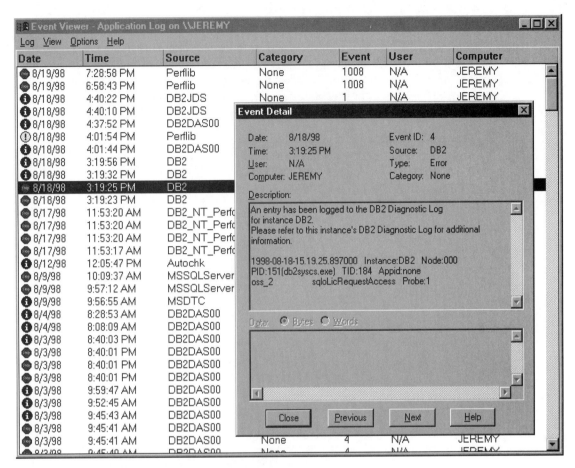

Figure 307. Viewing Windows NT Application Event Log

10.3.4.2 Archive Windows NT Event Logs (.evt)

You may want to archive Windows NT Event Logs for a period of time in order to be able to trace the origin or cause of a problem. It is also a good idea to archive the Event Log to prevent an Event Log full condition. If this error occurs logging is stopped until the log is cleared (this assumes of course that you have not set the event log to overwrite previous events).

When archiving the log contents you may want to archive based on the Event Log type such as System, Security, Application for more efficient retrieval at a later date. To do so, use the "Save As" option of the Log window in the Event Viewer. The log will be archived as a *.evt file. To retrieve an archived Windows NT Event Log use the Open option of the Log window in the Event Viewer.

10.3.5 Database Analysis and Repair Tool

The Database Analysis and Repair Tool (DB2DART) is used to verify the architectural integrity of a database and its objects. This utility will examine the data and index objects as well as the database construct files to ensure that they are architecturally correct. DB2DART does not verify that the data is correct, or that all of the tables and indexes match, however it ensures that the database is in the correct architectural format.

The following symptoms may indicate database damage:

- The server consistently goes down when particular data is accessed.
- The server fails repeatedly.
- There is a DIA3700C error in the DB2DIAG.LOG file.

DB2DART, found in the SQLLIB\BIN directory, can be used to verify the architectural integrity of the database by scanning through all of the database objects. It can analyze databases, table spaces, tables and indexes to confirm that:

- The control information is correct in the object.
- There are no discrepancies in the format of the object.
- The data and index pages are the correct size and contain the correct column types.

The syntax for DB2DART is:

```
DB2DART <DB Alias> <option> ...
```

Some database inspection options include:

/DB	(default) Inspects entire database
/T	Inspects a single table.
/TSF	Inspects only the table space files and containers.
/TS	Inspects a single table space and the tables within.
/ATSC	Inspects constructs of all table spaces (but not their tables).
/UBPF	Updates the bufferpool file with a new specification.

Data formatting options:

/DD	Dumps formatted table data.
/DI	Dumps formatted index data.
/DTSF	Dumps formatted table space file information.

/DEMP Dumps formatted EMP information for a DMS table.

/DBPF Dumps formatted bufferpool file information.

/DDEL Dumps formatted table data in delimited ASCII format.

Repair options (make sure database is offline):

/MI Mark index as invalid.

/IP Initialize data page of a table as empty.

Help option:

/H Display help text.

Input value options:

/OI	Object ID.
/TN table-name	Table name.
/TSI	Table space ID.
/PS number	Page number to start with (suffix page number with 'p' for pool relative).
/NP number	Number of pages.
/V Y/N	Y or N for verbose option.
/RPT path	Optional path to place report output file.
/CONN Y/N	Specify whether DB2DART processing includes operations that connect to database (Y) or not (N). Default (Y).
/SCR Y/N	(Y) output produced to screen. (N) minimize output to screen.
/ERR Y/N/E	(Y) normal error log DART.ERR file. (N) minimize output to error log DART.ERR file. (E) minimize DART.ERR file output, minimize screen output, only error information to report file. Default (Y).

If DB2DART discovers that an index is in error, you can mark the index as being invalid using the /MI option. The index will be rebuilt the next time the object is accessed using the index.

If DB2DART discovers that a table has been damaged, you have two options:

• The best option is to restore a backup and rollforward to the end of the logs. This is the only option that will preserve the data and ensure that the database remains consistent.

- If no backup is available or log retention is not enabled, you may consider reinitializing/clearing the damaged pages with DB2DART using the /IP option. This should only be done under the guidance and recommendation of DB2 UDB Support. This option will result in the loss of data and is not recommended for production databases, but in an emergency will restore the database to a connectable state. Prior to initializing the page you should dump the available data on the page using the /DDEL option to dump the page data in delimited ASCII format. Following this operation you must export all your data from this table(s), drop your table(s) and recreate them to ensure you have a valid and consistent database. If this is not done, the consistency of your database cannot be guaranteed.

DB2DART should only be used for emergency analysis and repair. In most instances it should only be used at the request of DB2 UDB Support. Using it to repair your database must *only* be done under the guidance of DB2 UDB Support personnel.

10.4 Examining the Diagnostic Information

Once the appropriate diagnostic information has been gathered you need to examine the information to determine the source of the error. We will now look at how to examine the different sources of diagnostic information we have previously discussed.

10.4.1 DB2DIAG.LOG File Entry Format

Let's look at an example of a DB2DIAG.LOG file to understand its format and the type of information recorded. For our example, our DIAGLEVEL is set to 4. For this example we are using the SAMPLE database with the default SMS table space USERSPACE1. The department table is in the USERSPACE1 table space. To force an error we have purposely manipulated the container where the department table resides.

We then issued the following commands:

```
db2 connect to SAMPLE
db2 select * from department
```

These commands produced the following DB2DIAG.LOG entries. Only a portion of the file is shown here. We've used bold numbers in parentheses following each element of the log to label them for purposes of clarity.

```
1998-07-27-11.25.07.216000(1)  Instance:DB2(2) Node:000 (3)
PID:192(db2syscs.exe)(4)TID:259(5)  Appid:*LOCAL.DB2.980727162504(6)
buffer_pool_services(7)sqlbStartPools(8)Probe:0(9)Database:SAMPLE (10)

Starting the database.
```

Each DB2DIAG.LOG entry includes these elements:

- (1) Timestamp of the error or information message
- (2) Instance name - Here it is DB2.
- (3) For DB2 UDB Enterprise-Extended Edition systems, the partition generating the message. (If not DB2 UDB EEE or if another version of DB2 is being used, the value is "000".)
- (4) Process id - In this example, it is identified by pid(XXX) where XXX is the process ID. The process being executed here is db2syscs.exe.
- (5) Thread id - This is identified by tid(XXX) where XXX is the actual thread ID.
- (6) Application ID - Identification of the application for which the process is working. In this example, the process generating the message is working on behalf of an application with the ID *LOCAL.DB2.980727162504. The application ID will indicate if the connection is local or remote.
- (7) Component identifiers - This is the component that has sent the message. In our example, it was buffer pool services.
- (8) Function name - This is the function within the component that sent the message. In this example sqlbStartPools.
- (9) Probe ID - This is an indicator of the line of code which reported the error. In our example, this was indicated by Probe:0.
- (10) Database name - The database is SAMPLE.

This example shows the first entry to DB2DIAG.LOG created during the first connection to a database. The next example is a DB2DIAG.LOG entry where an error has occurred.

```
1998-03-26-09.47.08.258000    Instance:DB2    Node:000
PID:186(db2syscs.exe)    TID:190    Appid:*LOCAL.DB2.980326144448
buffer_pool_services   sqlbDMSAcquireContainer    Probe:869   Database:SAMPL
DIA9999E An internal error occurred.

Report the following error code :"FFFF8139"(1)
```

In this example, we see the same components we did in the previous example, but we see additional information as well:

- **(1)** An internal return code. This return code will either be the actual SQL code or an internal DB2 return code. In either case the return code is always reported in hexadecimal format. In some cases, this return code may be byte-reversed. A hex value beginning with FFFF is in a valid format. If your value does not begin with hex FFFF then it is byte-reversed, and you must byte-reverse it prior to converting it to decimal. In this case the return code is in the correct order (FFFF8139).

The first step in analyzing the return code is to convert the return code to decimal and see if it is an SQL code. In this case FFFF8139 converts to -32455 which is not a valid SQL code. We then check to see if 8139 is a valid DB2 Internal Return Code. These codes are documented in the *DB2 UDB Troubleshooting Guide*, Appendix C. When we look this up we find that 8139 means "Container is already being used". We will explain this error further in the analyzing the data section.

```
1998-07-28-14.45.20.326000   Instance:DB2   Node:000
PID:214(db2syscs.exe)   TID:281   Appid:*LOCAL.DB2.980728194518
buffer_pool_services   sqlbrdpg   Probe:1110   Database:SAMPLE
DIA3806C Unexpected end of file was reached.(1)

ZRC=FFFFF609 (2)

1998-07-28-14.45.20.476000   Instance:DB2   Node:000
PID:214(db2syscs.exe)   TID:281   Appid:*LOCAL.DB2.980728194518
buffer_pool_services   sqlbReadPage   Probe:71   Database:SAMPLE

** Failure on first attempt to read the page **   09f6 ffff (3)
```

In this example, we see the same components we did in the previous example, but we see additional information as well:

- **(1)** An error message indicating that while DB2 was reading a file it reached the end of the file prior to reading all of the information that was expected.

- **(2)** A return code. This return code will either be the actual SQL code or an internal DB2 return code. In either case the return code is always reported in hexadecimal. In some cases, this return code may be byte-reversed. A hex value beginning with FFFF is in a valid format. If your value does not begin with hex FFFF then it is byte-reversed, and you must byte-reverse it prior to converting it to decimal.

- **(3)** In this case the return code is byte-reversed. Byte reversal of the value 09 F6 FF FF yields: FF FF F6 09.

The first step in analyzing the return code is to convert the return code to decimal and see if it is an SQL code. In this case FFFFF609 converts to -2551 which is a valid SQL code, however, when we examine the message for the SQL Code we see that it does not make sense for this error condition. We then check to see if F609 is a valid DB2 Internal Return Code. These codes are documented in the *DB2 UDB Troubleshooting Guide*, Appendix C. When we look this up we find that F609 means "Data does not exist".

Converting Return Codes

To convert a return code of the format FFFF nnnn to decimal, where nnnn is a hex number, subtract nnnn from FFFF, and add 1. The resulting number can be converted to decimal using a tool such as the calculator that comes with Windows NT. For instance, to convert FFFF F609, subtract F609 from FFFF to get 9F6, add 1 to get 9F7. In the NT calculator, click on view and select **Scientific**. Click on the **Hex** radio button, enter 9F7 in the entry field, and then click on the **Dec** radio button. This will give you the decimal equivalent.

Use the following DB2 command line processor or DB2 Command Window command to check to see if it is an SQLCODE:

```
db2 ? SQLXXXXX
```

where xxxxx is the 4 or 5-digit number of the SQLCODE.

10.4.2 Dump Files

Dump files are written by DB2 when an error occurs for which additional internal information, such as internal control blocks that would be useful in diagnosing the problem, are required. When a dump file is written, an entry is made in the DB2DIAG.LOG that will indicate the timestamp, the filename and the internal DB2 structure(s) written to disk. Since this information is written in binary format and is written in an internal DB2 structure it is not of use to database administrators in solving DB2 problems. These files are intended for use by the DB2 UDB Support team.

We'll look at some examples of DB2DIAG.LOG entries that indicate that data has been written to dump files. These files may be named in two different manners, depending on where they are encountered.

1. The file name will be made up of the process id (pid) concatenated to the thread id (tid), with a numeric extension. If you are using DB2 UDB EEE

the extension identifies the partition number, otherwise the extension is 000.

2. The file name will be made up of the process id (pid) concatenated to the thread id (tid), with an extension of DMP.

DB2 will dump all available diagnostic information which is relevant to the problem at the moment the error occurred. Here is an example of a DB2DIAG.LOG entry that indicates that a dump file has been created. In this case the pid and the tid are concatenated to produce the filename, 214281.000. The entry also indicates that the data being written into the dump file is the SQLB_PAGE structure.

```
1998-07-28-14.45.23.841000    Instance:DB2    Node:000
PID:214(db2syscs.exe)    TID:281    Appid:*LOCAL.DB2.980728194518
buffer_pool_services    sqlbReadPage    Probe:35    Database:SAMPLE

DiagData
0000 0000                                      ....

Dump File:d:\sqllib\DB2\214281.000 Data:SQLB_PAGE
```

10.4.3 Trap Files

Under severe error conditions DB2 may also issue an exception to itself to dump additional diagnostic information. All exceptions initiated by DB2 or encountered by DB2 are reported in a trap file.

The trap file will contain a stack trace back (this is a list of the functions that have been called by the process) showing the current function flow at the time the exception occurred as well as the current data on the process' stack. Each trap file will contain a single exception that was encountered by, or initiated by DB2. This file will be written in regular ASCII format, however, determining what data is on the process' stack requires access to internal structures. The DB2 UDB Support team can use this information to learn which exception was issued and the last steps that were performed.

Trap files will be stored in the same subdirectory as the DB2DIAG.LOG file. These files may be named in two different manners, depending on where they are encountered.

1. The file name will be made up of the letter t, followed by the process id with a numeric extension. If you are using DB2 UDB EEE the extension identifies the partition number, otherwise the extension is 000.

2. The file name will be made up of the process id with an extension of DMP

In the following example, you will see that the function which encountered the exception was sqloDumpEDU. The actual address within the library containing the sqloDumpEDU function which reported the exception is at 17DA8658. This address will aid the DB2 UDB Support team in determining the actual line of code which encountered the exception.

```
Exception C0010002 Occurred
Exception Address  =  17DA8658          sqloDumpEDU

Registers dump:
---------------

GS  : 0000     FS  : 150B     ES  : 0053     DS  : 0053
EDI : 0DAF4DD0 ESI : 0040E1AC EAX : 00000000 EBX : 12DE95D4
ECX : 00000004 EDX : 0040DE68
EBP : 0040DEA0 EIP : 17DA8658 EFLG: 00082202 ESP : 0040DE58
CS  : 17DD005B   SS  : 400053

Instruction dump:
-----------------

 17DA8658 : 83 C4 04 89 45 F8 0B C0 0F 84 95 00 00 00 50 B9
 17DA8668 : 05 00 00 00 83 EC 0C BA 5F 00 00 00 B8 4A 00 00
 17DA8678 : 00 E8 8A 21 02 00 83 C4 10 89 45 F8 E9 72 00 00
 17DA8688 : 00 8D 40 00 8B 5D 08 8B C3 E8 56 8B 01 00 0B C0
 17DA8698 : 0F 84 5D 00 00 00 8D 4B FF 53 8B D1 BB 01 00 00

Stack calling chain:
--------------------
 16923CBF 00000007 00000000   sqldLoadTCB__FP7sqleacbP8SQLD_TCBi
 16923765 0DAF4DD0 005F6340   sqldFixTCB__FP7sqleacbiN32PcT2T6T2PP8SQLD_TCB

DLL Addresses:
--------------

Code Address range for DB2ABIND is 16830000 .. 16842724
Code Address range for DB2APP   is 16D70000 .. 16DF2760
...

Date/Time: 1997-11-27-16.58.33

Thread slot 121 , Id 7 , priority 200
Stack Base   : 003D0000 ;Stack Top   : 00410000
Process Id   : 130
Process name : C:\SQLLIB\BIN\DB2SYSC.EXE

/*----- Stack Bottom ---*/
 0040DE58 :0040DE68 00000007 00000E83 00000000
 0040DE68 :C0010002 00000000 00000000 17DA8658
 0040DE78 :00000000 00000007 00000000 00000000
```

10.4.4 Formatting the DB2 Trace

The trace file, whether it was written directly or was written from memory is a binary file and cannot be analyzed without formatting. The trace facility can format the trace in two different styles. To convert the trace dump file to a readable format you must specify the format or flow subcommand for db2trc.

- *flow* - Represents the flow of control and an overview of invoked functions and return codes (or error codes), and is broken down by process and thread.

- *format* - Represents each trace entry in formatted form in the sequence they occurred regardless of process or thread.

The following example is a fragment of the flow and corresponding formatted entries from the same trace showing some of the trace entries.

```
Flow:

1435    |sqlodelq   fnc_entry    ...
1436    |sqlodelq   fnc_data     ...
1437    |  |sqlofmblk  cei_entry   ...
1438    |  |sqlofmblk  cei_data    ...
1439    |  |sqlofmblk  cei_retcode  0
1440    |sqlodelq   fnc_retcode  0


...


Format:

1435    DB2 fnc_entry     oper_system_services sqlodelq (1.30.15.196) ---------(1)
        pid 49; tid 1; cpid 0; time 197028; trace_point 0
        called_from 17DF6733

1436    DB2 fnc_data      oper_system_services sqlodelq (1.35.15.196) ---------(2)
        pid 49; tid 1; cpid 0; time 197028; trace_point 1
        0600 0000 0100 0100 50c4 3c0e        ........P.<.

1437    DB2 cei_entry     oper_system_services sqlofmblk (1.20.15.62) ---------(1)
        pid 49; tid 1; cpid 0; time 197028; trace_point 0
        called_from 17DF66EB

1438    DB2 cei_data      oper_system_services sqlofmblk (1.25.15.62) ---------(2)
        pid 49; tid 1; cpid 0; time 197028; trace_point 1
        c400 3c0e 50c4 3c0e                  ..<.P.<.

1439    DB2 cei_retcode  oper_system_services sqlofmblk (1.23.15.62) ---------(3)
        pid 49; tid 1; cpid 0; time 197028; trace_point 254
        return_code = 000000 = 0

1440    DB2 fnc_retcode  oper_system_services sqlodelq (1.33.15.196) ---------(4)
        pid 49; tid 1; cpid 0; time 197028; trace_point 254
        return_code = 000000 = 0
```

There are several types of trace entries shown in this example:

- Entry - Note that in the trace file, both `fnc_entry` and `cei_entry` denot an entry trace point.
- Data - This is where variable values are recorded at different trace poir within a function and dumped to a trace file.
- Exit/Return - This is when the function ends and its return code is recorded.
- Error - While not shown above, this is where any additional information relevant to an error condition is recorded and dumped to the trace file.

10.4.5 The Format of a Trace Entry

Each trace entry contains information in a predefined format. Let's look at sample formatted trace entry:

```
(1)339  (2)DB2  (3)cei_errcode  (4)oper_system_services  (5)sqloopenp  (6
(1.6.15.140)

(7)pid 44;  (8)tid 11;  (9)cpid 44;(10)time 500247;(11)trace_point 254

        return_code = (12)0xffffe60a = -6646 = SQLO_FNEX
```

- (1) Trace Entry sequence number. The trace entry is assigned a sequence number as it is recorded. The sequence always starts with one (1) and grows to the end of the trace file.
- (2) Product Indicator. (DB2)
- (3) Type of trace entry.
- (4) Component to which function being executed belongs
- (5) Function being executed.
- (6) Mask identifying (<Product>.<Event>.<Component>.<Function>) - This can be used to filter the trace collection, but only for specific Events, Components or Functions. Mask settings should be used as advised by a DB2 UDB Support analyst. The mask setting only affects the formatting of the trace. All entries will be recorded in the trace buffer/file no matter what mask is specified.
- (7) Process Id of the process under which the function was executed.
- (8) Thread Id of the thread executing the function.

- (9) Companion Process Id - This is the process id of the process whose child is the process being traced. Frequently the companion process is a DB2 System Controller (DB2SYSC.EXE) process).

- (10) A time place holder. A parameter must be set to gather real time information. This slows down the system and is not recommended.

- (11)Trace point number - This entry uniquely identifies the trace entry within DB2. The DB2 UDB Support analyst having access to function source code can determine the exact line of code which reported this trace entry. This information is required if any data is written with the trace entry so that the analyst can decipher the data correctly.

- (12) The return code is represented as a hexadecimal value. This value must be analyzed the same way as return codes within the DB2DIAG.LOG file. First see if it is the correct order or is byte reversed. Once it is in the correct format convert it to decimal and see if it is a valid SQL code. If not a valid SQL code look up the hex value in the *DB2 UDB Troubleshooting Guide*, Appendix C. For some of the internal return codes, a symbolic name is also shown. Frequently, this symbolic name makes the identification of the problem much easier. In this example, SQLO_FNEX means File Not EXist (i.e., the file does not exist).

10.4.6 Trace Information That is Not Captured

The collecting and capturing of trace information does not imply that the trace information will help diagnosing the error.

There are a number of reasons why a trace may not capture the error information you are looking for. For instance:

- The trace buffer size you specified was not large enough to hold a complete set of trace events. Since you specified a fixed buffer or file size, the trace buffer or file will eventually fill. Once it is filled entries will be lost. Depending on whether the trace was started with the -l or -i parameter the earliest (-l) or latest (-i) entries will be lost. This situation is frequently called "trace wrapped".

- The error condition was not reproduced while the trace was turned on.

- The error situation was recreated, but the error did not occur on the machine where you turned on the trace.

To verify that the trace contains a complete set of trace events and has not wrapped you can format the binary trace file. When the file is being formatted or flowed the function will indicate how many records were in the trace and if it has wrapped or not. An example of the trace flow subcommand and its output follows. In this case we will flow the trace to the NULL device as we are not interested in the output at this point.

```
C:\>db2trc flw example.trc nul

Trace wrapped : YES -------------------------------------------(1)
Size of trace : 65510 bytes
Records in trace: 1265
Records formatted : 828 (pid: 72; tid: 11)
Records formatted : 215 (pid: 122; tid: 1)
Records formatted : 148 (pid: 133; tid: 1)
Records formatted : 36 (pid: 72; tid: 9)
Records formatted : 4 (pid: 72; tid: 13)
Records formatted : 34 (pid: 134; tid: 1)
```

The output of the trace flow command indicates that this trace has wrapped. It is always best to provide a trace which has not wrapped to minimize the possibility of the required information not being captured. In this case it would be advisable to recapture this trace, specifying a larger trace buffer, before proceeding with any further verification of the trace.

There are times when it will be impossible for the trace not to wrap. In these cases do not specify a buffer/file size which is so large that it can not be transmitted to the DB2 UDB Support team. One other note is that when formatting a trace, the formatted version typically is four to five times larger than the binary trace file. Therefore specifying a buffer/file size too large will make analysis of the problem very long and complicated. Typically it is sufficient to provide the binary dump file to the DB2 UDB Support team along with the level of DB2 for Windows NT code under which the trace was obtained.

10.4.7 Verifying That the Error Has Been Captured

The obvious sign that the problem being traced has indeed occurred and was captured in the trace is the occurrence of the error code being reported in the trace. Unfortunately, error codes reported to the user are SQL codes. In the formatted trace, you are likely to find internal error codes reported by different functions called by the DB2 engine. However, you can examine the trace for entries written in the DB2DIAG.LOG file. If you look for sqltfast2 trace entries, you will see the actual DB2DIAG.LOG file entry.

10.4.8 Examining a CLI/ODBC Trace

We are including an example of a DB2 CLI trace from an unsuccessful attempt to connect to a DB2 database from an ODBC application.

For our example, the application has returned an SQL1403N error message indicating that the username and/or password supplied is incorrect. Let's examine the DB2 CLI trace to get more details.

```
SQLAllocEnv( phEnv=&73068 ) ---------(1)

SQLAllocEnv( phEnv=1 )
    ---> SQL_SUCCESS   Time elapsed - +0.000000E+000 seconds (2)

SQLAllocConnect( hEnv=1, phDbc=&73064 )
    ----> Time elapsed - +1.000000E-002 seconds
SQLAllocConnect( phDbc=1 )
    ---> SQL_SUCCESS   Time elapsed - +1.000000E-002 seconds
SQLGetInfo( hDbc=1, fInfoType=SQL_DRIVER_ODBC_VER,
rgbInfoValue=&3ed58, cb
InfoValueMax=6, pcbInfoValue=&3ed56 )
    ----> Time elapsed - +0.000000E+000 seconds
SQLGetInfo( rgbInfoValue="02.10", pcbInfoValue=5 )
    ---> SQL_SUCCESS   Time elapsed - +2.000000E-002 seconds
 (3)
SQLDriverConnect( hDbc=1, hwnd=10027236, szConnStrIn="DSN=SAMPLE;UID=grant;DBQ=",
cbConnStrIn=-3, szConnStrOut=&3f12c, cbConnStrOutMax=256, pcbConnStrOut=&3f3f6,
fDriverCompletion=SQL_DRIVER_COMPLETE_REQUIRED )
    ----> Time elapsed - +0.000000E+000 seconds ---(4)

SQLDriverConnect( )
    ---> SQL_ERROR    Time elapsed - +5.471800E+001 seconds (5)

SQLError( hEnv=0, hDbc=1, hStmt=0, pszSqlState=&3ec5c,
pfNativeError=&3ec58, pszErrorMsg=&3ec64, cbErrorMsgMax=511, pcbErrorMsg=&3ec56 )
    ----> Time elapsed - +0.000000E+000 seconds ---(6)

SQLError( pszSqlState="08004", pfNativeError=-1403,
pszErrorMsg="[IBM][CLI Driver]
SQL1403N
The username and/or password supplied is incorrect.  SQLSTATE=08004
", pcbErrorMsg=97 ) (7)
    ---> SQL_SUCCESS   Time elapsed - +3.000000E-002 seconds -----(6)
```

1. Statement `SQLAllocEnv` is invoked with the address of a variable which, upon completion, will contain an environment handle which will be used by subsequent statements.

2. Upon completion, `SQLAllocEnv` returned an environment handle (in this case handle 1). This statement completed successfully as can be seen from the return code of `SQL_SUCCESS`.

3. Statement `SQLDriverConnect` is invoked with a previously acquired connection handle and other parameters describing the data source name (`SAMPLE` is the alias of the database we are trying connect to; `grant` is the identification of the user, and no authorization data is provided. Note the Null Pointer instead of an authorization string.)

4. Here we have additional information to diagnose this problem. The password was not supplied. An SQL error message of SQL1403N was received. It indicates that the username and/or password is incorrect.

From the CLI trace, we found that user did not specify a password during the connection request to the database.

5. Upon completion, `SQLDriverConnect` returned `SQL_ERROR`. This indicates a non-zero return code which indicates that this function was not successful.

6. When the return code `SQL_ERROR` is returned it is the responsibility of the application developer to invoke the `SQLError` function to gather additional information about the error reported. Until the SQLError function is called we only know that the last function did not complete successfully. In this case, `SQLError` is invoked with the addresses of the variables which will contain further description(s) of the error.

7. Upon completion, the `SQLError` function returned the value of the SqlState=08004, SQLCODE (-1403), as well as a full description of the error. Note that `SQL_SUCCESS` is returned as the return code of the `SQLError` function. It only means that the `SQLError` function completed successfully!

This was a simplified example which could have been diagnosed from the SQL Code alone if the application was written to return the SQL Code to the users.

10.4.8.1 Other CLI/ODBC Diagnostic Parameters
This section lists some additional keywords that you can specify in your DB2CLI.INI file which may be helpful in verifying that the application catches all error conditions and deals with them correctly.

The default value for each keyword is underlined (if one exists).

- **APPENDAPINAME** = 0 | 1

  Controls whether the DB2 CLI function (API) that generated the error is appended to the error message retrieved using `SQLError()` or `SQLGetDiagRec()`. The function name is enclosed in curly braces {}.

  - 0 = Do not display the DB2 CLI function name (default).
  - 1 = Display the DB2 CLI function name.

  Example:
  ```
  "[IBM][CLI Driver]" CLIxxxx: < text >
  "SQLSTATE=XXXXX {SQLGetData}"
  ```

  You can use APPENDAPINAME in the DB2CLI.INI file or in the ODBC.INI file (i.e., x:\WINNT\ODBC.INI).

- **POPUPMESSAGE** = 0 | 1

Controls whether a message box is displayed when DB2 CLI generates an error that can be retrieved using `SQLError()` or `SQLGetDiagRec()`. This can be useful when debugging applications that do not report messages to users.

- 0 = Do not display message box (default).
- 1 = Display message box.

You can use `POPUPMESSAGE` in the DB2CLI.INI file or in the ODBC.INI file. See also `SQLSTATEFILTER` and `APPENDAPINAME`.

- **SQLSTATEFILTER** = "'S1C00','XXXXX',..."

Use with `POPUPMESSAGE` to prevent the DB2 CLI from displaying errors associated with the states listed (only applicable when POPUPMESSAGE is active).

You can use `SQLSTATEFILTER` in the DB2CLI.INI file or in the ODBC.INI file.

An ODBC/CLI trace is helpful when diagnosing ODBC or CLI specific problems, or when we suspect that something abnormal is happening with the ODBC driver manager or DB2 ODBC driver rather than in the DB2 client or server software.

10.4.8.2 ODBC Trace Example

The following example illustrates how an ODBC trace can be helpful in determining the source of a problem. An application developer has reported that an application is producing unexpected results.

As the database administrator, you might first want to set the `DIAGLEVEL` to `4`. If the DIAGLEVEL is changed you will need to stop and start the instance and reproduce the problem so that you can view the contents of the DB2DIAG.LOG file for more information.

Unfortunately (in this example), the DB2DIAG.LOG file has not recorded any information that can be used to diagnose the application problem. As the next step you might consider executing the application against a non-production database, such as SAMPLE. To simplify the analysis you may also wish to modify the application so that it only contains the function that is experiencing the problems. Then execute the modified application against the SAMPLE database. In this case the smallest recreatable scenario is an SQL `SELECT` statement against the ORG table in the SAMPLE database.

Issuing the select statement using the command line processor returns the expected number of rows.

```
C:\>db2 select * from org

DEPTNUMB    DEPTNAME     MANAGER DIVISION    LOCATION
-----------------------------------------------------
      10    Head Office      160 Corporate   New York
      15    New England       50 Eastern     Boston
      20    Mid Atlantic      10 Eastern     Washington
      38    South Atlantic    30 Eastern     Atlanta
      42    Great Lakes      100 Midwest     Chicago
      51    Plains           140 Midwest     Dallas
      66    Pacific          270 Western     San Francisco
      84    Mountain         290 Western     Denver

  8 record(s) selected.
```

However, when the ODBC application executes and tries to select all of the rows in the ORG table, different results are obtained:

```
C:\>SQLLIB\samples\cli>adhoc
>Enter Database Name:
sample
>Enter User Name:
grant
>Enter Password:
>grant
>Connected to sample
Enter an SQL statement to start a transaction (or q
to Quit):
select * from org
DEPTNUMB DEPTNAME      MANAGER      DIVISION    LOCATION
10       Head Office       160      Corporate   New York
15       New England        50      Eastern     Boston
20       Mid Atlantic       10      Eastern     Washington
38       South Atlantic     30      Eastern     Atlanta
Enter an SQL statement (or q to Quit):
q
Enter c to COMMIT or r to ROLLBACK the transaction
c
Transaction commit was successful
Enter an SQL statement to start a transaction (or q
to Quit):
q
Disconnecting...

C:\SQLLIB\samples\cli>
```

When issuing an SQL SELECT statement from the ODBC application the application completes successfully but does not return all of the expected records.

The following is an excerpt from the ODBC/CLI trace for this select statement.:

```
SQLAllocConnect( hEnv=1, phDbc=&3ff94 )----> Time elapsed - +0.000000E+000 seconds
SQLAllocConnect( phDbc=1 )---> SQL_SUCCESS   Time elapsed - +1.000000E-002 seconds
SQLSetConnectOption( hDbc=1, fOption=SQL_AUTOCOMMIT, vParam=0 )
----> Time elapsed - +5.000000E-002 seconds
SQLSetConnectOption( )---> SQL_SUCCESS   Time elapsed - +1.000000E-002 seconds
SQLConnect( hDbc=1, szDSN="SAMPLE", cbDSN=-3, szUID="grant", cbUID=-3,
    szAuthStr="*****", cbAuthStr=-3 )----> Time elapsed - +0.000000E+000 seconds
SQLConnect( )---> SQL_SUCCESS   Time elapsed - +1.372000E+000 seconds
SQLAllocStmt( hDbc=1, phStmt=&3fe6c )----> Time elapsed - +4.822900E+001 seconds
SQLAllocStmt( phStmt=1 )---> SQL_SUCCESS   Time elapsed - +1.000000E-002 seconds
SQLSetStmtOption( hStmt=1, fOption=SQL_MAX_ROWS, vParam=3 ) -----------------------(1)
----> Time elapsed - +0.000000E+000 seconds
SQLSetStmtOption( )---> SQL_SUCCESS   Time elapsed - +1.000000E-002 seconds
SQLExecDirect( hStmt=1, pszSqlStr="select deptname, location from org", cbSqlStr=-3 )
----> Time elapsed - +0.000000E+000 seconds
SQLExecDirect( )---> SQL_SUCCESS   Time elapsed - +2.610000E-001 seconds
SQLNumResultCols( hStmt=1, pcCol=&3fe6a )----> Time elapsed - +0.000000E+000 seconds
SQLNumResultCols( pcCol=2 )---> SQL_SUCCESS   Time elapsed - +1.000000E-002 seconds
SQLDescribeCol( hStmt=1, iCol=1, pszColName=&3fe30, cbColNameMax=32, pcbColName=&3fe2c,
    pfSQLType=&3fe2e, pcbColDef=&3fc94, pibScale=&3fc92, pfNullable=NULL )
----> Time elapsed - +0.000000E+000 seconds
SQLDescribeCol( pszColName="DEPTNAME", pcbColName=8, pfSQLType=SQL_VARCHAR, pcbColDef=14,
pibScale=0 )---> SQL_SUCCESS   Time elapsed - +7.000000E-002 seconds
SQLColAttributes( hStmt=1, iCol=1, fDescType=SQL_COLUMN_DISPLAY_SIZE, rgbDesc=NULL,
    cbDescMax=0, pcbDesc=NULL, pfDesc=&3f864 )----> Time elapsed - +1.000000E-002 seconds
SQLColAttributes( pfDesc=14 )---> SQL_SUCCESS   Time elapsed - +2.000000E-002 seconds
SQLBindCol( hStmt=1, iCol=1, fCType=SQL_C_CHAR, rgbValue=&e53e50, cbValueMax=15,
    pcbValue=&3fb00 )
----> Time elapsed - +0.000000E+000 seconds
SQLBindCol( )---> SQL_SUCCESS   Time elapsed - +1.000000E-002 seconds
SQLDescribeCol( hStmt=1, iCol=2, pszColName=&3fe30, cbColNameMax=32, pcbColName=&3fe2c,
    pfSQLType=&3fe2e, pcbColDef=&3fc94, pibScale=&3fc92, pfNullable=NULL )
----> Time elapsed - +1.000000E-002 seconds
SQLDescribeCol( pszColName="LOCATION", pcbColName=8, pfSQLType=SQL_VARCHAR, pcbColDef=13,
    pibScale=0 )---> SQL_SUCCESS   Time elapsed - +2.000000E-002 seconds
SQLColAttributes( hStmt=1, iCol=2, fDescType=SQL_COLUMN_DISPLAY_SIZE, rgbDesc=NULL,
    cbDescMax=0, pcbDesc=NULL, pfDesc=&3f864 )----> Time elapsed - +0.000000E+000 seconds
SQLColAttributes( pfDesc=13 )---> SQL_SUCCESS   Time elapsed - +1.000000E-002 seconds
SQLBindCol( hStmt=1, iCol=2, fCType=SQL_C_CHAR, rgbValue=&e53e70, cbValueMax=14,
```

```
    pcbValue=&3fb04 )
  ----> Time elapsed - +0.000000E+000 seconds
SQLBindCol( )---> SQL_SUCCESS    Time elapsed - +2.000000E-002 seconds
SQLFetch( hStmt=1 )----> Time elapsed - +0.000000E+000 seconds
SQLFetch( )---> SQL_SUCCESS    Time elapsed - +1.000000E-002 seconds
( iCol=1, fCType=SQL_C_CHAR, rgbValue="Head Office", pcbValue=11 )
( iCol=2, fCType=SQL_C_CHAR, rgbValue="New York", pcbValue=8 )
SQLFetch( hStmt=1 )----> Time elapsed - +2.000000E-002 seconds
SQLFetch( )---> SQL_SUCCESS    Time elapsed - +1.000000E-002 seconds
( iCol=1, fCType=SQL_C_CHAR, rgbValue="New England", pcbValue=11 )
( iCol=2, fCType=SQL_C_CHAR, rgbValue="Boston", pcbValue=6 )
SQLFetch( hStmt=1 )----> Time elapsed - +2.000000E-002 seconds
SQLFetch( )---> SQL_SUCCESS    Time elapsed - +0.000000E+000 seconds
( iCol=1, fCType=SQL_C_CHAR, rgbValue="Mid Atlantic", pcbValue=12 )
( iCol=2, fCType=SQL_C_CHAR, rgbValue="Washington", pcbValue=10 )
SQLFetch( hStmt=1 )----> Time elapsed - +3.000000E-002 seconds
SQLFetch( )---> SQL_SUCCESS    Time elapsed - +0.000000E+000 seconds
( iCol=1, fCType=SQL_C_CHAR, rgbValue="South Atlantic", pcbValue=14 )
( iCol=2, fCType=SQL_C_CHAR, rgbValue="Atlanta", pcbValue=7 )
SQLFetch( hStmt=1 )----> Time elapsed - +1.999999E-002 seconds
SQLFetch( )---> SQL_NO_DATA_FOUND    Time elapsed - +1.000000E-002 seconds-------(2)
SQLFreeStmt( hStmt=1, fOption=SQL_DROP )----> Time elapsed - +0.000000E+000 seconds
SQLFreeStmt( )---> SQL_SUCCESS    Time elapsed - +1.000000E-002 seconds

SQLDisconnect( hDbc=1 )
  ----> Time elapsed - +1.883000E+000 seconds
SQLDisconnect( )
    ---> SQL_SUCCESS    Time elapsed - +1.000000E-002 seconds

SQLFreeConnect( hDbc=1 )
  ----> Time elapsed - +1.000000E-002 seconds
SQLFreeConnect( )
    ---> SQL_SUCCESS    Time elapsed - +0.000000E+000 seconds

SQLFreeEnv( hEnv=1 )
  ----> Time elapsed - +0.000000E+000 seconds
SQLFreeEnv( )
    ---> SQL_SUCCESS    Time elapsed - +0.000000E+000 seconds
```

Reviewing the trace we find some details that shed light on the problem:

1. The function SQLSetStmtOption was invoked with a parameter limiting the number of output rows. Setting the parameter SQL_MAX_ROWS to a value = 3 causes an end-of-data signal when the number of rows fetched is greater than SQL_MAX_ROWS. In our example, the fourth row would generate the end-of-data signal.

2. The fourth call to the SQLFetch() function returned an SQL_NO_DATA_FOUND return code. Therefore the application is working as it was coded. Although it is not returning all of the records, it has been explicitly coded to return only three (3) records from the result set.

10.5 Determining the Source of the Problem

In many cases, the cause of the problem is readily apparent in the DB2DIAG.LOG file or other diagnostic information, and you will be able to recover without assistance. In other cases, you may need additional information in order to recover from the problem. Two valuable sources of problem resolution information are:

- DB2 Online help
- The DB2 Technical Library

This section describes how to access the DB2 online help facility and interpret SQL error messages. We will also look at the help available on the WWW DB2 Technical Library.

10.5.1 Online Help

The DB2 online help facility should be the first tool to use whenever you need additional information about an error condition. It will provide you with a detailed explanation of the error message, and will indicate what to do to recover from this condition. The DB2 Command Line Processor (CLP) has online help that provides information about general topics, command syntax and SQL error messages. You can also use the DB2 Command Center to accomplish the same tasks. For the purposes of this discussion, we focus on the DB2 Command Line Processor approach.

There are two modes for using the CLP in the Windows NT environment:

- *DB2 Command Window mode.* This is a regular Windows NT command prompt window that has been initialized for the DB2 CLP environment. From a DB2 Command Window, you can enter DB2 commands or certain SQL statements by preceding them with "db2". For example:

```
db2 connect to sample
```

The DB2 Command Window is useful if you want to issue DB2 commands and regular Windows NT commands from the same window. It can be initiated in one of two ways:

1. Open the DB2 for Windows NT program group, and click on **Command Window**.
2. From any Windows NT command prompt, enter db2cmd.

The DB2CMD Command

db2cmd.exe calls a batch program, db2env.bat, (which should be located in your SQLLIB\BIN directory) and passes to it the pid (process id) of the background process that has been created. db2env.bat sets the environment variable DB2CLP to be this pid.

- *Interactive mode.* Interactive mode is a window that uses db2=> as the prompt. DB2 commands and some SQL statements can be directly entered in interactive mode.

    Interactive mode can be initiated in one of two ways:

    1. Open the DB2 for Windows NT program group, and click on **Command Line Processor**.
    2. At a DB2 Command Window, enter db2.

There are several different kinds of help available through the CLP.

General Help provides a list of the commands that are available. To get General Help, type ? from CLP interactive mode or db2 ? from a DB2 Command Window.

Syntax Help provides help text for the Command Line Processor command syntax. To get Syntax Help in the CLP, type ? <phrase> from interactive input mode, where <phrase> is a Command Line Processor command. To get help on a command, type ? <command> where <command> can be the first few keywords. For example:

```
? catalog database
```

displays help for the catalog database command, whereas:

```
? catalog
```

displays help for all the catalog commands.

SQLSTATE and *class code Help* provides help text for SQLSTATES and class codes. From the Command Line Processor interactive mode, issue the command:

```
? <sqlstate>
```

or:

```
? <class code>
```

where `<sqlstate>` is a valid five digit SQL state or `<class-code>` is a valid two-digit class code. Here is an example of using the CLP to get additional help for a SQLSTATE and a class code:

```
DB2 CLP                                                    _ □ X
C:\>
C:\>db2 ? 08003

SQLSTATE 08003: The connection does not exist.

C:\>db2 ? 08

 08: Connection Exception

C:\>
```

Message Help is available for DB2 messages, describing the cause of the message and any action that should be taken to resolve the problems.

Help for the following kinds of DB2 messages are available through the DB2 Command Line Processor:

Table 9. Messages Available from the Command Line Processor

PREFIX	DESCRIPTION
CLI	Call Level Interface messages
DBA	Error messages generated by the Control Center and the Database Administration utility
DBI	Error messages generated by installation and configuration
DB2	Error messages generated by the Command Line Processor

PREFIX	DESCRIPTION
SQL	SQLCODEs generated by the database manager when an error condition has been detected or a warning or informational message is to be reported.

Message identifiers consist of a three character message prefix (CLI, DBA, DBI, DB2, SPM, or SQL), followed by a four or five digit message number. The single letter at the end describing the severity of the error message is optional.

To get Message Help from the Command Line Processor interactive mode, issue the command:

```
? <message number>
```

where <message number> is in the format XXXnnnnn, XXX representing the prefix and nnnnn the message number. For example, ? SQL30061N provides help on the SQL30061N SQLCODE:

```
DB2 CLP                                                    _ □ X
C:\>
C:\>
C:\>db2 ? SQL30061N

 SQL30061N The database alias or database name "<name>" was
           not found at the remote node.

Cause:  The database name is not an existing database at
the remote database node.

The statement cannot be processed.

Action:  Resubmit the command with the correct database
name or alias.

DataJoiner users: check to ensure that the entry in
SYSCAT.SERVERS correctly specifies the database name of the
data source.

sqlcode:  -30061

sqlstate:  08004

C:\>
```

Note that the message identifier accepted as a parameter of the db2 command is not case sensitive, and the terminating letter is not required to have the message information retrieved.

The following is an example of using the interactive input mode to obtain online help:

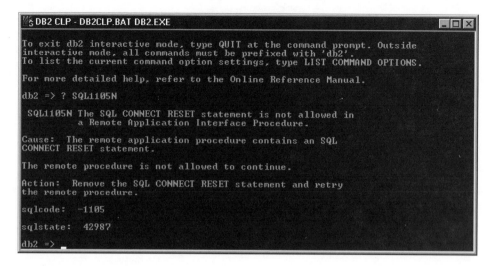

```
M  DB2 CLP - DB2CLP.BAT DB2.EXE                              [_][□][X]

To exit db2 interactive mode, type QUIT at the command prompt. Outside
interactive mode, all commands must be prefixed with 'db2'.
To list the current command option settings, type LIST COMMAND OPTIONS.

For more detailed help, refer to the Online Reference Manual.

db2 => ? SQL1105N

 SQL1105N  The SQL CONNECT RESET statement is not allowed in
           a Remote Application Interface Procedure.

Cause:  The remote application procedure contains an SQL
CONNECT RESET statement.

The remote procedure is not allowed to continue.

Action:  Remove the SQL CONNECT RESET statement and retry
the remote procedure.

sqlcode:  -1105

sqlstate:  42987

db2 => _
```

10.5.2 DB2 Technical Library on the Web

The DB2 Product and Service Technical Library lets you access information such as README files, the DB2 publications, technical notes, DB2 fixes, and frequently asked questions. The library can be very useful in problem determination since it allows you to search for similar problems or errors that have been encountered in the past.

The DB2 Technical Library can be directly accessed by opening the DB2 for Windows NT product group, clicking on **Information Center**, and going to the **Web** tab. Double-click on DB2 Technical Library to start your web browser and go directly to the DB2 Technical Library web page.

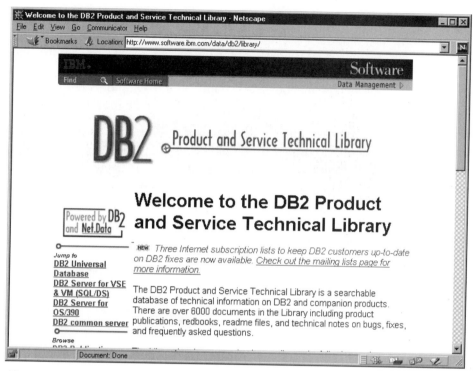

Figure 308. Web Page of DB2 Technical Library

10.5.2.1 The Information You Can Access

There are a number of methods available to access the information available in the library:

- **Library Search** lets you find documents containing keywords and will let you limit your search to one or more types of documents. To get to the search screen, click on the product name (DB2 Universal Database).

- **Users' Picks** shows those documents that answer the questions that are most frequently asked by DB2 users.

- **Recent Additions** lists the newest documents added to the library.

- **DB2 Publications** lets you link to the core set of DB2 books.

- **Debugging Tips** gives some tips on how solving problems to make DB2 work for you.

10.5.2.2 Searching for DB2 Problems

When debugging DB2 problems using the DB2 Product and Service Technical Library, there are a few basic principles to keep in mind when structuring your search. By listing them here, we hope that they will help you use the library more effectively.

1. When specifying your search terms, you should always attempt to use keywords that reflect the symptoms of the problem that you are encountering. Since the number of possible causes of a problem can be infinite, it is better to search on the symptoms because there are a finite number of symptoms. This provides the most effective way of narrowing your search to the information you need.

   Possible problem symptoms include:

   - Return codes and messages
   - Hang situations
   - Abends, access violations, and segmentation faults
   - Incorrect output
   - Poor performance

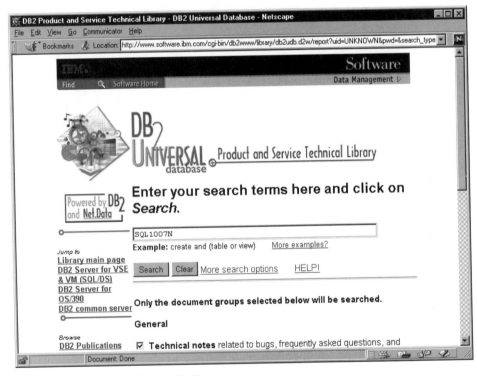

Figure 309. DB2 Library Search Facility

2. Return codes are by far the best search items to use in specifying your search. Return codes are most likely to lead you to information that will help in identifying your particular problem situation.

When using return codes as your search criteria, it is important to enter the return code exactly as it appears. For example, an SQL0805N error message *should not* be spelled as SQL0805 or SQL805N.

3. If your searches have been yielding a small number of documents, it may be possible that your search string is too specific. You may wish to use wild-card characters to increase the result set of your searches, allowing for variations in style across documents. An asterisk (*) is the wild card for multiple characters, and a question mark (?) is the wild card for a single character.

   For example, to search for documents related to an SQL2003C message, you may wish to search using the following term:

   ```
   *2003*
   ```

4. Problems involving poor performance and incorrect output can be much harder to search on due to the wide variation of operating environments and data among users. While many attempts have been made to use the words 'poor performance' in all documents related to such problems, you might also search using keywords such as 'slow'.

   It is also useful to use other keywords to indicate what task you are attempting to perform or which application program you are using.

   For example, if getting poor performance backing up your DB2 UDB database to a tape drive, you should use the following search terms:

   ```
   performance and backup and tape
   ```

5. Many return codes and messages have sub-codes or additional reason codes that further identify the problem. If searching on the primary return code yields too many documents, you should use the secondary return code to further restrict the set of documents returned.

   For example, if you encounter an SQL0902C error with reason code 59, you should search using the following terms:

   ```
   SQL0902C and 59
   ```

6. It is not necessary to describe your complete operating environment when constructing your search. If you have chosen to search for documents containing all of your search terms, this can have the effect of narrowing your search too much. For the most part, searching based on a concise set of symptoms, such as SQL codes, should return a useful and compact result set.

   For example, when getting an SQL1403N error attempting to connect to an MVS database from an NT client, you should initially use only the following search term:

```
sql1403n
```

Searching on 'sql1403n and MVS and NT' may exclude a document from being included that describes a similar problem encountered on a DOS client where the cause was the same.

7. Search terms that are enclosed in double quotes are searched "as is" with no Boolean operator inserted between them. Use double quotes (") to find search terms composed of multiple words. For example:

```
"declare cursor"
```

8. When searching on problems related to DB2 Text Extender or Net.Data and not using return codes specific to these products, it may be useful to include the name of the product as a search argument.

For example, to look for documentation related to the DB2 Net.Data macro reports, you should use the following search:

```
net.data and reports
```

Figure 310 on page 483 shows a technical note related to a problem. The problem was searched for using the keyword SQL0567N. The technical note includes the Symptom, Cause, and Action to solve the problem.

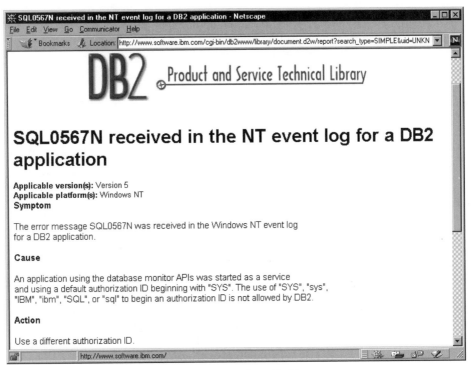

Figure 310. Example of a Technical Note Related to a Problem

10.6 Installation Problems

In this chapter we have discussed how you should go about debugging DB2 problems once your system is up and running. We will now take a look at what types of problems can occur during the installation of DB2 and how you can resolve these problems.

DB2 keeps a log (DB2.LOG) that tracks all DB2 install and deinstall activities and records information on any errors encountered during product installation or deinstallation. The log is stored in the DB2LOG directory on the boot drive of the system. If this directory already exists, the Setup program will write the file in this directory, otherwise, the Setup program creates the directory on the boot drive and creates the DB2.LOG file. If space constraints or other errors prevent the log from being written, the install or deinstall will still continue.

10.6.1 Common Installation Errors

If an error occurs while you are installing DB2 UDB, you should first read the error message text to find the probable cause and possible solution for the problem. You will find additional information in the x:\DB2LOG\DB2.LOG file.

The setup program copies some files from the install media to your destination drive/directory. You should try to ensure that nothing else is running on the Windows NT machine when you do the DB2 UDB installation as files may be open and locked by other processes which will prevent the setup program from updating them. Anti-virus programs in particular have been known to cause problems if running during a DB2 UDB install and should be stopped until the installation is complete.

On Windows NT, services that are running can also lock shared DLLs and cause some installation errors. Try stopping all services that are running, and ensure once again that no other applications are running (including the Control Panel). In particular, we have found that the OLE32 service locks the ODBC DLLs and can cause DB2 UDB installation errors.

The following table lists installation errors that you may encounter and the action you should take to resolve the problem.

Table 10. DB2 for Windows NT Common Installation Errors

ERROR	ACTION
Insufficient authority to run the Setup program or the user name is not valid.	1. Logon with a user name that has administrator authority on the local machine and follow the naming rules. 2. Reinstall the product.
Windows NT program groups or short-cuts cannot be created.	To create program groups or shortcuts: 1. From the task bar, select **START**, then **SETTINGS**, then **TASK BAR**. The TASKBAR PROPERTIES window appears. 2. Select the **START MENU PROGRAMS** tab. 3. Select **ADD**. 4. In the COMMAND LINE field, type the path to the program's executable file. 5. Select **NEXT**. 6. Select **NEXT**. 7. Select an existing folder or create a new folder. 8. Select **NEXT**, then **FINISH**, then **OK**. You do not need to re-install the product.

ERROR	ACTION

Windows NT program groups or items cannot be created.	To create a new program group, do the following:
	1. Create a common program group:
	   a. Go to the PROGRAM MANAGER FILE item.
	   b. Select **NEW.**
	   c. Select **COMMON PROGRAM GROUP.**
	   d. Select **OK.**
	   e. Specify the properties of the group to be made.
	2. Create a program item in that group:
	   a. Go to the PROGRAM MANAGER FILE item.
	   b. Select **NEW**.
	   c. Select **PROGRAM ITEM**.
	   d. Specify the properties of the new item to be made.
	You do not need to reinstall the product.

DB2 Security Service cannot be registered.	To register the DB2 Security Service, run DB2REGSC, specifying "I" for install, as follows: $DB2PATH\misc\db2regsc I You do not need to reinstall the product.
Environment variables cannot be added or updated.	In most cases, the setup program will try to recover from this error and continue processing. The error message indicates if the install program continues or terminates. 1. If it continues, you may need to correct some values. Correct the environment variables using the System program group within the PROGRAM MANAGER CONTROL PANEL. You do not need to reinstall the product. 2. If it does not continue, you need to correct the cause of the error before reinstalling.
Process environment variables may not be set.	This error may cause other install steps to fail. The error message gives the name of the environment variable that needs to be updated. If the setup program gives errors, update the process environment variable using the SET command. Then uninstall and reinstall the product.
Default instance cannot be created, or the service for default instance cannot be registered.	If the default instance, DB2, could not be created, run DB2ICRT to create it, as follows: $DB2PATH\bin\db2icrt DB2 You do not need to reinstall the product.

ERROR	ACTION
Key cannot be added to the registry.	In most cases, the setup program will try to recover from this error and continue processing. The error message includes the following information: 1. The key, subkey, and value names. 2. The operation that was executing at the time of error, for example, OPEN, QUERY, or SET. 3. The return value from the operation. 4. Whether the installation process continues or terminates. If the setup program continues after an error, you do not need to reinstall, but you may need to correct the software key in the registry. If it does not continue, you may need to correct the cause of the error before reinstalling.
The HELP file cannot be loaded. The environment variables are set properly in NT (System properties, Environment). However, %help% does not seem to pick up the value set in SystemProperties/Environment. The other variables, like DB2INSTANCE, and so forth are correct.	DB2 sets the system environment variables during install. However, on NT, the user environment variables take precedence. Check the following: 1. The user environment variable HELP is set to a value and does not also pick up the system settings. For instance, the user variable help should be set to something like HELP=%help%;<path> and not HELP=<path>.
Each time you try to start a CLP window from the shortcut, you get an error message stating the environment variable is not set or something like that.	DB2CMD.EXE calls a batch program db2env.bat (which should be located in your sqllib\bin directory) and passes to it the PID of the background process that has been created. Then db2env.bat sets the environment variable DB2CLP to be this PID. Check the following: 1. The DB2CMD is working correctly from the command line. 2. If so, check the properties of the Shortcut. The working directory should be the %db2path%\bin directory, and you should ensure that db2env.bat is in that director.

We strongly advise you to set the DIAGLEVEL configuration parameter to 4 whenever you are changing any DB2 configuration parameters. This setting will give you a greater level of detail in the DB2DIAG.LOG file if any problems occur.

10.7 Information to Collect for IBM Support

Once you have determined that you have to call IBM for support, you should gather and have ready necessary information that will help IBM to investigate further your problem. We discussed the various pieces of information earlier. Here we summarize once again the information you should gather before calling DB2 UDB Support.

10.7.1 What to Collect

The necessary information you gather may be staged in two phases:

1. An initial set of files and information that will allow the DB2 UDB Support to start investigating your problem, and hopefully it will be sufficient to find a fix to your problem.

   - A detailed description of the problem situation, which will include all the SQL codes and any Reason codes (if applicable). For example, the SQL error code -903 has several possible reason codes as shown below:

```
SQL0903N COMMIT statement failed, transaction rolled back.
Reason code: "<reason-code>"
Cause: One or more of the servers participating in the current
unit of work was unable to prepare the database to be committed.
The COMMIT statement has failed and the transaction has been rolled back.
Possible reason codes are:
01 - A connection to one of the databases participating in the unit of
work was lost.
02 - One of the databases participating in the unit of work was accessed,
but unable to prepare to commit.
Action: If a connection to a database was lost, reestablish the connection.
If the failure was not connection related, reference the error diagnostic
logs on the remote system to determine the nature of the failure and what
action might be required. Rerun the application.
sqlcode:  -903
sqlstate: 40504
```

   - The **DB2DIAG.LOG** file
   - All the dump files, if any
   - All the trap files if any
   - The Database Manager configuration information
   - The database configuration information (if applicable)
   - The DB2 Service Level you have installed on your machine.

- An additional set of files and information which might be necessary in case the first set of information you have provided is not sufficient to fix your problem. This set includes:

  - The Windows NT Application Event Log (either in a binary format file (.evt) or in a text format file or in a comma-delimited text format file (.txt)

  - The database directory information.

  - The node directory information (if applicable)

  - The DCS directory information, if DB2 Connect is installed on this workstation.

  - Network Configuration information about your workstation. You can find this information by going to the Control Panel and clicking on the **Network** icon.

  - \HKEY_LOCAL_MACHINE\SYSTEM\ControlSet001\Services\Tcpip \ parameters

  - The Services file. This file provides TCP/IP connection information.

  - A dump of the Windows NT Registry subkey, HKEY_LOCAL_MACHINE, for your machine.

10.7.2 History of Reported Problems

Technical support requires a certain amount of record keeping. In particular, you should establish and maintain problem-related records.

IBM recommends that you maintain a history of reported problems and actions taken to resolve or identify them. This information can help you isolate some problems and anticipate or avoid others. This information may also be of use when contacting DB2 UDB Support.

In particular, you should:

1. Record the information you gather related to the problem.

   The information includes:

   - The problem symptoms

   - The problem number (or Problem Management Record (PMR) number)

   - The problem description

   - Configuration of the hardware and software

   - The latest Program Temporary Fix (PTF) or service level installed on each user's system

- The message displayed and the results of the corrective action
- Should you be directed to contact IBM to resolve your problem, the information helps IBM respond to you in a prompt and effective manner. Information should be sent to IBM for analysis only upon direction from the IBM Support Center. Additional information is provided by Contacting IBM for Support and Maintenance.

2. Record the resolution of problems for later reference.

Appendix A. Related Publications

The publications listed in this section are considered particularly suitable for a more detailed discussion of the topics covered in this book.

A.1 International Technical Support Organization Publications

These are related ITSO publications:

- *DB2 Meets Windows NT, SG24-4893-00*
- *Migrating to DB2 Universal Database Version 5, SG24-2006-00*
- *DB2 Universal Database Certification Guide, SC09-2465-01*
- *The DB2 Cluster Certification Guide, SC09-2734-00*

A.2 Other Publications

These publications are also relevant as further information sources:

- *DB2 Universal Database Quick Beginnings for Windows NT, S10J-8149*
- *DB2 Universal Database Extended Enterprise Edition for Windows NT Quick Beginnings, S09L-6713*
- *DB2 Universal Database Administration Guide, S10J-8157*
- *DB2 Universal Database Command Reference, S10J-8166*
- *DB2 Universal Database Troubleshooting Guide, S10J-8169*

Index

A

Access Profiles   123, 165
   Client   150, 170
   Server   165
Active-Active   312
Active-Passive   311
Adapter number   94, 114, 146, 179
Add Database Smartguide   150
Administration Tools   194
AIX   8, 10, 13
Alert Center   194, 425, 427
Alert Messages   213
Alert mode   403, 408
APPC   10, 83, 92, 123, 146, 148
APPENDAPINAME   469
Authentication   23
   Client   62
      Master Account Domain   78
      Single Domain   75
      Workgroup   74
   DCE   63
   DCS   63
   local   55
   Methods   61
   Server   62
      Single Domain   77
      Workgroup   75
   types   61
authid   67
Authorities
   database   60
AUTORESTART   224

B

Backup
   Database   233
   Database Notebook   234
   Database SmartGuide   249
   File Format   237
   Table Space   233
   to Tape   259
Backup and Recovery   223
Backup Domain Controller   24, 31

C

C++   14
Call Level Interface   14
CATALOG ADMIN NODE   143
Certification   194
Chart mode   403, 404
CLI/ODBC
   Common Parameters   174
   registration   150
   Traces   451
Client
   local   3
   remote   3
   Settings   150, 174
   untrusted   62
Client Configuration Assistant   123, 125, 148, 194
CLUSTER_NAME   316
COBOL   14
Command Center   194, 206
Command Line Processor   194
Command Window   147, 194
Computer name   146, 181
Connection port   95
Control Center   123, 143, 186, 194, 196
   autostart   91
Coordinator Node   265
CREATE EVENT MONITOR   433

D

DAS instance
   Configuring   143
   owner   84, 96, 139
   service   91
DAS Instance Owner   285
DAS Node Manager   108
database   263
database manager   263
database partition   263
database partition server   263
DB2
   Administration Server   123, 125, 133
   AIX   1
   Authority Levels   56
   CAE Client Pack   4
   CLI   451
   Client Application Enabler   3, 87, 110
   Client/Server Communications   123

Common Server 85, 112
Connect 3, 9, 10, 87
   Enterprise Edition 3, 12
   Personal Edition 3, 11
Developer's Edition 3, 13
Discovery 123
   Configuring 130
   Known 128
   Search 125, 126
Extenders 14
Family 1
Fixpack 118
Governor 105, 107
Graphical Tools 191
Groups 67
HP-UX 1
in a Domain 72
in a Workgroup 71
Installation 83
instance
   autostart 91
   service 91
Java Applet Server 105, 107
naming rules 97
on a Backup Domain Controller 73
on a Non-Domain Controller 72
on a Primary Domain Controller 72
OS/390 1, 8, 10
OS/400 1, 8, 10
Performance Counters 402
Personal Developer's Edition 3, 13
Processes 108
Publications 479
Security Server 105, 107
Software Developer's Kit 14, 110
Sun Solaris 1
Support Information 193
Tape Support 254
Technical Library 443, 478
Trace Facility 441
UDB Enterprise Edition 3, 8, 87
UDB Enterprise-Extended Edition 3, 9, 301
UDB Monitoring 418
UDB Personal Edition 3, 5
UDB Workgroup Edition 3, 6, 87
Uninstalling 106
Universal Database 1
Universal Database (UDB) 3
Universal Developer's Edition 3, 13

Users 67
VSE/VM 1, 8, 10
Windows NT
   Authentication and Security 53
   environment 66
   Group Resolution 53
   Scenarios 17
DB2_FALLBACK 339
DB2_GRP_LOOKUP 55, 76, 79, 80, 81
DB2_LOGON_PASSWORD 316
DB2_LOGON_USERNAME 316
DB2_NODE 317
db2admin 68, 84, 96
db2admin create 138
db2bp.exe 108
db2cc.exe 108
db2cca.exe 108
db2cDB2 95
DB2CLI.INI 452
db2clpex.exe 346
DB2CLUSTER 342
DB2CLUSTERLIST 342
DB2COMM 129, 159
DB2CPOST.BAT 347
db2cpre.bat 346
DB2DART 456
DB2DAS00 92, 134
DB2DIAG.LOG 441
DB2DMNBCKCTLR 73
db2drvmp 334
db2govds.exe 108
db2iclus 330
DB2ICRT 329
db2icrt 271
db2iDB2 95
db2idrop 280
db2ilist 275
DB2INSTANCE 277, 402
db2ipxad.exe 183
db2iupdt 274
db2jds.exe 108
db2licd.exe 108
DB2MSCS 315
   input file 315
DB2NCHG 337
db2ncrt 332
db2ndmgr 108
db2nlist 267, 281, 338
DB2NODE 265, 282

db2perfc 418
db2perfi 402
db2perfr 418
db2sec.exe 108
db2start 276
db2stop 276
db2syscs.exe 108
DB2TRC 445
db2trc 446
DB2WOLF.DLL 311
db2wolfi 322
DBADM 59
DFT_MON_BUFPOOL 419
DFT_MON_LOCK 419
DFT_MON_SORT 419
DFT_MON_STMT 419
DFT_MON_TABLE 419
DFT_MON_UOW 419
DIAGLEVEL 444
Disaster Recovery Considerations 262
DISCOVER (parameter) 130
DISCOVER_COMM 130, 159
DISCOVER_DB 130
DISCOVER_INST 130
Discovery 125
DISK_NAME 318
Documentation subcomponent 90
Domain
    Admins 36
    Controller 24
    Guests 36
    Models
        Complete Trust 52
        Master 48
        Multiple Master 50
        Single 46
    Sychronize 32
    Users 36
Domino Go WebServer 14
DRDA 3, 123
    Application Requester 10
    Application Server 10, 12
    description 10
Dump Files 461

E
Embedded SQL 13
Event Analyzer 194

Event monitoring 418, 430
Event Monitors 418, 430
    Create 432
    record types 430, 434
EVENTMONITORS 434
EVENTS 434
Export Chart 416

F
Failover Support 301
First Steps 102, 194, 298
FORTRAN 14

G
GET SNAPSHOT 428
Graphical Tools component 89
GROUP_NAME 317
groups
    Account Operators 38
    Administrators 38
    Backup Operators 38
    Everyone 38
    global 34
    Guests 38
    local 34, 37
    Power Users 38
    Print Operators 38
    Replicator 38
    Server Operators 38
    Users 38

H
Help 443
Hostname 146, 176
Hot Standby 311, 323
HP-UX 8, 13
HTML Search Server 102, 105, 195
HTTPDL.EXE 109

I
IBM Communications Server for NT 83, 110
IBMCATGROUP 266
IBMDEFAULTGROUP 266
IBMTEMPGROUP 266
IMNSVDEM.EXE 109
Information Center 194, 478
INITIALIZE TAPE 257

Installation Errors   483, 484
Installation Types
  Compact   88
  Custom   88
  Typical   88
instance   263
INSTPROF_DISK   318
Internet Connection Server Lite   106
Internetwork address   146, 183
Interrupt port   95
IP address   176
IP_ADDRESS   317
IP_NAME   317
IP_NETWORK   317
IP_SUBNET   317
ipconfig   176
IPX/SPX   92, 123, 146, 147
IPX_SOCKET   147

J
Java   14
Java Development Kit   14
JDBC   4, 14
Jobs
  History   214
  Pending   214
  Running   214
Journal   194, 213
  monitoring   214

L
LAN Manager   29
License daemon   108
License Use Runtime   103
LIST ADMIN NODE DIRECTORY   143
Local workstation name   179
Log mode   403, 411
LOGBUFSZ   231
LOGFILSZ   231
Logging
  archival   229
  circular   228
LOGPATH   245
LOGPRIMARY   229, 231
LOGRETAIN   231
Logs
  Active   230
  Off-line archived   230

  On-line archived   230
LOGSECOND   229
Lotus Approach   14, 452
LotusScript   14

M
Manual Configuration   175
Message Reference   443
Microsoft Access   452
Microsoft SNA Server   83, 110
MINCOMMIT   231
Models of Domain Trust   46
MS Cluster Administrator   321
MS Cluster Server   301
  cluster   302
  dependency   302
  group failover period   308
  group failover threshold   308
  Looks Alive/Is Alive polling   302
  node   302
  quorum resource   302
  resource   302
  resource module   302
  resource type   302
  state   302
  Virtual Server   307
multiple logical nodes   265
Mutual Takeover   312, 325

N
Named Pipes   92, 123, 146, 147
Nbf binding   180
NET NAME   181
Net.Data   7, 8, 14
NetBIOS   92, 123, 145, 147
NETNAME_DEPENDENCY   318
NETNAME_VALUE   318
NetQuestion   106, 109
NETWORK_NAME   318
NEWLOGPATH   231
NNAME   94, 147
node   263
node configuration file   267
Nodegroups   265
Nodelock Administration   103
NTFS   29

O

ODBC 4, 14, 451
    Trace 451
Online Information
    Help 443
    Message Reference 443
OS/2 7, 11, 13
OS/390 9
OS/400 9
OVERFLOWPATH 232

P

partitioned database system 263
Partitioning 269
partitioning key 269
partitioning map 269
Performance Graph 426
Performance Monitor 195
Performance Monitoring 401
Permissions
    Change 28
    Full Control 28
    No Access 28
    Read 28
POPUPMESSAGE 469
Port number 94, 146, 176
Primary Domain Controller 24, 30
Priority Levels 28
privileges 23
    control 59
    Implicit 59
    Individual 59
    ownership 59
Problem Determination 193, 441
Protocol Tester 164

R

Recovery
    Concepts and Issues 227
    crash 223
    History 213
    History File 248
    Point of 228
    Restore 225
    Roll-forward 226
Registration 194
Release Notes 194
Remote Administration

Enabling 195
Remote Monitoring 417
REORG 214
Report mode 403, 414
RESTART DATABASE 224
Restore
    Database 239
    Database Notebook 240
    Database SmartGuide 252
    from Tape 260
    Redefining Containers 247
    Table Space 239
REWIND TAPE 257
REXX 14
RUNSTATS 214

S

SCO UnixWare 4, 7, 8
Script Center 194, 209
    creating 211
    scheduling 212
SECONDLOG 231
Security 23
    Overview 23
Security Access Manager 30
Server workstation name 179
Service name 146
SET TAPE POSITION 257
SETMARKS 257
Shared Disk 310
Shared Nothing 264, 310
shares
    ADMIN$ 28
    administrative 28
    default 28
    hidden 28
    NETLOGON 28
Silicon Graphics IRIX 4
Single Domain Model 46
Single Signon 62
SmartGuides 195, 196, 217
Snapshot Monitor 195, 418
Snapshot Monitoring 418, 419
Socket Number 146
SQL_NO_DATA_FOUND 474
SQL_SUCCESS 468
SQLAllocEnv 468
SQLDriverConnect 468, 469

SQLJ 14
SQLSTATEFILTER 470
Sun Solaris 8, 10, 13
SVCENAME 94, 147
Symbolic destination name 185
SYSADM 57
SYSADM_GROUP 57, 80
SYSCTRL 57
SYSCTRL_GROUP 58
SYSMAINT 57
SYSMAINT_GROUP 58
system catalog views
    SYSCAT.EVENTMONITORS 434
    SYSCAT.EVENTS 434

T
Tape Device
    Properties 256
    SCSI Adapter 255
TAPEMARKS 257
TCP/IP 10, 92, 123, 146, 147
thresholds 425
Tools Settings 194
TPNAME 148
Trace
    DB2 Trace Entry Format 464
    db2trc 445, 446
    ODBC 451
    point 445
    Starting a DB2 Trace 450
TraceFileName 452
TraceFlush 452
Transaction 227
Transaction program 147
Trap Files 462
Trust Relationships 42
TRUST_ALLCLNTS 62
TRUST_CLNTAUTH 76
Trusted Domain 18, 20, 42
Trusted Domains 42
Trusting domain 18

U
Uninstall Utility 195
Unit of Work 227
UPDATE ADMIN 147
User Accounts 34
USEREXIT 232

V
Visual Age for Java 14
Visual Explain 195
VSE/VM 9

W
Windows 3.x 11
Windows 95/98 11
Windows NT 16, 23
    Add/Remove Programs 85
    Administration Tools 97
    Administrators Group 139
    Authentication 40
    Backup Domain Controller 17
    Control Panel 91, 176
    Domains 29
    Event Log 453
        Archive 455
    Everyone Group 27
    Explorer 26
    Groups 33
    Introduction 16
    Member Server 17
    My Computer 26
    Performance Monitor 401
    Permissions 24, 27
    Primary Domain Controller 17
    Programs folder 101
    Registry 104, 116
    Registry Editor 85, 104, 118
    Right 24
    Server 17, 23
    Server Manager 32
    Services 105, 116, 195
    services file 95
    shares 25
    System Startup folder 91
    Task Manager 107
    User Account 139
    User and Group Support 349
    User Authentication 33
    User Manager 97
    Workstation 16, 23
Wolfpack 301
Workgroup 17, 25
Workstation name 114, 145, 179

IBM International License Agreement for Evaluation of Programs

Part 1 - General Terms

PLEASE READ THIS AGREEMENT CAREFULLY BEFORE USING THE PROGRAM. IBM WILL LICENSE THE PROGRAM TO YOU ONLY IF YOU FIRST ACCEPT THE TERMS OF THIS AGREEMENT. BY USING THE PROGRAM YOU AGREE TO THESE TERMS. IF YOU DO NOT AGREE TO THE TERMS OF THIS AGREEMENT, PROMPTLY RETURN THE UNUSED PROGRAM TO IBM.

The Program is owned by International Business Machines Corporation or one of its subsidiaries (IBM) or an IBM supplier, and is copyrighted and licensed, not sold.

The term "Program" means the original program and all whole or partial copies of it. A Program consists of machine-readable instructions, its components, data, audio-visual content (such as images, text, recordings, or pictures), and related licensed materials.

This Agreement includes Part 1 - General Terms and Part 2 - Country-unique Terms and is the complete agreement regarding the use of this Program, and replaces any prior oral or written communications between you and IBM. The terms of Part 2 may replace or modify those of Part 1.

1. License

Use of the Program

IBM grants you a nonexclusive, nontransferable license to use the Program.

You may 1) use the Program only for internal evaluation, testing or demonstration purposes, on a trial or "try-and-buy" basis and 2) make and install a reasonable number of copies of the Program in support of such use, unless IBM identifies a specific number of copies in the documentation accompanying the Program. The terms of this license apply to each copy you make. You will reproduce the copyright notice and any other legends of ownership on each copy, or partial copy, of the Program.

THE PROGRAM MAY CONTAIN A DISABLING DEVICE THAT WILL PREVENT IT FROM BEING USED UPON EXPIRATION OF THIS LICENSE. YOU WILL NOT TAMPER WITH THIS DISABLING DEVICE OR THE PROGRAM. YOU SHOULD TAKE PRECAUTIONS TO AVOID ANY LOSS OF DATA THAT MIGHT RESULT WHEN THE PROGRAM CAN NO LONGER BE USED.

You will 1) maintain a record of all copies of the Program and 2) ensure that anyone who uses the Program does so only for your authorized use and in compliance with the terms of this Agreement.

You may not 1) use, copy, modify or distribute the Program except as provided in this Agreement; 2) reverse assemble, reverse compile, or otherwise translate the Program except as specifically permitted by law without the possibility of contractual waiver; or 3) sublicense, rent, or lease the Program.

This license begins with your first use of the Program and ends 1) as of the duration or date specified in the documentation accompanying the Program or 2) when the Program automatically disables itself. Unless IBM specifies in the documentation accompanying the Program that you may retain the Program (in which case, an additional charge may apply), you will destroy the Program and all copies made of it within ten days of when this license ends.

2. No Warranty

SUBJECT TO ANY STATUTORY WARRANTIES WHICH CANNOT BE EXCLUDED, IBM MAKES NO WARRANTIES OR CONDITIONS EITHER EXPRESS OR IMPLIED, INCLUDING WITHOUT LIMITATION, THE WARRANTY OF NON-INFRINGEMENT AND THE IMPLIED WARRANTIES OF MERCHANTABILITY AND FITNESS FOR A PARTICULAR PURPOSE, REGARDING THE PROGRAM OR TECHNICAL SUPPORT, IF ANY. IBM MAKES NO WARRANTY REGARDING THE CAPABILITY OF THE PROGRAM TO CORRECTLY PROCESS, PROVIDE AND/OR RECEIVE DATE DATA WITHIN AND BETWEEN THE 20TH AND 21ST CENTURIES.

This exclusion also applies to any of IBM's subcontractors, suppliers or program developers (collectively called "Suppliers").

Manufacturers, suppliers, or publishers of non-IBM Programs may provide their own warranties.

3. Limitation of Liability

NEITHER IBM NOR ITS SUPPLIERS ARE LIABLE FOR ANY DIRECT OR INDIRECT DAMAGES, INCLUDING WITHOUT LIMITATION, LOST PROFITS, LOST SAVINGS, OR ANY INCIDENTAL, SPECIAL, OR OTHER ECONOMIC CONSEQUENTIAL DAMAGES, EVEN IF IBM IS INFORMED OF THEIR POSSIBILITY. SOME JURISDICTIONS DO NOT ALLOW THE EXCLUSION OR LIMITATION OF INCIDENTAL OR CONSEQUENTIAL DAMAGES, SO THE ABOVE EXCLUSION OR LIMITATION MAY NOT APPLY TO YOU.

4. General

Nothing in this Agreement affects any statutory rights of consumers that cannot be waived or limited by contract.

IBM may terminate your license if you fail to comply with the terms of this Agreement. If IBM does so, you must immediately destroy the Program and all copies you made of it.

You may not export the Program.

Neither you nor IBM will bring a legal action under this Agreement more than two years after the cause of action arose unless otherwise provided by local law without the possibility of contractual waiver or limitation.

Neither you nor IBM is responsible for failure to fulfill any obligations due to causes beyond its control.

There is no additional charge for use of the Program for the duration of this license.

IBM does not provide program services or technical support, unless IBM specifies otherwise.

The laws of the country in which you acquire the Program govern this Agreement, except 1) in Australia, the laws of the State or Territory in which the transaction is performed govern this Agreement; 2) in Albania, Armenia, Belarus, Bosnia/Herzegovina, Bulgaria, Croatia, Czech Republic, Georgia, Hungary, Kazakhstan, Kirghizia, Former Yugoslav Republic of Macedonia (FYROM), Moldova, Poland, Romania, Russia, Slovak Republic, Slovenia, Ukraine, and Federal Republic of Yugoslavia, the laws of Austria govern this Agreement; 3) in the United Kingdom, all disputes relating to this Agreement will be governed by English Law and will be submitted to the exclusive jurisdiction of the English courts; 4) in Canada, the laws in the Province of Ontario govern this Agreement; and 5) in the United States and Puerto Rico, and People's Republic of China, the laws of the State of New York govern this Agreement.

Part 2 - Country-unique Terms

AUSTRALIA:

No Warranty (Section 2): The following paragraph is added to this Section: Although IBM specifies that there are no warranties, you may have certain rights under the Trade Practices Act 1974 or other legislation and are only limited to the extent permitted by the applicable legislation.

Limitation of Liability (Section 3): The following paragraph is added to this Section: Where IBM is in breach of a condition or warranty implied by the Trade Practices Act 1974, IBM's liability is limited to the repair or replacement of the goods, or the supply of equivalent goods. Where that condition or warranty relates to right to sell, quiet possession or clear title, or the goods are of a kind ordinarily acquired for personal, domestic or household use or consumption, then none of the limitations in this paragraph apply.

GERMANY:

No Warranty (Section 2): The following paragraphs are added to this Section: The minimum warranty period for Programs is six months.

In case a Program is delivered without Specifications, we will only warrant that the Program information correctly describes the Program and that the Program can be used according to the Program information. You have to check the usability according to the Program information within the "money-back guaranty" period. Limitation of Liability (Section 3): The following paragraph is added to this Section: The limitations and exclusions specified in the Agreement will not apply to damages caused by IBM with fraud or gross negligence, and for express warranty.

INDIA:

General (Section 4): The following replaces the fourth paragraph of this Section: If no suit or other legal action is brought, within two years after the cause of action arose, in respect of any claim that either party may have against the other, the rights of the concerned party in respect of such claim will be forfeited and the other party will stand released from its obligations in respect of such claim.

IRELAND:

No Warranty (Section 2): The following paragraph is added to this Section: Except as expressly provided in these terms and conditions, all statutory conditions, including all warranties implied, but without prejudice to the generality of the foregoing, all warranties implied by the Sale of Goods Act 1893 or the Sale of Goods and Supply of Services Act 1980 are hereby excluded.

ITALY:

Limitation of Liability (Section 3): This Section is replaced by the following: Unless otherwise provided by mandatory law, IBM is not liable for any damages which might arise. NEW ZEALAND:

No Warranty (Section 2): The following paragraph is added to this Section: Although IBM specifies that there are no warranties, you may have certain rights under the Consumer Guarantees Act 1993 or other legislation which cannot be excluded or limited. The Consumer Guarantees Act 1993 will not apply in respect of any goods or services which IBM provides, if you require the goods and services for the purposes of a business as defined in that Act. Limitation of Liability (Section 3): The following paragraph is added to this Section: Where Programs are not acquired for the purposes of a business as defined in the Consumer Guarantees Act 1993, the limitations in this Section are subject to the limitations in that Act.

UNITED KINGDOM:

Limitation of Liability (Section 3): The following paragraph is added to this Section at the end of the first paragraph: The limitation of liability will not apply to any breach of IBM's obligations implied by Section 12 of the Sales of Goods Act 1979 or Section 2 of the Supply of Goods and Services Act 1982.

LICENSE AGREEMENT AND LIMITED WARRANTY

READ THE FOLLOWING TERMS AND CONDITIONS CAREFULLY BEFORE OPENING THIS SOFTWARE MEDIA PACKAGE. THIS LEGAL DOCUMENT IS AN AGREEMENT BETWEEN YOU AND PRENTICE-HALL, INC. (THE "COMPANY"). BY OPENING THIS SEALED SOFTWARE MEDIA PACKAGE, YOU ARE AGREEING TO BE BOUND BY THESE TERMS AND CONDITIONS. IF YOU DO NOT AGREE WITH THESE TERMS AND CONDITIONS, DO NOT OPEN THE SOFTWARE MEDIA PACKAGE. PROMPTLY RETURN THE UNOPENED PACKAGE AND ALL ACCOMPANYING ITEMS TO THE PLACE YOU OBTAINED THEM FOR A FULL REFUND OF ANY SUMS YOU HAVE PAID.

1.   **GRANT OF LICENSE:**   In consideration of your payment of the license fee, which is part of the price you paid for this product, and your agreement to abide by the terms and conditions of this Agreement, the Company grants to you a nonexclusive right to use and display the copy of the enclosed software program (hereinafter the "SOFTWARE") on a single computer (i.e., with a single CPU) at a single location so long as you comply with the terms of this Agreement. The Company reserves all rights not expressly granted to you under this Agreement.

2.   **OWNERSHIP OF SOFTWARE:**   You own only the magnetic or physical media (the enclosed CD-ROM) on which the SOFTWARE is recorded or fixed, but the Company retains all the rights, title, and ownership to the SOFTWARE recorded on the original CD-ROM copy(ies) and all subsequent copies of the SOFTWARE, regardless of the form or media on which the original or other copies may exist. This license is not a sale of the original SOFTWARE or any copy to you.

3.   **COPY RESTRICTIONS:**   This SOFTWARE and the accompanying printed materials and user manual (the "Documentation") are the subject of copyright. You may not copy the Documentation or the SOFTWARE, except that you may make a single copy of the SOFTWARE for backup or archival purposes only. You may be held legally responsible for any copying or copyright infringement which is caused or encouraged by your failure to abide by the terms of this restriction.

4.   **USE RESTRICTIONS:**   You may not network the SOFTWARE or otherwise use it on more than one computer or computer terminal at the same time. You may physically transfer the SOFTWARE from one computer to another provided that the SOFTWARE is used on only one computer at a time. You may not distribute copies of the SOFTWARE or Documentation to others. You may not reverse engineer, disassemble, decompile, modify, adapt, translate, or create derivative works based on the SOFTWARE or the Documentation without the prior written consent of the Company.

5.   **TRANSFER RESTRICTIONS:**   The enclosed SOFTWARE is licensed only to you and may not be transferred to any one else without the prior written consent of the Company. Any unauthorized transfer of the SOFTWARE shall result in the immediate termination of this Agreement.

6.   **TERMINATION:**   This license is effective until terminated. This license will terminate automatically without notice from the Company and become null and void if you fail to comply with any provisions or limitations of this license. Upon termination, you shall destroy the Documentation and all copies of the SOFTWARE. All provisions of this Agreement as to warranties, limitation of liability, remedies or damages, and our ownership rights shall survive termination.

7.   **MISCELLANEOUS:**   This Agreement shall be construed in accordance with the laws of the United States of America and the State of New York and shall benefit the Company, its affiliates, and assignees.

8.   **LIMITED WARRANTY AND DISCLAIMER OF WARRANTY:**   The Company warrants that the SOFTWARE, when properly used in accordance with the Documentation, will operate in substantial conformity with the description of the SOFTWARE set forth in the Documentation. The Company does not warrant that the SOFTWARE will meet your requirements or that the operation of the SOFTWARE will be uninterrupted or error-free. The Company warrants that the

media on which the SOFTWARE is delivered shall be free from defects in materials and workmanship under normal use for a period of thirty (30) days from the date of your purchase. Your only remedy and the Company's only obligation under these limited warranties is, at the Company's option, return of the warranted item for a refund of any amounts paid by you or replacement of the item. Any replacement of SOFTWARE or media under the warranties shall not extend the original warranty period. The limited warranty set forth above shall not apply to any SOFTWARE which the Company determines in good faith has been subject to misuse, neglect, improper installation, repair, alteration, or damage by you. EXCEPT FOR THE EXPRESSED WARRANTIES SET FORTH ABOVE, THE COMPANY DISCLAIMS ALL WARRANTIES, EXPRESS OR IMPLIED, INCLUDING WITHOUT LIMITATION, THE IMPLIED WARRANTIES OF MERCHANTABILITY AND FITNESS FOR A PARTICULAR PURPOSE. EXCEPT FOR THE EXPRESS WARRANTY SET FORTH ABOVE, THE COMPANY DOES NOT WARRANT, GUARANTEE, OR MAKE ANY REPRESENTATION REGARDING THE USE OR THE RESULTS OF THE USE OF THE SOFTWARE IN TERMS OF ITS CORRECTNESS, ACCURACY, RELIABILITY, CURRENTNESS, OR OTHERWISE.

IN NO EVENT, SHALL THE COMPANY OR ITS EMPLOYEES, AGENTS, SUPPLIERS, OR CONTRACTORS BE LIABLE FOR ANY INCIDENTAL, INDIRECT, SPECIAL, OR CONSEQUENTIAL DAMAGES ARISING OUT OF OR IN CONNECTION WITH THE LICENSE GRANTED UNDER THIS AGREEMENT, OR FOR LOSS OF USE, LOSS OF DATA, LOSS OF INCOME OR PROFIT, OR OTHER LOSSES, SUSTAINED AS A RESULT OF INJURY TO ANY PERSON, OR LOSS OF OR DAMAGE TO PROPERTY, OR CLAIMS OF THIRD PARTIES, EVEN IF THE COMPANY OR AN AUTHORIZED REPRESENTATIVE OF THE COMPANY HAS BEEN ADVISED OF THE POSSIBILITY OF SUCH DAMAGES. IN NO EVENT SHALL LIABILITY OF THE COMPANY FOR DAMAGES WITH RESPECT TO THE SOFTWARE EXCEED THE AMOUNTS ACTUALLY PAID BY YOU, IF ANY, FOR THE SOFTWARE.

SOME JURISDICTIONS DO NOT ALLOW THE LIMITATION OF IMPLIED WARRANTIES OR LIABILITY FOR INCIDENTAL, INDIRECT, SPECIAL, OR CONSEQUENTIAL DAMAGES, SO THE ABOVE LIMITATIONS MAY NOT ALWAYS APPLY. THE WARRANTIES IN THIS AGREEMENT GIVE YOU SPECIFIC LEGAL RIGHTS AND YOU MAY ALSO HAVE OTHER RIGHTS WHICH VARY IN ACCORDANCE WITH LOCAL LAW.

ACKNOWLEDGMENT

YOU ACKNOWLEDGE THAT YOU HAVE READ THIS AGREEMENT, UNDERSTAND IT, AND AGREE TO BE BOUND BY ITS TERMS AND CONDITIONS. YOU ALSO AGREE THAT THIS AGREEMENT IS THE COMPLETE AND EXCLUSIVE STATEMENT OF THE AGREEMENT BETWEEN YOU AND THE COMPANY AND SUPERSEDES ALL PROPOSALS OR PRIOR AGREEMENTS, ORAL, OR WRITTEN, AND ANY OTHER COMMUNICATIONS BETWEEN YOU AND THE COMPANY OR ANY REPRESENTATIVE OF THE COMPANY RELATING TO THE SUBJECT MATTER OF THIS AGREEMENT.

Should you have any questions concerning this Agreement or if you wish to contact the Company for any reason, please contact in writing at the address below.

Robin Short
Prentice Hall PTR
One Lake Street
Upper Saddle River, New Jersey 07458

ABOUT THE CD

CONTENTS

The CD included with this book contains the DB2 Universal Database for Windows NT product. This product is provided in trial mode. Once this product has been installed, it will continue to operate for 60 days. To use this product past the 60 days requires a DB2 license which is not included.

The version of DB2 Universal Database for Windows NT that is provided on this CD is version 5.2 and is English only.

INSTALLATION

You can install this product by placing the CD in your CD drive. The automatic install program will be started. If you do not see the program started automatically, you can also try to explore the CD and run the setup.exe program located on the CD to install the product.

The installation options provided for you are to install:
¥DB2 Universal Database for Windows NT Enterprise Edition
¥DB2 Universal Database for Windows NT Workgroup Edition
¥DB2 Client Application Enabler for Windows NT

SYSTEM REQUIREMENTS

To install DB2 Universal Database for Windows NT Version 5.2, you require Windows NT 3.51, Windows NT 4.0 or later.

TECHNICAL SUPPORT

Technical support is not provided by Prentice Hall nor the authors. If, however, you feel that your CD is damaged, please contact Prentice Hall for a replacement: disc_exchange@prenhall.com.